Literature and the Growth of British Nationalism

Literature and the Growth of British Nationalism

The Influence of Romantic Poetry and Bardic Criticism

FRANCESCO CROCCO

McFarland & Company, Inc., Publishers
Jefferson, North Carolina

LIBRARY OF CONGRESS CATALOGUING-IN-PUBLICATION DATA

Crocco, Francesco, author.
    Literature and the Growth of British Nationalism :
the Influence of Romantic Poetry and Bardic Criticism /
Francesco Crocco.
      p.   cm.
    Includes bibliographical references and index.

    ISBN 978-0-7864-7847-7 (softcover : acid free paper) ∞
    ISBN 978-1-4766-1600-1 (ebook)

    1. English poetry—19th century—History and criticism.
2. English poetry—18th century—History and criticism.
3. Romanticism—Great Britain.   4. National characteristics,
English, in literature.   I. Title.

PR590.C696 2014
821'.709—dc23   2013050569

BRITISH LIBRARY CATALOGUING DATA ARE AVAILABLE

© 2014 Francesco Crocco. All rights reserved

*No part of this book may be reproduced or transmitted in any form
or by any means, electronic or mechanical, including photocopying
or recording, or by any information storage and retrieval system,
without permission in writing from the publisher.*

On the cover: John Martin, *The Bard*, oil on canvas, 50" × 40", 1817

Manufactured in the United States of America

*McFarland & Company, Inc., Publishers
  Box 611, Jefferson, North Carolina 28640
    www.mcfarlandpub.com*

To Jackie and Joe

Table of Contents

Acknowledgments   ix
Preface   1
Introduction   3

1. Bardic Criticism, the Canon and the Invention of the Poet-Bard   19
2. Wordsworth's Bardic Poetics in *Lyrical Ballads*   52
3. Wordsworth and Class (Un)Consciousness   88
4. Coleridge, Religious Nationalism and the Anxiety of Empire   120
5. Patriot Women and the Future of Empire   153

Conclusion: William Blake's Prophecies and the Limits of Nationalism   182
Chapter Notes   193
Bibliography   225
Index   241

Acknowledgments

This book would not have been possible without the constant and caring support of my mentors, colleagues, family, friends, and comrades. First and foremost, I would like to thank my wonderful mentors, Jackie DiSalvo and Joe Wittreich, who helped me to conceive this project and make the perilous journey from dissertation to book. I could not have written this book without their sage instruction, valuable feedback, and generous support. Next, many thanks to the various faculty members at the Graduate Center of the City University of New York who, at one point or another, helped me develop my manuscript, specifically Alan Vardy, Meena Alexander, David Richter, Josh Wilner, Alyson Bardsley, Glenn Burger, and Steven Kruger. Thanks to Barbara Foley for her guidance drafting an early version of Chapter 3 and also for raising my consciousness. Thanks to Marilyn Gaull for her feedback on parts of Chapter 5 and for her helpful advice en route to a book contract. Thanks to Orrin Wang for his feedback on another part of Chapter 5. And thanks to Kate Broad for her skillful copy editing of the final manuscript. To James, Michael, Brooks, Nikhil, and the rest of my graduate school writing group I owe a tremendous debt of gratitude for helping me write through the hard times and offering valuable suggestions for revision. There are many other people who contributed in less direct but nonetheless profound ways to this project. Many thanks to Mrs. Jones and Professor Dell for making an English major out of me. Thank you as well to Ellen for helping me stay focused on my goals. Thank you to my furry friends, Fritz and Amelie, for keeping me company through the lonely hours of research and writing. Thank you to my close friends for keeping me sane. I am forever indebted to my parents, Giuseppe and Rosina, for their unwavering emotional and financial support. I wrote this dissertation partly to show that the doors of the academy must remain open to the sons and daughters of immigrants and workers. Most of all, thank you to my loving partner, Nichole, for believing in me when I did not, and for shouldering the burden of parenting so that I could be a full-time scholar. I promise to return the favor. Thank you to everyone else who, in one way or another, contributed to the labor of this project, especially my comrades, past and present, who inspire me to struggle for a better world. If I have seen further and more clearly, it is only because I have stood on the shoulders of giants. Finally, I wish to acknowledge the many staff members of the New York Public Library, Alexander Library, Mina Rees Library, A. Philip Randolph Memorial Library, and the British Museum who assisted with my research for this book.

Preface

This study explores how British Romantic poetry—the writing, reading, and critical reception of it—reinforced British nationalism in the nineteenth century, ripening the political processes of nationhood that began with the first Act of Union in 1707. It makes an original contribution to the conversation on Romantic poetry and British nationalism in several ways. On the one hand, my study documents the rise of *bardic criticism* in the eighteenth century, a style of literary criticism that reinvented the vernacular poet as a national bard and promoted a vernacular English canon over the traditional European and Latin canon. Within this framework, I argue that the reception of Romantic poetry was deeply colored by nationalism and served the growing demand for vernacular literature in compulsory public education programs and an expanding literary marketplace. By highlighting the complicity between bardic discourse and nationalism, this study therefore adds a rich political dimension to the recent investigations of the formative influence of minstrelsy and the ballad revival on Romantic poetry, which includes prominent studies such as Richard Gravil's *Wordsworth's Bardic Vocation*, Maureen McLane's *Balladeering, Minstrelsy, and the Making of British Romantic Poetry*, and Erik Simpson's *Literary Minstrelsy*. On the other hand, this study also advances the conversation about the ways that Romantic poets contributed to the production of British state nationalism, and thereby serves as a complement to works that emphasize instead the Romantic-era literary production of ethnic nationalisms opposed to the state, such as Katie Trumpener's *Bardic Nationalism*, Leith Davis's *Acts of Union*, and Julia M. Wright's *Ireland, India, and Nationalism in Nineteenth-Century Literature*. In chapters on William Wordsworth, Samuel Taylor Coleridge, Felicia Hemans, and Anna Letitia Barbauld, I examine how Romantic poets dealt with matters of class, race, gender, religion, and empire within a nationalist framework that corroborated the public image of poets as *bona fide* national bards. Finally, throughout this study, I stress the Romantics' unintentional participation with the project of British nationalism, even when they intentionally set out to oppose or reform it. My approach departs from studies that explore the ways Romantics stridently raised the flag, such as Anne Frey's *British State Romanticism* and David Aram Kaiser's *Romanticism, Aesthetics, and Nationalism*. Ultimately, my aim is to illuminate new dimensions of nationalism in British Romantic poetry and thereby advance the broader conversation about the complex relationship between literature and nationalism.

Introduction

> O Britons! O my brethren! I have told
> Most bitter truth, but without bitterness.
> —S.T. Coleridge[1]

M.H. Abrams wrote that the Romantics "developed new modes of organizing experience, new ways of seeing the outer world, and a new set of relations of the individual to himself, to nature, to history and to his fellow men."[2] This study examines the ways that the Romantics and their critics produced "modes of organizing experience" that contributed to the development of British nationalism. They did so by situating the poet as a bard-like national figure who wrote to and for "his fellow men" and women. Samuel Taylor Coleridge's adoption of the patriot's voice in "Fears in Solitude" is one salient example of this process: when he exclaims, "O Britons! O my brethren!" he is expressing a sentiment buried deep within many Romantic poems—the notion that the inspired solitary poet speaks to and for a singular people or nation.[3] By addressing a national collective about a presumably shared national experience, Coleridge also helps to weave modern Scots, Welsh, Irish, and English into a community of Britons.

This study explores how the writing, reading, and critical reception of British Romantic poetry helped to foster British nationalism in the nineteenth century, ripening the political processes of nationhood that began with the first Act of Union in 1707. It advances the conversation on Romanticism and British nationalism by tracing the connection between British nationalism and aesthetics back to the early eighteenth century and the rise of *bardic criticism*, a style of literary criticism that portrayed the vernacular poet as a national bard and promoted a vernacular national canon over the traditional European and Latin canon. Within this framework, I argue that Romantic poets were uniquely situated to exploit the poet's new-found reputation as celebrated national bard and meet the growing demand for vernacular poetry in the literary marketplace, while the subsequent introduction of canonical literature in the curriculum for compulsory public education in the nineteenth century enabled their work to have a lasting effect on national culture. While the first chapter historicizes the growth and development of bardic criticism from the mid-eighteenth to the late-nineteenth century using selections from antiquarian texts, contemporary reviews, and studies of English poetry and language, in later chapters I explore the bardic poetics and reception of William Wordsworth, Samuel Taylor Coleridge, Felicia Hemans, and Anna Letitia Barbauld using case studies of their poetry. I examine how they deal with matters of class, race, gender, religion, and empire within a nationalist framework, thereby corroborating the public perception established by bardic critics that vernacular poets were *bona fide* national bards.

A major contention of this study is that the Romantic poets' participation with nationalist culture was more often than not subterranean and unconscious rather than overt and explicit. Furthermore, even when nationalism and the nation appeared as explicit targets of Romantic critique, the manner of criticism upheld a conservative nationalist politics. For instance, on the surface, Wordsworth's aesthetic program set out in the Preface and accomplished in *Lyrical Ballads* does not appear to be particularly nationalist in sentiment or tone. Yet, in Chapter 2 I explain that several key elements in his program—an authentic poetic diction couched in the "real language of men," a renewed vision of the poet as "a man speaking to men," and a celebration of local characters and places—are informed by a civic discourse attuned to the prevailing nationalism of the era.[4] Similarly, in Chapter 3 I demonstrate that Wordsworth's complex relationship with class discourse in the 1805 *Prelude* and *Lyrical Ballads* contributes to a reification of class inequality that rescues nationalism from the divisive politics of class struggle. When the nation does come under scrutiny by Romantic poets, as I argue in my reading of Coleridge's "Fears in Solitude" in Chapter 4 and Barbauld's *Eighteen Hundred and Eleven* in Chapter 5, their recourse to a counter-patriotic discourse that appropriates patriotic devotion as a basis for criticism paradoxically reinforces nationalist politics. This is also true of Hemans' more explicitly conservative patriotic poem *Modern Greece*, which, in Chapter 5, I argue contains an admonition to the nation that rouses rather than rejects nationalism. Chapters 4 and 5 thus demonstrate how seemingly neutral or oppositional politics end up co-opted by and collapsing back into conservative nationalism. To further underscore the fluidity of nationalist politics in this era, I conclude with a reading of Blake's continental prophecies that demonstrates the reverse process—the cooptation of nationalist symbolism and mythos on behalf of a progressive internationalism. Blake's vision reveals that, while nationalism was a powerful ideology often operating beneath the surface of Romantic poetry, it was possible for Romantic poets to critique these politics by exploring utopian alternatives.

This study engages two recent trends in Romantic scholarship concerned with the subject of nationalism. Some scholars have examined the complex relationship between Romanticism and the nationalisms subsumed by the British Empire, particularly the Welsh, Scottish, Irish, and Indians, thereby shifting attention away from the focus on English nationalism that occupied earlier scholarship.[5] This body of work includes Katie Trumpener's *Bardic Nationalism*, Leith Davis's *Acts of Union*, and Julia M. Wright's *Ireland, India, and Nationalism in Nineteenth-Century Literature*. They complicate our understanding of British nationalism by demonstrating the degree to which it was a zone of contention and negotiation between Englishness and the national aspirations of subordinated groups, often expressed in literature through adaptations of local dialect, popular genres, and bardic iconography. On a different tack, other scholars have focused on historicizing the influence of specific elements of popular or provincial culture in Romantic texts. Richard Gravil's *Wordsworth's Bardic Vocation*, Maureen McLane's *Balladeering, Minstrelsy, and the Making of British Romantic Poetry*, Steve Newman's *Ballad Collection, Lyric, and the Canon*, Erik Simpson's *Literary Minstrelsy*, and Terence A. Hoagwood's *From Song to Print: Romantic Pseudo-Songs* explore Romantic appropriations of popular minstrelsy and the ballad tradition, while James M. Garrett's *Wordsworth and the Writing of the Nation* and Fiona Stafford's *Local Attachments* consider the interplay of local, regional, and national identities in Romantic poetry.

I place these conversations in dialogue with each other and with earlier conversations about the history of British nationalism and English studies programs to provide a broader understanding of how Romanticism contributed to the development of a hegemonic British state nationalism. In doing so, I take issue with some key arguments, particularly Katie Trumpener's claim that contemporary appropriations of bards and balladry were fundamentally counter-hegemonic. Trumpener writes that for Scottish, Irish, and Welsh patriots, "the bard is the mouthpiece for a whole society, articulating its values, chronicling its history, and mourning the inconsolable tragedy of its collapse," whereas for English poets she contends that the bard played a more atomistic role as "an inspired, isolated, and peripatetic figure."[6] Throughout this study, however, I demonstrate instances of bardic nationalism among English and non–English poets and critics who appropriate bards and balladry precisely in the collectivist and nationalist ways that she restricts to counter-hegemonic authors. In the process, I demonstrate how these poets and critics appropriate the elements of popular and provincial culture discussed by Gravil et al. to advance a hegemonic British state nationalism that is decidedly English in style and character.

This book also departs from existing arguments about Romantic poetry and criticism that stress the self-conscious intentionality of authors engaged in the various discourses of or about nationalism. For example, in *British State Romanticism* Anne Frey argues that major Romantic poets like Wordsworth and Coleridge were "State Romantics" who, believing that national identity "is imposed through a mesh of interlocking administrative systems," instrumentalized literature to serve state-sanctioned nationalism as the formal state apparatus contracted during the period of laissez faire policies from 1815 to 1870.[7] Similarly, in *Romanticism, Aesthetics, and Nationalism* David Aram Kaiser promulgates the concept of "aesthetic statism" to describe the work of aestheticians in England and Germany who sought to use the power of the Romantic symbol to negotiate a universal, liberal high culture with a popular, national low culture.[8] However, the diversity of political orientations represented by the poets and critics in this study suggests that Romantic complicity with state nationalism was not always or even primarily a matter of intent. Rather, it often reflected an un-self-conscious conformity to an increasingly hegemonic worldview in which the nation was perceived as the natural organizing unit of culture, an idea reinforced among authors by the formative landscape of political and economic forces that produced and shaped the national literary markets and canons within which they were able to operate and thrive as bardic critics and poets. This is not to suggest that British nationalism was monolithic; as Trumpener and others have noted, the rise of literary nationalism in Britain was fraught with controversy, especially as a result of the tension between the diverse and conflicting groups subsumed under the artificial category of "Britons." Nonetheless, I refrain from suggesting, as Yoon Sun Lee does in *Nationalism and Irony*, that Romantic-era literary nationalism was primarily an ironic performance—a "conspicuous social deference—a self-serving, self-conscious deference possessed of an indeterminate political meaning"— that disguised antipathy or contempt for British nationalism.[9] No doubt, many poets and critics genuflected at the altar of nationalism in their writing for fear of political or economic reprisal; but this argument cannot be true of all. Furthermore, by casting patriotic writing as ironic subversion one assumes a degree of authorial self-consciousness about nationalism that reinforces the notion that participation with nationalism was primarily a matter of deliberation and choice rather than of habit and custom.

My approach to understanding the relationship between Romanticism and nationalism agrees with that of Suvir Kaul. In his book-length study of eighteenth-century poetry and nationalism, *Poems of Nation, Anthems of Empire*, Kaul describes how nationalism "is *naturalized* into a matter-of-fact, everyday conversational consensus ... in and through the work of poets; it pervades their sense of self and vocation; it becomes an inescapable part of the paraphernalia of their craft."[10] Similarly, I proceed from the point of view that neither Romantic poets nor their readers and critics were always or ever aware of the pervasive nationalist medium within which they produced and consumed literature. Therefore, I approach nationalism as a kind of political horizon for the period, even if, as I suggest in my conclusion on William Blake, some poets were able to imagine international forms of community.

Nationalism, Poetry and the Canon

The approach to nationalism that informs this study is predicated on a syncretization of two schools of thought. Since the seventeenth century, proponents of nationalism and its organizational form, the nation-state, have put forward the idea that nations are organic and indivisible communities of blood, language, custom, or religion. This idea has been refined in the work of contemporary scholars who emphasize the importance of ethnicity for the rise of nations. A central study in the ethnicist school of thought is Anthony D. Smith's *The Ethnic Origins of Nations*, which posits that the formation of modern nation-states required pre-existing ethnic communities with a shared set of cultural, linguistic, originary, religious, and territorial traits. Smith calls this primordial grouping an *ethnie*, which he defines as a "collective cultural unit" that precedes and enables the formation of "modern national units and sentiments."[11] In this formulation, the institutions that comprise the nation-state and regulate its population take root organically, deepening and strengthening already existing ethnic ties.

However, since at least the late nineteenth century, scholars in the modernist camp have disputed ethnicist claims and contended that nations are convenient fictions used to legitimate the hegemony of the nation-state. This position is evident as early as 1882, when Ernest Renan delivered his groundbreaking lecture, "What Is a Nation?" Renan challenges the Romantic illusions about inveterate, ethnic communities trafficked in the nationalist movements of his day, declaring that nations are "something fairly new in history" in which "unity is always effected by means of brutality."[12] Modern scholarship on nationalism has taken a similar view. In his oft-cited book, *Imagined Communities*, Benedict Anderson contends that the nation is "an imagined political community" emerging after the destruction of dynastic monarchies during the Enlightenment and distinguished not by the falsity or genuineness of claims to a qualifying heritage, "but by the style in which they are imagined."[13] Anderson attributes the emergence of national consciousness to the adoption of a vernacular language of state, print capitalism, the creation of a public infrastructure for trade and transit, and state instruments like map, census, and survey, which both measure and define the population. In similar fashion, Michel Foucault traces the origins of the modern nation-state to the eighteenth century, when a new technology of power he calls "biopower" emerged as a way to control populations by premising the authority of the state upon its fulfillment of human biological needs.[14] Echoing Renan, Homi K. Bhabha writes, "Nations, like narratives, lose their origins in the myths of time and only fully realize their horizons in the mind's eye"; he proposes that the narrative-like nature of nationalism ensures that it will be a contested field, what he calls "the Janus-faced discourse of the nation."[15] Ernest Gellner's *Nations and Nationalism* and John Breuilly's *Nationalism and the State* also deconstruct Romantic arguments about monolithic nationalities and national sovereignty. Stressing the place of class in this conversation, Eric J. Hobsbawm in *Nations and Nationalism Since 1780* contends that nation-states are eighteenth-century inventions created to serve the economic interests of elites while using the myth of a national community to contain and control the lower classes. In short, the modernist position challenges Romantic notions about the age-old origins of nations and stresses the crucial role of state institutions in forming and controlling national populations.

The case of Great Britain provides a unique occasion for a nuanced understanding of nationalism that engages both ethnicist and modernist viewpoints on nationalism. Drawing upon the work of Anderson and company who stress the social construction of national identity, I contend that Britain is an "imagined community" forged into being by various political and cultural acts of union that nominally joined a population of English, Scots, Welsh, and Irish otherwise divided by the normative markers of nationality—ethnicity, language, custom, religion, and dynastic affiliation—as well as by class. The objective of this unification process was to produce an entity that could field and maintain an empire of trade and colonies, and the primary agents and beneficiaries of this imperial project were the landed and monied elites—drawn unevenly from the English, Scottish, and Welsh upper classes—who stood to profit most from this new imperial configuration. While it lasted, the empire was able to solidify a sense of exclusive national community and patriotic loyalty to the state by affording average Britons opportunities for material success in the colonies and by fomenting a them-and-us attitude whereby nominal Britons, who were divided by ethnic and class antagonisms, came to identify with each other and the state contra colonized others and imperial rivals. Linda Colley has elaborated on the role of empire in the construction of British nationalism in her acclaimed study, *Britons: Forging a Nation, 1701–1837*. Taking a modernist position on nationalism, Colley proposes that Britain is "an invention forged above all by war."[16] She argues that the empire enabled Britons to define themselves as a community against three specific out-groups:

They defined themselves as Protestants struggling for survival against the world's foremost Catholic power. They defined themselves against the French as they imagined them to be, superstitious, militarist, decadent and unfree. And, increasingly as the wars went on, they defined themselves in contrast to the colonial peoples they conquered, peoples who were manifestly alien in terms of culture, religion and colour.[17]

In return for embracing anti–Gallicanism, Protestantism, and colonialism, Colley demonstrates that marginalized Britons were able to secure economic gains and win rights and privileges from the state, thus bolstering their devotion to patriotism. Her study suggests that, given the reality of internal fissures, the viability of a British nation was premised on the success of the empire. Consequently, as Tom Nairn and others have argued, the spectacular decline of the empire after World War II removed a crucial vent for internal dissent, unleashing a resurgence of Scottish and Welsh nationalism that threatened to unravel the union.[18]

The ersatz nature of the British imperial nation is most poignantly revealed by the etymology of the word *Britain*. There were no aboriginal ethnic communities on the island who laid claim to the moniker *Britons*. Rather, the name derives from the island's Roman conquerors; they named it *Britannia* after the Greeks, who called the island *Pretanoi* to describe the peculiar body-painting habits of its Celtic inhabitants.[19] After the Roman retreat, the word *Britannia* and its various derivatives—*Britain*, *British*, and *Briton*—became a rallying cry for successive groups on the island seeking to promote inclusivity, conciliate difference, or justify efforts at forced unification. For instance, in *An Exhortation to the Scottes to Conforme Themselfes to the ... Union betweene ... England and Scotland* (c.1547) J. Harrison symbolically erases centuries of ethnic strife between the English and Scots by imagining a time "when these hateful termes of Scottes and Englishemen, shalbe abolished, and blotted oute for euer, and we shal al agre in the onely title and name of Britons."[20] Harrison's vision would come to pass in 1603 when King James I united the thrones of England and Scotland, thenceforth taking on the title "King of Great Britain." The name would be institutionalized a century later with the first Act of Union.

And yet, if Britain is an "imagined community," it is also one in which the influence and imperatives of a particular *ethnie* dominated politics and culture. Michael Hechter has argued that a situation of English "internal colonialism" prevailed from the outset of the unification process and often threatened to unravel the fragile ties of empire.[21] To this effect, Krishan Kumar has interpreted the peculiar English habit of subsuming *British* under *English* as a furtive sign of England's awareness of its dominant position within Great Britain.[22] "The English," he writes, were an imperial nation in a double sense. They created a land empire, Great Britain or the United Kingdom, formed by the expansion of England from its southern position at the base of the group of islands off the north-western coast of Europe.... And they created an overseas empire....[23]

Similarly, Gerald Porter has written, "The historical creation of Great Britain was the establishment of a Greater England."[24] The situation of a dominant English *ethnie* within the British imperial amalgam lends credence to Smith's idea that modern nation states are preceded and catalyzed by strong, proto-nationalist *ethnie*. In this case, an English *ethnie*, directed by elite circles, dominated the project of British nationhood, and this explains why the stamp of an English hegemon is evident in British politics, culture, and literature. In later chapters, I demonstrate the prevalence of an English *ethnie* in the British canon, which privileges English language, authors, and texts.

Overall, then, Britain as a whole is an imperial construct that exemplifies the claims of modernists, but an ethnicist framework is also necessary to account for internal power dynamics and inequities. Far from the Romantic unities proffered by nationalists, since the beginning the idea of Britain has been inseparable from the history of conquest and empire. It began as the Roman colony Britannia, morphed into a rallying cry that gave ideological cover to English internal colonialism, and finally matured into a formidable imperial state in its own right that bore the imprint of English hegemony in many ways. Given this history, it's not surprising that eighteenth-century Britons came to define themselves, as Colley has argued, by what they were not—French, Catholic, colonial other—rather than by what little they shared.

The establishment of an English vernacular British canon, within which Romantic poetry came to have a prominent role, began in earnest after the first Act of Union and helped to catalyze British nationalism over the next two centuries. On this note, Thomas F. Bonnell writes:

> In the last third of the eighteenth century, through successive developments both gradual and abrupt, publishers in Great Britain represented the nation to itself in a new light, delivering proof of its majority, of its arrival at a new stage of cultural maturity. This coming of age was expressed in distinctly material terms, as the poets of the nation—its classics, its worthies—began to be reprinted and sold to the public in one extensive multi-volume collection after another.[25]

Bonnell records that more than a dozen multi-volume collections of British poetry appeared during the second half of the century, registering "the fullest manifestation ever of an English poetic canon."[26]

Several factors contributed to the advent of an English vernacular literature in Britain during the eighteenth century: the invention of stereotyping print technologies that made cheap reprints commercially viable; the liberalization of copyright law; the growth of a literary marketplace in response to the growing demand for vernacular literature issuing from the nation's rising middle class; increased competition between publishing houses, which drove down costs and engendered elaborate marketing schemes; the founding of free public libraries; and the rise of English studies programs that promulgated a canon of vernacular literature for the nation. These factors freed literature from the exclusive circles and tastes of elite patrons and converted it into a commodity available to a broad swath of Britons. It was during this period of rich ferment in print culture, explains John Brewer, that debates over "high" and "low" art originate, reflecting a rift between the "low culture" of commercialized popular art (ballads, novels, etc.) and what was seen as the established "high culture" of Neoclassicism.[27] Wordsworth's declared rupture with Augustan "pre-established codes of taste" in the "Advertisement" to the first edition of *Lyrical Ballads* (1798) reflects this rift. Ultimately, the demand for a vernacular literature won out, and the profession of literary criticism would come to play a key role in this victory by nationalizing poets and poetry.

As I argue further in Chapter 1, the discourse of bardic criticism that began in the latter half of the eighteenth century institutionalized the literary practice of mingling nationalism with matters of aesthetic judgment, especially in regards to poets and poetry. As such, bardic criticism is an example of Terry Eagleton's contention that aesthetics began operating in the eighteenth century as a "supremely effective mode of political hegemony" because it inserted "social power more deeply into the bodies of those it subjugated."[28] In this case, the "social power" leveraged by bardic criticism was the ideology of nationalism. Thomas Carlyle offers a candid glimpse into this discourse when he exclaims, "It is a great thing for a Nation that it get an articulate voice; that it produce a man who will speak-forth melodiously what the heart of it means!"[29] Bardic critics inherited many of their tropes and techniques from eighteenth-century antiquarian discourse. Antiquarian collections of traditional and modern ballads, such as Thomas Percy's celebrated *Reliques of Ancient English Poetry*, satisfied a growing popular demand for vernacular literature. They also developed a cult of the artist around the iconic figure of the bard. Bardic critics would borrow both of these prerogatives, promulgating the importance of vernacular poetry for a national canon and converting the modern poet into a celebrated national bard. Again and again in contemporary reviews of Romantic poetry, critics refer to poets as "bards," a cliché that few could resist, even if tongue in cheek at times. In reviews, anthologies, philological histories, and critical treatises from the mid-eighteenth century to the late nineteenth century, one discovers the emergence of a tradition of bardic criticism, and the rise to national prominence of Romantic poetry was facilitated by this vibrant discourse.

In foregrounding the prominence of Romantic poets and poetry in the discourse of British nationalism, I do not diminish the role played by other genres. Popular novelists, such as Sir Walter Scott, strongly influenced the direction of national culture, and many profoundly important studies have established the broad cultural significance of novelistic prose for the shaping of British subjectivity.[30] My exclusive focus, however, on the relationship between poetry and nationalism in the Romantic period recognizes the powerful cult of the artist that took shape in Britain largely around poets. This phenomenon is evident in the practice of selecting a national poet laureate, an institution that began in 1668 with the nomination of John Dryden. The cult of the artist came to maturity in the eighteenth century with the prevalence of Romantic theories about originality and individual creativity, which engendered the invention of copyright and the legal persona of the author.[31] The fact that Robert Southey and William Wordsworth held the position of poet laureate of Britain for thirty-seven years between them highlights both the continuing fascination with the cult of the artist in nineteenth-century Britain, and the way it came to become closely associated with Romantic poets. By the height of the Victorian period, working class students, Scottish and Irish officers, and colonial subjects alike were all required to perform their nationality with proficiency in the poetry of the Lake District. Reciting Wordsworth would become simultaneously a marker of one's delicate sensibilities and proud national affiliation.

There are many reasons why Romantic poetry appealed to nineteenth-century Britons, chief among them its personal, lyrical quality. In a world of modern industrial capitalism characterized by the turmoil of political strife, economic competition, social dislocation, rapid technological change, secularization, materialism, alienation, and the dehumanizing rationalization of everyday life, Romantic poetry offered an oasis of sensitivity and emotional connection unavailable outside of scant family ties and fleeting romances. It voiced the egotism, isolation, and despair of the bourgeois subject, but also the heartfelt desire for a sense of genuine integration and community that transcended the base nexus of "callous 'cash payment'" ruling the marketplace.[32] This paradox coheres with Theodor Adorno's argument that lyric poetry mediates between the alienated consciousness of the modern subject and the generality of collective experience:

> The descent into individuality raises the lyric poem to the realm of the general by virtue of its bringing to light things undistorted, ungrasped, things not yet subsumed—and thus the poem anticipates, in an abstract way, a condition in which no mere generalities (i.e., extreme particularities) can bind and chain that which is human. From a condition of unrestrained individuation, the lyric work strives for, awaits the realm of the general.[33]

For a modern, secular society, the Romantic poet succeeds the priest and the prophet as the privileged mediator between individuated subjects and the greater social whole. Romantic lyricism cuts through the ideological constraints of individuation and reconnects individuals within a matrix of shared experiences and emotions, networking and sustaining community.

Among the bardic critics I discuss in the first chapter, Matthew Arnold comes closest to appreciating the essential social utility of lyric poetry: "More and more mankind will discover that we have to turn to poetry to interpret life for us, to console us, to sustain us. Without poetry, our science will appear incomplete; and most of what now passes with us for religion and philosophy will be replaced by poetry."[34] The life of John Stuart Mill is a case in point. In his *Autobiography*, Mill explains how Wordsworth's rustic and lyrical poetry ultimately rescued him from the dark abyss of depression and suicide.[35] Mill's testimony is a reminder of the poet's uncanny powers of expression. Thomas Percy described the ancient bards as the unparalleled "Smoothers and Polishers of language."[36] By the same token, Wordsworth would define the poet as "a man speaking to men ... endued with more lively sensibility, more enthusiasm and tenderness, who has a greater knowledge of human nature, and a more comprehensive soul, than are supposed to be common among mankind."[37] Little wonder, then, that literary critics would make bards of poets, and that the state would elect poet laureates to represent the people.

Ultimately, Romantic poetry complemented the political processes of unification by providing a new "structure of feeling" capable of positively networking alienated and nominal Britons into a distinct community of sensibility. Raymond Williams defines structures of feeling as "affective elements of consciousness and relationships" that are "often indeed not yet recognized as social but taken to be private, idiosyncratic, and even isolating." He explains that these seemingly private experiences are only visible as hegemonic social formations much later, "when they have been formalized, classified, and in many cases built into institutions and formations."[38] The national institutionalization of a Romantic "structure of feeling" occurred gradually as Romantic poetry entered the markets, canons, and curricula of British society. When Romanticism emerged as a coherent cultural formation at the turn of the nineteenth century it was channeled through these social arteries and produced a new cultural hegemon whose structure of feeling could be felt in everything from the arts and humanities to education and urban planning.[39]

The influence of a Romantic structure of feeling upon British society in the nineteenth century is most apparent in the significant ways it influenced the study of literature, educational theories, and the canon. Writing about the profound impact of Romanticism on the study of literature, Jerome McGann has famously charged that literary critics have uncritically absorbed a "Romantic ideology" characterized by extreme forms of historical displacement and idealization.[40] More recently, Ian Reid has explored the impact of Wordsworth and his writing on English studies. He notes, for example, that when University College London became the first secular, modern institution of higher education in 1828, Wordsworth and his contemporaries denounced its vocational curriculum for middle- and lower-class students as a "profane utilitarian enterprise."[41] Reid goes on to elucidate how nineteenth-century English scholars and critics from F.D. Maurice to Matthew Arnold and David Masson absorbed Wordsworthian ideas about literariness, including an emphasis on sentiment, imagination, high seriousness, and transcendence as the proper qualities of English literature. As proof of the existence of a Romantic hegemony in the study of literature, Stephen Potter cites the eminent literary historian George Saintsbury, Masson's successor at the University of Edinburgh, who proclaimed, "Poetry should be Wordsworthian, Romantic, of high seriousness."[42]

The Romantic structure of feeling is also evident in nineteenth-century educational theories and practices for primary education. Alan Richardson argues that popular Romantic notions about childhood engendered a veritable cultural revolution in early childhood education, enshrining several beliefs that continue to hold sway:

> That literacy should be universal, even considered a right; that schooling should be state-supported and available to all; that imaginative experience is important if not essential to proper development; that schools should divide children into classes by age and measure their progress and proficiency with tests; that fantasy is the proper literature for young children; that education does not end with adolescence, but should inform an entire life span; that childhood constitutes the "magic years," a period crucial for psychic development, an Edenic time to be treasured and, later, nostalgically regretted.[43]

Richardson traces the provenance of these ideas to poems such as Wordsworth's *Intimations Ode* (1807) and *The Excursion* (1814), and Romantic treatises such as Jean-Jacque Rousseau's *Emile* (1762), Mary Wollstonecraft's *Thoughts on the Education of Daughters* (1787), Anna Letitia Barbauld's *Evenings at Home* (1792–96), and Maria Edgeworth's *Practical Education* (1798).

The rapid prevalence of Romantic poetry in the canon for anthologies of national poetry is perhaps the most stunning material indication of its hegemony as a structure of feeling for British society. According to William St. Clair, "By the 1890s, as part of the effort towards universal education, the Romantic poets were made available, in abridged form, throughout the country at one penny each, less than the price of a loaf of bread or a pint of beer."[44] St. Clair reports that nineteenth-century publishers produced a staggering array of anthologies, readers, and miscellanies of canonical poetry priced for all sections of society, from the country gentleman to the urban pauper. There were nationalist and celebratory titles like *English Classics*, *Golden Treasury of English Verse*, *National Poets*, *British Poets*, *Standard Poets*, *Popular Poets*, and *People's Editions*.[45] The Romantics came to dominate the roster of authors appearing in these anthologies so completely that St. Clair speculates by the end of the century they were read and esteemed on a level equal to that of the Bible.[46]

In his longitudinal study of school poetry anthologies from the sixteenth century to the late nineteenth century, Ian Michael corroborates St. Clair's conclusions by demonstrating a gradual but perceptible shift in the educational canon from a preponderance of eighteenth-century writers to a prevalence of Romantics. The frequency of Romantic selections in school anthologies rose precipitously in the 1830s, and by the 1850s and 1860s, Wordsworth, Byron, Scott, Southey, and Hemans were dominating the rosters, with Coleridge, Shelley, and Blake enjoying more moderate success. Aggregating the contents of all school anthologies from 1805 to 1875, Michael reveals that five of the thirteen most represented authors in this period were British Romantics (Wordsworth, Byron, Scott, Southey, and Hemans) and one other was an American Romantic (Longfellow), with Wordsworth and Byron tied for second place behind Shakespeare.[47] In a relatively short period of time, then, Romantic poetry came to dominate the canon, thereby asserting its powerful and enduring impact on British culture.

Chapter Organization and Content

The meteoric rise of Romanticism to national prominence would not have been possible without the poetry itself possessing qualities that rendered it fertile soil for nationalism. This study addresses several major Romantic-era poets and texts that display the key features of British nationalism identified earlier—anti-Gallicanism, Protestantism, colonialism, the prevalence of bourgeois class interests, and the hegemony of an English *ethnie* due to England's leading role in British unification. These characteristics may be considered the *ideologemes* of British nationalism, a term that Fredric Jameson coined to describe discrete units of an ideology and which I borrow because it provides a useful handle for organizing the chapters that follow.[48] After the first chapter, which grounds the study in an investigation of the phenomenon of bardic criticism that established poetry as part of the discipline of nationalism, each subsequent chapter demonstrates instances of Romantic poets engaging one or more ideologemes of British nationalism.

Chapter 1 examines the phenomenon of *bardic criticism*, the practice of assessing and canonizing vernacular authors based on their putative expression of national characteristics that converted the private act of reading and writing poetry into a nationalist past-time. I trace this phenomenon from its origins in eighteenth-century antiquarian discourse about bards and balladry to its permutations in the first English studies programs, reviewery, and literary criticism. I articulate a tradition of bardic criticism from Samuel Johnson to Matthew Arnold, and discuss when and why this tradition comes to a terminus in the early twentieth century. I also highlight the hegemony of an English *ethnie* in the British canon that emerges from this process. The chapters that follow continue to foreground the influence of bardic criticism on the poets under discussion in order to weave a more complete narrative of this phenomenon.

Chapters 2 and 3 focus on William Wordsworth's contributions to the culture of nationalism. In Chapter 2, I argue that Wordsworth models the radical poetics of *Lyrical Ballads* (1798/1800) upon antiquarian accounts of the "first poets"—the celebrated bards. In the Preface (1802) and *Lyrical Ballads*, he fashions and deploys a *bardic poetics* that imitates the demotic style and substance of the bards. This involves a reform of language and a preference for rusticated pastoral settings and themes, while eschewing conventional diction and urban tastes, which he regards as alien and threatening influences from continental Europe and the colonies. Consequently, these poetics demonstrate the features of anti–Gallicanism and colonial *alterity* identified by Colley. They also display a markedly English sensibility in their form and content, thereby inscribing Englishness at the center of Romanticism and, subsequently, British nationalism. Chapter 3 examines Wordsworth's bardic poetics in *Lyrical Ballads* from a different perspective, revealing how Wordsworth subverts his ostensibly demotic goals by promoting a form of bourgeois individualism that reifies and idealizes scenes of class inequality. In so doing, he occludes a class-conscious perspective that would otherwise pose a challenge to the imagined community promoted by the classless ideology of nationalism.

Chapters 4 and 5 shift attention to the connection between nationalism, religion, and empire. In Chapter 4, I examine the idea of British exceptionalism—that the Protestant British are united as the elect of God—and trace its manifestation in literature from the eighteenth century to the Romantics. Though frequently deployed to justify British imperialism, I show that dissonant voices challenge the narrative of divinely ordained empire by citing historical and biblical precedents about the folly of empire. I present Samuel Taylor Coleridge's "Fears in Solitude" (1798) as an example of the latter, simultaneously demonstrating that he uses it to expiate his radical past and publically mark his embrace of Protestant nationalism.

Chapter 5 explores two ways that Romantic women writers entered the fray of national politics to weigh in on matters of war and empire. Because of the gendered construct of feminine morality, they did so either as moral supporters, evident in Felicia Hemans's *Modern Greece* (1817), or as moral critics, evident in Anna Letitia Barbauld's *Eighteen Hundred and Eleven* (1812). In both cases, I highlight that these writers suffered public censure from male reviewers for deigning to speak publically about national politics. As the examples of Coleridge and Barbauld demonstrate, these two chapters are also linked by the theme of *counter-patriotism*—the use of nationalist rhetoric to critique the state. This suggests that nationalism does not have a static political valence. Sometimes it appears in the service of the state; other times it is appropriated to challenge and reform the state.

I conclude the study by posing the question of whether Romantic-era writers had alternatives to the ideological framework of nationalism. To this effect, I cite the case of William Blake. Misunderstood by literary critics as a proponent of English nationalism and British imperialism for his trafficking in English millenarianism and his use of mythological figures such as Albion, Blake's prophecies illuminate a path beyond nationalism, adumbrating a set of international politics that appropriate and rework elements of pre-national ideology. Though less pronounced, elements of these politics are present among Blake's Romantic contemporaries, from the counter-patriotism of Coleridge and Barbauld to the internationalism of Lord Byron and Percy Bysshe Shelley. Collectively, these poets contribute to the historical development of egalitarian forms of consciousness that move beyond the constraints of nationalism.

One caveat to bear in mind when studying the relationship between nationalism and literature is that the politics of nationalism may be present in unfamiliar and subterranean forms. This complexity follows Karl Marx's pronouncement about ideology:

> A distinction should always be made between the material transformation of the economic conditions of production, which can be determined with the precision of natural science, and the legal, political, religious, aesthetic or philosophic—in short, ideological forms in which men become conscious of this conflict and fight it out.[49]

Analogously, this study posits a distinction between overtly political statements of nationalist propaganda, which can be determined more or less with precision, and the more subtle and equivocal forms that nationalism may take in aesthetic productions. In other words, the ideologemes of British nationalism may be present even when they are not obvious or even intended. Sometimes, as in the case of Coleridge and some bardic critics, nationalism is purposely instrumentalized; other times, as in the case of Wordsworth, nationalism operates in the background as a kind of *zeitgeist*, in this case informing novel expressions of ethnic nationalism and the suppression of class consciousness. Furthermore, when authors do "become conscious" of nationalism and "fight it out," they don't always assume a position of conventional patriotism as evidenced by the examples of counter-patriotism in Coleridge and Barbauld's poetry. The examples in this study demonstrate that nationalism can serve a variety of nuanced and even conflicting political ends ranging from conservative state nationalism to liberal or radical critiques of the state. Ultimately, this study suggests that nationalism formed part of the political unconscious of British poets and critics over the two centuries following the first Act of Union such that literature and criticism came to function as an accessory to more obvious forms of nationalism.

CHAPTER 1

Bardic Criticism, the Canon and the Invention of the Poet-Bard

> Yes, truly, it is a great thing for a Nation that it get an articulate voice; that it produce a man who will speak-forth melodiously what the heart of it means!
> —Thomas Carlyle[1]
>
> By nothing is England so glorious as by her poetry.
> —Matthew Arnold[2]

In *English Bards and Scotch Reviewers* (1809) a young Lord Byron satirizes contemporary poets and their positive reviewers for perpetrating what he perceives to be a poetic devolution from the great Neoclassical works of Pope and Dryden. "No dearth of Bards can be complained of now," writes Byron, who inveighs against the preponderance of what he calls "Pseudo-bards" trafficking in hackneyed ballads, graveyard elegies, simple lays, and gothic romances.[3] At the end of the satire, he laments, "Oh! would thy Bards but emulate thy fame, / And rise, more worthy, Albion, of thy name!"[4] Byron clearly displays a disdain for the way that the antiquarians of the previous century transformed the landscape of British poetry by revitalizing popular forms like the ballad over-and-against Neoclassical modes of writing. But, in his wish for a poet-bard worthy of the nation (here figured as the mythical Albion), he also reinforces one of the primary, yet little noted, effects of that revival—the tendency among critics and readers to ascribe bard-like qualities to poets by upholding them as representatives and *vox populi* of the nation, a status that the antiquarians had previously succeeded in bestowing upon the popular bards. To delineate this mode of critical reception from those before and after, I call it *bardic criticism*.

This chapter explores transformations in British literary criticism and culture during the two centuries following the first Act of Union in 1707 that established a nationalist trope for the reception and canonization of poetry. As such, it sets up later chapters by exploring the ways that these changes facilitated, promoted, and institutionalized the Romantic reinvention of poets and poetry along nationalist lines. Beginning in the mid-eighteenth century with the revival of popular ballads, broadsides, gothic metrical romances, and the bards associated with these productions, antiquarian discourse began to shift British literary tastes away from prevailing classical and Neoclassical modes and authors and toward vernacular poets and poetry, which it invested with nationalist significance. The rise of English studies over the next century operated within this nationalist discourse and extended its reach by canonizing modern poets as latter-day neo-bards, imbuing them with the nationalist significance that the antiquarians had ascribed to the original bards. I refer to the common mode of criticism that prevailed among diverse literary scholars, critics, and reviewers in this period as *bardic criticism* both because of the formal and ideological continuities between antiquarianism and early English studies, but also in recognition of the fact that they commonly referred to poets as "bards." Bardic critics were cultural mediators with various political backgrounds and affiliations who uniformly responded to the popular call for a national literature by investing native authors and texts with nationalist import throughout their many and sundry critical productions, which included literary compilations, biographies, histories, reviews, and philological essays. By crafting a national canon, they satisfied the demand for a homegrown literature emanating from a growing number of literate, middle-class readers while also helping to legitimate the authority of the nation-state. The national canon helped to cohere an imagined community of Britons by anchoring it to a literary tradition stretching from the ballad-mongering bards of antiquity to the Romantic poet-bards, thus retrofitting a linear narrative of national history to a nation divided by past and present internal conflicts. Having solidified a national canon and nationalist modes of literary study, by the late nineteenth century bardic criticism receded into the background of literary study, making way for new modes of critical investigation that responded to new concerns.

By shifting the lens from poets to critics, this chapter adds to our understanding of British literary nationalism in the period before, during, and after the Romantic poets. Specifically, I add to Katie Trumpener's concept of "bardic nationalism," Leith Davis's dialogic "acts of union," and Ann Frey's critique of the state function of poetic production by exploring the ways that bardic criticism set the stage for poetic mediations of nationalist identity, whether within or against the state. Likewise, by foregrounding the ways that criticism aided and abetted the nationalist production and appropriation of poetry, this chapter adds new dimensions to studies of poetry and empire, such as those by Julia Wright, Suvir Kaul, and Saree Makdisi. Furthermore, by tracing the origins of bardic criticism to the antiquarian ballad revival, this chapter also bridges studies of literary nationalism with studies of popular culture and Romantic appropriations of it, such as those proffered by Maureen McLane, Erik Simpson, Steve Newman, Terence A. Hoagwood, Richard Gravil, and Michael Gamer. In arguing for the existence of a nationalist-oriented bardic criticism originating with antiquarian studies, I confirm Maureen McLane's contention that "it was precisely through their vexed engagement with the multiply-mediated, historical situation of poetry that eighteenth-century antiquarians, poets, and historians formulated crucial arguments about cultural nationalism, the status of vernaculars, and emergent British historiography."[5] If it is true, as Matthew Arnold claims, that criticism "tends to establish an order of ideas,"[6] then what bardic criticism did for Romantic poetry was to establish a nationalist order both for its production as a sort of ersatz organ of nationalism crafted from vernacular materials and for its consumption as a kind of popular commodity that fostered nationalist sentiment while promoting a cult of nationalism around the poet-bard. By creating a critical infrastructure for the production of a vernacular canon, bardic criticism also enabled the relatively speedy canonization of Romantic poetry after less than a century of circulation among the reading public.

As a study of criticism, this chapter also contributes to a body of scholarly work on the relationship between the institutionalization of English language and literature programs and the rise of nationalism. Scholars have noted that, with the waning cultural prominence of religion during the Enlightenment, the formal study of vernacular English language and literature offered a secular path to the cultural assimilation of national subjects.[7] From its origins, instruction in vernacular English language and literature helped to manufacture an exclusive national identity by linking prescriptions about rhetorical style and aesthetic judgment with nationalist, racist, religious, and class-based prejudices.[8] Consequently, it helped to preserve class stratifications by offering differential training (basic literacy for the working class; cultural capital for the elites) while inculcating a common set of national values that served to defuse class conflict.[9] The use of instruction in the English vernacular to promote nationalism dates back to the Tudors, who relied on it as part of an overall effort to accelerate England's separation from Roman Catholicism.[10] A half-century later, King James I, in an effort to unify the court, encouraged the Anglicization of Scottish nobles and courtiers.[11] During the seventeenth century, the study of vernacular English literature became professionalized,[12] and, by the eighteenth century, English literature had become an acknowledged academic subject with a growing canon of teachable texts. As several studies have made clear, Scottish intellectuals played a prominent role in this process.[13] Adam Smith delivered the first university lectures on English literature at the

University of Edinburgh from 1748–1751: not coincidentally, they were delivered at the same time as the Highland Clearances, helping to defuse ethnic resistance by assimilating middle-class Scots into English society, where they could seek opportunities in cities across the empire.[14] Throughout the next century, university English studies programs continued to promote nationalism, often by emphasizing an essential link between language, race, and creed.[15]

Instruction in English vernacular language and literature also served the British empire. In his study of linguistic imperialism, Robert Phillipson cites Crusoe's teaching of English to Friday in Daniel Defoe's *Robinson Crusoe* (1719) as a seminal moment in the global hegemony of English.[16] A century later, Guari Viswanathan observes, "As early as the 1820s ... English as the study of culture and not simply the study of language had already found a secure place in the British Indian curriculum."[17] Instruction in the British canon helped to co-opt local Indian elites by teaching them to internalize British tastes and habits of mind. Furthermore, Viswanathan's research reveals that the colonies functioned as a laboratory for developing an English studies curriculum, which was then exported back to Britain and became part of the curriculum for compulsory public education in the 1880s. In response to public opinion in the same decade, English literature joined the roster of subjects for the British Civil Service Examination, which was a gateway to administrative positions in the empire.[18] Thus, less than two centuries after the first Act of Union, familiarity with the canon had already become a requirement for British students, soldiers, and subjects alike.

Bardic criticism emerged in the context of institutional and popular support for vernacular language and literature that followed the formation of the British nation-state in 1707. Its origins coincide with nationalist movements on the continent, which, aided by nationalist theories of culture such as Johann Gottfried Herder's concept of the *volk*, achieved the apotheosis in national folklore and ballad collections. Eric Hobsbawm observes that nationalist movements historically thrive upon the dissemination of a vernacular language and the construction of a canon of vernacular literature, as was the case in Germany, Russia, Poland, Hungary, and the Scandinavian countries in the nineteenth century.[19] The case of Britain in the century following the first Act of Union in 1707 follows suit. During this century, standard English was codified, literacy peaked, the literary marketplace thrived, and the study of English literature became institutionalized, replete with disciplinary standards and a national canon. There are numerous signs of these developments in popular culture. For instance, the century witnessed an explosion of treatises on aesthetic judgment that sought to define proper literary tastes for a growing, literate, middle-class reading public.[20] In the same period, popular editions of Shakespeare's works ballooned, as did his reputation as a national bard.[21] By the 1720s, a broad array of English authors and texts were popularly held to be "classics" on par with canonical Latin, Greek, and French texts; busts of Shakespeare and Milton adorned private gardens in the 1730s; and by the 1760s there was even a flourishing business in trading cards featuring popular vernacular authors. The lifting of perpetual copyright in 1770, which substantially reduced the price of collections of English literature, satisfied a growing demand for English classics; a proliferation of collections ensued, with sales increasing five-fold.[22] Hence, by the late eighteenth century, Britain had already become a highly literate society with a middle-class reading public that attached personal and cultural value to vernacular authors and texts.

Operating within this context, bardic critics from the antiquarians to the Victorians vetted native talent and delivered vernacular texts to a reading public that embraced its new-formed British identity partly through a shared knowledge of and appreciation for the British canon. Through the canon, critics rescued popular specimens of English vernacular literature from becoming the ephemera of history. They also helped to belie the artificial and politically unstable nature of British nationhood by positing an organic, shared literary tradition reified in the canon. The practice of canon formation in the British experience illustrates two main dynamics: (1) the canon was both unconsciously and also at times self-consciously an act of invention that involved the creation of a "neo-tradition" of national literary models promoting an imagined community premised on a tradition of literature, language, and culture that transcended class, race, and ethnic differences; (2) an English *ethnie* dominated the construction of this neo-tradition in alignment with the practices of "internal colonialism" that shaped other aspects of culture, policy, and economy in Great Britain.

In sociological terms, the canon is a paramount example of what Eric Hobsbawm and Terence Ranger have dubbed a *neo-tradition*, which they define as "a set of practices ... which seek to inculcate certain values and norms of behaviour by repetition, which automatically implies continuity with the past." They argue that one should expect the invention of tradition "to occur more frequently when a rapid transformation of society weakens or destroys the social patterns for which 'old' traditions had been designed."[23] The multiple crises of ethnic resistance to national unification, colonial and imperial wars, profound economic and technological transformations, multiple class conflicts, and secularization that characterized British society in the two centuries after the first Act of Union made it a ripe breeding ground for the stabilizing efforts of neo-traditionalism. In this respect, the canon as neo-tradition offered a tremendous ideological contribution to the inculcation of "certain values and norms of behaviour" by linking Britons as one community of readers with literary tastes and a literary tradition running unbroken from the ancient bards to the modern poets, what Mathew Arnold euphemistically refers to as the "stream of English Poetry."[24]

Arnold's euphemism reveals another important aspect of canon construction by bardic critics—the fact that it reinforced existing inequalities between the different *ethnies*—Anthony D. Smith's term for ethnic cultural units—within Great Britain.[25] For Arnold, the "stream of English poetry" is quite literally a lineage of poets who are ethnically English (from Chaucer to Wordsworth). The preponderance of English authors in the British canon is consistent with the reality of English cultural, political, and economic supremacy within Great Britain, what Michael Hechter refers to as England's status of "internal colonialism" within the British amalgam.[26] For the most part, the British canon featured male, middle-class, Protestant, English authors, thereby reflecting the actual hegemony of these groups in British society. Hence, it serves as an example of the way that bardic critics approached internal differences by hierarchy and exclusion rather than pluralism and inclusion. When viewed as a neo-tradition that reproduced elements of existing hegemony, then, one can understand, for instance, why the bardic critics discussed in the following pages primarily studied English poets, even though some of these critics were not English themselves.

The following analysis is organized as a chronological investigation of the rise and decline of bardic criticism. I begin with an examination of antiquarian discourse in the mid-eighteenth century in order to illustrate its conflation of poetry, bards, and nationalism. I continue by examining the ways that several major literary critics over the next century adopted antiquarian methods and terminology for ranking, classifying and describing national poets. Specifically, I examine canonical selections from Samuel Johnson, William Hazlitt, Thomas Carlyle, and Matthew Arnold. I focus my analysis on this select group of authors from the period for several reasons. First, since this study is concerned with mapping critical reading habits that shaped the field and the canon by normalizing the reading of literature through a nationalist lens, these critics are the best candidates for such a study because their work was formative of national tastes and reading practices in their own day. The fact that they continue to be read today as part of a veritable "canon of critics" by scholars entering the field further corroborates this formative role. Second, these critics span the period from the rise of antiquarian bardology to the climax and denouement of bardic criticism in the late Victorian period, thereby bracketing the chronological limits of the study. Third, several of these critics are particularly germane for the study of Romantic nationalism because they furthered the canonization of Romantic poets such as Wordsworth. Finally, because these critics represent a variety of political orientations—a staunch Tory, an early nineteenth-century radical, a post–Reform Tory Radical, and a mid–Victorian moderate, respectively—this diverse selection intentionally demonstrates the pervasiveness of nationalist modes of thought among a rich literary community. As the conclusion to the chapter argues, the decline of bardic criticism only came about at the end of the nineteenth century when more timely concerns warranted different critical modes.

The Antiquarian Roots of Bardic Criticism

The conceit of the poet as national emblem and *vox populi* derives from the work of antiquarians who sought in vernacular texts, histories, and lore an image of the ancient Bards and Druids that depicted them as national symbols for a mythical fraternity of ancient Britons. This work was only part of a broader rash of antiquarian studies that furnished modern Britons with a spurious national heritage. Antiquarian modes of inquiry concerning matters of British national origin developed between the period from the late sixteenth century to the first decade of the nineteenth century. The dating is significant because the rise of this phenomenon coincides with several key events that culminate in the production of a modern British nation state: the English Reformation and break from papal authority, the Civil War, and the two Acts of Union. With the passage of these events, a territorially unified British nation-state emerged and the world found itself facing a new global empire. During this period, then, the ideological needs of the fledgling nation-state would have been most urgent. The interests of antiquarianism, therefore, cannot be divorced from the political climate of the era, which both fed these interests (materially and ideologically) and fed upon them.

Antiquarian investigations were based upon the authority of written sources and archaeological discoveries. According to Stuart Piggott, popular interest in the ancient Britons began with the Renaissance revival of classical texts on Gaul and Britain.[27] Texts like Julius Caesar's *Gallic Wars* and Geoffrey of Monmouth's *Historia Regum Britanniae* generated interest in the history and culture of the ancient Britons and their druidic orders. The Bible also became a reference point for anthropological and historical inquiries concerning the ancient Britons. For instance, seventeenth-century Puritan theologians, working from literal interpretations of scripture, propagated the myth that the sons of Noah peopled Britain and the West in general after the great flood.[28] Piggott notes that these texts exerted a controlling influence on the development of archaeological investigations.[29] In this vein, he describes the archaeological work of William Stukeley (1687–1765), an early eighteenth-century antiquarian who toured the countryside taking precise notes, measurements, and drawings of the megaliths and stone circles left by the ancient

Britons.[30] His renderings and speculations built upon prior authorial speculations about the Britons and helped to promote the Romantic image of Druids so common today, including the idea that stone circles like Stonehenge were ancient Druidic temples.

Piggott's study focuses on the role that scriptural and classical texts played in the formation of antiquarian studies, but neglects the importance that later antiquarians placed on vernacular texts, particularly texts attributed to ancient and medieval bards and minstrels. By the eighteenth century, these texts were also being accorded historical authority and played a central role in the shaping of a unified British culture. Antiquarian compilations of medieval minstrel songs and ballads collected from manuscripts and transcriptions of oral performances became quite popular in the eighteenth century and were part of a national revival that included such phenomena as the rise of gothic novels, art, and architecture (as evidenced, for instance, by Horace Walpole's mid-century construction of an imitation gothic castle at his home on Strawberry Hill). Such broad cultural phenomena demonstrate that antiquarianism was more than just an academic eccentricity; rather, it operated within a political moment in which nominal Britons were actively seeking to define a unified national identity by "rediscovering" their roots in and through vernacular literature, folklore, art, architecture, and even oral performances. By late century, such interests would eventually culminate in the production of an authoritative national canon. A central trope in the rise of a vernacular literature was the ballad-mongering bard, who operated metonymically as a *vox populi* and national symbol.

Thomas Percy's three-volume *Reliques of Ancient English Poetry* (1765), a phenomenally popular and seminal work of eighteenth-century literary antiquarianism that offered the first significant collection of English and Scottish traditional ballads and broadsides, jump-started a ballad revival that reshaped the literary landscape and popularized the association of bards with nationalism.[31] Despite allegations of forgery and embellishment (more or less true),[32] the *Reliques* played a crucial role in helping to shift national literary tastes away from Neoclassicism by popularizing the traditional ballad forms and subject matter that would later inform the Romantic break from established poetic modes. The *Reliques* directly inspired many Romantic texts, such as Scott's successful ballad collection *The Minstrelsy of the Scottish Border* (1802) and Wordsworth's experimental *Lyrical Ballads*. From a young age, Scott was deeply affected by Percy's *Reliques*, relating in his autobiography that he would beguile his schoolfellows with "tragic recitations from the Ballads of Bishop Percy."[33] Furthermore, in the introductory remarks to the 1830 edition of *The Minstrelsy* he claims the *Reliques* contributed a "great and important service to national literature."[34] Wordsworth, too, was profoundly influenced by the

Reliques and thought them to be formative of a new generation of British poetry. He testifies to both effects in the critical history of English poesy that makes up the bulk of the "Essay Supplementary to the Preface" (1815):

> I have already stated how much Germany is indebted to his latter work; and for our own country, its poetry has been absolutely redeemed by it. I do not think that there is an able writer in verse of the present day who would not be proud to acknowledge his obligations to the "Reliques"; I know that it is so with my friends; and, for myself, I am happy in this occasion to make a public avowal of my own.[35]

By establishing a lineage from the ancient bards, whom it depicted as venerated national symbols, to the modern poet, the *Reliques* also profoundly altered the popular and critical reception of contemporary poets. Percy establishes this lineage in the prefatory "Essay on the Ancient Minstrels in England" that begins the first volume.[36] The essay serves both as a critical exegesis of minstrel songs and an ethnographic study of minstrelsy in England, discerning its roots among the hallowed bards and their cognates, the scalds, of pre–Norman society. In Percy's account, the itinerant minstrels of the fifteenth and sixteenth century, who made a living by delighting courtiers and commoners with their songs and mimes, are a degraded version of the revered bards who frequented the great halls and battlefields of England and continental Europe several centuries earlier. This lineage is still evident in the songs and performances of the minstrels, whose "songs tended to do honour to the ruling passion of the times, and to encourage and foment a martial spirit."[37] Their predecessors, the ancient scalds and bards, however, were accorded much more respect and admiration by the ancient Celtic, Gothic, and Teutonic tribes.

Percy tells us that the name for scald literally meant "Smoothers and Polishers of language,"[38] suggesting the seminal and influential role that they played in shaping a national language and culture. According to Percy, the bards and scalds were virtually worshipped by their people for their god-like ability to shape language:

> The origin of their art was attributed to Odin or Woden, the father of their gods; and the professors of it were held in the highest estimation. Their skill was considered as something divine; their persons were deemed sacred; their attendance was solicited by kings; and they were everywhere loaded with honors and rewards. In short, Poets and their art were held among them in that rude admiration, which is ever shewn by an ignorant people to such as excel in intellectual accomplishments.[39]

By Percy's account, the bard or scald was thus considered a hallowed figure by king and commoner alike. Their orphic skill with words was deemed a thing surely divine, while their intellect and knowledge placed them on par with monastic erudition. Additionally, the strong annalistic and martial qualities of their songs and declamations linked them to the halls of power and fields of battle. To the different strata of medieval society, the bard was entertainer, poet, oral historian, and field marshal, thereby earning respect where he (and sometimes she) went. To illustrate this point, Percy recounts the tale of Colgrin, son of a Saxon king, who was shut up in York under siege by Arthur, then king of the Britons. To gain access to the besieged city and apprise his brother of the reinforcements forthcoming from Germany, Balduph, brother of Colgrin, disguised himself in bardic attire, replete with harp and tonsured head. Playing and singing British songs of heroism and mirth, Balduph was able to pass through the enemy's trenches and enter the city unmolested.[40] Percy provides several other marvelous tales of this nature, all of which serve to illustrate the high privilege and respect accorded to the bards by their people. Percy's reverent characterizations of the ancient bards and scalds suggest that the bardic practices of shaping language and reciting local lore were essential for defining a people, and the bards who did this well became emblematic and celebrated figures of their society. For Percy, then, the shaping of language and the shaping of the nation were apposite and interrelated processes.

In his descriptions of bards and scalds, Percy slips easily from the label "scald" to "poet," thereby promoting a genealogical relationship between these two figures that would establish the poet's nationalist credentials. He deduces that both the minstrel and the poet derive from the bards and scalds, from which they evolved into two separate roles:

> Thus the Poet and the Minstrel early with us became two persons. Poetry was cultivated by men of letters indiscriminately, and many of the most popular rhymes were composed amidst the leisure and retirement of monasteries. But the Minstrels continued a distinct order of men for many ages after the Norman Conquest, and got their livelihood by singing verses to the harp at the houses of the great.[41]

Percy clearly perceives the minstrel as more of an entertainer for the elites, a figure that evokes the Augustan poets and their well-heeled sponsors; conversely, he accords the poet a more independent and hallowed role as the learned composer of language and rhyme, a role more on par with the scald's orphic "polishing" of language that he associates with national service. By establishing a lineage from one to the other, Percy set the stage for eighteenth-century appropriations of the poet as a national symbol. Just as the medieval British king retained bards to chronicle important events, inspire troops, and counsel from the wisdom of the nation's lore, so too the modern British nation-state and literate bourgeoisie who sponsored and steered national culture celebrated the poet for the ability to unite and define the nation in and through autochthonous and polished verse.

The *Reliques* spawned a host of antiquarian collections, imitations, and forgeries that contributed to the transformation of the poet's public image from a sophisticated Augustan courtier to a popular national bard. By far the most popular collection after Percy's was Scott's *Minstrelsy of the Scottish Border*, a collection of border ballads that won instant acclaim and went through five revised editions from 1802 to 1830, spanning the entirety of Scott's phenomenal literary career. The collection observes discursive practices established by Percy's *Reliques*, such as the inclusion of an historical and philological prefatory essay to the 1830 edition entitled "Introductory Remarks on Popular Poetry and on the Various Collections of Ballads of Britain, Particularly Those of Scotland." In the essay, Scott reinforces the association between nation and bard. He describes the bards as "aboriginal poets" who possessed a command of the language and the ability to arrange words according to "the recognized structure of national verse."[42] The bards produced and recycled a canon of tropes, expressions, and phrases that Scott describes as a "joint stock for the common use of the profession."[43] For Scott, this joint stock had exclusively national properties. While giving a cursory history of the varieties of national poetry, he explains, "Though poetry seems a plant proper to almost all soils, yet not only is it of various kinds, according to the climate and country in which it has its origin, but the poetry of different nationals differs still more widely in the degree of excellence which it attains."[44] Going further, Scott theorizes that the progress of a nation's poetry, materialized in the canon, can also serve as a chronicle of its history:

> Yet the investigation of the early poetry of every nation, even the rudest, carries with it an object of curiosity and interest. It is a chapter in the history of the childhood of society, and its resemblance to, or dissimilarity from the popular rhymes of other nations in the same stage must needs illustrate the ancient history of states; their slower or swifter progress towards civilization; their gradual or more rapid adoption of manners, sentiments, and religion.[45]

In many respects, Scott's stadial theory of the progress of poetry coincides with Scottish Enlightenment theories about the stadial development of human civilization. However, contrary to this vein, Scott is careful to explain that the progress of poetry is more indebted to individual talent than to the workings of impersonal social laws: "But the progress of the art is far more dependent upon the rise of some highly-gifted individual, possessing in a pre-eminent and uncommon degree the powers demanded, whose talents influence the taste of a whole nation, and entail on their posterity and language a character almost indelibly sacred."[46] Ultimately, then, for Scott, the individual poet plays a central role in defining the tastes and culture of the nation.

The commercial popularity of ballad collections spurred numerous ballad imitations and forgeries. The list of notables includes James Macpherson's

Poems of Ossian (1765) and Thomas Chatterton's *Rowley Poems* (1777), which, despite being exposed as forgeries, were treated to popular acclaim and added to the cult of the bard. James Beattie's *The Minstrel: Or, the Progress of Genius* (1768), while neither a ballad forgery, nor an imitation, also drew upon the antiquarian vogue for bards and balladry by deploying a minstrel narrator. Perhaps the most stridently nationalist instance of bardophilia was Thomas Gray's "The Bard" (1757). The poem is set in 1283 and narrated by an anonymous Welsh bard who curses the English army as it marches home after the bloody conquest of Wales. Amidst a host of slain Welsh warriors and bards, the lone bard celebrates his fallen comrades and prophesizes a redemptive future that "warms the nations with redoubled ray."[47] Gray's "The Bard" reveals the fault lines of British nationalism that poetry could alternatively conceal or reveal depending on the poet's political bent. But it also reinforces the bard's situational and social relevance as a national poet by asserting that the bard is not only the keeper of national collective memory—in this case the memory of a vanquished nation—but also a visionary who grasps and shapes its future.

The ballad revival had a profound effect on the production and reception of pre-Romantic and Romantic poetry, infusing the latter with the nationalist import of the former. Part of the allure of balladry and minstrel songs for contemporary poets was the emphasis on a lost collective oral tradition, which appealed to a society undergoing rapid industrialization and prone to sentimentalizing about a simpler, more idyllic national past. Accordingly, Maureen McLane argues that the ballad revival provided a "new literary orality" that offered poets the "romance and technique of a popular, apparently collective, still-living oral tradition" of folk ballads and minstrel songs.[48] Similarly, in his study of "Romantic pseudo-songs" Terence A. Hoagwood links this newfound fascination with orality and tradition to commercial interests: "As printed commodities grow more numerous in the nineteenth century, poets often exploit that nostalgic preference amongst a customer-base that had become 'a reading nation.'"[49] Erik Simpson and Michael Gamer have argued for a more conflicted relationship between balladeering and Romantic poetry. Simpson contends that, while Wordsworth and Coleridge's early careers are characterized by provisional experimentation with popular national genres like minstrelsy and the ballad, they recant this style in favor of a more mature, high philosophical style that they developed against the low populism of the minstrel mode.[50] Gamer makes a similar argument about Romantic appropriations of the gothic, a genre that gained popularity in the late eighteenth century and shared features in common with ballad imitations and forgeries; while the Romantics were not above borrowing commercially successful elements from this genre, they considered their own style more elevated.[51] Whatever the case, Steve Newman argues that the complex relationship between the ballad revival and poetry profoundly altered *poeisis* and the English canon. He concludes: "The lesser lyric of the ballad changed lyric poetry as a whole and, in so doing, helped to transform 'literature' from polite writing in general into the body of imaginative writing that becomes known as the English literary canon."[52] I would add that the ballad revival also transformed poetry from an elite preoccupation to a popular genre with a distinctly national character and wide commercial appeal.

Ultimately, by investing bards and balladry with national import, the profusion of antiquarian treatises, ballad collections, imitations, and forgeries succeeded in transforming the writing, consumption, and critical reception of literature into acts of nation-building. For a nation that lacked a central, unifying narrative, the popularization of folk ballads and broadsides, either assiduously gathered from local songs and dusty manuscripts, or reproduced in numerous imitations and forgeries, provided an opportunity to manufacture a national tradition. Like the bards whom they celebrated as national symbols, the antiquarians who fostered this national discourse themselves became bards of a sort by writing the nation into being. Yet, the practice of bardic criticism was not confined to antiquarianism and the vogue for ancient bards and ballads. Spurred by the interest in vernacular texts generated by antiquarianism, the academic field of English studies that emerged in the latter half of the eighteenth century and matured throughout the nineteenth century adopted many of the critical habits and practices of bardic criticism developed by its antiquarian predecessors.

The Rise of Bardic Criticism

In the century between Thomas Percy and Matthew Arnold, a vernacular English literature supplanted the traditional Greek and Latin classics that had dominated the canon in Britain. This shift to the vernacular in literature coincided with the codification of the English language and its normalization as the language of instruction, developments that consolidated the rise of English as the language of state and commerce earlier in the century. The literary scholars operating in this period helped to consolidate earlier efforts to institutionalize a vernacular language by performing philological/literary investigations that traced the nation's linguistic roots to the thirteenth-century poets. Furthermore, from this linguistic origin, they also traced a tradition of vernacular literature for the fledgling amalgamation that was the British nation. To distinguish this vein of criticism from the modes that came before it, which emphasized classical texts and rhetoric, but also to highlight its relationship to the antiquarians, I have called it *bardic criticism*.

Bardic criticism shared many things in common with the antiquarianism of the preceding era. Like the antiquarians, bardic critics applied the techniques of philology, historiography, and biography to select, collate, and annotate collections of national poetry, replete with introductory essays and appendices that conflated language, literature, and nation. They also shared the desire to rescue vernacular authors from the margins of critical opinion and popular memory to which they had been relegated as a result of the prevalence of Neoclassical influence over the canons of taste since the Renaissance. To this effect, Francis Jeffrey commented that what he perceived as the major studies and collections of English literature of his day—Thomas Warton's *The History of English Poetry* (1774), Samuel Johnson's *Lives of the English Poets* (1781), George Ellis's *Specimens of the Early English Poets* (1790), and Thomas Campbell's *Specimens of the British Poets* (1819)—ranked with Percy's *Reliques* as part of a movement to recover the nation from "that strange and ungrateful forgetfulness of our older poets."[53] Jeffrey's sentiment illustrates the strong ideological affinity between antiquarianism and bardic criticism as both sought to elevate vernacular authors and literature to the status of the established classics of Greco-Roman antiquity.

One marker that visibly linked bardic criticism to antiquarianism was the prevalent conflation of "poet" and "bard" by many, though not all, critics and reviewers writing about living or canonical national poets. This practice was a transliteration from the nomenclature of the antiquarian ballad revival, in which the term "bard" took on a nationalist aura that made it a readily transferable moniker for modern poets. To wit, in a passage of the *Letters on Chivalry and Romance*, the Bishop Richard Hurd refers to contemporary national poets as "modern bards."[54] As a popular moniker for poets, the term "bard" actually had several connotations in common usage. "Bard" could be used as a generic moniker for all poets (following Hurd's usage), as a title of honor for superlative poets, or as a term of derision used ironically to denote a poet who is unworthy—a poetaster.

The period of Romantic reviewery, which marks an important mid-point in the lifespan of bardic criticism, is rife with examples of all three usages. The generic connotation is evident in a review for *European Magazine* (May 1819) that classed Wordsworth "in the first rank of the bards of our own day"; similarly, a reviewer for the *Monthly Repository* (1835) reflected on the fact that common opinion, which once denigrated the poet, now ranked him among the highest "bards of his age and country" and an anonymous reviewer for the *Eclectic Review* (November 1842) dubbed Wordsworth "the head of all living bards."[55] The superlative usage is illustrated in a review by John Wilson for *Blackwood's* (October 1817) in which he honored Scott by describing him as "like some ancient Bard awakened from his tomb"; likewise, a reviewer for

New European Magazine (1822) exalted Wordsworth by calling him "our great mountain Bard."[56] On the other hand, the ironic usage appears in a review by John Stoddart for the *British Critic* (February 1801), where he favorably compared the Romantic poets to the Darwinian "Bards of Science" and their brethren the "Bards of Insipidity."[57] Cutting in the other direction, John Montgomery for the *Eclectic Review* (August 1809) contemptuously referred to Wordsworth, Coleridge, and Southey as the "Westmoreland triumvirate of Bards" and a reviewer for the *Monthly Review* (1819) made an underhanded jab at Southey when in the course of a particularly acrimonious review of *Peter Bell* he deemed the unfit poem "worthy of the bard to whom it is offered,"[58] namely Southey. The poets corroborated their own bardification by labeling each other bards. Consider, for instance, Coleridge's superlative reference to Wordsworth as the "great bard" in "To William Wordsworth"[59] or Byron's satirical treatment of the Romantic bards in *English bards and Scotch Reviewers*. All in all, the practice of conflating the terms "poet" and "bard," regardless of usage and connotation, semantically conjoined the realms of poets and poetry with that of bards and balladry, inflecting the former with all of the nationalist import attached to the latter.

While the antiquarian revival of traditional ballads and romances helped to pave the way for bardic criticism, nonetheless, a key difference existed between the two groups that amplified over time. The antiquarians mainly sought to preserve and popularize a particular genre of traditional poetry that appealed to the emerging consciousness of nationalism within British culture, and they largely succeeded in this endeavor. Despite their popularity, however, these traditional forms and later spin-offs, such as the gothic novel, for the most part failed to make the transition to canonical status. Ironically, this was due largely to the efforts of bardic critics and reviewers, who deemed these popular forms below the intellectual standard of high literature. Unlike their antiquarian predecessors, the bardic critics were mainly interested in the canonicity of vernacular authors and texts. Some, like Arnold, chose to use the classics as "touchstones" to authorize the canonization of vernacular texts.[60] Others, like Hurd, preferred to argue that canonical vernacular authors like Spenser and Milton derived their genius more from the ballads and romances of their homeland than from the classics.[61] All, however, shared the belief that a national canon should record a nation's highest literary accomplishments. The canon would be a literary genealogy of the nation—albeit selective since it left out many popular genres—whose imaginary organicism would lend credibility to the nation's claim to a rich and inveterate heritage.

Accordingly, one generic feature of bardic criticism that developed in the century after the antiquarians was the notion that canonical literature, particularly poetry, should be treated as an article of national pride. Thomas

Campbell stridently conveyed this sentiment in the introduction to his *Specimens*: "No human pursuit is more sensible than poetry to national pride or mortification."[62] Two decades later, in a passage celebrating Shakespeare's contributions to the nation, Thomas Carlyle made a similar connection between poetry and national pride: "Yes, truly, it is a great thing for a Nation that it get an articulate voice; that it produce a man who will speak-forth melodiously what the heart of it means!"[63] And another three decades after that, Arnold summed up the feeling of intense pride that he experienced due to the nation's poetic achievements when he declared, "By nothing is England so glorious as by her poetry."[64] In each case, poetry is treated in a nationalist manner, as something that transcends the personal and historical conditions of its production because it comprises a grand narrative of national literary achievement. Arnold captured this perspective most poignantly when he described the canon as a "stream of English poetry,"[65] thus providing through the canon an organic, linear metaphor for the nation.

Many of the chief literary scholars and critics from the late eighteenth century to the late nineteenth century exhibited and further refined the critical habits and practices of bardic criticism foreshadowed by the antiquarians. Chief among these critics are Samuel Johnson, William Hazlitt, Thomas Carlyle, and Matthew Arnold. Collectively, they comprise a veritable canon of critics because of the influence they exerted in their own day, but also because their work continues to be read and debated today among literary scholars of English as part of an acknowledged canon of criticism. As a result, these four critics helped to normalize the mindset of bardic criticism within the profession, establishing paradigms and assumptions that subsisted until the canon wars of the 1960s finally brought critical scrutiny to bear on them.

As major exponents of bardic criticsm, Johnson, Hazlitt, Carlyle, and Arnold exemplify the mode of bardic criticism in the way they, like the antiquarians before them, promulgate an intimate relationship between poetry and the nation. For instance, Samuel Johnson established a model for the canonization of national authors in his literary biography of Shakespeare based on the degree to which the poet supposedly exhibits national characteristics. William Hazlitt upgraded this method of canonization by celebrating Wordsworth's poetry on the basis that it arose organically from the territory of the nation. Furthermore, Hazlitt put forward the claim that poetry is an expression of the "spirit of the age," thus propagating the antiquarian conceit that poetry conveys the shared experience of a people. Thomas Carlyle corroborated this claim by arguing for a direct correspondence between poetry and culture; going further, he also advanced the notion that poetry ideologically sustains nationalism and empire. Finally, the work of Matthew Arnold in many respects consolidated the efforts of previous bardic critics. Like Hazlitt and Carlyle, Arnold perceived a symbiotic relationship between poet and nation, such that the level of nationalism determined the level of poetic genius. He consolidated Johnson and Hazlitt's methods of bardic canonization by corroborating the claim that poetry subsumes culture, land, and verse. He repeated Carlyle's claim that poetry serves nation and empire. And he consolidated a national canon by mapping an ostensibly organic "great tradition" of vernacular poets from Chaucer to Wordsworth. But Arnold took bardic criticism to a new level by reflecting on its function, which he defined in terms of cultivating national culture and canonizing national poets. In the next few sections, I focus on the most important works by each of these four critics, both to identify where and how they perform bardic criticism, and to narrate the discourse of bardic criticism.

Johnson and the Methods of Bardic Canonization

Samuel Johnson contributed much to the development of British nationalism in the eighteenth century. As a lexicographer for the nation, he helped codify what Pierre Bourdieu calls the "legitimate language." Bourdieu writes, "One must not forget the contribution which the political will to [national] unification ... makes to the *construction* of the [legitimate] language."[66] Noah Webster, who was in this respect Johnson's double in the United States, was quite explicit about the "political will to unification" behind the publication of his *American Dictionary* in 1828, stating in his Introduction that language "is a band of national union."[67] Johnson, too, was explicit about the nationalist political will behind the publication of his two-volume *A Dictionary of the English Language* in 1755. In the Preface he states that the work is devoted "to the honour of my country, that we may no longer yield the palm of philology, without a contest, to the nations of the continent." But the *Dictionary* served British nationalism in more ways than just inflating philological pride. In the same passage from the Preface, Johnson writes, "The chief glory of every people arises from its authours."[68] This was no empty platitude for Johnson: the *Dictionary* demonstrates his veneration for national authors with the innovative use of no less than 114,000 literary quotations as illustrations for word entries. Significantly, the authors most frequently cited are Shakespeare, Milton, and Dryden, the same authors whom Johnson would later extol in his biographies and critical collections. The publication of the *Dictionary*, then, signaled Johnson's transition from nationalist lexicographer to bardic critic.

In his criticism, Johnson imported the antiquarian conceit that the poet is a representative of the nation. Accordingly, he developed a method of canonizing poets based on their expression of ostensibly nationalist characteristics, both in terms of the poet's personal character and literary style. In some places, this method borders on a sort of patriotic idolatry, such as in the "Life of Milton" (1781), where he treats Milton as a synecdoche for the nation when he states, "For what Englishman can take delight in transcribing passages, which if they lessen the reputation of Milton, diminish in some degree the honour of our country."[69] Johnson's high regard for Milton notwithstanding, the most sustained example of bardic criticism in his opus can be found in the Preface to *The Plays of William Shakespeare* (1765). In the Preface, Johnson highlights Shakespeare's autochthonous qualities and draws attention to the intimate relationship between the language, plot, and style of his dramatic poetry and the culture of the nation.

The case of Shakespeare offers a prime example of the role that bardic criticism played in manufacturing canonicity. As Jack Lynch has argued, Shakespeare's meteoric rise to national bardom was not *sui generis*:

> The man from Stratford wrote *Hamlet* and *King Lear* more or less on his own, but it took the combined efforts of countless actors, editors, scholars, readers, and teachers to turn Shakespeare, the provincial playwright and theatrical shareholder, into Shakespeare, the universal bard at the heart of English culture.[70]

Johnson contributed to Shakespeare's transformation from a popular Elizabethan playwright to the most celebrated national bard, but he also operated within a tradition of critical praise for Shakespeare dating back at least a century. For instance, in *An Essay of Dramatic Poesy* (1668) Dryden credits Shakespeare with being "the Homer, or father of our dramatic poets."[71] Similarly, Johnson, in the Preface, writes of Shakespeare, "The form, the characters, the language, and the shows of the English drama are his."[72] But Johnson was not content to make genealogical statements only in his praise for the great bard, and instead went on to outline several ways in which Shakespeare captured the spirit of the nation in his poetry and personality.

In the Preface to *The Plays of William Shakespeare*, Johnson explains that Shakespeare's language and style possess quintessential national qualities. To support this claim, he elaborates a proto–Wordsworthian theory of language to identify the quintessential language and style befitting each nation:

> If there be, what I believe there is, in every nation, a stile which never becomes obsolete, a certain mode of phraseology so consonant and congenial to the analogy and principle of its respective language as to remain settled and unaltered; this stile is probably to be sought in the common intercourse of life, among those who speak only to be understood, without ambition of elegance.[73]

Johnson regards Shakespeare as the master of this unique national idiom, going so far as to declare that he "deserves to be studied as one of the original masters of our language."[74] This claim echoes the antiquarian argument most acutely expressed by Percy, who called the ancient poets "smoothers and polishers" of language because of their double role as masters and creators of the national tongue. In a similar vein, Johnson commends Shakespeare's poetry for its quality as "a faithful mirrour of manners and of life,"[75] which raises another antiquarian conceit—the image of the inspired bard who conveys the thoughts and manners of the nation. In Johnson's reckoning, then, what makes Shakespeare great is his bard-like ability to communicate the manners and life of the nation in the ordinary language and style of the people.

Johnson further explores Shakespeare's national qualities in a biographical sketch of the poet, linking the poet's literary genius to his upbringing among the people. For instance, since Shakespeare possessed very little formal training or exposure to classical models, Johnson conjectures that his poetic and dramaturgical talents must derive from a keen and intimate knowledge of the attitudes and mannerisms of the common people. In this vein, he observes that Shakespeare possessed a "vigilance of observation and accuracy of distinction which books and precepts cannot confer," and that this talent enabled Shakespeare to write about "not what he knew himself, but what was known to his audience."[76] Therefore, to understand Shakespeare, Johnson suggests one must "look for his meaning sometimes among the sports of the field, and sometimes among the manufacturers of the shop."[77] Johnson's high esteem for Shakespeare's rootedness in the language, land, and people compel him to admit that, apart from Shakespeare, "there were no writers in English, and perhaps not many in other modern languages, which shewed life in its native colours."[78] This assertion again returns to the bardic discourse of the antiquarians, who esteemed the bard to be a kind of *vox populi*, the more so because he was of the people.

Although Johnson's appraisal of Shakespeare is mixed, even his criticism of the poet's peccadilloes and literary flaws militate toward a positive rendering of Shakespeare as an iconic national poet. Johnson points out several perceived flaws in Shakespeare's writing and character: the desire to please the audience at the expense of virtue and decorum; loose plots; anachronistic characters; excessive vulgarity; exaggerated passion; pompous diction; feckless oratory; a neglect of the classical unities; and a personal tendency to be quarrelsome in public and private life.[79] However, Johnson blunts the impact of his censure by creatively interpreting these aesthetic and personal blemishes as further signs of Shakespeare's intimacy with and upbringing among the people. He argues that many of these flaws were in fact a deliberate accommodation to "the state of the age in which he lived," which "was yet struggling to emerge from barbarity."[80] As the argument goes, because Shakespeare's Elizabethan audience was mostly illiterate and "could not have followed him through the intricacies of the drama, had they not held the thread of the story in their hands," Johnson explains that Shakespeare sought to accommodate his audience by drawing his plots from popular sources—familiar fables, myths, legends, and romances, dispensing with the alien strictures of the classical unities, and making use of common language and idioms.[81] Therefore, "his English histories he took from English chronicles and English ballads," writes Johnson, and, "his plot, whether historical or fabulous, are always crouded with incidents, by which the attention of a rude people was more easily caught than by sentiment or argumentation."[82] In Johnson's estimation, then, even Shakespeare's flaws can be interpreted as signs of the poet's deep investment in the nation because they reflect his familiarity with and respect for the tastes and desires of a broad national audience.

In presenting Shakespeare as a bard-like man of the people who wrote in the language, idioms, and tropes organically suited to an Elizabethan audience, Johnson's canonization of Shakespeare established a model for later bardic critics. Hazlitt, Carlyle, and Arnold would each pick up the strands of Johnson's critical appraisal of national poets in their own ways by further refining and elaborating the practice of bardic canonization illustrated in Johnson's Preface on Shakespeare.

Hazlitt, Wordsworth and the Spirit of the Age

William Hazlitt is not known for his patriotism, much less for his patriotic writings about the poets. In what is perhaps his most memorable work of criticism, *The Spirit of the Age, or, Contemporary Portraits* (1825), he presents portraits of contemporary figures that are brimming with acerbic wit. For instance, in one particularly cheeky passage about Coleridge, he concludes, "If Mr. Coleridge had not been the most impressive talker of his age, he would probably have been the finest writer."[83] Yet, Hazlitt's well-known portrait of Wordsworth, which is not without similar moments of critical censure, is remarkable for the critic's insistence that there is an organic and indivisible connection between the poet's verse and the land and people of his upbringing. This claim resembles the one made by Johnson about Shakespeare, but goes farther by emphasizing the poet's rootedness in the natural environment of the nation. Like Johnson, Hazlitt uses this claim to Wordsworth's bard-like connection to the land and people as evidence to support the poet's merit as a canonical poet. In so doing, he helps to redeem Wordsworth's reputation from nearly two decades of critical disdain.

The plan of *The Spirit of the Age* is itself an exercise in bardic criticism because it is based on the belief that individuals can embody and express the "spirit of the age," a notion that resonates with the antiquarian portrayal of bards as representatives and spokespersons for the nation. The text consists of a collection of eighteen essays that present twenty-three biographical portraits of living or recently deceased subjects—all men, almost all Britons (excepting Washington Irving)—whom Hazlitt deems to be representative of the age. Given the virtual monopoly of British subjects in his collection of portraits, the "age" that Hazlitt has in mind is that of the nation rather than of history or some other universal signifier. The list of British subjects includes notable philosophers, statesmen, political economists, clergymen, philologists, critics, and poets.[84] The preponderance of poets in Hazlitt's roster of subjects might seem unusual for a work that purports to represent the culture of a particular moment in the history of the nation; however, it can be interpreted as yet another aspect of his inclination towards antiquarian modes of thought, which normalized the practice of promulgating poets as representative national figures.

Of all the portraits, the essay on Wordsworth, entitled "Mr. Wordsworth," stands out for its frank assertion of the poet's superlative quality as a representative of the age, a point Hazlitt declares in the first sentence: "Mr. Wordsworth's genius is a pure emanation of the Spirit of the Age."[85] For Hazlitt, no other poet captures the revolutionary spirit that captivated British intellectuals, artists, and progressives after the outbreak of the French Revolution. He finds this spirit in Wordsworth's experimentation with common subjects and diction in *Lyrical Ballads*, which he argues is modeled on "the political changes of the day,"[86] a reference to the egalitarian politics of the Revolution. He famously declares Wordsworth's muse "a levelling one" that "proceeds on a principle of equality, and strives to reduce all things to the same standard."[87] He continues, "His popular, inartificial style gets rid (at a blow) of all the trappings of verse, of all the high places of poetry.... All the traditions of learning, all the superstitions of age, are obliterated and effaced. We begin *de novo* on a *tabula rasa* of poetry."[88] To Hazlitt, Wordsworth is so much a representative of the revolutionary spirit of the age that "had he lived in any other period of the world, he would never have been heard of."[89]

The close association between Wordsworth's poetic system and the spirit of the age did not help the poet to garner a positive reputation among critics and reviewers. Indeed, Francis Jeffrey went so far as to suggest that what made Wordsworth and his Lake Poet brethren so disagreeable was precisely their aesthetic expression of a revolutionary spirit. In a review of Southey's *Thalaba* for the *Edinburgh Review* (October 1802), he presents the aesthetic experimentation pursued by Wordsworth and the Lake Poets as tantamount to sedition, describing them as "*dissenters* from the established systems in poetry and criticism," of "*German* origin," who obeyed principles borrowed from "the great apostle of Geneva," namely, Rousseau, the philosopher most closely associated with the ideals of the French Revolution.[90] For the most part, however, criticism of Wordsworth's poetic experiments tended to revolve around charges of simplicity, bathos, dogmatism, and egotism. For example, in a review of the first edition of *Lyrical Ballads* (1798) a reviewer for the *New London Review* (January 1799) criticizes Wordsworth's "simple style"[91]; in the *Satirist* (November 1807), a reviewer of *Poems, in Two Volumes* (1807) mockingly compares the poems to "Mother Bunch's tales and Mother Goose's melodies"[92]; in another review of *Poems*, a tart reviewer in *Poetical Register* (1811) describes the poems as "driveling nonsense" and bemoans Wordsworth's mechanical allegiance to an "incomprehensible system of poetry"[93]; and a reviewer of *Memorials of a Tour on the Continent* (1820) writing for *Literary Gazette* (April 1822) decries what he calls Wordsworth's "teemings of egotistical complacency."[94] Even Hazlitt, of course, criticizes Wordsworth for his egotism, remarking, "He takes a subject or a story merely as pegs or loops to hang thought and feeling on; the incidents are trifling, in proportion to his contempt for imposing appearances; the reflections are profound, according to the gravity and aspiring pretensions of his mind."[95] Hazlitt conjectures that a surfeit of negative reviews produced in Wordsworth a "sense of injustice and of undeserved ridicule" that soured his public disposition. Regardless, he explains, "[Wordsworth] did not court popularity by a conformity to established models, and he ought not to have been surprised that his originality was not understood as a matter of course."[96]

Hazlitt, of course, was among those who did understand and appreciate the value of Wordsworth's originality, going so far as to declare Wordsworth "the most original poet now living."[97] His essay on Wordsworth helped to change the critical discourse on the poet, a process that ultimately transformed Wordsworth from a provincial Lake Poet with a cult-like popular following to a canonical national poet. He intimates that this process was already underway at the time he was writing his essay on Wordsworth: "The tide has turned much in his favour of late years. He has a large body of determined partisans...."[98] Indeed, Hazlitt was among the ranks of these determined partisans. His partisanship dates back to a moment in his childhood when he first encountered the soon to-be poet of *Lyrical Ballads*. The event is described in "My First Acquaintance with the Poets" (1823), where Hazlitt paints Wordsworth in a visionary light as "Don Quixote-like" with "a fire in his eye."[99] In the same essay, he also describes how he was treated to a preview of the as yet unpublished *Lyrical Ballads* while on a visit with Coleridge to Alfoxden in the summer of 1798. The experience stirred in him a "deep power and pathos" as "the sense of a new style and a new spirit in poetry came over me. It had to me something of the effect that arises from the turning up of the fresh soil, or of the first welcome breath of Spring."[100] The "new spirit in poetry" to which Hazlitt refers later becomes the impetus for his charge that Wordsworth, more than any other national figure, embodies the "spirit of the age," a claim that contributes to a critical reassessment of the poet. But what sets Hazlitt apart from Wordsworth's other critical admirers is his bardic tendency to perceive in Wordsworth's poetry a salient attachment to the land and people.

At the same time that Hazlitt trumpets Wordsworth as the poet who best captures the national "spirit of the age," he also celebrates Wordsworth's attachment to a particular place and people in the nation, suggesting that Wordsworth's provincialism adds to rather than subtracts from his status as a bard-like representative of the nation. Hazlitt alludes to Wordsworth's provincialism by describing his poetry as "vernacular,"[101] not just because of his choice of common diction, but also because his themes, subjects, and settings are vernacular, too, in the sense that they convey the ordinary manners, feelings, and experiences of people from his native Lake District. Accordingly, he explains that Wordsworth's poetry delivers "household truths."[102] He also upgrades Wordsworth's muse from a "levelling one," which suggests a universal habitation, to a local one rooted in the pastoral locale and community of the Lakes: "[Wordsworth] has struck into the sequestered vale of humble life, sought out the Muse among sheep-cotes and hamlets, and the peasant's mountain-haunts, has discarded all the tinsel pageantry of verse, and endeavoured (not in vain) to aggrandize the trivial, and add the charm of novelty to the familiar."[103] He attributes Wordsworth's vernacular qualities to the poet's devotion to the land and people of his upbringing among the lakes: "He has dwelt among pastoral scenes, till each object has become connected with a thousand feelings, a link in the chain of thought, a fibre of his own heart."[104] In effect, Hazlitt presents Wordsworth as a sort of aboriginal native of the Lakes whose poetry cannot help but be vernacular. Furthermore, he does not see a conflict between Wordsworth the provincial poet of the Lake District and Wordsworth the "spirit of the age." Rather, for Hazlitt, the two identities mutually reinforce each other as the former lends credence to the latter by instancing the poet's bard-like ability to represent the people. Going further, one may conjecture that for Hazlitt, Wordsworth's particular affinity for the pastoral environs of the Lake District makes him an even more desirable candidate for the "spirit of the age" because of the fact that this part of the country features so prominently in the sentimental narratives of merry-old England that permeate British literary culture.

Perhaps the most striking feature of Hazlitt's bardic rendering of Wordsworth is his tendency to read place into Wordsworth's poetry even when it is not explicitly mentioned:

> Nursed amidst the grandeur of mountain scenery, he has stooped to have a nearer view of the daisy under his feet, or plucked a branch of white-thorn from the spray: but, in describing it, his mind seems imbued with the majesty and solemnity of the objects around him. The tall rock lifts its head in the erectness of his

> spirit; the cataract roars in the sound of his verse; and in its dim and mysterious meaning the mists seem to gather in the hollows of Helvellyn, and the forked Skiddaw hovers in the distance. There is little mention of mountainous scenery in Mr. Wordsworth's poetry; but by internal evidence one might be almost sure that it was written in a mountainous country, from its bareness, its simplicity, its loftiness and its depth![105]

Hazlitt's certainty that there is invisible "internal evidence" for a correspondence between the features of Wordsworth's style (e.g., simplicity, loftiness, and depth) and the features of the landscape augments Wordsworth's bardic status by advancing the notion that his poetry is literally a part of the landscape, extending the natural features of the nation into its literature. It also augments Hazlitt's status as a bardic critic because it underscores his tendency to conflate poetry, place, and people.

Hazlitt's use of a critical framework that naturalizes the association between poets and the national "spirit of the age" together with his depiction of Wordsworth as a vernacular poet whose verse subsumes land, language, and culture contributed to the development of bardic criticism by further elaborating the bardic conceit that poets are representatives of the people. Carlyle will take this conceit a step further by attaching an imperial instrumentality to the national poet.

Carlyle's National Poet-Hero and the Literary Sinews of Empire

Thomas Carlyle's "The Hero as Poet," which is collected in *On Heroes, Hero-Worship and the Heroic in History* (1841), offers a salient example of bardic criticism in the mid-nineteenth century. At first glance, the text's universalist pronouncements about the role of poets and other "great men" in the making of history may make it appear to be a poor candidate for an analysis of nationalism in the critical discourse on poets and poetry. However, beneath the veneer of Carlyle's universalist philosophy is a strong undercurrent of partisan nationalism, most poignantly expressed in his bardic rendering of Shakespeare as a figurehead and rallying point for both the nation *and* the empire.

On Heroes is often cited for its delineation of a "great man" theory of history in which "Universal History" or "the history of what man has accomplished" is defined in terms of "the History of the Great Men who have worked here."[106] While the essay outlines various types of men who drive human history towards ever-greater deeds and accomplishments, these types are also determined by the material conditions of their age, and in that sense they are also representative of their age. Hence, in lecture three on "The Hero as Poet," he writes, "The Hero can be Poet, Prophet, King, Priest or what you will, according to the kind of world he finds himself born into."[107] In Carlyle's narrative, after reformations and republican politics have tarnished the prestige of king and priest, and after the prophet's halo has been stripped by skeptical philosophy and natural science, the role of hero falls to the poet.

Carlyle's rendering of the poet-hero emphasizes the poet's vatic powers of insight, and this description at first appears to ratify a universalist rather than a nationalist view of the poet. In Carlyle's scheme, the poet does not merely supplant previous incarnations of the hero, such as the prophet, but instead incorporates them into a greater whole. He describes the poet as a kind of modern prophet with privileged access to the "sacred mystery of the Universe."[108] The conflation of poet and prophet is not, of course, original to Carlyle, but is consistent with the philosophy of Romanticism. For instance, in *The Prelude* (1805), Wordsworth proposes that poets and prophets are "connected in a mighty scheme of truth."[109] When Carlyle avers that the poet is able to "*see*" and "discern the inner heart of things, and the harmony that dwells there," he is echoing a phrase from Wordsworth's "Tintern Abbey" (1800) in which the poet, caught in a moment of sublime reverie, describes how "we see into the life of things."[110] The upshot of these Romantic intimations about the poet's privileged access to universal truths hidden in the "inner heart of things" is that the poet is a kind of transcendent oracle unfettered by nationalist sympathies, belonging to a specific age of human development rather than to a period of national development. But Carlyle deconstructs this universalist reading by presenting Shakespeare as a key example of the poet-hero while also highlighting his nationalist qualities. In so doing, his conception of the poet-hero as an oracular figure begins to approach and merge with the antiquarian view of the bard as a prophet of the nation in the manner of Gray's "Bard."

Carlyle's rendering of the poet as a universal hero is contradicted by the way he uses Shakespeare to illustrate his point, which reveals a decidedly more nationalist purview for the poet. At the conclusion to "The Hero as Poet," Carlyle's theory of the poet hero flaunts its national colors when he asserts that "it is a great thing for a nation that it get an articulate voice; that it produce a man who will speak-forth melodiously what the heart of it means!"[111] As previously argued, this expression of national pride in poetry is a mainstay of bardic criticism. One realizes now that the poet's visionary gleam does not penetrate so much into the heart of nature, but into the heart of the nation. Hence, while Carlyle assures us that Dante embodies the nebulous religious impulse of the Catholic Middle Ages, which is itself only a Eurocentric phenomenon and not nearly a universal one, Shakespeare, the provincial "Stratford Peasant," on the other hand, embodies "that strange outbudding of our whole English Existence, which we call the Elizabethan Era."[112] In this vein, Carlyle states that "there is a noble Patriotism" in Shakespeare's verse, and concludes, "A true English heart breathes, calm and strong, through the whole business."[113] Such declarations concerning the poet's supposed patriotic leanings really disclose the critic's desire to appropriate the poet as an icon of the nation. Accordingly, he declares that "King Shakespeare" who shines "in crowned sovereignty, over us all" is the "strongest of rallying-signs" for the nation.[114] By conflating the hero as poet with the hero as kingly figurehead and rallying sign for the nation, Carlyle emphasizes the key role that literature plays in holding together the nation.

Carlyle further deconstructs his universalist theory of the poet hero by explaining that Shakespeare's world-historic role is not to unite all of humanity in one grand vision of universal truth, but to unite all of "Saxondom," a euphemism for the British Empire. He expresses this sentiment in the form of a rhetorical question:

> Before long, this Island of ours, will hold but a small fraction of the English: in America, in New Holland, east and west to the very Antipodes, there will be a Saxondom covering great spaces of the globe. And now, what is it that can keep all these together into virtually one Nation, so that they do not fall-out and fight, but live at peace, in brotherlike intercourse, helping one another?[115]

The answer, of course, is Shakespeare. Carlyle's portrayal of Shakespeare as a rallying-sign for both the nation and the empire registers a recognition of the role that literature can—and in fact did—play in the maintenance of empire, both in terms of sustaining national loyalty among the agents of empire and assimilating its colonized victims.

The stridently patriotic depiction of Shakespeare, the poet hero, found in Carlyle's essay contradicts the overstated universalist basis of his theory of heroes and history. His bardic rendering of the poet reveals that Shakespeare's universality actually consists in the degree to which he is universally beloved by the nation, and thereby serves as a convenient hub for its empire. Arnold will return to this theme in his treatment of Milton; but he will also dwell on the nationalist function of criticism itself.

Arnold and the Consolidation of Bardic Criticism

More than any other critic, Matthew Arnold helped to shape the critical habits and practices of the emerging profession of English studies in the nineteenth century. In relation to previous bardic critics, he also served to consolidate the core features of bardic criticism and implant them into the profession. For instance, in his key works of criticism, Arnold espoused the belief that literature and the nation shared a symbiotic relationship, and that literature could be used to promote the cultural unification of the nation, including its empire. Going further, Arnold advanced the work of bardic criticism by formalizing an English canon and pressing for its institutionalization. With his idea of "touchstones" and reliance on Aristotelian "high seriousness" as a category of evaluation, Arnold developed a comparative system of aesthetic judgment to delineate a "great tradition" of English literature dating back to Chaucer and the rise of an English vernacular over two centuries after the Norman conquest. Furthermore, as a strong proponent of compulsory public education,[116] he sought to make the canon a core feature of the national curriculum, envisioning that literature would standardize a quality national education because, in his words, "in literature we have present, and waiting ready to form us, the best which has been thought and said in the world."[117] Arnold also envisioned a national role for the critic, who would be fundamental for establishing standards of taste, much in the way of the French Academy, an institution that Arnold admired for its role "as a sort of centre and rallying-point" for the profession.[118] And he theorized the crucial role that critics played in canonizing national authors, thus making explicit the critical habits and practices of bardic criticism that others had performed more or less un-self-reflexively in the past.

Arnold's belief in the basic tenet of bardic criticism, that the poet functions as a national *vox populi* in the manner of the legendary bards, is evident from the very beginning of his academic career. Elected to the position of Chair of Poetry at Oxford in 1857—where, significantly, he was the first to lecture in vernacular English rather than the traditional Latin of the academy—Arnold's inaugural lecture "On the Modern Element in Literature" (1857) proffers a theory of aesthetic judgment based on how adequately an author represents the character of the nation at a particular moment in its history, what he calls "epochs."[119] For instance, during an investigation of the qualities of two Roman poets, Lucretius and Virgil, Arnold asks, "*Is he adequate? Does he represent the epoch in which he lived, the mighty Roman world of his time, as the great poets of the great epoch of Greek life represented theirs, in all its fullness, in all its significance?*"[120] Arnold applies to the classical poets the yardstick that Percy and the antiquarians developed in regard to the ancient bards, whom they perceived as spokespeople for the nation. Using this yardstick, Arnold declares that Aeschylus and Sophocles are, indeed, great poets, but Lucretius and Virgil are not because they fail to represent the characteristics of the nation during their age.

In "The Function of Criticism at the Present Time" (1865), Arnold expands on the concepts espoused in "On the Modern Element in Literature." Though the central claim of the essay is that critics play a vital role by seeding and preparing the nation for periods of great literary production, Arnold's subordinate claim—that there exists a dialectical relationship between authors and nations—is less evident, but equally significant for the way it reinforces the bardic conceit shared by Hazlitt and Carlyle that literature is an expression of the "spirit of the age." The essay presents a schema for the way Arnold thinks about the interrelationship of authors, critics, and nations. In Arnold's formulation, literary periods follow the vicissitudes of national history, and authorial talent is subordinate to the pitch of national culture. What Arnold calls "classic" literature, a euphemism for canonical literature, only emerges during periods of intellectual and spiritual growth within the nation, periods he calls "epochs of expansion."[121] Conversely, during "epochs of concentration,"[122] Arnold explains that the creative impulse in the nation is stifled and the critical faculty must be engaged to prepare for another age of creative production.

Arnold suggests that some parts of the world (again, read "Europe") might be entering epochs of expansion characterized by great movements of literary *sturm und drang*, while other parts might be receding into epochs of concentration characterized by a diminution of literary genius and a greater need for the function of criticism. Working backwards from the illustrations that Arnold provides for these epochs, one discerns that the theory of cultural expansion and contraction is, in fact, a nationalist construction because the type of epoch is determined by the degree of nationalism. For instance, he positively cites the "nationally diffused life and thought of the epochs of Sophocles or Shakespeare," stating: "In the Greece of Pindar and Sophocles, in the England of Shakespeare, the poet lived in a current of ideas in the highest degree animating and nourishing to the creative power; society was, in the fullest measure, permeated by fresh thought, intelligent and alive."[123] In other words, he proposes that these periods—the heyday of Grecian antiquity and Elizabethan England—produced great poets because in each case nationalism had achieved a high level of development and was diffused throughout every aspect of life.

On the other hand, Arnold demonstrates that epochs of concentration arise when national culture is as yet unformed, premature, or divided. He cites Goethe's Germany as a case in point: "There was no national glow of life and thought there as in the Athens of Pericles or the England of Elizabeth. That was the poet's weakness." Yet, despite the prematurity of the German nation-state at the time of Goethe, Arnold concedes that there was an equivalency in "the complete culture and unfettered thinking of a large body of Germans" whose popular nationalism stamped German Romanticism with a relatively high degree of quality.[124] Arnold is less forgiving when it comes to British Romanticism, describing it as an ultimately doomed "burst of creative activity in our literature" that had about it "something premature."[125] Arnold attributes this prematurity to that fact that the nation had entered an epoch of concentration as a result of the political reaction, sectarianism, and division unleashed by the domestic furor over the French Revolution: "The great force of that epoch of concentration was England; and the great voice of that epoch of concentration was Burke."[126] Justifying his role as a critic, Arnold contends that the nation is only now exiting that epoch of concentration, aided, of course, by the meticulous work of disinterested critics like himself.

Central to Arnold's formulation of the author/critic/nation relationship is the idea of "atmosphere":

> But [literary genius] must have the *atmosphere*, it must find itself amidst the order of ideas, in order to work freely; and these it is not so easy to command. This is why great creative epochs in literature are so rare, this is why there is so much that is unsatisfactory in the productions of many men of real genius; because for the creation of a master-work of literature two powers must concur, the power of the man and the power of the moment, and the man is not enough without the moment; the creative power has, for its happy exercise, appointed elements, and those elements are not in its own control.[127]

This claim establishes the central premise for the role of the critic, whose function is to cultivate the right atmosphere for periods of great artistic ferment by professing, in a disinterested manner, "*the best that is known and thought in the world.*"[128] Arnold writes, "These new ideas reach society, the touch of truth is the touch of life, and there is a stir and growth everywhere; out of this stir and growth come the creative epochs of literature."[129] Applying his theory of atmosphere, he attributes the efflorescence of literary genius in the Elizabethan Age, what he later calls "national glow,"[130] to the intellectual and spiritual ferment engendered by the critical spirit of the Renaissance and Reformation.

The author/critic/nation paradigm proffered by "The Function of Criticism at the Present Time" exhibits two more features of bardic criticism. First, Arnold's paradigm extends national borders to the cultural and ideational dimensions by setting up a dualistic inside/outside relationship between ideas out there in the "world"—which, in offhand remarks scattered throughout the essay, he actually delimits to the European world of ideas derived from the Greco-Roman tradition[131]—and ideas that grow in a greenhouse-like national "atmosphere." While the cultural membrane surrounding the nation must be permeable if critics are to import "the best that is known and thought in the world," the upshot of Arnold's paradigm is to further cement the notion of a symbiotic relationship between authorial production and national culture. Second, Arnold theorizes a direct connection between the critic's work and the making of canonical authors and texts, such that what becomes canonical is itself largely a function of the critic's careful efforts behind the scenes rather than the spontaneous outcome of popular decree. Arnold expounds this view when he explains, "The creation of a modern poet, to be worth much, implies a great critical effort behind it...."[132] Significantly, here we find a kind of meta-consciousness about the canon-making function of bardic criticism that is lacking in the writings of previous critics. In effect, the process of canon-formation is the modern equivalent of medieval sainthood. Just as the hagiographic writings of the clergy legitimated the popular worship of individual saints by formally canonizing them, the writings of bardic critics like Johnson and Hazlitt, for instance, legitimated the national appreciation of Shakespeare and Wordsworth, respectively, by helping to bring them into a formal national canon.

If Arnold's early essays are significant because they elaborate a bardic theory of literature premised on the interrelationship between authorial talent, national culture, and the nurturing work of criticism, his later essays also deserve mention because they go on to advance a theory of the canon that emphasizes its organic cohesiveness as a living record of national accomplishment that is instrumental for shoring up nationalism. In "The Study of Poetry" (1880), Arnold conveys the idea of a linear, organic national literary tradition through the use of a watery conceit—the "stream of English poetry." Reflecting his sympathies for comparative literature, Arnold explains that this stream is but one tributary feeding the "world-river of poetry," which, once again, he defines in terms of a Greco-Roman and European tradition.[133] Yet, within this tradition, he argues that English poetry has distinctive qualities and a unique origin all its own. Pressing his metaphor almost to the point of silliness, Arnold tracks the origin of the English stream to Chaucer, the "well of English undefiled," whose current of "liquid diction" and "fluid movement" he tells us streams through the great works of Spenser, Shakespeare, Milton, and Keats.[134] By means of this watery conceit, Arnold dispatches five hundred years of religious, class, and ethnic strife, much of which is embodied in the very men constituting his great tradition, replacing this troubled history with a fantasy of linear and orderly continuity dating back to the origins of the English tongue itself. In short, Arnold fabricates a neo-tradition of English poetry whose stream feeds not so much the world-river of poetry, but the local pond of nationalism, which is fed, in turn, by the tributaries of philology and literary criticism.

For evidence of Arnold's direct attribution of nationalist instrumentality to poetry, one must turn to his remarks on the individual poets. "Milton" (1888) is the text of an address delivered at a service in St. Margaret's Church, Westminster, to commemorate the donation of a Memorial Window in honor of Milton given by an American enthusiast, George W. Childs. Fittingly, the address is a rumination on the power of Milton's verse to bind together a diaspora of Anglo-Saxon communities dispersed across the past and present territories of the British Empire. Arnold proudly declares that Milton is a quintessential Englishman who ennobled his nation by mastering the "great style" of antiquity. Reminiscent of Carlyle's presentation of Shakespeare as the great unifier of Saxondom, Arnold concludes that through a shared appreciation of Milton's great style "his hearers on both sides of the Atlantic, are English, and will remain English."[135]

Similar themes arise in Arnold's Preface to *The Poems of Wordsworth* (1879), in which Arnold moves from an appreciation of the poet's style to the exaltation of the poet into a kind of national icon. His unmitigated praise for Wordsworth runs contrary to previous remarks about the prematurity of Romantic writers expressed in the "The Function of Criticism at the Present Time." It also illustrates the remarkable appeal of the national cult of the poet. In the Preface, Arnold declares himself a "Wordsworthian" and delves into a paean that betrays a deep well of national affinity rooted in place: "It is not for nothing that one has been brought up in the veneration of a man so truly worthy of homage; that one has seen him and heard him, lived in his neighbourhood, and been familiar with his country." Arnold's paean ends on a high note of nationalism in which he, like Campbell and Carlyle before him, declares that poetry is the highest article of national pride: "[Wordsworth] is one of the very chief glories of English Poetry; and by nothing is England so glorious as by her poetry."[136] Finally, Arnold's bardification of Wordsworth into "one of the very chief glories of English Poetry" also completes the work of canonization begun by Hazlitt many decades earlier.

Arnold's pronouncements about the national scope and importance of criticism, together with his promotion of poetry as an instrument of national assimilation and focal point for national pride, brought the ideological assumptions of bardic criticism into the mainstream of literary culture. The concomitant institutionalization of English studies as a standard part of the curriculum for grammar schools and universities throughout the empire further amplified the bardic notion that literature engaged national identity. These assumptions would not begin to be challenged until nearly a century later with the radicalization of the profession in response to powerful movements for social justice. But, until then, Arnold's "great tradition" would persist as the central paradigm for the study of literature, ensuring that many more Britons would come to know each other as avowed "Wordsworthians" and fans of Milton's "great style."

The Decline of Bardic Criticism?

Because of its preoccupation with nationalist concerns, which precipitated the reinvention of modern poets as neo-bards and the establishment of a vernacular national canon, I have described literary criticism in the roughly two centuries since the first Act of Union as bardic criticism. This process took several forms: philological investigations that conflated nation, race, and language; the writing of quasi-hagiographic biographies of the poets that emphasized their bardic qualities; the drawing up of national standards for vernacular canonical texts; and the construction of a grand narrative for the nation's literary accomplishments that suggested a long and glorious national history while belying its recent amalgamation. The British canon that culminated from these efforts gave material substance to the ideology of nationalism. The canon functioned as a sort of ersatz state apparatus that influenced the national and colonial reading public, working through the everyday, intellectual labor of reading to network individuals into an imagined community of Britons by virtue of a shared familiarity with and affinity for the canon.

By the dawn of the twentieth century, bardic criticism was already being superseded by a different kind of criticism, one less concerned with the priorities of nation-building, which had more or less been met, and more concerned with shoring up the profession in a sprawling university culture organized along the lines of the German model of scientific research. Accordingly, men like I.A. Richards, F.R. Leavis, and William Empson traded in the techniques of philology, literary history, and biography that had been the trademarks of their bardic predecessors for ostensibly more empirical methods of inquiry that favored close reading and the use of interpretive schemas derived from the domains of semiotics and psychology. This cohort later inspired, and in some cases directly trained, the New Critics on both sides of the Atlantic, who continued to transform the discipline of English in similar ways by choosing aesthetic considerations like form and style over and against more political avenues of inquiry dealing with historical and social context. Richard Ohmann, among others, has linked this methodological shift to a convergence of factors—the reactionary politics of the Cold War and the conservative influence of a rapid rise in academic salaries during the post-war education boom.[137] Whatever the case, the New Critical methodology, which shaped the profession in Britain and the United States during mid-century, both subsumed and mellowed the nationalist preconceptions embedded in the study of literature by their bardic predecessors.

It's worth mentioning that, like their British counterparts, the American New Critics were also preceded by several generations of bardic critics dating back to the American Renaissance. In 1837, Ralph Waldo Emerson delivered the text of "The American Scholar" before a rapt audience of Harvard honor students. At the end of his speech, he sounded the bell for a uniquely American canon by declaring, "We have listened too long to the courtly muses of Europe."[138] Within a century, American universities had heard the call and were routinely training students in the classics of British *and* American literature. Robert Scholes and Gerald Graff have traced the history of this process, pointing out that elite universities like Yale, Harvard, and Brown led the way in the nineteenth century, first by replacing the study of Greek and Roman classics with the study of British literature, later by developing a separate canon for American authors.[39] Thus, Emerson and the American bardic critics revised Arnold's dream of an Anglophone nation by placing American specimens alongside the classics of British literature.

Sparked by a powerful convergence of events, the culture wars of the 1960s reactivated debates over the canon that had been dormant for nearly a century on both sides of the Atlantic. A new generation of scholars influenced by social justice movements, national independence movements, and theories ranging from post-structuralism to post-colonialism and feminism critiqued the racist, class-based, phallogocentric, and Eurocentric biases implicit (and often explicit) in the canon's grand narrative. Ironically, however, it can be argued that the culture wars were an upgrade of rather than a challenge to the nationalist assumptions and practices of bardic criticism that shaped the traditional canon. In Britain, the reconstitution of the canon was driven by the hopes of ethnic Scots, Welsh, and Irish who, having been culturally marginalized or subsumed by English hegemony, were now emboldened by the decline of the empire and inclusion within a new federated European Union to pursue greater autonomy either with the creation of distinct national canons of their own or by pressing for greater representation within the existing canon. In the United States, the shake-up of the canon was carried out under the banner of the new pluralist, multicultural hegemony, which sought to modernize the canon by including traditionally marginalized groups in order to make it more representative of the nation's actual diversity. In both cases, it can be argued that the spirit of bardic criticism persisted, albeit in new forms and among formerly subaltern or marginalized groups. Ultimately, then, though new songs are now sung, the nationalist impulse that initially kindled the profession continues to inform debates over the canon. Most likely, bardic criticism in some form or another will remain part of the critical landscape of English studies so long as nationalism continues to be the primary category for cultural and political organization.

***

From Percy's apotheosis of the bard as national icon, to Arnold's propagation of Wordsworth as England's chief glory, bardic criticism succeeded in redefining the role of poets and poetry along nationalist lines. This process had repercussions for the Romantic poets. By normalizing nationalist modes of literary study and reception, bardic criticism saturated Romantic production with nationalist import. Furthermore, the critical infrastructure erected through the process of bardic canon-making created pathways for the speedy canonization of Romantic poetry, and thereby ensured a broad dissemination to the reading public. The next few chapters go on to illuminate several ways that Romantic poetry promulgated nationalism through new modes of Romantic authorship that keyed into popular forms and beliefs.

CHAPTER 2

Wordsworth's Bardic Poetics in *Lyrical Ballads*

> What is a Poet? To whom does he address himself?
> And what language is to be expected from him?
> He is a man speaking to men....
> —William Wordsworth[1]

> In the first rank of the bards of our own day,
> Mr. Wordsworth may justly be classed.
> —*European Magazine*[2]

In his homage "To William Wordsworth," Coleridge conveys his esteem for the poet by hailing him "O great Bard!"[3] Wordsworth had yet to publish *Poems in Two Volumes*, and *Lyrical Ballads* had been treated to as much criticism as acclaim for its daring transgression of the "pre-established codes of decision,"[4] yet Coleridge's salutation would prove to be prophetic. In later years, critics would echo Coleridge's superlative view of the experimental poet, writing of Wordsworth that he is "in the first rank of the bards of our own day," "our great mountain Bard," "amongst the [highest rank of the] bards of his age and country," and "at the head of all living bards."[5] William Hazlitt, known for his acerbic criticism, nonetheless dubbed Wordsworth "the Spirit of the Age," and Matthew Arnold did him one better by honoring Wordsworth as "one of the very chief glories of English Poetry."[6]

These declarations illustrate the degree to which Wordsworth's reception was colored by the canon-making practices of bardic criticism examined in the last chapter. However, they also tacitly acknowledge the success of Wordsworth's *bardic poetics*, a mode of poetic composition outlined in the Preface and deployed throughout his opus—beginning with *Lyrical Ballads*—that reinforces British nationalism. Like the bards celebrated by eighteenth-century antiquarians, who were credited to be chroniclers and representatives of the people, Wordsworth sought to redefine poetry as an act of speaking for and to the people in a language and style that is common and accessible, and about ordinary shared experiences. Wordsworth's bardic poetics were directly inspired by antiquarian bardology, particularly Thomas Percy's *Reliques* (1765).[7] In the "Essay Supplementary to the Preface" (1815), he remarks that British poetry was "absolutely redeemed" by the *Reliques*, and admits, "I do not think that there is an able writer in verse of the present day who would not be proud to acknowledge his obligations to the 'Reliques'; I know that it is so with my friends; and, for myself, I am happy in this occasion to make a public avowal of my own."[8] In the expanded 1802 Preface, Wordsworth bases his radical experimentation with language on the plain language and natural style of "the first Poets,"[9] an allusion to Percy's bards and scalds whose name, Percy relates, literally meant "Smoothers and Polishers of language."[10] Wordsworth's experiment with poetic diction, style, and subject matter is presented therefore as a revival of the bardic tradition so inflected with nationalist import by antiquarians since the ballad revival. *Lyrical Ballads* exemplifies Wordsworth's bardic poetics by combining the simple language and style of the popular ballads with rustic characters and pastoral imagery. In so doing, Wordsworth appeals to forms of continental Romantic nationalism that evoked nationalist images of country folk and to anti-urban populism in Britain that developed in reaction to the dislocating effects of urbanization, industrialization, and immigration. *Lyrical Ballads* further enacts its nationalism by positing a link between landscape and the collective memory of an *ethnie*, thereby producing national space. Finally, the prevalence of English characters and places drawn from the Lake District for an ostensibly demotic bardic poetics reinforced the existing hegemony of an English *ethnie* within representations of the British nation.

In general, Wordsworth critics interested in questions of nationalism have tended to focus on the more pronounced nationalism of his later topographical writing and the *Ecclesiastical Sonnets* rather than on the subtler nationalism of *Lyrical Ballads*' bardic poetics.[11] The many scholars who have written about *Lyrical Ballads*' complicated relationship with the eighteenth-century ballad revival mostly have not made the connection between the ballad revival and the politics of eighteenth-century British nationalism in which the ballad revival played a role by nourishing a populist culture formed around native art.[12] Richard Gravil's *Wordsworth's Bardic Vocation, 1787–1842* stands out from the crowd by linking what he calls Wordsworth's "bardic vocation"—a sublimated but persistent antiquarian "impulse" that he traces throughout Wordsworth's major works—to English nationalism.[13] Yet, while he hails Wordsworth as "England's last *national* poet," his chapter on *Lyrical Ballads* is less concerned with the nationalism of Wordsworth's bardic vocation than with what he calls the "mastered irony" of *Lyrical Ballads*' negotiation of republican and conservative ideas.[14]

Katie Trumpener's *Bardic Nationalism: The Romantic Novel and the British Empire* explicitly makes the connection between nationalism and the antiquarian revival of bards and balladry. According to Trumpener, "English literature, so-called, constitutes itself in the late eighteenth and early nineteenth centuries through the systematic imitation, appropriation, and political neutralization of antiquarian and nationalist literary developments in Scotland, Ireland, and Wales."[15] She describes how Scottish, Irish, and Welsh patriots promulgated the bard as symbol of an oppressed, but determined national minority similar to the role of the last minstrel in Grays "The Bard." For these groups, she writes, "the bard is the mouthpiece for a whole society, articulating its values, chronicling its history, and mourning the inconsolable tragedy of its collapse." She contrasts the bardic nationalism of these marginalized groups to the urbane bardism of the English poets, who, situated in the hegemonic center and lacking an historical memory of collective suffering, therefore construed the bard as "an inspired, isolated, and peripatetic figure" rather than a focal point for collective struggle.[16] While I concur that Wordsworth's appropriation of the bardic mode does, in fact, reinforce the hegemony of an English *ethnie* by featuring English subjects and places, I also demonstrate that it does so in the service of a radical agenda that combines the elements of ballad populism and pastoral poetry with folk nationalism and republican evocations of the Lakes as a "pure Commonwealth"[17] in order to challenge elitist Neoclassical aesthetics and to resist what he perceives as harmful and foreign gothic influences emanating from cosmopolitan urban centers.

Wordsworth, of course, wasn't the only bard behind the composition of *Lyrical Ballads*. Admittedly, Coleridge's "Rime of the Ancient Mariner" is technically the finest example of a formal ballad in the collection. Yet, Coleridge's contributions, as he himself professes in the *Biographia Literaria* (1817), are limited to speculations on the "dramatic truths" evinced by supernatural events.[18] His four contributions—"Ancient Mariner," "The Foster-Mother's Tale," "The Nightingale," and "The Dungeon" exhibit this tendency in their reliance on supernatural elements. This temperament is consistent with the elements of superstition contained in the popular ballads, but Coleridge's reliance on sensational and exotic topoi jars with the local and quotidian themes that characterize their typical subject matter. Rather, Coleridge's contributions to *Lyrical Ballads* more closely resemble the gothic elements that Wordsworth explicitly rejects in the Preface. Coleridge identifies the difference between the two poets in terms of subject matter, writing that for Wordsworth's part,

> subjects were to be chosen from ordinary life; the characters and incidents were to be such, as will be found in every village and its vicinity, where there is a

meditative and feeling mind to seek after them, or to notice them, when they present themselves.[19]

Wordsworth's charge, then, was to demonstrate what was extraordinary about the seemingly mundane and ordinary scenes of everyday life. This strategy produced the rich admixture of aesthetics and ethnography that characterize his bardic poetics in *Lyrical Ballads*.

Wordsworth was conscious of the fact that conventional readers and reviewers might reject the unconventional populist style of *Lyrical Ballads*. In the "Advertisement" to the first edition, he describes it as a democratic experiment in poetic diction meant "to ascertain how far the language of conversation in the middle and lower classes of society is adapted to the purposes of poetic pleasure."[20] He confronts his fear that such experimentation would provoke resistance:

> Readers accustomed to the gaudiness and inane phraseology of many modern writers, if they persist in reading this book to its conclusion, will perhaps frequently have to struggle with feelings of strangeness and aukwardness: they will look round for poetry, and will be induced to enquire by what species of courtesy these attempts can be permitted to assume that title.

In a democratic gesture, Wordsworth appeals to the higher sensibilities of his readers and asks them "to be pleased in spite of that most dreadful enemy to our pleasures, our own pre-established codes of decision." Instead, he asks them to judge the collection on whether it "contains a natural delineation of human passions, human characters, and human incidents."[21] Fear that the poems will be judged by conventional measures arises again in the "Preface," in which he mounts "a systematic defence of the theory, upon which the poems were written" because the poems are so "materially different from those, upon which general approbation is at present bestowed."[22]

Early reviews were drawn over the merit of *Lyrical Ballads*. *The Critical Review* granted that the author's talents "certainly rank him with the best of living poets," yet bluntly concluded, "the 'experiment,' we think, has failed ... because it has been tried upon uninteresting subjects."[23] Slightly more acerbic, *The Monthly Review* offered a back-handed compliment, writing that while "we have been extremely entertained with the fancy, the facility, and (in general) the sentiments, of these pieces, we cannot regard them as *poetry*, of a class to be cultivated at the expence of a higher species of versification."[24] Despite its own detractions, the *British Critic* did offer a favorable endorsement: "The attempt made in this little volume is one that meets our cordial approbation; and it is an attempt by no means unsuccessful." They preferred its simplicity and unadorned tales "to all the meretricious frippery of the *Darwinian* taste."[25] But, as Wendell Harris notes, it was not until 1832 that a reviewer finally praised *Lyrical Ballads* unconditionally on the merits of its experimental poetics.[26]

Wordsworth sought comfort from his detractors by comparing himself to Shakespeare and Milton, two canonical poets who experienced similar rejection by established critics. Writing in the "Essay Supplementary," he reflects,

> At all events, it is certain that these Poems of Milton are now much read, and loudly praised; yet were they little heard of till more than 150 years after their publication; and of the Sonnets, Dr. Johnson, as appears from Boswell's Life of him, was in the habit of thinking and speaking as contemptuously as Steevens wrote upon those of Shakespeare.[27]

That Wordsworth viewed himself as part of a great tradition of English poetry embodied by these two luminaries is evident in his declaration,

> We must be free or die, who speak the tongue
> That Shakespeare spake; the faith and morals hold
> Which Milton held.[28]

Consequently, Wordsworth anticipated that, after a similar delay in popularity, his novel poetry would eventually find "fit audience" among readers and critics.

Indeed, by the end of the century, Wordsworth's *Lyrical Ballads* and much of his later poetry would become a staple of the British canon. In this regard, the modest commercial success of the second edition of *Lyrical Ballads* would prove revelatory. Wordsworth himself took notice of the difference in sales from that of the first edition, remarking in the Preface, "The result has differed from my expectation in this only, that I have pleased a greater number, than I ventured to hope I should please."[29] For a collection of experimental provincial poetry from a small Bristol publisher, sales of *Lyrical Ballads* were quite impressive: after four years and three editions, nearly 2,000 copies were sold.[30] These figures are comparable to those of prestigious poetic contemporaries, such as Scott's *Minstrelsy of the Scottish Border* (1802), which sold 2,990 copies after four years and three editions, and Southey's *Madoc* (1805), which sold 2,500 copies after ten years, three editions, and a poet laureateship to boot.[31] Of course, the success of *Lyrical Ballads* was not epiphenomenal, but rather amplified over time. Ian Michael's study of British literature anthologies and school readers in the nineteenth century provides material evidence for Wordsworth's relatively speedy rise to canonical status. By the 1830s, Wordsworth and other Romantic poets were already among the most anthologized poets, and by the 1870s, Wordsworth ranked only behind Shakespeare and Cowper for the most anthologized British poet.[32]

These figures demonstrate the immense popularity of Wordsworth's poetry at the national level, and thus controvert claims that challenge

Wordsworth's relevance to nationalism based on the provincial or English features of his poetry. No doubt, it is true, as Jonathan Bate has argued, that Wordsworth's poetry of place need not contribute to nationalism because "love of the land may be differentiated from institutionalized patriotism."[33] Yet, the very fact that such provincial poetry became canonical within less than a century suggests how broadly applicable the literary exploitation of local attachments were for nourishing and sustaining nationalism across the empire. It was precisely the power of local attachments that gave, for instance, copies of A.E. Housman's *A Shropshire Lad* (1896) such currency among the many British soldiers—most of whom were not from anywhere near Shropshire—who carried it to their deaths in the First World War. Wordsworth's poetry was similarly able to eclipse its local boundaries by becoming part of the required reading for countless school-age children throughout the empire who, from reading his canonical poetry, attached their conception of Britain to quaint pastoral images of a Lake District they had never seen. Certainly, there must have been tourists and residents of the Lakes who appreciated Wordsworth's poetry on an experiential level, trading zings about its accuracy or guffawing at the literary documentation of a silly local story or personage. However, like the provincial poetry of Burns and Scott, whose hyper-local leitmotif enabled it to become an iconic expression of Scottish nationalism, Wordsworth's poetry of place transcended its local and even its English origins by becoming a staple of the English-dominated British canon, in which the expression of English nationalism, overt or implied, was not inconsistent with British nationalism in the ways that Scottish, Welsh, or Irish nationalism were.

The following analysis is divided into four sections and explores the elements of Wordsworth's bardic poetics as explained in the Preface and exemplified in *Lyrical Ballads*. Part one examines prefatory material and focuses on Wordsworth's reinvention of the poet as a nationalist bardic figure who speaks to and for the nation in a language and style that is common, accessible, and derived from the plain style and ordinary language of the ancient bards. Part two situates Wordsworth's preference for rustic English scenes and subjects in *Lyrical Ballads* within the folk politics of continental Romantic nationalism and anti-urban Romantic nostalgia for the English countryside in Britain. Part three highlights the ways that *Lyrical Ballads* embodies an English folk nationalism by incorporating pastoral and ballad elements that valorize folk culture. Finally, part four specifically looks at the aesthetics of place in *Lyrical Ballads* in order to discern how Wordsworth produces national space by emphasizing local attachments to the landscape.

The Bardic Reinvention of the Poet in Wordsworth's Preface

In the 1802 Preface, Wordsworth asks the question, "What is a poet?" Throughout the rest of the Preface, he proceeds to answer this question in a manner that reinvents the poet in the image of the mythical bards trafficked several decades earlier by antiquarians who perceived the bard as an inspired poet and *vox populi*. With this radical reinvention of the poet's role in society, Wordsworth embarks on the transformation of poetry from an act of personal lyricism to a nationalist act focused on the building of community. This new view of the poet's place in society implies a radical critique of the contemporary state of the profession, which Wordsworth viewed as stultified by the patronage system. Rather, Wordsworth's new poet is a demotic being who writes not for court or cast, but for the common man and the broad community of citizens:

> [The Poet] is a man speaking to men: a man, it is true, endued with more lively sensibility, more enthusiasm and tenderness, who has a greater knowledge of human nature, and a more comprehensive soul, than are supposed to be common among mankind.[34]

Wordsworth's reinvention of the poet in the passage above displays two bardic qualities. First, like the fabled bards who spoke by, for, and of the people, Wordsworth presents the new poet as a "man speaking to men." This principle authorizes a popular reform of poetic diction back to the vernacular style attributed to the bards, what Wordsworth calls the "real language of men."[35] Second, Wordsworth's assertion that the poet is possessed of "a more comprehensive soul" invokes the representative qualities of the mythical bards by indicating a degree of empathy capable of mediating between the individual and the collective.

Wordsworth's experiment with the "real language of men" in *Lyrical Ballads* is intended as a democratic rejoinder to the patronage system that had for centuries confined the writing and reception of poetry to an aristocratic pastime. With the maturation of print capitalism in eighteenth-century Britain, a national market for vernacular literatures emerged, enabling experimentation with vernacular language and popular content that loosened the Neoclassical standards of poetic diction and topoi set by court and manor. In this new economy, Wordsworth was able to substitute the "language of conversation in the middle and lower classes," which appealed to a middle-class reading public, for the "gaudiness and inane phraseology" of court poets. Accordingly, in the Preface he explains, "There will also be found in these volumes little of what is usually called poetic diction; I have taken as much pains to avoid it as others ordinarily take to produce it; this I have done for the reason already alleged, to bring my language near to the language of men..."[36] Wordsworth's program entails a wholesale abandonment of the rarefied poetic diction, rhyme, and meter of the Neoclassical school in favor of the "language of men," code for vernacular poetry. Consequently, his injunction "Poets do not write for Poets alone, but for men" is an affront to conventional poets whom he believes

> think that they are conferring honour upon themselves and their art in proportion as they separate themselves from the sympathies of men, and indulge in arbitrary and capricious habits of expression in order to furnish food for fickle tastes and fickle appetites of their own creation.[37]

Wordsworth figures the hegemonic Augustan court poetry of his day as involuted, egotistical, elitist, and servile to the poetic diction that titillated its wealthy, aristocratic patrons. In contrast, by eschewing poetic diction and upholding the "real language of men," Wordsworth is self-consciously establishing himself as a poet of the people, while denigrating conventional poets as elitist sycophants who aim only to please the narrow tastes of their court patrons.

Wordsworth's language politics in *Lyrical Ballads* has been a common area of study for Romantic scholars. For instance, Nigel Leask writes that Burns's experimentation with Scottish vernacular dialects offered Wordsworth "a strong ideological counterweight to the literary hegemony of London," but follows that Wordsworth went to great lengths to purify his language of any regional dialect in order to insist that it was a universal language for the nation.[38] David Simpson presents a similar argument about Wordsworth's eschewal of dialect and suggests that his effort to select and promote a "national English" was part of a broader agenda to reform the language of poetry along "'republican' lines."[39] He explains that Wordsworth's "language of men" is actually modeled after the "plain, biblical English" of the King James Bible, which offered Wordsworth a "new standard diction for a poetry of civic virtue."[40] Along the same lines, Olivia Smith concludes that the references to rusticity and the "language of men" in the Preface are leveling gestures intended to substitute a semantically less vitiated "'native' English" for conventional poetic diction while also asserting its inherent worth and scientific value *vis-à-vis* classical languages and the refined English used by the upper classes.[41]

As Simpson, Smith, and others have pointed out, Wordsworth's project to promote a single national vernacular is riddled with class-based assumptions. In this case, Wordsworth's "language of men" is in fact the language of his middle-class, Protestant background, interspersed with common and archaic idioms for effect. Going further, Susan Manly adds that the radical implication of Wordsworth's experiment with common language is further undercut by a streak of Burkean conservatism in the form of an endemic solipsism that undermines his effort to represent the common thoughts and experiences of the rustic poor whom he purports to represent.[42] Yet, these limitations do not blunt the impact of Wordsworth's republican critique of the conventions of Neoclassical court poetry, which he viewed as an elitist institution that was a perversion of the original poetry of the nation dating back to the earliest poet-bards.

Wordsworth was inspired to pursue vernacular forms of poetic diction by antiquarian accounts of the vernacular language and ballad style used by the first poets, the ancient bards. Wordsworth indicates his conversancy with antiquarian discourse in "Essay Supplementary to the Preface" (1815), where he expresses his debt to Percy for enabling the rejuvenation of national poetry and the invention of his own poetic style by reviving the popular ballads.[43] Just as Percy describes how the original "Smoothers and Polishers of language" were celebrated bards whose style and importance devolved over the ages as they transitioned from *vox populi* to minstrel entertainers, so too does Wordsworth in his "Appendix on Poetic Diction" to the 1802 Preface cite the vernacular language of the "earliest Poets" as a precedent for his experimentation with the "real language of men," and historicizes the progress of poesy as a transition from this natural language to the corrupted and over-refined poetic diction evident in later periods:

> It is indeed true that the language of the earliest Poets was felt to differ materially from ordinary language, because it was the language of extraordinary occasions; but it was really spoken by men, language which the Poet himself had uttered when he had been affected by the events which he described, or which he had heard uttered by those around him.... The first Poets ... spake a language which, though unusual, was still the language of men.[44]

Wordsworth's assertion that the first poets composed in the language "really spoken by men" lends credence to his experiment with the "real language of men."

Wordsworth uses his history of poetry to reinforce his critique of poetic diction. He asserts that, over time, the poets "became proud of a language which they themselves had invented," moving poetry further away from the "real language of men." In this vein, he explains, "metre of some sort or other was superadded" and "adulterated phraseology" was introduced by which the "taste of men was gradually perverted."[45] He continues,

> Abuses of this kind were imported from one nation to another, and with the progress of refinement this diction became daily more and more corrupt, thrusting out of sight the plain humanities of nature by a motley masquerade of tricks, quaintnesses, hieroglyphics, and enigmas.[46]

Following this narrative, "the progress of refinement" eventually leads to the "gaudiness and inane phraseology" of the Augustan court poets. Wordsworth's radical reform of poetic diction is therefore couched as a conservative move to reject "the progress of refinement" and restore the "language of men" traditionally used by the earliest poet-bards. This formulation is consistent with modes of Enlightenment radicalism premised on the idea that republican values are a restoration of the "natural rights" that once existed in a primeval egalitarian society. Similarly, Wordsworth posits his reform of poetic diction as a restoration of the egalitarian language used by the original poet-bards.

Wordsworth addresses the "progress of refinement" of poetic diction in moral terms as the progress of social corruption, which suggests that his eschewal of poetic diction is part of a broader critique of society. Simpson notes that Wordsworth's reform of poetic diction was meant to encourage a reform of national culture in the face of "the negative effects of urbanization and the debasing of 'popular' culture."[47] Indeed, in the Preface Wordsworth links his critique of the "gaudiness and inane phraseology" of conventional poetry to his critique of urbanization and popular culture, in which he focuses on the "encreasing accumulation of men in cities" and their addiction to the "gross and violent stimulants" trafficked in "frantic novels, sickly and stupid German Tragedies, and deluges of idle and extravagant stories in verse."[48] Hence, for Wordsworth the corruption of poets and poetry follows the breakdown of society, while the restoration of the original "language of men" used by the first poet-bards is a path to the restoration of society in general.

If Wordsworth's alternative to vitiated court poetry is a decidedly more plebian poetry modeled after the vernacular style of the ancient bard, the corresponding form for his experiment with the "real language of men" is, not surprisingly, the ballad, whose revival he praised in the "Essay Supplementary to the Preface" (1815). Wordsworth's appropriation of ballad form and content connected his poetic experiments in *Lyrical Ballads* to the populism associated with the ballad revival, thereby adding weight to his radical critique of established poetic diction. Yet, his high opinion of the ballad set him against powerful critics, who looked upon the ballad revival with disdain and considered ballads to be trite and undeserving. Even Coleridge, his partner in *Lyrical Ballads*, was critical of Wordsworth's formal appropriations from the ballad.[49] Nonetheless, in the Preface, he defends his preference for the ballads, citing, for instance, "The Babes in the Wood," a popular broadside that Samuel Johnson had publicly censured for its lack of artistry, as an exemplary poem that conveys real human emotion in simple, but evocative language.[50] To facilitate oral transmission, the ballads rely on simple language, the repetition of established and memorable stanza structures, and the use of recognizable content, such as themes drawn from everyday experience and common myths (e.g., Arthurian legend and the tales of Robin Hood).[51] In *Lyrical Ballads*, Wordsworth sought to emulate these qualities in several ways: by utilizing simple language unladen by the classical allusions and Latinate forms of Neoclassicism; by recourse to ballad meter and natural blank verse, which Wordsworth compares to the "language of prose when prose is well written"[52]; and by attention to the value of familiar experiences, particularly the quotidian experiences of rural subjects.[53]

Later in the Preface, Wordsworth begins to limn a social theory of poetry that situates *Lyrical Ballads* on par with the popular ballads, which were believed to foster social cohesion by unifying a community through the collective act of oral reproduction and, in some cases, production.[54] Wordsworth relates that the immediate effect of poetry is the excitation of personal pleasure, which he explains is instrumental for producing sympathy: "We have no sympathy but what is propagated by pleasure."[55] On this basis, he counsels the poet to "express himself as other men express themselves" in order to "excite rational sympathy."[56] In Wordsworth's formulation, then, the aesthetic pleasure generated by reading poetry that is fitted to the real language and experiences of the nation's subjects ultimately functions as a catalyst for the sympathy that nourishes and sustains community.[57] The resulting structure of feeling binds the nation as a community of sensibility that contrasts with and excludes foreign modes of being. In this sense, Wordsworth's revolutionary poet functions much like the ancient bard: both are culture-workers whose manipulation of language, image, and affect shapes social consciousness and weaves the ideological weft of collective (in this case *national*) identity.

If the poet's first bardic quality is to craft poetry that is representative of common vernacular language and experience in order to bind a community of readers, the poet's second bardic quality aids and abets this enterprise, for it is the unique ability to perceive and express ambient emotion. Wordsworth perceives the poet to be one possessed of "more than usual organic sensibility" and "a greater readiness and power in expressing what he thinks and feels."[58] To avoid elitist ascriptions, Wordsworth claims that by "poet" is "implied nothing different in kind from other men, but only in degree."[59] Wordsworth's leveling belief that all men share the faculty of poetic expression is evident in his choice of epigraph for the first volume of the 1802 and 1805 editions, where he cites a line from Quintilian: "Feeling is what makes men eloquent, and force of imagination; and that is why *even the uneducated have no lack of words if only they are stirred by some emotion*."[60] The faculty of poetic expression cuts across class lines precisely because poetry is, as he writes in the Preface, the "spontaneous overflow of powerful feelings."[61] But these emotions are not simply privately held feelings; rather, they are the residue of collective experience because "the Poet thinks and feels in the spirit of the passions of men."[62] He cites examples of the poetic expression of common passions in *Lyrical Ballads*, such as the intensity of the maternal passions depicted in "The Idiot Boy" and "The Mad Mother," the solemnity of death evident in "The Forsaken Indian" and "We Are Seven," and the nobility of human attachment illustrated in "The Brothers" and "Simon Lee."[63] For Wordsworth, then, the poet is anyone who can sense the "spirit of the passions of men" and convey these feelings through a facility with language. In this way, Wordsworth's poet is a reincarnation of the mythical bards, whose talents as "Smoothers and Polishers of language" enabled them to do "honour to the ruling passion of the times."

Wordsworth's characterization of the poet as an individual who "thinks and feels in the spirit of the passions of men" jars with the normative view of poetry as a solitary and subjective act of personal lyricism and completes the realignment of the poet with the bard. The idea that poets weave poetry out of shared human emotion suggests that good poetry also functions as a kind of lyrical ethnography that bridges public and private, personal and social. In this respect, Wordsworth's definition of the poet as one who channels "the passions of men" instantiates Theodor Adorno's claim that lyric poetry escapes the ideological and psychological boundaries of individuation by operating at an emotional and empathic level that taps into the unmediated, generalized experience of humanity.[64] This redefinition of the poet as a kind of social empath who can speak for the people finally realigns the image of the poet with that of the bard, who, like Gray's protagonist in "The Bard," was popularly depicted in the eighteenth century as an inspired poet who possessed the uncanny ability to translate shared experience (the slaughter of a people in the case of "The Bard") into personal lyricism. In the final analysis, then, one can look to eighteenth-century popular portrayals of the bard for the answer to Wordsworth's question, "What is a Poet?"

The "Real" Britain: The Country and the City in Wordsworth's Bardic Poetics

For his experiment with democratic poetics in *Lyrical Ballads*, Wordsworth explains in the Preface that he planned "to chuse incidents and situations from common life, and to relate or describe them, throughout, as far as was possible, in a selection of language really used by men."[65] To this end, he selects scenes of "low and rustic life" in which "the passions of men are incorporated with the beautiful and permanent forms of nature."[66]

Given the prevailing winds of urbanization, industrialization, and colonial migration in the late eighteenth century, it is strange that Wordsworth should select such vanishing, rusticated subjects as English shepherds, huntsmen, cottagers, and country beggars for his tableau of "common life." Conversely, he depicts rising urban centers as marginal aberrations whose threatening plurality and heterogeneity require literal containment and purification. In *Biographia Literaria*, Coleridge suggests that Wordsworth chooses "a particular mode of pastoral life, under forms of property, that permit and beget manners truly republican,"[67] a remark confirmed in the *Guide to the Lakes* (1811), where Wordsworth describes his native Lake District in republican terms as a "pure Commonwealth."[68]

As the *Biographia* and the *Guide* make clear, Wordsworth's preference for "low and rustic life" in *Lyrical Ballads* involves an intentional politicization of aesthetics whereby the pastoral English countryside is transmogrified into the "pure Commonwealth" dreamt of yet still unrealized by republican politics. Lore Metzger explores the political implications of Wordsworth's turn to the pastoral in her study of the Romantic pastoral:

> English poets from Wordsworth to Shelley resorted to the pastoral repertoire of *topoi*, themes, and representative anecdotes for articulating their belief in the ideals of the French Revolution while also affirming that these goals were attainable without revolution.... That is to say: pastoral most frequently functions in English Romantic poetry to articulate radical ends of social reform attenuated by an insistence on conservative means.[69]

Borrowing the conventions of the Neoclassical pastoral enables Wordsworth to pose the English countryside as a natural and available alternative to the failed republican politics of London and revolutionary France. It also, as Annabel Patterson posits, allows him to key into the anti–Enlightenment politics of the genre.[70] What Raymond Williams calls the "green language" of Wordsworth's poetics implies a trenchant critique of industrialization, urbanization, enclosure, and other aspects of modernization.[71] Still, for a democratic poetics ostensibly predicated on depictions of "common life," Wordsworth's privileging of pastoral scenes and characters drawn from a Romanticized, even radicalized English countryside seems oddly out of place.

The preference for "low and rustic life" in *Lyrical Ballads* ultimately reveals another facet of literary nationalism in Wordsworth's bardic poetics, the idea that the "real" Britain is not to be found in urban centers, which he depicts as disturbing sites of corruption and alienation, but in the English countryside, particularly his native Lake District, which he depicts in idyllic terms throughout the many pastoral ballads that litter the collection. Wordsworth symbolically recenters the English countryside at the heart of the nation as the "real" Britain, reinforcing the hegemony of English culture in representations of the nation even as he rejects urban modernity. These poetics are consistent with Romantic nationalism on the continent, which developed through folk movements that idealized the common peasantry and village life, presenting them as emblems of national culture over and against urban cosmopolitanism. They are also consistent with contemporary cultural politics in Britain, where a "back-to-the-country" movement of sorts sprang up as a backlash to the rise of cosmopolitan urban culture.

Aira Kemiläinen has described Romantic nationalism as a "reaction against 18th-century Cosmopolitanism" that used folk-songs, folklore, customs, and local poetry to define an essential national identity.[72] The most pronounced expression of this movement can be found in Johann Gottfried Herder's concept of the *Volk*.[73] Herder popularized the idea that the folk or common peasantry represented the highest expression of national culture, and that nations could only achieve their highest form of development by pursuing their own unique national characteristics, which were embodied by the folk.[74] Conversely, he believed the cosmopolitanism and multiculturalism of the Enlightenment stunted a nation's development. Furthermore, like Montesquieu, Herder promoted the blood-and-soil notion that geographic features shape national culture.[75] This genetic connection creates an unbreakable link between a people and its "fatherland." According to Herder, only by pursuing the unique path of national development could each nation contribute to the total growth of humanity. For this reason, he lamented that contemporary Germans aped French culture and scorned their own native traditions, which for him explained why Germany yet remained insignificant and fragmented into many rival territories.

Herder believed that the broad dissemination of popular folklore and traditional ballads would hasten the rise of German nationalism, which would lead to the formation of a unified German nation-state. Supporting Vico's contention that folklore and poetry contained a genetic record of its history, language, and traditions, Herder called for Germany to revive its folk literature and develop national poets in the order of Homer or Shakespeare, whom he admired for their incorporation of folklore, vernacular language, and native style.[76] For Herder, "poetry is the expression of the weaknesses and perfections of a nationality, a mirror of its sentiments, the expression of the highest to which it aspired."[77] He considered the folk ballads in particular to be "the archive of a nationality," "the imprints of the soul" of a nation, and "the living voice of the nationalities" from which "one can learn the mode of thought of a nationality and its language of feeling."[78] Inspired by Percy's *Reliques* and Macpherson's *Poems of Ossian*, he published a collection of German folk poems, which later influenced the work of the Brothers Grimm.[79] William A. Wilson has traced the influence of Herder's folk theories and publications on *Sturm and Drang* and German Romanticism, which produced poetry that became emblematic of German nationalism a century later.[80]

On the other side of the pond, eighteenth-century travel guides, picturesque painting, neo-pastoral poetry, and ballad collections contributed to the depiction of the English countryside as an idyllic national heartland, the imag-

ined locus of an essential folk identity and singular national culture. Conversely, in popular culture, the cities were construed as wicked, dirty, and dangerous contact zones characterized by cheap commercialism, social dislocation, and a threatening cultural pluralism consisting of Frenchified elites, working class roughs, and exotic specimens from the colonies. Understood in these moral and nationalist terms, the "countryside" in the popular British imagination excluded areas such as the Scottish Highlands, for instance, which were still commonly Romanticized as primitive, wild, and dangerous. The apotheosis of the countryside in British culture was therefore as much an apotheosis of Englishness as it was a condemnation of the city.

Donna Landry has written that the invention of the "countryside" as a popular concept corresponds to the rise of urban, middle-class culture from 1671 to 1831.[81] This correspondence suggests that disdain for the city actually concealed a growing sense of anxiety about rapid modernization. Only a century earlier, many more Britons had lived relatively stable, unchanging lives as farmers and villagers in the countryside, which was also the traditional seat of aristocratic power. The agricultural, industrial, and political revolutions of the long eighteenth century altered the traditional rhythm of life by dislocating people from their traditional lands and livelihoods and removing social and political power to the cities. Meanwhile, the concomitant growth of empire further alienated Britons by exposing them to new peoples and cultures. In the face of these changes, a double-consciousness emerged among socially mobile urban middle-class Britons. Though they relied on the opportunities afforded by urban life, they also rejected identification with urban culture, which they viewed with fear, suspicion, and hostility. Consequently, Gerald MacLean, Donna Landry, and Joseph P. Ward propose, "Urbanity itself came to involve a rejection of life in the city for the country estate, house, or cottage."[82]

Social caricatures of the era vividly portray the depth and complexity of British antipathy toward urban culture.[83] Political cartoonists routinely satirized the *beau monde* of London's high society for its unabashed Francophilia, over-refinement, epicene manners, and unwholesome enjoyments. They also portrayed the urban masses as alien, criminal, and morally depraved. On the contrary, country village life was depicted as wholesome and patriotic, but also threatened by infection from the culturally alien cities. For instance, L.P. Boitard's *The Present Age, 1767* (1767) lampoons the activities of London's fashionable elite. As indicated in the subtitle, these include dressing, ogling, playing, gambling, dancing, boxing, swearing, and humming. A numbered

Opposite: L.P. Boitard, *The Present Age, 1767* (1767). © The Trustees of the British Museum.

explanation beneath the image singles out various affronts to patriotic feeling, such as British nobility disguised in French fashions, a French valet insulting a beggared English soldier, and an industrious English tradesman thrust aside by a contemptuous highborn gambler. The sign above the theatre advertises "A Mock Tragedy. To which is added a Farce call'd The Pregnant Rabbit Woman, Together with the Adventures of the Bottle Conjurer and Polish Jew." The performances suggest the depravity of urban taste. William Hogarth's *Southwark Fair* (1733) depicts a similar scene, but this time the object of satire is not limited to the upper class. Mixed in with fashionable men and women is a lowbrow and exotic urban

J.H. Grimm, *Welladay! is this my son Tom!* (1770). © The Trustees of the British Museum.

spectacle of rope-dancers, conjurers, quack doctors, harlequins, Scottish bagpipers, and Moorish trumpeters. The scene makes urban street life appear alien and hostile, in many ways prefiguring Burke's characterization of the urban masses as a "swinish multitude."

On the other hand, two drawings by J.H. Grimm imagine what happens when the sons and daughters of stout and virtuous English farmers are exposed to the tantalizing corruptions of city life. *Welladay! is this my son Tom!* (1770) depicts a salt-of-the-earth John Bull–like farmer in distress after a chance encounter in the city with his son, now become a foppish macaroni. In the companion piece, *Be not amaz'd Dear Mother—It is indeed your Daughter Anne* (1770), the scene is moved to a farmhouse where a puritan-like, simply

Opposite: **William Hogarth, *Southwark Fair* (1733). © The Trustees of the British Museum.**

clad farmer's wife stands aghast as she realizes that the silly and immodest woman standing before her who is sporting a revealingly low-cut dress and ridiculously high-frizzured couture adorned with headdress is actually her once-plain daughter come from the city. Attending the fashionable young lady is an Indian valet bearing a regulation French poodle.

These caricatures cast the city as a foolish, debased, and alien place whose culture threatens to contaminate the virtuous world of the nation's iconic countryside. Furthermore, by the 1790s, the city was also perceived as a potential cauldron of sedition. Wordsworth's account of London in Book Seven of *The Prelude* (1805) resonates with these negative stereotypes of urban life. He describes the city as a "Babel din,"[84] sums up the *beau monde* as "Folly, vice, / Extravagance in gesture, mien and dress,"[85] and denigrates the street rabble as "all freaks of Nature," "jumbled up together to make up / This Parliament of Monsters."[86] The discovery of a cheap, commercialized version of the sad Maid of Buttermere legend from his youth prompts a diatribe about urban corruption and confirms his prejudice that the city perverts all that it touches. As a result, in Book Eight, Wordsworth's reaction is to escape to the pastoral and restorative environs of the Lake District. By mid-century, many Britons were taking a similar holiday from the city. For harried urban men and women of means, the countryside promised a pleasurable respite from the hustle and bustle of city life, and the Lake District was a favored locale. In *A Guide to the Lakes* (1778), Thomas West stresses the psychological comforts of a retreat to the countryside. He writes, "In the depth of solitude may be reviewed ... the hurry

J.H. Grimm, *Be not amaz'd Dear Mother—It is indeed your Daughter Anne* (1770). © The Trustees of the British Museum.

and bustle of busy life.... The contemplative traveler will be charmed with the sight of the sweet retreats, that he will observe in these enchanting regions of calm repose."[87]

But the pleasures of the Lake District numbered more than just natural beauties. In *A Fortnight's Ramble to the Lakes* (1792), Joseph Budworth invokes the charming hospitality of country folk and takes a kind of national pride in claiming them as fellow Britons.[88] Upon leaving Keswick, he feels compelled to remark, "I am amongst a people, who are too much my superiors to have justice done them.... I never met so unassuming or obliging a set of human beings before; and I congratulate my country on their belonging to it." He continues, "They are always ready to do a good turn to a stranger, and instead of expecting money for any trifling assistance, they will take off their hats, throw their heads at you, and wish you a good day."[89] Budworth contrasts this behavior to that of the "southerners," meaning Londoners, whose "rapaciousness to strangers is a disgrace to the country."[90]

Budworth's account of sincere and courteous country folk who bring honor to the nation suggests how much the country had become the locus of national sentiment by the turn of the century. This sentiment is even more apparent in Wordsworth's idealization of country life in his *Guide to the Lakes* as a "pure Commonwealth." He describes the country as "a perfect Republic of Shepherds and Agriculturists ... the members of which existed in the midst of a powerful empire like an *ideal society*."[91] For Wordsworth, these people were not just the beloved folk of his childhood; they were also a human alternative to the abstract and frustrated ideals of the revolution. In the *Convention of Cintra* (1809), he once again looks to the countryside for political inspiration and finds it in the humble farmer, whom he transmogrifies into a natural patriot:

> For he is in his person attached, by stronger roots, to the soil of which he is the growth: his intellectual notices are generally confined within narrower bounds: in him no partial or antipatriotic interests counteract the force of those noble sympathies and antipathies which he has in right of his Country.[92]

Such Herderian language of roots and soil symbolically presents country folk as true patriots because they are organic specimens of the nation.

In Wordsworth's political imaginary, then, the mountain-ringed village of Grasmere and its pastoral environs are the symbolic center or "heartland" of the nation, while urban places are decentered and envisaged as marginal sites of frightening hybridity that produce crises of identity requiring restorative trips to the countryside.[93] The recursive structure of *The Prelude* (1805) provides evidence for this dynamic. Whether recovering from the "Babel din" of London's carnivalesque streets in Book Eight or from disillusionment with

London radicalism after the failure of the French Revolution in Book Eleven, Wordsworth needs to spiritually recenter by continuously re-enacting a ritual "home-coming" whereby a return to the pastoral and insular countryside of Grasmere serves as an antidote to or inoculation against contamination by foreign and disturbing elements from the cities, continental politics, or the colonies. This recursive dynamic serves to mediate Wordsworth's own growing sense of double-consciousness, which he expresses in Book Two as an unsettling schizophrenia: "I seem / Two consciousnesses—conscious of myself, / And of some other being."[94] The narrative design of *The Prelude* is an attempt to achieve oneness by concentrating personal and political desires in the "pure Commonwealth" of Wordsworth's native English countryside.

For Britain, the construction of a Romantic nationalism in and around an idealized English countryside similarly functioned to keep at bay the imperiling threats to national identity posed by the cosmopolitan, radical, and alien influences issuing from the colonies, coasts, and cities. In the Preface, Wordsworth addresses some of the deleterious changes that have beset the nation, lamenting, for instance, how the "discriminating powers of the mind" have been reduced "to a state of almost savage torpor" by "the great national events which are daily taking place, and the encreasing accumulation of men in cities, where the uniformity of their occupations produces a craving for extraordinary incident which the rapid communication of intelligence hourly gratifies."[95] Desensitized by a persistent stream of "gross and violent stimulants," Wordsworth complains that urban readers, seeking escape from the whirligig of urban politics and culture, turn to the pages of "frantic novels, sickly and stupid German Tragedies, and deluges of idle and extravagant stories in verse."[96]

Wordsworth is not just concerned with what he considers the debased gothic literary tastes of this urban population. His animosity towards the gothic novel is couched as a desire to purge foreign contaminants from national culture at a time when Britain was still reeling from invasion scares and the Napoleonic army was beginning its march of conquest across the continent. In the same passage, he laments the fact that while urban readers seek escape in foreign literatures, "the invaluable works of our elder writers, I had almost said the works of Shakespeare and Milton, are driven into neglect."[97] In later years, he reflected on the dangers of German "extravagance" for his own artistic development and expressed concern for young poets "who are in danger of being carried away by the inundation of foreign Literature."[98] Wordsworth's response to the incursion of foreign tastes and genres is to look to the countryside for local alternatives. In *Lyrical Ballads*, he sells the country to the city, albeit a Romanticized version of it, in the form of nostalgic English pastorals that foreground folk characters and experiences, thereby mediating urban double-consciousness with the poetry of folk nationalism.

Wordsworth's recourse to "low and rustic life" in *Lyrical Ballads* is ultimately part of a program of national reform intended to cleanse and reconstitute national identity around folksy images of pastoral England.[99] Combined with the myriad of other cultural artifacts that promoted nostalgia for the countryside, *Lyrical Ballads* helped to foster what John Brewer calls a culture of "nostalgic primitivism":

> The enthusiasm for the recovery and preservation of primitive and less refined forms of expression—passionately pursued by some of the most refined folk of Europe—reflected a profound and growing ambivalence towards the sophistication of civilized life that became especially strong in the last quarter of the century.[100]

Brewer notes that nostalgic primitivism was most concentrated among sophisticated urbanites because "it was necessary to be civilized in order to appreciate the virtues of the primitive life."[101] Wordsworth's *Lyrical Ballads* became part of the primitivist trend in popular art enjoyed by the eighteenth-century urban middle-class "man of taste" who dominated the reading public.[102] It conveniently nourished a Rousseauian appetite for the "noble savagery" of folk life in a "high" lyrical mode that was recognizably sophisticated. Trained in this sensibility, polite urban readers, feeling alienated by the hectic pace of urban life or the brouhaha of politics, could, like J.S. Mill, seek refuge in the nostalgic pastoral world of *Lyrical Ballads*, or, like Matthew Arnold, go one step further and declare themselves spiritual Wordsworthians.

The Folk Nationalism of *Lyrical Ballads*

The poems of *Lyrical Ballads* bear the mark of Wordsworth's country/city binary and valorization of folk life. They feature pious English peasants and villagers in pastoral settings who, when forced into contact with urban sites, must resist corruptive influences or suffer tragedy. This portrayal is consistent with the politics of folk and countryside described above, which valorized the lives, beliefs, and attitudes of simple country folk while denigrating cosmopolitan urban culture as alien and unpatriotic. Stylistically, it borrows formal and topical elements from the ballads, keying into the folk politics and nationalist fervor associated with the ballad revival; it also borrows from the anti–Enlightenment and anti-urban valence of the Neoclassical pastoral. *Lyrical Ballads* enacts these politics in two major ways: (1) by celebrating the values and simple lives of local English folk; and (2) by incorporating folklore and popular superstitions, two staples of popular ballads and Herderian folk politics. A reading of selected poems demonstrates these strains of folk nationalism in *Lyrical Ballads*.

"Last of the Flock," "The Brothers," and "Michael" most acutely demonstrate the celebration of folk values in *Lyrical Ballads*. Combining the ballad "tale" format and its familiar sing-song metrics with pastoral conventions, these poems present country folk whose particular histories and features effectively dissolve into a timeless typology: stoic, resolute, pious, and stolidly moral, these characters perform the true-blue qualities of the nation's emblematic folk subject. Conversely, the poems also register a keen awareness that these traditional folk are being corrupted by influences from the cities and colonies, and are vanishing in the wake of modernization. The poems seek to rescue the memory of these folk in a manner that transmutes England's harsh agrarian past into the national mythology of a pastoral golden age.[103]

"Last of the Flock" is a case in point. Here, the bardic narrator proceeds to absorb the tale of a hapless shepherd into the nation's oral tradition. The narrator happens upon a woeful shepherd who walks the roads as a vagabond carrying a single ewe, the last of his flock. The shepherd is described as "a healthy man, a man full grown," insinuating the vigor of his occupation. Yet, in contrast to this physical vigor, he is also described as "weeping in the public roads alone," a rather queer comportment for one so hearty. The shepherd's sad tale revolves around the simple plot of having to sell off his lambs to feed his ten children, another sign of his manly virility. Yet, it is the offspring of this virility, which had once assured him a comfortable existence, that now becomes a burden in the new economy of commodity production. Unable to weather this new economy, one by one he is forced to sell off his stock of lambs to feed his starving family. His alienation from his labor grows as his stock dwindles, making him despondent. In his desperation to survive in this new economy, corruption sets in:

> To wicked deeds I was inclined,
> And wicked fancies cross'd my mind,
> And every man I chanc'd to see,
> I thought he knew some ill of me.[104]

Despairing, he is even moved to question his faith in God and church. His parish rejects his plea for alms, his god ignores his prayers, and he feels cursed by "an evil time" that makes him question even his sacrosanct love for his children. All the while, the cloudy fleece of his hard-earned flock "melts away" until but one remains.

This is a simple story, really. It is in large part a modern riff on the generic fable about wolves and sheep. This time, however, the metaphorical wolf is a capitalist economy hungry for cheap agricultural commodities to feed its super-exploited wage laborers in the cities. The result, however, is that the lowly shepherd, unable to compete in the economic arena, is driven into penury, tempted by corruption, and forced into vagabondage. It seems inevitable that he must add to the pool of surplus labor that sustains cheap industry. This modern fable is an allegory for the rapidly changing social landscape and its corrosive effects on the nation's rural heartland. Indeed, our diminutive shepherd contrasts sharply with Wordsworth's boyish recollections of country swain in Book Eight of *The Prelude* (1805). In his youthful imaginary, the shepherd is transmogrified into a force of nature. He is "As of a lord and master, or a power, / Or genius, under Nature, under God."[105] Yet, while far from the apogee of this archetypal shepherd, our fallen shepherd still retains the grandeur of his former years in his stoic resistance to the corruptive tide of urban life. This is symbolized by his steadfast grip upon the last of his flock and his resistance to the corruptive thoughts of crime and heresy. By highlighting his stubborn refusal to abandon the shepherd's way for the inevitability of urban conformity, Wordsworth presents him as an iconic reminder of the nation's folk traditions and values.

In a note appended to the poem, Wordsworth relates that "The Brothers, A Pastoral Poem" was intended to be the concluding poem of a series of pastorals set in the mountains of Cumberland and Westmoreland, two popular destinations for walking tours in the Lake District. The poem is at once inscribed within the genre of English travel narratives within which it was canonical to trope the British countryside as an insulated pastoral utopia surrounded by sheltering and picturesque mountain vistas.[106] Yet, the poem's plot raises the tragedy that befalls when capitalist property relations intrude upon these hermetic spaces, as well as the immunity to moral corruption that their ennobling forms of rustic life endow.

The story centers on the tragedy that befalls the Ewbanks, a family of yeoman farmers and shepherds destroyed by the new economy. It is told in the sage voice of the Priest of Ennerdale, who relates the tragic tale to a curious traveler. The Priest explains how Walter Ewbank heroically attempted to save the family's land:

> Year after year the old man still preserv'd
> A cheerful mind, and buffeted with bond,
> Interest and mortgages; at last he sank,
> And went into his grave before his time.[107]

Walter perishes, "too weak / To strive with such a torrent."[108] Upon his death, his estate, house, and sheep are all sold, leaving his two children, Leonard and James, orphaned and destitute. The poem's pastoral conventions are evident in how the Priest stresses the sale of the family's "pretty flock, and which for aught I know, / Had clothed the Ewbanks for a thousand years."[109] The invocation of shepherding is meant to inscribe the family within an inveterate pastoral tradition. This pastoral conceit is also traceable in the autochthonous description of Leonard as "a Shepherd-lad" whose "soul was knit to this his native soil."[110]

Leonard is forced into a seafaring life to earn a living for his brother and himself. Not yet thirteen, he risks his fortunes on the open seas as a mariner in the British Empire with his uncle, "a thriving man" who "traffick'd on the seas."[111] Yet, despite the allures of this new world, the poem stresses that Leonard still maintains a steadfast loyalty to his pastoral homeland:

> He had been rear'd
> Among the mountains, and he in his heart
> Was half a Shepherd on the stormy seas.[112]

The poem suggests that Leonard's wholesome upbringing immunizes him from the temptations and corruptions of the wider world. In the end, he returns home with riches from his journeys, but only to discover that in his absence his brother James has died. While Leonard was away, James had become "a child of all the dale," cared for by each family in turn.[113] James's unexpected death is not the result of any malice within this perfect community, but of a brotherly love so pure and strong that in his pining he stumbles off the summit of a high rock upon which he was wont to stand daily vigil for his brother's return.

"The Brothers" offers simple lessons about the virtue of integrity and the strength of devotion. This is most evident in Leonard, who remains morally incorruptible and unflinchingly committed to his family throughout the story, despite his many personal tragedies and the hazardous temptations of a seafaring life. The kindly Priest of Ennerdale and the community he shepherds also evince these qualities in their care for James and in their intimacy with the lives and stories of all those who belong to this community. So, too, does James in his constant devotion for his wayfaring brother. Yet, despite the exemplary moral conduct of these characters, exposure to the outside world nevertheless works its treacherous way into this pastoral heartland, resulting in the tragic destruction of the Ewbanks.

In "Michael," Wordsworth further explores the theme of corruption from without. Placed prominently at the end of the second volume of *Lyrical Ballads*, "Michael" is also explicitly labeled "A Pastoral Poem" by its subtitle. Surviving leaves of the *Christabel Notebook* show that Wordsworth originally conceived the poem as a ballad pastoral.[114] While Wordsworth later changed its meter and rhyme (to iambic blank verse), the poem still bespeaks its ballad origins in its use of folklore and locative markers. A sympathetic narrator tenderly recounts the tragic, but all too common tale of a local shepherd, Michael, whose family is brought to ruin by modernization and the moral corruption it purveys. In truth, the theme of the poem is really no different from that of "Last of the Flock" and "The Brothers," each of which treats the deleterious effects of modernity in its own way.

The poem's plot can be related in a few brief incidents. Michael, a stock pastoral character, lives with his wife Isabel, "a comely Matron," and his able son Luke in a hilltop cottage "Upon the Forest-side in Grasmere Vale."[115] This locative cue both situates the tale within the pastoral cradle of the mountain-ringed Lake District and corroborates its historicity. Michael's family is placed at the spiritual and geographic center of an idyllic folk community in the Lake District that looks to their hilltop cottage, meritoriously dubbed "The Evening Star," for a guiding light through literal and moral darkness. But Michael's pastoral bliss is shattered when he is called to discharge the debts of his brother's son, for whom he has accepted financial liability. Michael is reluctant to pay off these debts by selling portions of the patrimonial fields he has worked for seventy years. He wishes to bequest the land intact and unencumbered by lien or debt to his son, Luke, so that he too can be "free as is the wind / that passes over it."[116] Following the familiar plot conventions of the picaresque narrative in which the colonial outside is imagined to be a source of limitless wealth and potential, Michael decides that Luke, now turned eighteen, should depart overseas with a prosperous kinsman "thriving in trade" in order to amass enough wealth to return and pay off their kinsman's debts. Michael and his wife recall how other members of the community have grown "wond'rous rich" from their exploits "beyond the seas," and are convinced that Luke will do the same.[117] Like Leonard, Luke reluctantly accepts this responsibility for the sake of his family. Before departing, Michael decides that Luke will lay the corner stone of a sheepfold he is building as a symbol of their unity and a record of his promise to return and finish the work of the fold. This symbolic act ill prepares Michael for the disappointment to come. While Michael works diligently to build the fold,

> Meantime Luke began
> To slacken in his duty, and at length
> He in the dissolute city gave himself
> To evil courses: ignominy and shame
> Fell on him, so that he was driven at last
> To seek a hiding-place beyond the seas.[118]

Old Michael, hearing the news of his son's failure, in despair continues to habitually return to the work of the sheepfold, but "never lifted up a single stone." Utterly depressed, he dies seven years later, leaving the sheepfold unfinished. Isabel follows him to the grave three years after, and the estate is thereafter sold into a "stranger's hand." But one is comforted by the remains of the unfinished sheepfold that still may be seen "Beside the boisterous brook of Green-head Gill."[119]

As a specimen of Wordsworth's bardic poetics, the poem is remarkable for two reasons. First, it continues to harp on the dangers that cities and seafaring present to the nation's domestic core. Luke's corruption in the city and self-exile "beyond the seas" is an allegory for what happens when a people loses its identity. The ruins of the unfinished sheepfold offer a silent testament to this lesson. It functions as a symbol of the ruin that befalls Michael and his family. Second, it repeats the pattern of locative cues evident in folk ballads and popular in Lake District tour guides by providing the reader with exact walking directions to the ruin's secretive location in the first stanza. The locative introduction does more than just relate the spatial coordinates of the poem's action. It also invokes the power of memory to invest powerful feelings and stories in mundane places and objects, and thereby literally inscribe the land with the residue of its human inhabitants. The narrator will recall this "history / Homely and rude" not merely "For the delight of a few natural hearts" like his own, but more importantly,

> For the sake
> Of youthful Poets, who among these Hills
> Will be my second self when I am gone.[120]

The narrator's statement amounts to a frank admission to imitate the popular oral tradition of folk balladry by commemorating the parochial histories of simple folk in verse.

Wordsworth's representation of the folk in *Lyrical Ballads* also emphasizes the social traction of common superstitions and folklore, a feature best exemplified by "Heart-leap Well," "Lucy Gray," "We Are Seven," "Goody Blake and Harry Gill," "The Idiot Boy," "The Mad Mother," and "The Thorn." Similar to the popular folk ballads, these poems celebrate the pre-secular wisdom of the peasantry and weave the cultural integuments of British nationalism out of this cloth.

Superstition plays a causal role in "Heart-leap Well," a poem that notably begins the second volume of *Lyrical Ballads*. The narrator encounters a local myth that attributes the ruination of a promising estate to its unlucky founding upon the foot of a spring where an innocent hart was killed long ago. A local shepherd avers "the spot is curs'd" and names it "Hart-leap Well" in honor of the fallen hart.[121] Superstition also drives the ending to "Lucy Gray," whereupon townsfolk spread rumors that long-lost Lucy is not dead but lives "Upon the lonesome Wild."[122] "We Are Seven," which uses the regular ballad, plays on the folk belief in ghosts and hauntings. For the "little cottage girl," there is no distinction between earth and heaven, body and soul, so her siblings can still be with her, the more so because of the proximity of their graves to her home.[123] That the narrator is obviously confounded by her reason, or lack thereof, suggests the conflict between secular and pre-secular modes of thought.

In "Goody Blake and Harry Gill" and "The Idiot Boy," it is the narrator who propagates supernaturalism. "Goody Blake and Harry Gill" is essentially a Christian parable about the grace of charity and the wages of greed. The plot focuses on the tale of Harry Gill, a prosperous landowner who mistreats Goody Blake, an old pauper so poor she must comb his land for firewood. Goody Blake is caught stealing firewood by Harry Gill, but prays to heaven for a miracle, after which Harry Gill begins to suffer from an incurable shiver. The reader is led to believe that her miracle was answered in the form of divine retribution. The narrator ends the story with a warning to others who would place personal gain before charity. To lend credence to the story, Wordsworth appends the subtitle, "A True Story," and sincerely testifies in the Advertisement that the tale is "founded on a well-authenticated fact which happened in Warwickshire."[124] In "The Idiot Boy," superstition and miracle again feature prominently. The poem recounts the tale of Betty Foy who sends her idiot boy Johnny off on a pony to fetch a doctor for her ailing neighbor Susan. When Betty is racked by nightmares depicting her son in the clutches of sinister gypsies and devils, she and the narrator faithfully interpret these dreams as prophecies. While a frantic Betty combs the roads for Johnny, the ailing Susan has a miraculous recovery and rises up Lazarus-like from her bed, "As if by magic cured."[125]

Betty Foy's hysteric reaction to her missing son represents a common belief in folk ballads that women who have lost a child or lover also lose their mind. Gottfried August Bürger's macabre folk ballad, *Lenore* (1773), which was wildly popular throughout Europe and instigated a host of imitators, provides the most notable example of this convention. The poem explores the psychology of a woman longing for her lover, William, who has most likely died in war. One is told that "grief racked and tore the breast of Lenore, / And was busy at her brain."[126] A similar tale is conveyed in Wordsworth's "The Mad Mother," in which a poverty-stricken woman roams the forest with her beloved child, mourning the loss of her lover who is "gone and far away."[127] The poem adopts what Timothy Fulford defines as a common ballad-motif, the idea of "walking out" into the greenwood (or alternatively the city streets). Fulford suggests this is a "ballad-form of protest" against the rampant and unprecedented poverty levels of the 1790s, which—owing to population growth, bad harvests, capitalist employment practices, and continual war—generated more single mothers, beggars, and vagrants than ever before.[128]

A more developed version of this theme can be found in "The Thorn," in which Wordsworth pens a "loquacious narrator" to convey the story of an infanticide by a desperately poor single mother. The term "thorn" is a colloquialism that refers to the English hawthorn or white-thorn tree or bush. According to Mary Jacobus, the thorn has two common English literary associations: illegitimate birth and infanticide.[129] Wordsworth invokes this symbolism in the poem. A stunted thorn, covered by moss and lichens, stands atop a stormy mountain by a muddy pond. Under its small canopy is a hill of moss that marks the grave of a child who, had out of wedlock, is killed and buried by her desperate mother, Martha Ray, after her betrothed, Stephen Gill, leaves her for another woman. The trauma of this experience never leaves Martha Ray, who visits the gravesite frequently, bellowing, "Oh misery! oh misery! / Oh woe is me! oh misery!"[130] The superstitious narrator claims to have espied Martha Ray on one of these visitations. Obviously shaken by Martha's eerie cry, the loquacious narrator credulously conveys local rumors about the gravesite: that the moss is dyed scarlet from the infant's murder; that the infant's face can be seen reflected in the pond; that its spirit haunts the hilltop and scares away any meddlers; and that its restless and vengeful spirit animates the moss that strives to drag the thorn to the ground.

The *Fenwick Notes* reveal that the story was inspired by Wordsworth's encounter with a similarly dreary thorn sometime in 1798. Wordsworth writes that it "arose out of my observing, on the ridge of Quantock Hill, on a stormy day a thorn which I had often passed in calm and bright weather without noticing it." He continues,

> I said to myself, "Cannot I by some invention do as much to make this Thorn permanently an impressive object as the storm has made it to my eyes at this moment?" I began the poem accordingly and composed it with great rapidity.[131]

Dorothy's *Alfoxden Journal* of March 19th confirms that afterwards Wordsworth wrote some lines on a thorn: "William and Basil and I walked to the hill-tops, a very cold, bleak day. We were met on our return by a server hailstorm. William wrote some lines describing a stunted thorn."[132] Basil's presence suggests that his recently murdered mother might be a possible source for Martha Ray.

Aside from these biographical connections, "The Thorn" is primarily indebted to the genre of folk ballads. One folk ballad emulated by "The Thorn" is "The Cruel Mother," a traditional ballad that Fulford believes was most likely still being sung across the country at the time.[133] It dates from a broadside ballad of the 1680s, *The Duke's Daughter's Cruelty: Or the Wonderful Apparition of two Infants whom she Murther'd and Buried in a Forrest, for to hide her Shame*, which was included in the Pepys Library of broadside ballads.[134] A fragment of the ballad was included in David Herd's *Ancient and Modern Scottish Songs* (1776) under the title of "The Cruel Mother."[135] Rather than hearing it performed, Fulford suggests that Wordsworth first encountered the piece by reading Herd in 1798; he later transcribed the piece into his notebooks sometime in 1801.[136] The stanzas he copied from Herd's fragment contain the key elements of "The Thorn":

> Ah there she's lean'd her back to a thorn
>   O and alas-a-day, O and alas-a-day
> And there she has her baby born.
>   Ten thousand times good-night and be wi' thee
> She has houked a grave ayont the sun,
>   O and alas-a-day, O and alas-a-day
> And there she has buried the sweet babe in.
>   Ten thousand times good-night and be wi' thee.[137]

The forlorn thorn, the forsaken and woe-begotten woman, the make-shift grave of an infant child, and the repetition of phrases and sounds are all present and directly imitated by Wordsworth in "The Thorn." Jacobus reveals that another possible ballad source for the poem is William Taylor's translation of Bürger's "The Lass of Fair Wone" in an issue of the *Monthly Magazine* from 1796.[138] The gothic machinery of "The Thorn" is adapted from Bürger's poem, which deploys a haunted bower, gibbet, pond, and grave. Bürger's poem focuses on a spot haunted by past suffering and guilt, a "bower of yew" stained by infanticide and marked by the mother's execution for the crime.[139] Unlike Bürger, who forces us to dwell on the sensational facts of violence and pain, Jacobus argues, "Wordsworth plays down the gothicism of his source by transferring it to an everyday setting."[140] Indeed, he goes further to mitigate the blunt horror of the scene by forcing us to focus not so much on the tortured suffering of the phantasmagoric woman, nor on the cursed grave marked by the moss and stunted thorn, but on the effect of this experience on the narrator's superstitious mind.

The Production of National Space

According to Benedict Anderson, the census, map, and museum "profoundly shaped the way in which the colonial state imagined its dominion— the nature of the human beings it ruled, the geography of its domain, and the legitimacy of its ancestry."[141] Yet, state-sponsored events in Great Britain like the inauguration of the British Museum in 1757, the first Ordnance Survey in 1791, and the first population census in 1801 show that these categories apply as much to the center as to the periphery. Census, map, and museum were powerful tools for interpolating subjects, but Wordsworth resisted their tendency to produce an abstract and homogenous national identity absent of local color and variety. In *Lyrical Ballads*, he promulgates the moral and artistic value of local attachments by featuring poems indebted to characters, incidents, and places drawn from his native Lake District. For Fiona Stafford, Wordsworth's turn to the local in *Lyrical Ballads* was inspired by the provincial poetry of Burns and Scott and demonstrates the way that "'love of country' could draw strength from love of a particular part of 'the country.'"[142] James M. Garrett reveals that the stylistics of Wordsworth's post–1815 writing also stress the value of local attachments by symbolically resituating local customs, histories, and landscapes at the center of national identity.[143] Wordsworth's move from the general to the particular, the abstract to the concrete in his countenancing of local attachments is another aspect of his bardic poetics. In *Lyrical Ballads*, poems that memorialize incidences by indelibly etching them into local sites and landscapes effectively produce national space by literally scarring the landscape with the psychic resonance of its human inhabitants, past and present. The local attachments featured in Wordsworth's poetry of place become a means for colonizing space, but also for integrating Britons into a community who share a Herderian blood-and-soil affinity for the menagerie of local places that comprise the territorial space of the nation.

The praxis of associating places and things with feelings and memories can be linked to Wordsworth's contact with David Hartley's associationist theories of memory filtered through Coleridge.[144] Hartley believed that sensations recorded in the brain become braided with other sensations, forming a chain of associations imprinted in memory. Wordsworth espouses a poetics of association in the Preface, where he observes that pleasure is concentrated in pools of affect attached to some familiar object or place: "all men feel an habitual gratitude, and something of an honorable bigotry for the objects which have long continued to please them: we not only wish to be pleased, but to be pleased in that particular way in which we have been accustomed to be pleased."[145] In *Lyrical Ballads*, objects, but especially places, are associated with the events that have transpired there, thereby acting as mnemonic devices for past sensations. The physical world thus functions as a sort of cognitive map that registers collective experience.

In practice, the mapping of collective experience upon a landscape produces what Anthony D. Smith calls an *ethnoscape*, a landscape "endowed with poetic ethnic meaning through the historicization of nature and the territorialization of ethnic memories."[146] By indelibly inscribing places and objects in the Lake District with the psychic resonance of its inhabitants, Wordsworth's bardic poetics figuratively colonizes and transforms this territory from a stagnant political abstraction into a living ethnoscape that gives substance and meaning to national space, which, in turn, gives permanence to national identity. This practice follows Garrett's contention that "[i]ncreasingly for

Wordsworth, local identity was found to rely on local customs, folklore, and history, and so the depiction of the local landscape was itself an act of preservation, an artifact for the national museum."[147] In Wordsworth's landscape poetry, the landscape becomes a kind of "national museum" in which individual experiences associated with local ruins, places, and objects are preserved and assembled into a collective national heritage. Like the old folk ballads, Wordsworth's poems memorialize these associations in the vernacular language of the people, thus enmeshing language, territory, and experience.

The idea that land and folk share an intimate bond differs from those that precede it and from the hegemonic capitalist-instrumentalist idea of land that was replacing it in Wordsworth's time. Classical society imagined land to be guarded by spirits called geniuses and medieval society imagined places to be consecrated or desecrated by the good or evil spirits tied to them. Romantic nationalism carries over these traditions by imagining that space is scarred and haunted by the residue of folk and history. The association of places and objects with memories creates a living ethnoscape in which the nation's past is indelibly imprinted upon its territory. Marlon B. Ross explains how this sentimental folk attachment to the land, or what he calls a "Burkean romance of the land," is central to Wordsworth's Romantic nationalism. He writes,

> Wordsworth views the modern nation-state as an organic body, motivated by instinctual, tribal affection. Wordsworth's focus, however, is the supposedly *original* and *natural* attachment of the folk to the land that they inhabit.[148]

For Wordsworth, this "original and natural" attachment of the folk to their land stands in stark contradiction to the instrumental attachment to land practiced by bourgeois investors seeking profits or leisure, which is a central concern of the *Guide to the Lakes* (1811). In contrast, Wordsworth's poems invest land with personal meaning by associating places and objects with individual experiences or collective memory.

The importance of national space for Wordsworth is indicated by the notable absence of such a space that facilitates the tragic events of "The Borderers" (1795) and by the disrespect for national property that is the sub-text of the *Guide to the Lakes*. In the Advertisement to "The Borderers," he explains his choice of setting:

> As to the scene and period of action, little more was required for my purpose than the absence of established law and government; so that the agents might be at liberty to act on their own impulses.[149]

Set during the reign of Henry III, which was plagued by Scottish invasions and civil strife, Wordsworth imagines the border territory between Scotland and England to be a liminal space where moral chaos can ensue.[150] The English band of borderers, led by Marmaduke, is charged with enclosing national space in order to protect it from Scottish forays. But they cannot protect against internal conflict. In this sense, the national instability and turmoil of the period is mirrored by the psychological action between Marmaduke and Oswald, which resolves in a tragedy that scatters the borderers and weakens the nation.

The desire to consolidate national space from internal jeopardy is a central theme of Wordsworth's *Guide to the Lakes*. Ostensibly a tour guide intended to instruct Britons on how to discover the most pleasing prospects in the Lake District, Wordsworth confesses that his ulterior goal is "to reconcile a Briton to the scenery of his own country."[151] Wordsworth is concerned by his countryman's preference for Alpine or North American prospects and by the sale of Lake District lands to wealthy gentry of native and foreign descent who build homes in unsightly places and import foreign flora, either for decoration or for agribusiness. His solution is to inculcate British nationalism via the seemingly apolitical aesthetic of what he glibly refers to as "better taste" in a key passage from the third section, which is fittingly entitled "Changes, And Rules of Taste for Preventing Their Bad Effects." He writes,

> It is then much to be wished that a better taste should prevail among these new proprietors; and, as they cannot be expected to leave things to themselves, that SKILL and KNOWLEDGE should prevent unnecessary deviations from that path of simplicity and beauty along which without design and unconsciously, their humble predecessors have moved. In this wish the author will be joined by persons of pure taste throughout the whole island, who, by their visits (often repeated) to the Lakes in the North of England, testify that they deem the district a sort of national property, in which every man has a right and interest who has an eye to perceive and a heart to enjoy.[152]

Wordsworth is implicitly calling for the institution of aesthetic conditioning on a grand scale to instruct these nominal Britons in how to be British by outfitting them with national eyes with which to properly see and appreciate national prospects.[153] The result of this process will be the creation of a "national property" that will root British identity into the very soil of the nation.

A similar process is at work in the poems of *Lyrical Ballads*. Many of the poems in the collection implicitly present natural landscape in the Lake District as a "national property" that is territorialized by the poetic act of memorializing personal experiences and folklore associated with particular sites of human habitation. The sheer number of poems in *Lyrical Ballads* that invoke personal experiences and memories connected to historically significant places or ruins is staggering. I have already illustrated this phenomenon in "Heart-leap Well," "The Brothers," and "Michael" (the tale of Hart-leap Well communicated by the superstitious shepherd, the oral history of the Ewbanks graves shared by the Priest of Ennerdale, and the story of Michael's unfinished sheepfold in Greenhead Gill, respectively).[154] These ruins are haunted and possessed (literally and figuratively) by the tales of generations past, whose stories are transmogrified through oral history and bardic verse into a rich skein of collective memory. The nationalist evocation of ruins and natural landscapes is central to Anne Janowitz's understanding of how *The Prelude* merges the story of personal poetic growth with an epic of national redemption.[155] The same holds true of *Lyrical Ballads*, where native ruins and other places of local importance dissolve and lose their individuality within the greater psychic and territorial matrix of nationalism.

The poetic conceit of territorializing places by associating them with memory informs many other poems of *Lyrical Ballads*. The two "Inscription" poems memorialize sites with local import—the former spot of a hermitage on St. Herbert's Island and the structure of an outhouse on the Island of Grasmere. In this light, the poems' title has a double significance: it alludes both to the poems' genre and to the action, which is literally or figuratively to inscribe these locales with the memory of past events. Similarly, "Lines, Written with a Slate-pencil upon a Stone" commemorates the tale of Sir William's endeavor to build a "pleasure house" on the Island of Rydale, which can be read in the "hillock of misshapen stones" that mark the ruins of a quarry and unfinished foundation.[156] "Lines, left upon a Seat in a Yew-tree" also invokes the trope of ruins to encode memory into a place. The poem commemorates a seat of piled stones that is the only earthly monument to "one who own'd / No common soul," thus memorializing in verse the relationship between site and soul.[157] This is repeated to greater effect in "Tintern Abbey," where a special site located a few miles above the abbey is associated with the narrator's former self, which must now be reconciled with the man he has become:

> Five years have passed; five summers, with the length
> Of five long winters! and again I hear
> These waters rolling from their mountain-springs
> With a sweet inland murmur.[158]

These simple lines display the potency of memory and its tendency to cling like mist to the places where one has once been. By returning to this site, old memories that lay dormant, encoded in the ethnoscape surrounding the Abbey, stir back to life with all the freshness of novelty. This residue precipitates the poem's celebrated soul-searching journey and resolution.

Perhaps the most significant acts of territorialization are found among the "Poems on the Naming of Places," which colonize space by invoking the magic of naming. In the Advertisement to the "Poems," Wordsworth declares:

> Many places will be found unnamed or of unknown names, where little Incidents will have occurred, or feelings been experienced, which will have given to such

places a private and peculiar interest. From a wish to give some sort of record to such Incidents or renew the gratification of such Feelings, Names have been given to Places by the Author and some of his Friends, and the following Poems written in consequence.[159]

The act of naming a place cements location (space) with memory (time), creating a space/time bubble or wormhole that can repeatedly "renew the gratification" of the feelings associated with that place. In so doing, the namer lays claim to a degree of ownership over the place that cannot be erased by time or distance. In "It was an April morning," Wordsworth possesses a beloved natural retreat by naming it "Emma's Dell" after a young girl from Hawkshead, the village of his grammar school.[160] In "To Joanna," Wordsworth figures himself a "Runic Priest" of the ancient Britons who commemorates his affection for Joanna Hutchinson by chiseling out her name in "rude characters" upon a "native rock" that henceforth will be known as "Joanna's Rock."[161] By this act of ritual inscription, the Druid-like Wordsworth seizes ownership of the place from Roman conquerors, whose worn inscriptions can still be seen on the surrounding rocks as indicated in the note appended to the poem. In "A narrow girdle of rough stones and crags," the place is given the name "Point Rash-Judgment" to remember a lesson learned there not to rashly judge a man before one learns his circumstances.[162] And finally, in "To M.H." an isolated place of beauty "made by Nature for herself" is named "Mary" by Wordsworth to commemorate his love for Mary Hutchinson.[163]

By mapping a record of human experience, past and present, upon the landscape of the Lake District and memorializing this record in verse, Wordsworth's poetry of place contributed to the production of national space in British consciousness. Wordsworth centered pastoral images of the English Lake District within imaginings of national space, promoting a perception of Britain that emphasized its cultural cohesion and adherence to virtuous folk traditions. As a result, it mediated the social alienation generated by national integration, industrialization, urban cosmopolitanism, and contact with sharply different cultures in the far-flung colonies. It also gave substance to the tenuous idea of a British nation.

***

I have demonstrated Wordsworth's development of a bardic poetics modeled after the antiquarian revival of bards and balladry, and I have connected it to movements in Continental Europe and Britain that emphasized the symbolic nationalism of folk traditions and the essential national virtues of country life. Wordsworth's *Lyrical Ballads* expresses these qualities in its reorientation of the poet as a bardic figure speaking to and for a broad national audience in the vernacular language and style of the popular ballads. These poetics emphasize the universality of rustic subjects and locations drawn from English stock, thus inscribing idyllic images of the English countryside at the symbolic center of national life. In the next chapter, I examine how Wordsworth's bardic poetics not only privileges a particular national *ethnie*, but also mediates class differences by reifying class inequality in order to present Britain as a classless nation.

CHAPTER 3

Wordsworth and Class (Un)Consciousness

> Heroes of Truth pursue your march, uptear
> Th'Oppressor's dungeon from its deepest base;
> High o'er the towers of Pride undaunted rear
> Resistless in your might the Herculean mace
> Of Reason;
>
> —William Wordsworth[1]

> —She ceased, and weeping turned away,
> As if because her tale was at an end
> She wept;—because she had no more to say
> Of that perpetual weight which on her spirit lay.
>
> —William Wordsworth[2]

> [Culture] seeks to do away with classes; to make the best that has been thought and known in the world current everywhere; to make all men live in an atmosphere of sweetness and light, where they may use ideas, as it uses them itself, freely, —nourished, and not bound by them.
>
> —Matthew Arnold[3]

In 1793, a young radical issued the following bromide against his government:

> If it is true in common life, it is still more true in governments that we should be just before we are generous: but our legislators seem to have forgotten or despised this homely maxim. They have unjustly left unprotected that most important part of property, not less real because it has no material existence, that which ought to enable the labourer to provide food for himself and his family. I appeal to innumerable statutes whose constant and professed object it is to lower the price of labour, to compel the workman to be content with arbitrary wages, evidently too small from the necessity of legal enforcement of the acceptance of them. Even from the astonishing amount of the sums raised for the support of one description of the poor may be concluded the extent and greatness of that

oppression, whose effects have rendered it possible for the few to afford so much, and have shewn us that such a multitude of our brothers exist in even helpless indigence.[4]

The young radical in question, of course, is William Wordsworth. Having just returned from a stint in republican France, Wordsworth wrote the inflammatory *A Letter to the Bishop of Llandaff* (1793) in which he supported the regicide and advocated for revolutionary changes in Britain. Though never published, the letter reveals the degree to which Wordsworth had become sensitized to the plight of the working class. Not quite the labor theory of value, it also demonstrates a sophisticated understanding of economic exploitation. Wordsworth conceives of wages in terms of property rights that provide necessary access to the means of subsistence. He also perceives an ongoing class struggle in which state power is directed by the exploiting classes to protect traditional forms of property while pressuring wages down. According to the letter, this situation has yielded, on the one hand, extravagant wealth for the few, and, on the other hand, desperate poverty for the many. As a result, Wordsworth argues for the economic rights of the working class. In short, what we find in this unsent missive is a prescient statement of class consciousness that in many ways prefigures the proletarian uprisings of the 1840s.

Strangely, the acute sense of injustice towards oppression and inequality that one finds in *A Letter to the Bishop of Llandaff* is absent in his poetry of the late 1790s, replaced by what Raymond Williams has called the "green language" of the English pastoral.[5] Beginning with *Lyrical Ballads,* the overt class-consciousness of the earlier period is replaced by the aesthetic management or erasure of scenes of poverty that would otherwise challenge the narrative of community established by his bardic poetics. These poems recuperate the image of the poor by spiritualizing, idealizing, or universalizing their condition. The difference is perhaps most apparent when we compare his treatment of the female vagrant in "Salisbury Plain" (1795) with the same figure in "The Female Vagrant" (1798), a later redaction of "Salisbury Plain" that appears in the first edition of *Lyrical Ballads.* Where the former moves from shock, to sympathy, and finally culminates with outraged polemic that invokes Godwinian reason to bring about the fall of "Superstition's reign," a jibe at the tyranny of Church and State, the latter develops along a similar track but exchanges internal psychodrama for polemic. The female vagrant confesses that what ails her most is neither the wars that stole her family, nor the abject poverty caused by property relations, but the spiritual pain of losing a "clear and open soul, so prized in fearless youth."[6] The poem now foregrounds the vagrant's spiritual crisis rather than the social, political, and economic crises that have produced her condition of utter destitution.

This chapter explores Wordsworth's part in the production of a Romantic structure of feeling in *Lyrical Ballads* that disables class-consciousness. If, as described in the last chapter, Wordsworth's bardic poetics constitutes a democratization of poetic form and content, it also enables the literary erasure of signs of class conflict and social injustice that might threaten the imagined community of the nation-state. Wordsworth manages the social and political fallout of the 1790s not by the conventional strategy of exposing it, but by striving to transcend it altogether via sentimental images of poverty that sanitize and contain the impact of scenes of class oppression. This process is not self-conscious, but issues instead from a Romantic structure of feeling that seeks to resist the new order of industrial capitalism, yet ends up being co-opted by it as it seeks to mediate the psycho-social impact of exploitation and inequality. The structure of feeling that emerges in Wordsworth's *Lyrical Ballads* and later poetry reifies and naturalizes signs of poverty that challenge or contradict the ideal of community upon which nationalist discourse thrives, thereby relegating class-consciousness to the margins of the political unconscious. Reified images of idyllic poverty result from a subject position that treats others as part of the landscape for the contemplative Romantic subject. In so doing, the presence of poor laborers, vagrants, beggars, disabled veterans and other indigents who populate the national landscape is contained or concealed, and the imagined community of national subjects is preserved from the fissiparous reality of class antagonism.

The Romantic reaction to the new set of exploitative class relations engendered by modern industrial capitalism has elicited a rich divergence of opinions from scholars. The spectrum of positions runs the gamut from stern accusations of reactionary sentimentalism and bourgeois decadence to passionate defenses of an embedded, if not explicit, radical spirit. The iconic literary Marxist, Christopher Caudwell, stands squarely in the former camp, arguing that the Romantics were "bourgeois poets" and "mirror revolutionaries" whose "revolt of feeling and the sentiments against sterile formalism and the tyranny of the past" reflects the bourgeoisie's revolt against the remaining feudal restraints on personal freedoms and free trade. For Caudwell, Wordsworth's nature poetry is a privileged pose of the educated bourgeoisie for whom "the division of labour involved in industrialism has made it possible for sufficient surplus produce to exist to maintain a poet in austere idleness in Cumberland."[7] More measured, Gary Kelly has written that the Romantics represent "the interests, culture, and values of those [middle] classes as the 'national' interest, culture, and values while concealing the fact that it did so."[8] The New Historicism of the 1980s advanced the critique of Romanticism by exploring the way Romantic texts displace history, thereby obviating matters of class and other forms of social injustice.[9] In the words of Jerome J. McGann,

"The poetry of Romanticism is everywhere marked by extreme forms of displacement and poetic conceptualization whereby the actual human issues with which the poetry is concerned are resituated in a variety of idealized localities."[10] McGann and others also charged that Romanticists were guilty of an "uncritical absorption in Romanticism's own self-representations," thus perpetuating the historical displacements and depoliticization of poetry endemic to the Romantic ideology.[11]

Contrary to these opinions, ecocritics such as Jonathan Bate, Karl Kroeber, and James C. McKusick have argued for a reassessment of Romanticism on its own terms, as self-conscious nature poetry that serves as a forerunner to modern ecology and progressive environmentalism.[12] Similarly, Michael Löwy and Robert Sayre have described Romanticism as a progressive reaction to capitalist modernity that has informed a wide-range of events over the past two centuries—from the Luddite rebellions, Owenism, Chartism, trans–Atlantic intentional communities, and the 1848 revolutions, to the modern environmental movement, post-modernism, radical feminism, and twentieth-century utopian social movements.[13] These critiques build upon a tradition of scholarship dating back to the post–World War II period that emphasizes the progressive aspects of Romanticism. For instance, V.G. Kiernan called for a reassessment of the Romantic legacy in light of the Romantics' persistent and sympathetic attention to the plight of the poor.[14] Ernst Fischer went on to describe Romanticism as "a movement of protest—of passionate and contradictory protest against the bourgeois capitalist world, the world of 'lost illusions,' against the harsh prose of business and profit."[15] Terry Eagleton advanced the concept that the Romantic notion of the creative imagination poses "an image of non-alienated labour" implicitly opposed to the new capitalist social order.[16] Taking a diachronic view, Eric J. Hobsbawm proposed that Romanticism was initially a middle class revolt against the corruption of court and church, but became the "instinctive enemy" of the bourgeoisie after it came to power with the French and Industrial Revolutions.[17]

Raymond Williams has outlined a position on the subject that straddles both camps, and his position informs my own. Williams explains that Romanticism inherited the "melancholy consciousness of change and loss" which colored the late eighteenth-century poetry of sentimentalism, but was unable to achieve a systemic understanding of the structural relations between the outward manifestations of these troubling social changes and the inner processes of capitalist development.[18] For Williams, the main current of Romanticism is the desire to transform nature into an ideal of community, not through the will, but through the poetic imagination; the Romantic poet is a "man driven back from the cold world and in his own natural perception and language seeking to find and recreate man."[19] He calls this the "green language" of the new Romantic poetry, which is most evident in Wordsworth's poetry. Williams suggests that Wordsworth was the most attuned to this agrarian ideal, which he believed was receding "into a past which only a few surviving signs, and the spirit of poesy, could recall."[20] Yet, in turning from political to aesthetic forms of resistance rooted in the superiority of art and the imagination over the dehumanizing reality of modern society, Williams suggests that Wordsworth and the Romantics unintentionally opened the door to subjectivist theories that depoliticize art.[21]

Building on Williams, I suggest that the Romantic ideology described by McGann et al. and expressed above all in the works of Wordsworth is a structure of feeling that results from a flawed attempt to escape the alienation of modern industrial (and later on post-industrial) society by transcending it through the work of the creative imagination. Romanticism thus registers both the solipsism of the bourgeois subject and the desire to transcend this condition to a higher level of social integration by retreating even further into the imagination, what Williams has described as the elevation of "natural beauty and personal feeling" above "crude worldliness and the materialism of politics and social affairs."[22] Accordingly, Anne Janowitz remarks that Romanticism is "the literary form of a struggle taking place on many levels of society between the claims of *individualism* and the claims of *communitarianism*."[23] Disquieted by the ubiquitous conditions of social alienation under capitalism, the Romantic subject clings to the panacea of a more organic and natural world. Yet, in aiming to decohere from the existential condition of modernity by seeking an illusory escape from the ills of modern society in a contrived natural world—in Wordsworth's case predicated on an idealized agrarian past—Romanticism also enables an existential drift from being to reflection that converts the presence of others into part of a reified landscape. In this manner, signs of distress like rural poverty or urban squalor are contained instead of probed, relegated to the political unconscious, and ultimately made to serve the fanciful delusions of communal harmony so central to the politics of nationalism.

Romantic reification informs claims by Matthew Arnold and other cultural mediators that "[culture] seeks to do away with classes." Arnold desired that elements of culture, specifically canonical literature, should transcend social, economic, and political differences, uniting all of society around a shared appreciation of " the best that has been thought and known in the world."[24] A half century later, this sentiment would be echoed in the "Newbolt Report on the Teaching of English in England" (1921), which set the agenda for English studies programs throughout the nation's public schools. Set against the backdrop of Bolshevism and intensified class struggle at home, the report asserts that an education of this kind is the greatest benefit which could be conferred upon any citizen of a great state, and that the common right to it, the common discipline and enjoyment of it, the common possession of the tastes and associations connected with it, would form a new element of national unity, linking together the mental life of all classes by experiences which have hitherto been the privileges of a limited section.[25]

In other words, a common education in literature deemed canonical by the elite preachers of culture—the bardic critics discussed in an earlier chapter—would expose conflicting social classes to a hegemonic culture selected and vetted from above, the effect of which would be to diminish class consciousness and preserve the nation from the divisive effects of class struggle. As part of the canon, Romanticism contributed to the agenda of "linking together the mental life of all classes" by privileging a transcendental state of consciousness in which the material conditions of class society—which generated this condition in the first place in reaction to social alienation—are reified rather than examined and ameliorated.

In the following sections, I explore Wordsworth's production of a structure of feeling in *Lyrical Ballads* that reifies signs of class antagonism, bypassing the moral outrage that is so salient in early poems like "Salisbury Plain." The first section explores Wordsworth's fateful romance with radical republican politics in the 1790s in order to trace his political development toward conservatism and how this affected his poetic style. Specifically, I argue that Wordsworth's poetry beginning with *Lyrical Ballads* demonstrates the qualities of reification first described by György Lukács. Though distressed by the social and political crises fostered by the twin revolutions—the French and Industrial revolutions—Wordsworth's technique for dealing with the fallout of these crises inadvertently reinforces the forms of bourgeois subjectivity (i.e., alienation, individualism, idealism) whose material conditions (i.e., industrialization, urbanization, enclosure) he so vigorously opposes. The second section traces the impact of this failure in the poems of the two-volume *Lyrical Ballads*.

Wordsworth, Class-Consciousness and the Flight into Reification

If the 1790s was the decade of *Lyrical Ballads*, it was also, as E.P. Thompson has explained, the "crucible" out of which emerged working-class consciousness.[26] The agricultural and industrial revolutions of the preceding century set the stage for this event. Between 1700 and 1760, some 200 enclosure acts privatized nearly 300,000 acres of rural land inhabited by peasants or used in common; between 1761 and 1800, the rate increased tenfold, with 2,000 acts enclosing more than 2,000,000 acres.[27] The ensuing dispossession of the peasantry provided a captive workforce for the booming industrial towns, and the drop in food prices generated by the concomitant agricultural revolution enabled manufacturers to keep wages low. Those who couldn't find work swelled the ranks of the poor, contributing to the spike in urban crime or taking to the highways as rural vagabonds. By the 1780s, workers began organizing trade unions and corresponding societies to improve the miserable conditions they suffered in the "dark Satanic mills" and squalid factory towns, but also to lobby for more political rights. The state's response to these developments was two-fold. On the one hand, the passage of the Poor Law in 1795 set up a welfare system that supplemented inadequate wages. On the other hand, laws protecting property and outlawing vagabondage multiplied.[28] By the 1790s, workers associations were also coming under fire. A sharp uptick in political repression in the wake of the French Revolution led to the passage of the Corresponding Societies Act in 1799, which banned political associations. A year later, the Combination Act outlawed trade unionism. Thompson concludes,

> We can now see something of the truly catastrophic nature of the Industrial Revolution; as well as some of the reasons why the English working class took form in these years. The people were subjected simultaneously to an intensification of two intolerable forms of relationship: those of economic exploitation and of political oppression.[29]

A half century later, reflecting on the desperate condition of the working class in England, Frederick Engels would write, "Now, he who was born to toil had no other prospect than that of remaining a toiler all his life."[30]

Wordsworth knew firsthand the plight of the poor. "Grief was the making of Wordsworth," observes Duncan Wu in reference to Wordsworth's loss of both parents and his separation from his siblings at a young age.[31] The grief all around him also must have affected a sensitive child such as Wordsworth was. As a child growing up in the countryside, he probably witnessed the tragic and dislocating effects of enclosure up close, while in later years he certainly witnessed the viciousness and squalor of industrial towns and experienced the chill of political repression faced by those who dared to question the social order. Dorothy Wordsworth's *Grasmere and Alfoxden Journals* (1798–1803) record many casual run-ins with the poor and indigent, which suggests just how numerous and commonplace these encounters must have been all along. Mary Moorman describes an early encounter with prostitutes in June, 1787, which she conjectures "undoubtedly helped to nourish [Wordsworth's] interest in the outcasts of society."[32] Wordsworth would later write about this encounter in the 1805 *Prelude*:

> A barrier seemed at once
> Thrown in, that from humanity divorced
> The human form, splitting the race of Man
> In twain, yet leaving the same outward shape.³³

The sense of social and spiritual division registered in these lines resonates with Wordsworth's early writing, which evinces a tone of quiet indignation toward signs of poverty and injustice. For instance, "An Evening Walk" includes a scene in which a wandering beggar mother and her children are caught in a storm. Her husband lost to the American War, the vagrant mother

> Hath dragged her babes along this weary way;
> While arrowy fire extorting feverish groans,
> Shot stinging through her stark o'er-laboured bones.³⁴

The passage contains many features that will later become emblematic of Wordsworth's portrayal of the poor: a chance encounter with a wandering vagrant (often female), the bite of hunger and infirmity, the death of a loved one (in this case a spouse), suffering children, and the backdrop of coerced soldiering in foreign wars that extracts such heavy domestic costs.

In the years between "An Evening Walk" and *Lyrical Ballads*, Wordsworth became radicalized by the French Revolution, which sensitized him to the social causes of poverty. During his second trip to France in 1791–2, Wordsworth traveled with Michel Beaupuy, a member of the Royal Guard turned clandestine republican, who provided him with an ersatz political training in class struggle.³⁵ In an incident recorded in Book Nine of *The Prelude*, he describes how the two chanced upon the all-too-common sight of a hunger-bitten and destitute girl. Beaupuy exclaims, "'Tis against that / Which we are fighting."³⁶ Overcome by pity and passion, Wordsworth affirms his faith

> That a spirit was abroad
> Which could not be withstood, that poverty,
> At least like this, would in a little time
> Be found no more, that we should see the earth
> Unthwarted in her wish to recompense
> The industrious, and the lowly child of toil.³⁷

Moved by his vision of a better world, Wordsworth writes,

> I gradually withdrew
> Into a noisier world, and thus did soon
> Become a patriot—and my heart was all
> Given to the people, and my love was theirs.³⁸

Upon returning to England, he wrote the *A Letter to the Bishop of Llandaff*, in which he defended the regicide and issued a radical critique of exploitation.³⁹ The early drafts of "Salisbury Plain" were also written at this time. They contain motifs similar to "An Evening Walk" but go further in denouncing the social injustices that cause poverty and suffering. In 1794, Wordsworth traveled to London to join Godwin's circle of radicals. But his radical years would be brief, lasting only until 1795, when a falling out with Godwin caused Wordsworth to make preparations to retreat with Dorothy to Alfoxden, where they settled in 1796 and remained for the next few years as he and Coleridge collaborated to write *Lyrical Ballads*.[40]

It is canonical to speak of Wordsworth's political "apostasy" at this point in terms of his disillusionment with the French Revolution and republicanism generally, attitudes neatly documented in Book Ten of the 1805 *Prelude*. Yet, what is less commented on is the fact that this change in political outlook brings Wordsworth closer to embracing a nationalist perspective that undercuts his burgeoning class-consciousness.[41] This perspective is evident as early as the 1802 sonnets. Written during the Peace of Amiens on a trip to Calais to visit his former lover Annette Vallon, the sonnet cycle begins with predictably harsh denouncements of Buonopartist France, but then shifts into a progressively more patriotic mode in which England becomes the antithesis of despotic France. Wordsworth is, at first, reluctant to make this transition. For instance, in "England! The time is come when thou shouldst wean," Wordsworth chastises England's imperial trespasses in Greece, Egypt, India, and Africa, but concludes that England must be supported as the lesser evil against French imperialism because

> Far, far more abject is thine Enemy:
> Therefore the wise pray for thee, though the freight
> Of thy offences be a heavy weight:
> Oh grief! That Earth's best hopes rest all with Thee![42]

One registers no grief in "Composed by the Sea-Side, near Calais, August 1802," where Wordsworth now looks optimistically to England as a bastion of freedom. Upon crossing the channel, his tone becomes even more patriotic. In "Composed in the Valley, near Dover, On the Day of Landing," he describes the "perfect bliss, to tread the grass / Of England once again."[43] In "September 1802," one finds England now numbered among the "great and free" and posed in stark contrast to a tyrannical and expansionist French empire.[44] The later sonnets deliver a picture of England as the antithesis of France: it stands for freedom against tyranny, without any qualification of its own transgressions at home and abroad, as occurs in the earlier sonnets.

Years later, Wordsworth would explicitly affirm his belief in the tenets of nationalism in the *Convention of Cintra* (1809), a pamphlet he published in outrage to the favorable terms of surrender that Britain granted to France after its stunning victory at Vimeiro in the Peninsular War. In the document,

Wordsworth unleashes a torrent of censure for the conduct of British statesmen and military leaders, but he is careful to present himself as an unequivocal patriot. In one passage, he waxes patriotic about his country's commitment to liberty:

> Now, liberty—healthy, matured, time-honoured liberty—this is the growth and peculiar boast of Britain; and nature herself, by encircling with the ocean the country which we inhabit, has proclaimed that this mighty nation is for ever to be her own ruler, and that the land is set apart for the home of immortal independence.[45]

Wordsworth's ideological commitment to nationalism goes beyond loyalty to his own nation. In a later passage, he describes the formation of nation-states in patently nationalist terms, writing of "the solemn fraternity which a great nation composes—gathered together, in a stormy season, under the shade of ancestral feeling."[46] He celebrates the formation of the British nation-state, but also looks forward to the emergence of nation-states throughout Europe: "Who does not rejoice that former partitions have disappeared [in the British Isles].... And it will be a happy day for Europe, when the natives of Italy and the natives of Germany ... shall each dissolve the pernicious barriers which divide them, and form themselves into a mighty People."[47] Accordingly, he couches his opposition to French imperialism in terms of the right to national self-determination: "Perdition to the Tyrant who would wantonly cut off an independent Nation from its inheritance in past ages: turning the tombs and burial-places of the Forefathers into dreaded objects of sorrow, or of shame and reproach, for the Children!"[48]

The *Convention of Cintra*, then, demonstrates that what remained of Wordsworth's commitment to radical republicanism was a persistent faith in the inviolable "solemn fraternity" of the nation. Shorn of the radical egalitarianism intrinsic to the republican doctrine, however, Wordsworth's commitment to nationalism would prove to be a gateway to conservative politics. Specifically, it would spell the jettisoning of his earlier critique of class inequality, which posed an insuperable threat to the concept of a solemn national fraternity. In retrospect, the signs and symptoms of this shift are already evident by the time of *Lyrical Ballads*. By adopting the Neoclassical pastoral mode to present idealized images of the rural poor, the disturbing presence of class conflict, instead of becoming an opportunity for a polemic against the social establishment, as in the early drafts of "Salisbury Plain," is used as a foil for urban dissolution or, alternatively, as an opportunity for reflection on the human condition that transcends history, and thereby precludes social critique. Kenneth R. Johnston has summed up the difference thusly:

> Between 1793 and 1798, Wordsworth "revolves" from an initially conventional poetry and conventional politics, through a stage of radical politics and conven-

tional but unstable poetry, into a period of radical poetics and unstable but increasingly conventional liberal to conservative politics.[49]

This formulation explains why Wordsworth's radical experiment with a bardic poetics in *Lyrical Ballads* meant to challenge the elite "pre-established codes of taste" also incorporates a conservative slant that minimizes the impact of exploitation and oppression.[50]

Wordsworth's construction of Nature in *Lyrical Ballads* provides insights into his shift from radical politics/conservative poetics to radical poetics/conservative politics. In *The Politics of Nature*, Nicholas Roe relates that the Romantics inherited a nature discourse developed in the eighteenth century in which nature signified an initial state of consciousness characterized either by moral purity, as Shaftesbury and Rousseau believed, or by selfish egoism and amorality, as Hobbes and Burke believed. Using this schema, *Lyrical Ballads* ostensibly deploys a positive version of nature that contrasts with the negative culture of modern society. For Raymond Williams, the nature/culture binary is intrinsic to Romanticism, whose worldview is based on a postlapsarian ontology that is in "perpetual retrospect to an 'organic' or 'natural' society."[51] Likewise, Timothy Morton has described the nature/culture binary that emerges in the Romantic period as "a way of symbolically healing what modern society has rent asunder through alienation—the subject and the object."[52] Yet, as James K. Chandler contends, Wordsworthian "Nature" does not signify the *tabula rasa* imagined by Rousseauian radicals as the starting point for an egalitarian society, but the "second nature" of ingrained custom and habit central to the rhetoric of Burkean conservatives.[53] If so, as the bardic poetics outlined in the Preface suggests, Wordsworthian "second nature" is dressed in the customs and habits of "low and rustic life," a coded reference to his native community in the rural Lake District, which, as I have argued in the last chapter, he idealizes and upholds as the bearer of an essential national culture. This conservative view of Nature as a reference to the positive values of Lake District culture rather than to a pre-cultural state of perfection helps to explain why *Lyrical Ballads* relies on a pastoral mode that, since antiquity, has been used to express concern about life in the metropolis by contrasting it with an idealized agrarian culture.

For Wordsworth, then, Nature becomes a Romantic signifier for an agrarian mode of production and contingent state of consciousness nearly obliterated by the rapid rationalization of land, labor, and industry under capitalism. Faced with an unregenerate world growing increasingly more repressive, Wordsworth makes recourse to the "beautiful and permanent forms of Nature"[54] to countervail the disturbing scenes of moral and social dissolution most acute in the cities. As opposed to the callous "getting and spending" of commercial society, Wordsworth seeks to restore what he perceives as the more humane customs and traditions of England's agrarian past, which he finds still extant in the Lake District. Therefore, for Wordsworth, Nature is not a thing or a place, so much as a state of consciousness and set of traditions that inform a poetic grammar through which to express resistance to the oppressive new social order of industrial capitalism. The "mighty heart" of the final line of "Westminster Bridge" is a salient example of the way in which even the city, the place most abhorred by Wordsworth, can, with the right accents, and under the magical aura of twilight, invoke this natural grammar just as effectively as a scene laid in the Lake District.

And yet, Wordsworth's natural grammar ultimately fails in its design because it reinforces the very forms of bourgeois subjectivity whose material conditions he so adamantly opposes. When faced with the incomprehensible totality of the crisis of modernity that he finds most acute in the cities, Wordsworth psychologically (and often physically) retreats into the constructed utopian space of Nature. Saree Makdisi describes this process as the "immaterial exploitation" of Nature—a counterpart to the material exploitation of nature that accelerated during the eighteenth century—and points to the fabled "spots of time" episodes as key moments in this process.[55] Makdisi follows that this reaction ultimately fails to provide a real alternative to capitalist modernity precisely because it is framed in terms of the "phenomenological and cognitive space of the bourgeois subject."[56] In other words, in fleeing from the material conditions of capitalist modernity into transcendent "spots of time" catalyzed by the Romantic construct of Nature, Wordsworth reinforces the hallmark features of bourgeois subjectivity—alienation, individualism, and idealism. These features are evident in the way Wordsworth relegates the physical and social landscape to a static backdrop for the self-reflexive Romantic subject. So, whereas the sign of the other in "Salisbury Plain" catalyzes a moment of negative capability expressed as socially-engaged polemic, the sign of the other in "The Female Vagrant" and later poetry becomes an occasion for a moment of recognition leading to self-reflexivity that bypasses social and historical considerations altogether. In terms of class and nation, Wordsworth's subjective turn finally precludes class-consciousness, thus making viable the happy notion of a "solemn fraternity" that he comes to locate in the nation.

The concept of reification is central to understanding how and why Wordsworth's escape into Romantic Nature promotes the class unconsciousness of bourgeois subjectivity that sustains nationalist appeals to an imaginary "solemn fraternity." The theory of reification was first proposed by György Lukács in *History and Class Consciousness* (1923) as an effect produced by the novel, but the theory can also be applied to poetry. Lukács defines reification as the psychological effects of capitalism and commodity fetishism:

> The commodity character of the commodity, the abstract, quantitative mode of calculability shows itself here in its purest form: the reified mind necessarily sees it as the form in which its own authentic immediacy becomes manifest and—as reified consciousness—does not even attempt to transcend it. On the contrary, it is concerned to make it permanent by "scientifically deepening" the laws at work. Just as the capitalist system continuously produces and reproduces itself economically on higher and higher levels, the structure of reification progressively sinks more deeply, more fatefully and more definitively into the consciousness of man.[57]

Reification is the process by which capitalist ideology is reproduced at the level of consciousness. It is through reification that one's perception of the world becomes dehistoricized, naturalized, and universalized—in short, one succumbs to the immediacy of reality. That immediacy is consonant with commodity fetishism—the core of capitalist ideology according to Marx. *Commodity fetishism* means that a relationship between things takes the place of a relationship between people. Hence, when one goes shopping, one is not immediately presented with the social conditions of the labor that produced the commodity for sale, but rather with the commodity itself, represented chiefly by its exchange value, or price, which decontextualizes it from the exploitative social relations of production and recontextualizes it within the callous cash nexus of getting and spending. The commodity is thus a broken signifier attached to a new order of signification that no longer registers its organic history—the history of its production—but instead registers the history of its consumption in the form of prices and marketing. For Lukács, a fierce proponent of social realism, the role of artists should be "to pierce the surface to discover the underlying essence, i.e., the real factors that relate their experiences to the hidden social forces that produce them" and thus overcome the false consciousness and fragmentation generated by the immediacy of experience.[58] Lukács charges art with the mission of exfoliating the reified layers of ideology in order to make the actual social relations apparent.

In *History and Class Consciousness*, Lukács traces the origin of reification to the rationalization of production and division of labor under modern industrial capitalism, which renders incomprehensible a totalizing understanding of social relations that would otherwise empower real social agency.[59] Unable to comprehend the social totality, the modern bourgeois subject turns inward and assumes a contemplative stance towards the outside world, a phenomenon that Lukács would later describe in "The Ideology of Modernism" as the "flight into psychopathology."[60] The contemplative stance produces an artificial dualism between the external, objective world, and the inner subjective world of thought.[61] In this condition, the external world becomes a static landscape for the contemplative subject alienated from its social and physical environment:

When nature becomes landscape—e.g., in contrast to the peasant's unconscious living within nature—the artist's unmediated experience of the landscape (which has of course only achieved this immediacy after undergoing a whole series of mediations) presupposes a distance (spatial in this case) between the observer and the landscape.[62]

The landscape effect converts ambient space and the presence of others into a mirror for the self, placing an understanding of the totality of social relations further out of reach. The bourgeois subject in search of meaning is left to embrace a narcissistic egotism, or accept fate, chance, or some supernatural agent as the mysterious minister of an incomprehensible world.

The signs and symptoms of reification are evident in Wordsworth's poetry. Unable to comprehend the totality of the forces causing the crisis of modernity, Wordsworth places his faith in the poetic imagination to produce a restorative version of Nature that facilitates transcendental spots of time. Within this psychic-scape, he assumes a contemplative stance towards his surroundings, turning it and those within it into a reified landscape for self-meditation. Wordsworth's complicity with the landscape effect can be traced throughout much of his poetry, where people and nature alike are displayed in unmediated fashion as aesthetic phenomena valued solely for the emotional residue they leave with the spectator. The spectator assumes a contemplative stance toward their plight that rarely moves beyond a self-gratifying pity. The result is a poetry that everywhere conceals the social conditions wreaking havoc upon society. When confronted with scenes of injustice, gross poverty, or profound misery, Wordsworth mitigates the severity by deploying the imagination either to creatively alter, recuperate, or reflexively internalize the scenes before him, aiding and abetting where necessary the progress of reification. The poetic imagination is an epistemological adaptation to the incomprehensible reality of industrial capitalism, and a reified Nature/landscape is its palette. The contemplative Romantic subject flees from the terrible spectacles of city life into an idealized Nature because it cannot or will not comprehend the titanic social forces that are radically transforming its environment. It bemoans the loss of an imaginary, organic, natural past without ever penetrating beneath this nostalgia to understand why or how such a change has happened in the first place, and in so doing reifies the conditions of existence for itself and others, who become part of the landscape for its solipsistic reflections.

Wordsworth's encounter with the blind beggar in Book Seven of the 1805 *Prelude* illustrates the flight into psychopathology symptomatic of reification. In panicked flight from the incomprehensible "Babel din" of London's roiling street life, Wordsworth experiences a spot of time in which "the shapes before my eyes became / A second-sight procession."[63] In this out-of-body-like condition, he chances upon a blind beggar who

> with upright face,
> Stood propped against a wall, upon his chest
> Wearing a written paper, to explain
> The story of the man, and who he was.[64]

Instead of contemplating the injustice of such pauperism, Wordsworth veers off into a self-referential discourse about the impossibility of self-knowledge and total understanding:

> My mind did at this spectacle turn round
> As with the might of waters, and it seemed
> To me that in this Label was a type,
> Or emblem of the utmost that we know,
> Both of ourselves and of the universe.[65]

The blind beggar, clad with his self-narrative sign, is reified, objectified, and dehumanized, becoming a signifier for a universal human condition characterized by incomplete knowledge and existential dread. This order of signification coheres with the troubled state of mind that has pushed Wordsworth into a meditative spot of time. In this condition, Wordsworth is unable to meet the beggar as another human being. Wordsworth's confession that "My mind did at this spectacle turn round" insinuates an inward turn precisely at the moment when a sympathetic narrator would be reaching out to the suffering, blind beggar to understand his condition and perhaps provide some assistance.

As the gap widens between the subject and the reified object that has become part of the landscape for the contemplative self, the possibility for true communication and empathy disappears, and the other becomes a mirror for the self's own thoughts and feelings. Hence, Wordsworth describes how the beggar's eyes become mirrors that reflect his own sense of existential guilt: "I looked, / As if admonished from another world."[66] This guilt-ridden reaction could potentially trigger deeper engagement with the social nexus—perhaps the sting of guilt might signify Wordsworth's complicity with the exploitative social order—but this possibility ultimately collapses as Wordsworth shifts the subject from the impoverished beggar before him to the ontic and epistemic limitations of self-knowledge. Wordsworth takes a subjectivist inward turn and begins to ponder how "outward things" are in fact "such structures as the mind / Builds for itself."[67] A rumination on the incomprehensibility of the vast, teeming social life of the city follows, in which he describes the city as a "Parliament of Monsters," further reifying, objectifying, and dehumanizing the beings around him.[68] Ultimately, unable to overcome the feeling of "blank confusion" brought about by "trivial objects ... / That have no law, no meaning, and no end," Wordsworth turns in retreat to the panacea of a contrived Nature that promises "Composure and ennobling harmony," thus setting up the return to the Lake District in Book Eight.[69]

If *The Prelude* sheds light on the effects of reification upon Wordsworth's consciousness, an analysis of "The Solitary Reaper" is instrumental for understanding how reification operates in his poetry, and thus functions as a touchstone for understanding the dynamics of reification in *Lyrical Ballads*, a topic that will be explored at length in the next section. The ostensible subject of the poem, an encounter with a lone Highland lass singing unintelligibly while she reaps, is eclipsed by the spectator's memory of the *feeling* that her unintelligible song evokes, thus reifying the reaper as part of the landscape for the contemplative narrator.[70] This inward turn is evident in the poem's final stanza, where the narrator recalls,

> Whate'er the theme, the Maiden sang
> As if her song could have no ending;
> I saw her singing at her work
> And o'er the sickle bending;—
> I listened, motionless and still;
> And, as I mounted up the hill
> The music in my heart I bore,
> Long after it was heard no more.[71]

Wordsworth does not dwell on the fact that the reaper's song is rendered unintelligible not because it is infused by incomprehensible sadness, but because it is sung in her native Gaelic, a language suppressed and displaced by the hegemonic English language of state. Nor is he troubled by the fact that her solitude is probably not a Romantic posture, but actually the direct result of the brutal Highland Clearances that decimated the Scottish peasantry after The Forty-Five, dispersing them into industrial cities to occupy the lowest rung of exploited wage-laborers. Rather than examine the underlying political crises that determine the reaper's unintelligibility and thus occasion the very melancholia of the poem's ending, he is content to seal the envelope of history with a gratifying gesture of self-reflection.

This treatment of the reaper substantiates the criticisms made by Wordsworth's contemporaries that his poetry betrays a narrow self-reflexivity. John Keats famously referred to the "Wordsworthian or egotistical sublime," which he defined as an explosion of the self that occludes true sympathy.[72] Against this he contrasted the "negative capability" of the "camelion Poet" who has no ego of her own, and thus can inhabit any subject position.[73] Keats was following the sentiments of his mentor, William Hazlitt, who disparagingly wrote,

> [Wordsworth] takes a subject or a story merely as pegs or loops to hang thought and feeling on; the incidents are trifling, in proportion to his contempt for

imposing appearances; the reflections are profound, according to the gravity and aspiring pretensions of his mind.[74]

The criticisms levied by Keats and Hazlitt apply to "The Solitary Reaper." By turning from the reaper to the pleasurable melancholia elicited by the reaper's alterity and unintelligibility, Wordsworth de-materializes the reaper and converts her into an object of aesthetic pleasure for the narrator and the reader. In short, her unintelligibility is aestheticized instead of probed. In this sense, the poem's stanzaic structure imitates the same move enacted by the revisions to "Salisbury Plain," which proceed from a passionate, almost Shelleyan recognition of the other's painful historicity to an aestheticization of the other that universalizes and depoliticizes her condition. By this operation, rather than become a catalyst for greater social awareness, the other is converted into a source of pleasure for the contemplative subject.

For the contemplative subject, then, the reaper exists as phenomenon rather than noumenon because her presence has meaning only in relation to the observer's emotions. Wordsworth's privileging of the spectator's subjectivity is consistent with his declaration in the Preface that "all good poetry is the spontaneous overflow of powerful feelings."[75] Wordsworth is not trying to solve the dilemma of how to authentically represent the reaper's condition. Instead, he is more interested in how to frame his contact with the reaper as a self-reflexive event.[76] While this procedure might seem harmless, or indeed even laudable for its attempt to achieve an emotional connection with elements of one's environment, it must be understood as an act of reification. The spontaneous emotional pleasure elicited by the reaper's aestheticization signals that the reaper has become an object of connotative meaning determined by the gazing subject. It also signals an embrace of the immediacy of the external world (for poet and reader), reifying rather than exfoliating the layers of history and ideology that mask the various forms of exploitation and oppression denoted by the reaper—class exploitation, ethnic cleansing, and cultural-linguistic marginalization.[77] Therefore, whereas the encounter with the reaper might trigger a reassessment of the unjust social norms that govern life in the nation, instead it leaves these norms altogether untouched, preserving the pleasurable fantasy of a national "solemn fraternity."

Reification in *Lyrical Ballads*

Although "The Solitary Reaper" displays the hallmarks of Wordsworthian reification, the reification effect appears much earlier in *Lyrical Ballads*. However, whereas the former displays these features in concentrated form, the latter provides a more distributed sampling of the reification effect. Specifically, *Lyrical Ballads* exhibits three distinct modalities of Romantic reification, which I group into three categories of poetry: (1) the poetry of the rustic poor; (2) the poetry of nature(alization); and (3) the poetry of transcendence. This section will explore representative samples of each type. "Goody Blake and Harry Gill," "Simon Lee," and "The Old Cumberland Beggar" offer examples of the reification of the rustic poor. "Lines Written in Early Spring" and "The Tables Turned" offer examples of Wordsworth's retreat into a reified nature/landscape. Finally, "Tintern Abbey" combines aspects of the other two types with the transcendent sublime of Wordsworth's signature "spots of time" to produce the most complete degree of Romantic reification.

The reification effect in Wordsworth's poetry of the rustic poor displaces the violence of poverty by removing it from its social conditions in order to make it seem part of a natural, moral economy. Gary Harrison has explicated the dynamics of this process. Harrison relates that, although Wordsworth's poetry is "couched in an iconoclastic poetics that argues for transgressing cultural boundaries," it nonetheless

> appears to reinforce the ideological and social boundaries it purports to break down. Drawing upon both pastoral and picturesque conventions even as it denounces them, Wordsworth's poetry is implicated in an ideology that confirms and perpetuates the pauperization of the agricultural laborer and the idealization of rustic poverty that interferes with genuine concern over the welfare of the poor.[78]

Harrison outlines two discursive strategies for representing the poor that were available to Wordsworth. The first is "a strategy of containment rooted in the aristocratic conventions of the pastoral and the georgic." It involves "a 'rustification' of poverty, a displacement of poverty into a scriptural space that attenuates its shock and violence."[79] The second is "a strategy of normalization rooted in middle-class conventions of capitalism and industry," which involves "the writing of values, like thrift, patience and industriousness, onto the working-class body."[80] According to Harrison, Wordsworth both normalizes and contains the experiences of the poor, while at the same time empowering them by offsetting material deprivation with moral surplus. Wordsworth's rustic poor are made powerful precisely because they appear to be so powerless.[81]

One finds this discursive strategy at work in "Goody Blake and Harry Gill," subtitled "A True Story," a parable in which Wordsworth bypasses class consciousness and the politics of class struggle by valorizing the spiritual economy of Goody's surplus morality over the material economy of Harry's surplus value, accumulated in the form of monetary wealth. The poem opens by describing Harry Gill, a wealthy landowner who was once

> a lusty drover,
> And who so stout of limb as he?
> His cheeks were red as ruddy clover;
> His voice was like the voice of three.[82]

In contrast,

> Old Goody Blake was old and poor;
> Ill fed she was, and thinly clad;
> And any man who passed her door
> Might see how poor a hut she had.[83]

Goody Blake is Wordsworth's classic poor old woman, whose poverty is thrown into strong relief when juxtaposed with the wealth and vigor of "Young Harry."

However, Wordsworth relates that Harry Gill now suffers from a mysterious and debilitating ailment:

> Oh! what's the matter? what's the matter?
> What is't that ails young Harry Gill?
> That evermore his teeth they chatter,
> Chatter, chatter, chatter still!
> Of waistcoats Harry has no lack,
> Good duffle grey, and flannel fine;
> He has a blanket on his back,
> And coats enough to smother nine.[84]

Wordsworth gradually reveals the cause of Harry Gill's ailment. He begins by describing how on cold evenings Goody Blake retrieves sticks from Harry Gill's property to use for kindling a fire in her hut to keep her warm "when frost was past enduring, / And made her poor old bones to ache."[85] Harry eventually discovers that Goody has been trespassing and violently apprehends her, at which point Goody drops to her knees and prays "To God that is the judge of all."[86]

At this point, the poem shifts from a comical folk tale to a parable about the dangers of greed and materialism and the virtues of pious poverty. Goody calls upon "God! who art never out of hearing," and invokes his divine justice so that Harry "may he never more be warm!"[87] From that moment on, Harry Gill is incessantly plagued by a chill that makes his teeth chatter. Goody, powerless to resist Harry, appeals to a supernatural agent for redemption. She is backed by what Harrison calls a "moral surplus," and so her wish is actualized.

Despite the fact that the wealthy landowner has gotten his just desserts in the end, one must wonder what such a maudlin display of morality really accomplishes. Wordsworth has not challenged the economic system that keeps Goody impoverished while it gives Harry a disproportionate share of social wealth. Nor has he returned to Goody any of the welfare that is her due. By ignoring the determinants that regulate poverty, Wordsworth naturalizes the predicament in which one finds these two characters. The claim that a "moral surplus" is an adequate substitute for political power is hardly justifiable, especially since the supposed power it affords originates in an immaterial, transcendental agent. In fact, power in itself is not the issue at all, since it is significantly determined by wealth. "Goody Blake and Harry Gill" illustrates Wordsworth's roundabout way of dispensing justice to the poor without understanding or challenging the system that produces poverty. He succeeds in reifying the image of poverty by normalizing the social relations that produce and perpetuate it.

Another of Wordsworth's poems of the common poor, "Simon Lee," begins with a chance encounter with an old and unemployed huntsman, Simon Lee, "In the sweet shire of Cardigan, / Not far from pleasant Ivor-hall."[88] Simon Lee is still proudly dressed in the tattered livery coat of his former master, but Ivor Hall now sits in quiet ruin because his master, having died without a son, cannot fulfill the medieval primogeniture law, which required that manorial estates succeed to the firstborn son. As a result of this untended contradiction within feudal inheritance laws, the manor indefinitely awaits legal adjudication before it can be mortgaged to a new owner, most likely a gentlemen of the rising monied class.

For Wordsworth, Ivor Hall's inactivity and slow erosion signifies more than just what is wrong with feudalism, but also operates within a larger field of signification that insinuates what is wrong with the society replacing it. This critique is most redolent in Simon Lee's tattered livery coat, which simultaneously evokes a sense of loyalty to and nostalgia for a bygone era of feudal *noblesse oblige* while visually demonstrating the instability and penury introduced by the new system of market relations. Simon Lee's tragic infirmity—we are told that the old man degenerates to the point where his aged wife, Ruth, must "do what Simon cannot do"[89]—and even more tragic obsolescence betoken a society that denies even the most rudimentary measures of social welfare. The narrator describes the deleterious effects of this transition with a heavy heart:

> But, oh the heavy change!—bereft
> Of health, strength, friends, and kindred, see!
> Old Simon to the world is left
> In liveried poverty.
> His Master's dead,—and no one now
> Dwells in the Hall of Ivor;
> Men, dogs, and horses, all are dead;
> He is the sole survivor.[90]

Simon Lee is the last vestigial survivor of a bygone age of feudal obligation who now dwells in a new society, that of industrial capitalism, which has no place for him. His infirmity and obsolescence thus represent both the decline of feudalism and the vicious effects of a market economy whose ruthless efficiency forecloses any quaint sentiments of loyalty and charity.

Having described Simon's plight, however, the narrator now turns his attention to the reader and the real subject of the poem:

> O Reader! had you in your mind
> Such stores as silent thought can bring,
> O gentle Reader! you would find
> A tale in every thing.[91]

Here is where the poem begins to drift away from its ostensible subject—poor Simon Lee—and move towards an investigation of the spectator's emotional reaction to what is encountered. Wordsworth encourages the reader to aestheticize the people and scenes that one meets, and thereby draw a "tale" from even the most common experiences. Yet, to reduce reality to a set of phenomena that serve only to excite pleasure or pain is to implicate oneself in reification.

This is indeed what he does to poor Simon Lee, for it is after this proclamation that the narrator enters the scene as the sensitive spectator:

> One summer-day I chanced to see
> This old Man doing all he could
> To unearth the root of an old tree,
> A stump of rotten wood.[92]

The narrator arrives just in time to catch the old man feebly trying to uproot a stump. Naturally, he lends a hand and severs the root for the old man, "At which the poor old Man so long / And vainly had endeavoured."[93] "The tears into his eyes were brought," avers the narrator,

> And thanks and praises seemed to run
> So fast out of his heart, I thought
> They never would have done.[94]

At this point, the poem shifts from dialogue to monologue. "Alas! the gratitude of men / Hath oftener left me mourning," exclaims the narrator in the final two lines of the poem.[95] Almost magically, Wordsworth succeeds in transmuting a poem about poverty and inequality into a poem about his contingent response to the image of such phenomena. Simon Lee and the entire context of feudalism slip into the background and become merely an occasion for the exploration of one's own subjectivity. Reality has been reduced to landscape for the emotional effusions of the contemplative subject.

Poverty is reified differently in the case of "The Old Cumberland Beggar." The poem is a perfect example of what Celeste Langan defines as the "freedom from" and "negative liberty" of liberalism that characterizes Romantic idealizations of vagrancy.⁹⁶ Wordsworth converts the trials and tribulations of itinerant poverty into an ideal of freedom by stressing the beggar's freedom from the captivity of an almshouse, the statesmen's utilitarian solution to the problem of vagrancy, which became institutionalized under the Poor Laws. The almshouse is like a miniature city whose "pent-up din" is "misnamed of industry," for it consumes rather than sustains life.⁹⁷ Against this, Wordsworth celebrates the beggar's freedom of mobility in Nature:

> And let him, *where* and *when* he will, sit down
> Beneath the trees, or by the grassy bank
> Of high-way side, and with the little birds
> Share his chance-gather'd meal, and, finally,
> As in the eye of Nature he has liv'd,
> So in the eye of Nature let him die.⁹⁸

The beggar's mobility, as Langan argues, offers only a simulation of freedom because the beggar is abstracted from the social conditions that produce his "residual economic freedom"—his subjection to the policies of a fiscal-military state that renders him part of the surplus labor pool for commodity production.⁹⁹ The beggar's mobility is therefore a reified abstraction that obfuscates his historical and social determinants.

While this is one aspect of Wordsworth's recuperation of the old beggar, another aspect is his placement of the beggar within a vanishing moral economy in which the beggar exchanges spiritual services for material goods. In the note appended to the poem, Wordsworth explains how the old man comes from a class of itinerant beggars who "will probably soon be extinct."¹⁰⁰ These beggars differ from the usual kind by traveling a well-worn circuit, which attaches them to the sympathies of a particular community. In exchange for material charity, the beggar offers the spiritual rewards of moral certainty and self-congratulatory praise that come along with being charitable. These rewards are repeatedly conveyed by the beggar's visibility in the community.

Philip Connell has pointed out that Wordsworth's insistence on the social utility of the beggar "might be read in critical counterpoint to a more crassly utilitarian, quasi–Malthusian view of the dependent poor as little more than a 'redundant population.'"¹⁰¹ On the other hand, James K. Chandler has commented on how this instrumentalization of the poor serves to endorse the social hierarchy that produces abject poverty: "The speaker's claims for the Beggar's 'use' to the villagers has ... to be seen as serving [the] larger quietistic argument about the limits of human wisdom, the vanity of political science, and the justice of the ways of God to man."¹⁰² What this suggests is that by emphasizing the beggar's use-value, his poverty is removed from the context of social injustice and resituated within a moralistic framework of good deeds where begging becomes a spiritual occupation within the greater social economy of the community. Thus, by both "liberating" the beggar from the economy of the almshouse and assigning him a specialized role in the community's division of labor, Wordsworth rescues the poem from a critique of the national politics that have produced the beggar's abject poverty.

Like many of Wordsworth's poems of the poor, the poem begins with a chance encounter. This time, the narrator recalls that the beggar is someone he remembers from childhood:

> Him from my childhood have I known, and then
> He was so old, he seems not older now;
> He travels on, a solitary man.[103]

The beggar is seemingly ageless; his course is as constant as the sun and moon; and his path is a lonely one. His constancy commands instant respect from the community. When he draws near, the toll-gate attendant instinctively lets him pass and the post-boy gives him right of way. The fact that the narrator remembers him at all suggests the status accorded to this figure.

The beggar's description emphasizes his solitude, humility, self-abnegation, and perseverance, all qualities befitting the asceticism of the penitent monk. Indeed, the beggar seems to have forsaken the pleasures of the flesh for those of the spirit:

> He travels on, solitary Man,
> His age has no companion. On the ground
> His eyes are turn'd, and, as he moves along,
> *They* move along the ground; and evermore,
> Instead of common and habitual sight
> Of fields with rural works, of hill and dale,
> And the blue sky, on little span of earth
> Is all his prospect. Thus from day to day,
> Browbent, his eyes for ever on the ground,
> He plies his weary journey.[104]

By emphasizing the beggar's self-denial of even the most free and simple pleasures—of companionship and pleasing vistas—the narrator leads us to believe that the beggar's poverty is self-inflicted. His physical poverty is interpreted as a sign of his greater spiritual wealth rather than as a sign of social injustice. Begging is thus erased from the list of social evils caused by class society and reinscribed within a Christian framework of sacrifice and holy works.

It is from this conceit—of beggar as holy man—that the narrator defends the old beggar from ne'er-do-well statesmen "who have a broom still ready in your hands / to rid the world of nuisances."[105] The statesmen claim that all beggars are useless nuisances, but the narrator contends that even from a utilitarian standpoint they offer a valuable social commodity. Already resonant in this statement is the central idea of Wordsworth's much later injunction against the Poor Law Amendment Act (1834), in which he defends the sacred institution of almsgiving against plans to institutionalize the administration of poor relief (an action not meant to eliminate poverty, but to remove it to the margins of society).[106] Adopting the logic of political-economy, the narrator recasts the beggar as an economic agent who barters blessings in exchange for material goods. The effect of this labor can be measured by observing what happens to those who grant him charity:

> While thus he creeps
> From door to door, the Villagers in him
> Behold a record which together binds
> Past deeds and offices of charity
> Else unremembere'd, and so keeps alive
> The kindly mood in hearts which lapse of years,
> And that half-wisdom half-experience gives
> Make slow to feel, and by sure steps resign
> To selfishness and cold oblivious cares.[107]

The old beggar is a living record of the charitable deeds committed over the years by the members of his community. In this economy of charity, the beggar is a bank or repository of the community's good will, and each member can draw moral interest from the beggar each time he returns. This is similar to the medieval practice of buying indulgences, only instead of requiring constant pre-payment to hedge against immorality, the beggar offers moral interest for charity given in the past. This is evident when the narrator writes,

> All behold in him
> A silent monitor, which on their minds
> Must needs impress a transitory thought
> Of self-congratulation, to the heart
> Of each recalling his peculiar boons
> His charters and exemptions; and perchance,
> Though he to no one give the fortitude
> And circumspection needful to preserve
> His present blessings, and to husband up
> The respite of the season, he, at least,
> And 'tis no vulgar service, makes them felt.[108]

The beggar is a "silent monitor" whose panopticon-effect enables others to feel again the transitory "self-congratulation" of past charities. And the good feeling generated by the beggar's presence acts to safeguard against the "selfishness and cold oblivious cares" that might otherwise unravel the social fabric of the community. Hence, the beggar's "vulgar services" provide both individual salvation and communal harmony. These services make his condition not only desirable, but socially necessary.

In "The Old Cumberland Beggar," then, we discover a clever inversion that reifies poverty by converting it into a necessary condition for the social maintenance of moral order. The abject and persistent poverty of the old beggar, far from being a living spectacle of national crimes whose ignominy cries out for redress, is instead a national treasure whose lifestyle ought to be preserved from the feckless plans of social reformers.

Nowhere is Wordsworth's landscape-effect more evident than in the poems of nature(alization). These poems are so named because in them one finds the process of naturalization by which ambient nature is converted into transcendental Nature and used as a foil for culture. Nature becomes a dehistoricized landscape for the contemplative subject in pursuit of emotional relief. Yet, what this accomplishes is not a clearer vision of the social ills that Wordsworth instinctively feels, but an illusory retreat into the solipsistic world of the creative imagination that further defers understanding and agency.

"Lines Written in Early Spring" is a salient example of this phenomenon. The narrator begins by describing his emotions while in nature's bowers:

> I heard a thousand blended notes,
> While in a grove I sate reclined,
> In that sweet mood when pleasant thoughts
> Bring sad thoughts to the mind.[109]

Characteristically, the poem is introduced as a poem about feelings. The narrator's melancholy is mitigated by nature's balms, yet all throughout the poem he cannot shake his sadness. One can see the struggle to overcome this mood in the second stanza:

> To her fair works did Nature link
> The human soul that through me ran;
> And much it grieved my heart to think
> What man has made of man.[110]

The vacillation that occurs in this single stanza is indicative of the mental maneuverings that Wordsworth will make throughout the rest of the poem. He grieves over the exploitative social relations that are becoming more prevalent in Britain as industrial capitalism steadily wipes out every last trace of what is perceived as a more humane agrarian past. As Raymond Williams suggests, he is mourning the loss of an organic or natural past. Hence, he seeks refuge in nature, the most explicit reminder of what has been lost.

But this nature is not merely a physical reality. For Wordsworth, it is imbued with a spirit and a presence—with, one could say, a mind of its own. The next few stanzas attest to this as the narrator struggles to convince himself that "Nature's holy plan" is to ensure pleasure.[111] He states, "And I must think, do all I can, / That there was pleasure there."[112] Here one can trace Wordsworth's recourse to a transcendent emancipatory agent in the form of "Nature." It is to "Nature" that he attributes the "holy plan" of a pleasurable world, a world that man has corrupted. "Have I not reason to lament / What man has made of man?," he questions, after comparing the pleasure of nature with the oppressive and exploitative reality of capitalist society.[113] Nature, as a transcendental signifier of pleasure and redemption, entirely loses its objective material reality. It becomes an otherworldly plane, a transcendent landscape, against which Wordsworth can unfavorably compare his sordid world. For him, Nature's grand plan has gone awry because of man's intervention. The fragmentation produced by the advent of industrial capitalism has left him with no alternative but to project onto nature a yearning for a total understanding of reality that is hopeful and promising, a vision of reality that is suffused with pleasure. Wordsworth can little understand "what man has made of man" other than to mourn the loss of a past that is somehow more "natural," more attuned to the grand design of a benevolent "Nature."

Ultimately, Wordsworth's conversion of nature—the historical product of changing social relations—into Nature—an immutable, pantheistic, and transcendental alternative to modernity—backfires. In "Lines Written in Early Spring," the Romantic subject, searching for a genuine emotional connection, has naturalized and reified nature, in the form of a transcendent landscape, and in turn has robbed it of its rich history and precluded any personal agency that might accrue from a better understanding of the real determinants behind the oppressive social relations that are the poem's main subject-matter. As Wordsworth relates in the Preface, the evocation of pleasurable feelings, after all, is the primary obligation of the poet. It would seem that what Wordsworth elicits in this poem is not some transcendent emancipation from reality, but the cultivation of pleasurable melancholy by brooding "in that sweet mood when pleasant thoughts / Bring sad thoughts to the mind." By reifying Nature into an idealized construct against which human society seems spoiled and unbearable, the Romantic subject succeeds in heightening the delicious intensity of melancholia, forcing the individuated subject further into a solipsistic monad.

"Tables Turned" is perhaps a more pronounced example of the naturalization of nature. The poem begins with a strong exhortation to lay aside books and venture out into nature for true knowledge. "Up! up! my friend, and quit your books," commands the narrator, "Come forth into the light of things, / Let nature be your Teacher."[114] Once again one finds nature transformed into a transcendent agent, who this time serves as a wiser teacher than books. The spirited narrator continues:

> One impulse from a vernal wood
> May teach you more of man,
> Of moral evil and of good,
> Than all the sages can.[115]

As in the previous poem, nature functions as a sort of antidote to the incompleteness of human knowledge. This incompleteness is the result of psychological fragmentation—an inability to attain a totalizing understanding of the material conditions within a mode of production that entails the division and specialization of labor. Hence, Wordsworth counsels us to seek a total understanding of the world in nature, which is ironically a vision of the world removed from the world of books and men.

In addition to indicating the incompleteness of human knowledge, Wordsworth further enjoins us to stop thinking because "Our meddling intellect / Mis-shapes the beauteous forms of things."[116] Wordsworth both recognizes the fragmentary nature of human knowledge and advocates in favor of keeping it that way! The last stanza fortifies this point:

> Enough of Science and of Art;
> Close up those barren leaves;
> Come forth, and bring with you a heart
> That watches and receives.[117]

In the place of an active striving for real knowledge, for a totalized understanding of one's material conditions, Wordsworth substitutes an image of nature. Nature, in objectified form—dehistoricized, naturalized, and universalized—becomes for Wordsworth the consummate repository of wisdom. Without actively considering the national history that has led to the current state of nature, he cannot claim to have any understanding of it other than a reified one. The wisdom that such a view of nature can bestow is an illusory one, meant to palliate the feelings of frustration and powerlessness that accompany the fragmentation of life, labor, and thought. Wordsworth advises us to quit the labor of learning and effectively shut-down, to unquestioningly accept the immediacy of the external world as truth rather than to strive in vain for an understanding of the historical processes that produce it and frame our consciousness of it.

Wordsworth's poetry of transcendence represents the pinnacle of Romantic reification. "Lines written a few miles above Tintern Abbey" is the most emblematic poem of this kind in *Lyrical Ballads*. The opening scene is laden with historical congruities and resonances, which are indicated by its subtitle, "On Revisiting the Banks of the Wye During a Tour, July 13, 1798," and by its opening lines,

> Five years have passed; five summers, with the length
> Of five long winters! and again I hear
> These waters, rolling from their mountain-springs
> With a sweet inland murmur.[118]

Wordsworth had visited the abbey five years earlier, during a walking tour from Salisbury Plain to the Wye and North Wales after returning from his second trip to France. In the interim, England and France had declared war, the Terror had erupted, and Wordsworth had begun to question his republican ideals and move back to a position of conditional patriotism. The meditative tone of the opening lines suggests a mind darkened and weighted by the gravity of these years. Wordsworth negotiates these troubling memories by recourse to a transcendent economy of "abundant recompence" in which a contemplative stance catalyzes a moment of sublimity that eclipses history, thereby enabling a restorative moment of self-renewal and re-invention.

Beginning with New Historicist re-readings of Romantic poetry in the 1980s, Wordsworth's representation of place and history in "Tintern Abbey" has elicited much critical controversy for the ways that it displaces history and reinforces hegemony. I rehearse this conversation here in order to contextualize my own position. At the center of this conversation was Marjorie Levinson's seminal essay, "Insight and Oversight: Reading 'Tintern Abbey.'" Levinson begins with the simple observation, initially offered by her students, that the abbey noted in the title was oddly absent from the poem. Her suspicions are further aroused by the palimpsestic political history of the poem's dating— July 13, 1798, almost marking the nine-year anniversary of the fall of the Bastille, the eight-year anniversary of Wordsworth's first visit to France, the five-year anniversary of Marat's murder, and the five-year anniversary of Wordsworth's first visit to the Abbey. Wordsworth's eschewal of these events for a searching meditation and pastoral aesthetic suggests to Levinson that Wordsworth is intentionally displacing history in order to escape from a complicated and impossible political scene:

> Given the sort of issues raised by "Tintern Abbey"'s occasion, it follows that the primary poetic action is the suppression of the social. "Tintern Abbey" achieves its fiercely private vision by directing a continuous energy toward the nonrepresentation of objects and points of view expressive of a public—we would say, ideological—dimension.[119]

Levinson concludes that, despite the poem's title, "The Abbey is precisely what gets looked over and overlooked, as does the significance of 13, 14, July 1798, 1793, 1790, and the actual appearance of the banks of the Wye."[120] She proposes that Wordsworth's pastoral prospect in the poem is "artfully assembled by acts of exclusion" in order to effect his escape from personal and social history.[121] Relying on descriptions from biographers and some contemporaries, Levinson reconstructs what Wordsworth must have actually witnessed in 1798 from his perch several miles above the abbey as the violent processes of de-monasticization, enclosure, and industrialization were ravaging the countryside. She conjectures that the abbey, which was a common refuge for vagrants and beggars at the time, was most likely omitted for this reason. The nearby iron forge is also missing, its plumes of toxic smoke replaced by innocent "wreathes of smoke" attributed to idyllic "vagrant dwellers" in the "houseless woods" and hermit's caves. Levinson further suggests that Wordsworth would have been downstream of the abbey on the 13th, but intentionally repositions himself above the abbey in the poem's timeframe to avoid the "ouzy, and discolored" waters polluted by the forge.[122] Levinson finishes her reading with a McGannian indictment that Romantic scholars have adopted a "facile sympathy" for the poem's sensibility, which produces "our enabling, alienated purchase on the poems we study."[123]

Not surprisingly, Levinson's analysis stirred up controversy among critics. For instance, Thomas McFarland has contested the significance she gives to the abbey's absence from the poem: "The abbey is not in the poem because Wordsworth is nowhere near the abbey, not because he is overlooking the abbey either visually or metaphorically."[124] He disproves Levinson's theory about Wordsworth's repositioning by showing that it is based on a factual inaccuracy, concluding, "If the 'few miles above Tintern Abbey' cannot be impeached as *locus* of the poem's origin, then there would seem to be no grounding for Levinson's arguments."[125] Ultimately, he dismisses Levinson's reading as an act of "sociological bad faith" that makes a "great poem ... seem not even a good one."[126] Yet, McFarland's critique is marred by an overstated antipathy to New Historical methods, which he categorically rejects in favor of a neo–Arnoldian focus on the quality of Wordsworth's intensity and achievement.

Nicholas Roe has critiqued Levinson's argument from a different perspective. He contends that Wordsworth's picturesque landscape is not intended to be escapist, but is instead a strategy for recouping the troubling history of the 1790s by invoking Milton's *Paradise Lost*, a kindred poem set in the equally picturesque bowers of Eden that functions as an allegory for recouping after the failure of revolution—this time the English Civil War.[127] Roe notes several factors that make the picturesque scene in the Wye Valley an appropriate place for a political retrenchment rather than a political escape. He contends that, for Wordsworth, the Wye Valley would have been coded with political meaning, making it the least effective candidate for the conceit of a Romantic sojourn into nature. For one thing, the signs of industrial activity, poverty, and tourism would certainly inhibit such a poetic conceit. So too would Wordsworth's memory of his initial visit, ebullient from his return from France and hopeful for a republican revolution in England. In addition, Roe argues that Wordsworth would have been cognizant of the contemporary political significance of Chepstow Castle, just downstream of the abbey, which he must have passed on his tour. Henry Marten, a republican and MP who supported the regicide during the English Civil War, served a sentence of life imprisonment in Chepstow after the restoration in 1660. Southey had written about Marten and Chepstow in his *Poems* (1797) because it appealed to disillusioned former supporters of the republican cause, like Wordsworth and himself, who felt a spiritual kinship with the suffering Marten.[128] Finally, Roe reminds us that Thelwall, a political exile and comrade of Wordsworth's, had toured the Wye Valley and written about his trip in the May and July 1798 issues of *The Monthly Magazine*.[129] Roe concludes that Wordsworth, far from feeling like a fugitive, must have felt much like the embittered Satan stealing into Paradise after his fall from Heaven. From Roe's account, then, we gather that Wordsworth's return to the picturesque setting of the Wye Valley was an attempt to force a reconciliation with the private and public failures of this post-lapsarian moment.

Following Roe, I suggest that, indeed, Wordsworth *is* actively wrestling with the shadow of his past. However, in the vein of Levinson's critique of the poem's exclusions and aporias, I also propose that his victory in this psychological agon hinges upon a declarative narrative act featuring a manufactured "sense sublime" that is deployed to willfully transcend and sublimate his previous memories of the Wye Valley. The result is that one set of associations—of London, France, and political turmoil—is replaced by another, less disquieting set that emphasizes the "green pastoral landscape" and his persistent filial affection for Dorothy. In this sense, the sublime catalyzes a moment of psychological restoration and renewal that allows Wordsworth to recoup his losses and move on with his life, but only at the expense of effacing his class-conscious republican former self. Ultimately, it is not the history of the abbey or of the surrounding landscape that is reified by the aesthetics of the sublime, but his own complicated personal and political history, which is eclipsed and abandoned in a singular moment of aesthetic euphoria.

Wordsworth's formulation of the "sense sublime" in "Tintern Abbey" as a hybrid phenomenon that the mind and body "half-create, and what perceive" anticipates his later theorization of the sublime in a fragmentary treatise entitled *The Sublime and the Beautiful* (1811). Contrary to Burke's empirical approach in *A Philosophical Enquiry into the Origins of Our Ideas of the Sublime and Beautiful* (1757), Wordsworth explains that the sublime is a moment of transcendence in which both the subject and the object must equally participate: "To talk of an object as being sublime or beautiful in itself, without references to some subject by whom that sublimity or beauty is perceived, is absurd."[130] He continues,

> It appears that even those impressions that do most easily make their way to the human mind, such as I deem those of the sublime to be, cannot be received from an object however eminently qualified to impart them, without a preparatory intercourse with that object or with others of the same kind.[131]

The "preparatory intercourse" is not carried out by the faculty of reason, but by the imagination. Reason, the exalted faculty of eighteenth-century philosophy, cannot comprehend the sublime, for sublimity implies transcendence to a point beyond human understanding. This formulation more closely follows 's model of the sublime in the *Critique of Judgment* (1790) whereby sublimity occurs precisely when the subject is unable to comprehend its experience. Wordsworth echoes this Kantian axiom when he writes, "Whatever suspends the comparing power of the mind [reason] & possesses it with a feeling or image of intense unity, without a conscious contemplation of parts, has produced that state of the mind which is the consummation of the sublime."[132] In summary, Wordsworth's sublime is actuated by the imagination's dialectical intercourse with the object, which produces a moment of intellectual suspension and self-transcendence.

Such a moment of blissful self-transcendence occurs at the apogee of "Tintern Abbey," after a sublime singularity precipitates "gleams of half-extinguish'd thought."[133] Burdened by the gravity of the past five years, which is synaesthetically conveyed by the diametrical extremes of "lonely rooms" and the "din / Of towns and cities,"[134] Wordsworth characteristically deploys the trope of Romantic Nature to achieve "tranquil restoration."[135] His description of a natural experience endowed with "aspect more sublime" coheres with McFarland's explication of the sublime as an experience of fragmentation that produces an overwhelming sense of euphoria.[136] Wordsworth writes of

> that blessed mood,
> In which the burthen of the mystery,
> In which the heavy and the weary weight
> Of all this unintelligible world,
> Is lightened:—that serene and blessed mood,
> In which the affections gently lead us on,—
> Until, the breath of this corporeal frame
> And even the motion of our human blood
> Almost suspended, we are laid asleep
> In body, and become a living soul:
> While with an eye made quiet by the power
> Of harmony, and the deep power of joy,
> We see into the life of things.[137]

In the sublime state of euphoria, the "burthen of the mystery" of this "unintelligible world" ceases to exist as consciousness is "laid asleep," permitting one to look beyond history and the self to "see into the life of things." Building on McFarland's theory, I propose that the fragmentation of consciousness produced by the sublime euphoria of this moment is analogous to how reification functions: a moment of aesthetic overload contracts the purview of consciousness to a single event that precludes a totalizing understanding of the phenomena under scrutiny, hence rendering it "unintelligible." Unable to translate the experience in rational terms, one "suspends the comparing power of the mind" and succumbs to a willful myopia that releases one from the burden of intelligibility. In other words, one achieves tranquility by transcending history through the experience of aesthetic joy.

When placed within the poem's many personal and political contexts, one can discern that the sublime machinery of this event conceals beneath the surface ripple of a powerful aesthetic experience an equally powerful experience of sublimation and self-renewal. If we take the opening stanza of "Tintern Abbey" as the deep sigh of a man weighted by five years of history, this moment then represents the spiritual and metaphorical release of all that psychic energy and the psychological equivalent of a rebirth. Here, we discern the telltale signs of Wordsworth's recourse to a transcendent economy in which the immediacy of an experience in nature provides "abundant recompence" for the frustrations and failures of his previous political engagements. These painful memories, which are overdetermined by the Wye Valley's palimpsestic landscape (and aptly decoded by Roe), generate unintelligible and burdensome contradictions that call for a suspension and fragmentation of consciousness metaphorically figured as sleep. In this state, a cynosure is substituted for a totalizing understanding of reality as history is contracted to the present moment, and the present moment is phenomenologically approached as the reified circle and circumference of "the life of things." In "Tintern Abbey," then, a singularity consisting of a sunny day with Dorothy on the picturesque banks of the Wye effaces layers of history and political meaning, leaving behind a psychological *tabula rasa* that signifies a conscious rejection of republicanism and class struggle in favor of "tranquil restoration" among the "green pastoral landscape" of an edenic British countryside because, unlike the former, "Nature never did betray / The heart that loved her."[138]

***

Wordsworth's retreat into a reified Nature sadly accelerates the disturbing social change that his poetry ostensibly abhors. The Romantic structure of feeling that it produces amplifies the effects of individualism, idealism, and alienation that comprise bourgeois subjectivity precisely because it seeks to humanize the plight of the poor in ways that dehistoricize and universalize their condition for a contemplative subject that cannot reach beyond the immediacy of personal experience. Instead of facilitating a greater awareness of the social contradictions that generate poverty, this technique is complicit with the forms of bourgeois ideology that mitigate or excuse the existence of poverty and other forms of class inequality that would otherwise challenge the myth of community intrinsic to nationalist discourse, what Wordsworth will later describe in glowing terms as a "solemn fraternity" founded on "ancestral feeling." In so doing, Wordsworth rescues this myth from the grim reality of class struggle, and thereby retards the development of a more objective class consciousness that can generate real alternatives both to the ideology of nationalism and to the depredations of capitalist modernity.

Chapter 4

Coleridge, Religious Nationalism and the Anxiety of Empire

> When *Britain* first, at heaven's command,
>   Arose from out the azure main
> *This* was the charter of the land,
>   And guardian angels sung *this* strain:
>   "Rule, *Britannia*, rule the waves;
>   *Britons* never will be slaves."
> —James Thomson[1]

> Therefore, evil days
> Are coming on us, O my countrymen!
> And what if all-avenging Providence,
> Strong and retributive, should make us know
> The meaning of our words, force us to feel
> The desolation and the agony
> Of our fierce doings?
> —S.T. Coleridge[2]

> Of his country he speaks with a patriotic enthusiasm,
> and he exhorts to virtue with a Christian's ardor.
> —Christopher Lake Moody[3]

"Mr. C., in common with many others of the purest patriotism, has been slandered with the appellation of an enemy to his country."[4] So writes a critic in an early review of Coleridge's "Fears in Solitude" (1798), reminding one that Coleridge's reputation had been, by 1798, seriously tarnished by his former republican sympathies. "The little Bristol Thelwall," as E.P. Thompson dubbed him for the radical speeches he delivered in Bristol in 1795, was, in the intervening years that brought him to settle in Nether Stowey with wife and babe, actively in retreat from Godwin's circle, London, and republican politics.[5] Yet, the damage to his reputation had been done. The now laughable "Spy Nozy" incident reveals the degree to which the British government was con-

4. Coleridge, Religious Nationalism and the Anxiety of Empire 121

vinced that he might indeed be "an enemy to his country." "Fears in Solitude" arrives at a moment of paranoia when Britons, tremulous with the fear of a threatened French Invasion thought to be aided and abetted by treasonous elements within the country, were mobilizing the greatest mass *levee* of volunteer militia in a decade. It also arrives at a moment when Coleridge was eager to prove his patriotic loyalty. Both fears are registered by the poem—the former the ostensible topic of the poem, the latter punctuated by repeated, impassioned, patriotic overtures: "O Britons!"; "O my brethren!"; "O my countrymen!"

Yet, the poem also registers that this return to patriotic orthodoxy is conditional, premised upon an equal return to Christian orthodoxy, which the author asserts the nation has sadly abandoned in pursuit of imperial spoils, and for which it is now being punished by the imminent French invasion that sets the occasion for the poem. Surprisingly, the immediate response from reviewers to a poem critical of the establishment by a poet suspected of treason was mostly positive. While one reviewer complained that the "retributive inflictions of providence" threatened in the poem are "not highly honourable to [the author's] feelings as a Briton,"[6] the reviewer concerned about Coleridge's status as "an enemy to his country" wrote that the poem was "sufficient to wipe away the injurious stigma."[7] Another favorably opined, "In urging his countrymen to unite to repel invading foes, [the author] takes care to remind them of that too prevalent degeneracy of manners, and those public crimes, which demand instant reformation, if they would wish their efforts to prove successful, and sanctioned by the great ruler of empires."[8] Yet another put the point more succinctly: "Of his country he speaks with a patriotic enthusiasm, and he exhorts to virtue with a Christian's ardor."[9] The fact that Coleridge, a suspected traitor, could negotiate a political rapprochement in verse that simultaneously critiqued national policy under the cover of Christian moral rectitude draws attention to the rich overlap of nationalism and religious faith in eighteenth-century Britain.

If nationalism is a "new secular religion," as theorists have contended, it is also one that tends to subsume older forms of faith. In the case of Great Britain, Linda Colley has demonstrated that adherence to Protestant Christianity, particularly the Anglican state church version, became a marker of mainstream patriotism. Using Coleridge's "Fears in Solitude" as an illustrative example, this chapter will explore how adherence to Protestant Christianity was an intrinsic part of the performance of British nationalism in the eighteenth century. The peculiar British belief in the nation's divinely chosen status as a "New Jerusalem" peopled by "New Israelites" underwrote the drive to expand its empire, which was figured in patriotic poems, such as James Thomson's "Ode: Rule, Britannia!" as a divine calling. However, "Fears in Solitude" taps into a counter-discourse dating back through the English Civil War period to antiquity and the Old Testament that expresses anxiety about the spiritual and social costs of empire. My reading of "Fears in Solitude" situates Coleridge's rhetorical commingling of "patriotic enthusiasm" and "Christian's ardor" within this longstanding discourse of faith-based critiques of empire, the ostensible subject of a poem that critiques the rapacity of Britain's continental and colonial exploits. In the poem, Coleridge presents the dreaded French invasion as a sign that Britons have lost their moral way, abandoning the Christian ideals believed to guide the nation. Within this paradigm of faith-based nationalism, the invasion is indeed rendered part of the "retributive inflictions of providence." The poem is an intervention in this process where Coleridge assumes the role of prophet and shepherd in order to lead the nation out of its moral wilderness and save it from spiritual and material calamity. Yet, because this foregrounded narrative also serves as a convenient vehicle for a humbled Coleridge to rehabilitate his reputation by disavowing the "folly" of his radical years and rejoining the national mainstream, the poem ultimately draws attention to the rich concatenation of patriotism and piety that colors British nationalism in this period.

As this reading suggests, "Fears in Solitude" serves as a fulcrum point for Coleridge's transition from radical Unitarian democrat to conservative Anglican Tory, a process that is mediated by a persistent devotion to Christian ideals. Several scholars—Kelvin Everest, John Gatta, Jr., and Alan Vardy, for instance—have contributed insightful readings about how the poem is significant as such a turning point for Coleridge.[10] This reading contributes to the conversation by specifically addressing how Coleridge's choice to perform his political apostasy in the character of a Christian patriot sheds light on his perception about the intimate relationship between religion, nationalism, and empire. Coleridge's thoughts on empire were not monolithic, but were subject to radical alterations throughout his intellectual and political development. The 1795 Bristol Lectures show that early in his political development he was sharply critical of what he saw as the dangerous excesses of empire—war, slavery, and tyranny (domestic and colonial). However, Coleridge's persistent religious devotion brought him to interpret the rise and decline of nations and their empires as evidence of a grand design in which primitive pagan societies give rise to advanced Christian nations. Consequently, Coleridge opposed secular histories of empire, such as Edward Gibbon's *The Decline and Fall of the Roman Empire* (1776), because they denied the legitimacy of this teleology.[11] In 1833, he would write of Gibbon's work, "I do not remember a single philosophical attempt made throughout the work to fathom the ultimate causes of the decline or fall of that empire."[12] In later years, Coleridge's millenarian view of empire would bring him to endorse the British Empire as essentially a benevolent force in history. This is confirmed by scholarship from Paul W.L. Arthur and Ian R. Scott, who draw attention to Coleridge's support of the Napoleonic Wars and British colonialism.[13] In relation to Coleridge's thoughts on empire, "Fears in Solitude" does not register so much an anti-imperialist position, but a position of concern about the excesses of colonial violence and their deleterious effects at home and abroad. This position is consistent with nationalist claims about the desirability and duty of empire, while simultaneously voicing concerns about its practice, specifically, whether it is consistent with the nation's Christian values. In the guise of a Christian patriot, then, Coleridge seeks to redeem the nation while simultaneously redeeming himself before a public that considers him "an enemy to his country," and the latter serves as an example for the kind of penitential humility required to save the nation from its terrible fate.

My analysis consists of three sections. The first section describes the positive view of empire as a divine calling that underwrites British liberty and prosperity. Against this, I identify a counter-discourse with religious and secular roots that expresses anxiety about the excesses of empire, often by deploying the "trope of luxury"—a conceit in which the luxuries afforded by empire are depicted as morally and physically corrosive. In the second section, I outline the political gyrations in Coleridge's radical years leading up to the unique blend of conditional patriotism and religious nationalism that characterize the critique of empire in "Fears in Solitude." Specifically, I chart his move from republican flirtations to his development of an associative theory of political praxis in which love of God fosters love of family and nation. The third section examines the manifestation of this triptych in "Fears in Solitude."

Religion, Nationalism and the Anxiety of Empire

The idea of British exceptionalism derives from an English tradition that dates back before the pre–Norman period, at least to Bede, who believed that "the English were God's new 'chosen' nation elected to replace the sin-stained Briton in the promised land of Britain."[14] In the early seventeenth century, Puritans and antiquarian scholars reactivated this discourse by attempting to establish a credible ancestral link between the English and the original chosen people of the Old Testament, the Jews. Using simple archaeological methods, they claimed to trace the origin of European peoples to the post-diluvial resettlements conducted by the sons of Japhet, a child of Noah.[15] Consequently, the Puritans popularized the belief that Britain was a "New Jerusalem" inhabited by a chosen race of "New Israelites." The Noachian "first plantations" were cited as scriptural precedent for the practices of English and later British imperialism. According to this genealogy, civilization advances from East to West through the auspices of a benevolent and divinely ordained system of colonialism in the tradition of the resettlements conducted by the sons of Noah.[16] Ironically, then, what began as a way of marking and elevating the English above the early "sin-stained Briton"—a reference to the island's original Celtic tribes—later became a way of assimilating all of these peoples into a modern Britain nation-state that projected an archetypal "sin-stained" status onto the indigenous peoples they now sought to colonize and exploit.

The Puritan belief in the nation's chosen status and its obligation to spread Christian civilization was a corollary of the spiritual ideas of election and calling that operated at the personal level, informing the stereotype of the "industrious Englishman" central to the new culture of capitalism. Derived from Calvinism, Puritans believed in the doctrine of predestination—that one was predestined at birth for heaven or hell. Contra Catholicism, no amount of good works could alter this destiny. Yet, to achieve certainty of salvation, one had to obey one's instinctive calling as ordained by God. Max Weber and R.H. Tawney have described how these religious ideas informed the "spirit of capitalism."[17] With the advent of Calvinism, Weber observes that a spiritual transvaluation occurs in which "the only way of living acceptably to God was not to surpass worldly morality in monastic asceticism, but solely through the fulfillment of the obligations imposed upon the individual by his position in the world."[18] He explains that the doctrines of spiritual election and calling found their material correlative in a work ethic that stressed industry and abstemiousness. The more diligently one labored and saved in the fulfillment of one's calling, the greater would be one's spiritual *and* material rewards. In this manner, prosperity was transfigured into a reliable signpost of election—what Weber calls *certitudo salutis* (the certainty of salvation). The wealthiest believers were assured to be the elect of God, while the status of the poorest was questionable. Similarly, Tawney explains that this ideology countenanced the new system of class relations: "[The Puritan] sees in the poverty of those who fall by the way, not a misfortune to be pitied and relieved, but a moral failing to be condemned, and in riches, not an object of suspicion ... but a blessing which rewards the triumph of energy and will.... He is the practical ascetic, whose victories are won not in the cloister, but on the battlefield, in the counting-house, and in the market." He concludes, "Success in business is in itself almost a sign of spiritual grace."[19]

If spiritual ideas informed the stereotype of the "industrious Englishman" who dutifully observed his calling to certify his election, it also reinforced the notion that Britons had a duty to obey their national calling to spread Christian civilization by expanding their empire, the benefits of which would serve as proof of its chosen status. These ideas are saliently expressed in James Thomson's patriotic "Ode: Rule, Britannia" (1740). The poem so thoroughly resonated with the new British populace that it was later put to music and became the unofficial national anthem.[20] In a bombastic address to the nation, figured as the pseudo–Athenian *Britannia*, Thomson exhorts Britons to "rule the waves," and thus triumphantly calls for an era of unfettered British imperialism.[21] The first line of the poem links this imperative to empire with a divine calling. The British Isles rise from the sea "at heaven's command" while "guardian angels" encourage it to "rule the waves."[22] British liberty and prosperity are pegged to the success of its imperial calling, and this guarantees "*Britons* never will be slaves."[23]

By the nineteenth century, the ideology that upheld imperial expansion as a divine calling became imbricated with racist discourse. This is evident in Rudyard Kipling's *The White Man's Burden* (1899), a parody of imperialist aims that nonetheless embodies imperialist attitudes about the racial, spiritual, and moral inferiority of non-white colonized peoples while asserting that the virtuous sacrifices of white colonizers working to civilize these peoples will be in vain. Though written in response to the U.S. debate over whether to invade the Philippines, a prospect that American imperialists presented as the next stage in the country's divinely ordained "manifest destiny," the poem is equally a summation of the attitudes developed by Britons over nearly four centuries of experience as colonizers. In a stanza that rings with racist *and* millenarian import, Kipling exhorts,

> Take up the White Man's burden—
> And reap his old reward:
> The blame of those ye better,
> The hate of those ye guard—
> The cry of hosts ye humour
> (Ah, slowly!) toward the light:—
> "Why brought ye us from bondage,
> Our loved Egyptian night?"[24]

The overt claim here is that the white soldiers of empire are actually liberators who should expect nothing but resistance and enmity from the uncomprehending races whom they are presumably serving by conferring upon them the benefits of Western civilization, here figured by the Enlightenment trope of moving them "toward the light." But there is something more going on here. The last two lines substitute this conventional Enlightenment metaphor with one from a religious tradition. The scriptural reference to Moses' deliverance of the Israelites from the dark night of Egyptian slavery becomes imbricated with the Enlightenment motif of progress as exposure to the light of reason and knowledge. The upshot is that, like the biblical Moses, the Britons have been divinely called to the millenarian purpose of delivering the non-white peoples of the earth from spiritual and cultural "darkness," even if those peoples will, as Kipling asserts, thwart all best intentions on the part of patriotic Britons who answer the call.

Religious arguments for the sanctity and duty of empire did not go unchallenged. A counter-discourse emerged, first in England, and later throughout Britain, that posed a fundamental incompatibility between morality and empire, and, furthermore, propagated the idea that empire diminished the liberty and prosperity of the nation. This discourse also perpetuated the centrality of religion to British nationalism, but it was rooted in parts of scripture that contested the call to empire by expressing an "anxiety of empire." This anxiety is acutely expressed in the Old Testament prophecies of Isaiah and Jeremiah, who warn about the spiritual and social peril brought about by imperial ambition. The scriptures relate how, having embarked down the same road of imperial conquest as their former Egyptian masters, the Israelites under the successors of King David began to reap the dual menace of oppressive class hierarchies and ruinous imperial wars. Jeremiah reads these social evils as signs and portents of divine abandonment, vehemently preaching the certainty of divine destruction for his people's ignominious and impious ways. Isaiah's polemic, however, takes another route, offering the prospect of redemption to the chosen people on the condition that they accept due punishment and recant their ways.[25]

The discourse of imperial anxiety also has classical roots in the argument that the sumptuary rewards of empire are corrosive luxuries that come at the high cost of impaired virtue and curtailed liberties. David Armitage has traced this secular discourse back to antiquity, in the writings of the Roman historian Sallust who argued that the Roman Republic's thirst for riches and glory led to the dictatorship of Sulla and eventually to the loss of republican freedoms under the dictatorship of the Caesars.[26] Armitage follows the Sallustian tradition, which places liberty at odds with empire, to Machiavelli's *Discorsi*, where he too remarks on the contradiction between liberty and imperial *grandezza*. Armitage demonstrates that this tradition resurfaces during the Cromwellian Protectorate, after Cromwell's failed bid to subject the Spanish Caribbean in 1654–5 as part of the so-called "Western Design," which resulted in a serious loss of faith in the Protectorate and its burgeoning empire.[27] Allusions to the Sallustian tradition, with Cromwell playing the role of the dictator Sulla, were common among critics of Cromwell during the Protectorate. For instance, Marchamont Nedham warned Republicans to heed the example of Rome, whose relentless drive for imperialist expansion brought with it the unintended consequences of enervating luxuries, moral corruption, and martial law.[28]

Milton, while acting as Cromwell's Latin Secretary, also warned against the ruinous temptations of imperial expansion in his prose and poetry, alluding to both classical and scriptural sources. Written at the time of the "Western Design" debacle, he posits this argument in the *Defensio Secunda* (1654). A few years later, during the collapse of the Protectorate, he identifies Cromwell with Sulla in the epigraph to *The Readie and Easie Way* (1660), where he quotes Juvenal: "Et nos/consilium dedimus *Syllae*, demus populo nunc" ("We, too, gave advice to Sulla; now we give it to the people").[29] The treatise, written after Cromwell's death, offers advice to the people on how to save their republic from the imminent danger of monarchic restoration. At the very end, he counsels the people on the dangers of seeking the luxuries of trade at the expense of the "forein or domestic slaverie" represented by the tyranny that will follow after the monarchy is restored.[30] The theme of liberty lost to corrosive luxury resurfaces in Milton's dramatic poem, *Samson Agonistes* (1671), which returns us full-circle to the Old Testament origins of imperial anxiety. During an imperial war to subdue the Philistines, Samson, the hero of the Israelite people chosen by God, risks his personal freedom and the freedom of his people for an assignation with Delilah, his Philistine lover. The story of Samson provides a warning parable that the sumptuary delights of empire come at the expense of liberty, virtue, and even the grace of God.

Milton's appropriation of the story of Samson, a warrior emasculated and weakened by his submission to the material temptations of empire—in this case figured as the lovely Delilah—illustrates the "trope of luxury," a conceit for expressing the anxiety of empire that presents materialism and over-refinement of manners as the hallmark symptoms of a moribund society on the verge of decline. Suvir Kaul has described this literary phenomenon in terms of an "antimaterialistic discourse" that served as shorthand for expressing class-based anxieties about unequal access to consumption in late seventeenth- and early eighteenth-century Britain.[31] Yet this trope also operated in a religious framework in which the sins of materialism and greed precipitate divine abandonment and retribution. For instance, Puritan criticism of court and high church in the build up to the Civil War involved charges that these institutions endorsed sinful material pleasures over spiritual discipline—the protracted debate over Sabbath sports comes to mind—leading Puritan critics to invoke a millenarian situation in which these sins would be remediated by divinely-willed retributive actions. Puritan vitriol was so extreme and pervasive in this period that Ben Jonson was moved to satirize it in *Bartholmew Fair* (1614), a play that features the cantankerous and hypocritical Puritan Zeal-of-the-land Busy.

Use of the trope of luxury continued well into the eighteenth century. Early in the century, the Bishop George Berkeley adopts it in *An Essay Towards Preventing the Ruin of Great Britain* (1721), where he issues a scathing condemnation of greed and speculation in the wake of the notorious South Sea Bubble fiasco of 1721. The South Sea Company, a massive joint-stock company formed in 1711, obtained exclusive British trading rights with Spanish South America for nearly a decade. On the promise of windfall future profits, it secured massive government and private investments. Through calculated fiscal projections and trumped-up publicity schemes, the corporation managed to incite a speculative bubble that saw stock prices skyrocket. One scheme involved the company's purchase of large shares of national debt and a promise to lower interest rates in exchange for high equity. But, in the wake of Britain's recent War of Succession with Spain, trade relations between the two powers became strained and the company realized minuscule profits throughout its decade-long period of operation. When it became clear that the company was insolvent, stocks plummeted and many over-extended investors became instant bankrupts. This precipitated the intervention of Parliament to indemnify against further economic collapse and restore public confidence in financial markets. Although the South Sea Bubble was only one among many "bubble" schemes arising throughout the early eighteenth century, Berkeley seizes upon the magnitude of this particular event as an ominous sign of the nation's decrepit economic, social, and moral condition.[32]

Ironically, Berkeley castigates the lazy and reckless speculation of the new monied class that caused the crisis by invoking the middle-class Puritan discourse of virtuous industry. He declares, "Industry is the natural sure way to wealth. This is so true that it is impossible an industrious free people should want the necessaries and comforts of life, or an idle enjoy them under any form of government."[33] As opposed to this diligent accumulation, he sternly admonishes "all projects for growing rich by sudden and extraordinary methods, as they operate violently on the passions of men, and encourage them to despise the slow moderate gains that are to be made by an honest industry, [and] must be ruinous to the public."[34] The target of this tract gradually comes into focus as the "monied men"—the monied class of financiers and speculators—who, by "cozenage and stock-jobbing," seek quick and easy profits "without producing labour and industry in the inhabitants."[35] Ironically, Berkeley appropriates anti-court Puritan rhetoric to stage a Tory counter-attack on the growing hegemony of an extravagantly wealthy and elite stratum of the bourgeoisie; the philippic thunders as he enumerates the "luxurious follies" that this class and its Whig party machine have introduced into culture and government. These include a preference for speculation ("gaming") over honest labor; wanton graft and corruption in public institutions; casual perjury by public officials; cynicism; sumptuous habits of dress and culinary delight; and an "atheistical narrow spirit, centering all our cares upon private interest, and contracting all our hopes within the enjoyment of this present life."[36]

Alluding to the recent debates between Lord Shaftesbury and Bernard Mandeville over the public effects of private interest,[37] Berkeley sides with Shaftesbury, arguing that private interest ultimately controverts the moral maxims of religion and undermines the public good:

> Men are apt to measure national prosperity by riches. It would be righter to measure it by the use that is made of them. Where they promote an honest commerce among men, and are motives to industry and virtue, they are without doubt, of great advantage; but where they are made (as too often happens) an instrument of luxury, they enervate and dispirit the bravest people.[38]

In Berkeley's analysis, wealth has no intrinsic virtue; if pursued for its own account, it produces enervating luxury rather than ennobling industry. Berkeley counsels that "frugality of manners is the nourishment and strength of bodies politic," whereas luxury is "the natural cause of their decay and ruin." He illustrates his theory with examples from antiquity, citing the decline of the Persian, Lacedaemonian, and Roman empires.[39]

Berkeley questions whether the cycle of rise and decline evident in previous empires is an historical law or a contingency based on choice: "Whether it be in the order of things that civil States should have, like natural products, their several periods of growth, perfection, and decay; or whether it be an effect as seems more probable, of human folly that, as industry produces wealth, so wealth should produce vice, and vice ruin.[40] The indeterminacy of this formulation allows for the possibility of recovery from the precipice of social decline. It suggests that a nation is responsible for its fate, and that it can choose to cultivate a Spartan and virtuous patriotism, what he calls "public spirit," or "run headlong into all those luxurious follies, which ... have been fatal to other nations, and will undoubtedly prove fatal to us also, if a timely stop be not put to them."[41] Berkeley situates his tract as an intervention at a moment that he frames as a crucial juncture: either the nation will continue to rush headlong into certain doom *or* it will heed his solemn counsel and foster "public spirit." For Berkeley, the latter will require a campaign that involves, among other things, the enforcement of sumptuary laws and the restoration of religious faith.

Should the nation continue on its path of self-destruction, Berkeley predicts an apocalyptic future. At the conclusion of his essay, he dons the persona of a sentimental British narrator from the future who reflects back on the ruins of Britain's former glory. In a eulogy that mingles patriotism with religious zeal, he poignantly captures the anxiety of empire: "Such were our ancestors during their rise and greatness; but they degenerated, grew servile flatterers of men in power, adopted Epicurean notions, became venal, corrupt, injurious, which drew upon them the hatred of God and man, and occasioned their final ruin."[42] In this narrative, the temptation of corrosive luxuries triggers Britain's moral and material decline. It implies that even the chosen can be abandoned by God and face divine retribution for irreverent behavior. Berkeley reinscribes the crisis of the South Sea Bubble within this apocalyptic narrative and poses Britons with a choice: continue down the sumptuous path of certain destruction, or return to the path of righteousness and redeem the nation.

The theme of materialism and greed leading to social decline would become secularized during the eighteenth century and resonate in many other writings. For instance, in "Of Simplicity and Refinement in Writing" (1742) David Hume warns against the "degeneracy of taste" produced by commercial and imperial success and points to past examples of over-refinement leading to imperial decline.[43] Similarly, in *The Decline and Fall of the Roman Empire* (1776) Edward Gibbon attributes the fall of the Western Roman Empire to "immoderate greatness" in which "Prosperity ripened the principles of decay."[44] Likewise, in *Ruins or Meditations on the Revolutions of Empires and the Law of Nature* (1791), a French text translated and popularized in Britain, C.F. Volney puts forward the theory that imperial decline is triggered by greed: "CUPIDITY had nevertheless excited among men a constant and universal conflict, which incessantly prompting individuals and societies to reciprocal invasions, occasioned successive revolutions, and returning agitations."[45] The poet William Cowper invokes similar themes in Book One of *The Task* (1785). Using the conceit of the evolution from simple stool to sumptuous sofa, Cowper traces a cultural history of the British Isles marked by degeneration from simplicity and plain virtue to meek over-refinement and moral turpitude. He contrasts the rough stool upon which "immortal Alfred sat," to the refined elbow chair framed from imported Indian cane, and, finally, to the luxurious sofa before him, inveighing, "Rank abundance breeds / In gross and pamper'd cities sloth and lust, And wantonness and gluttonous excess."[46]

Edmund Burke's parliamentary speeches against the abusive practices of the British East India Company also convey anxiety about the domestic costs of empire. Similar to Berkeley's critique of the relationship between easy speculation and the South Sea Bubble fiasco in the *Essay*, Burke's speeches link the Company's deadly commercial exploits in India to the decline of the social order back home, both of which are attributed to the rapacious greed of a new class of monied elites. Since the late 1600s, the Company had ruled over part of the Indian mainland with total impunity. However, the catastrophic death of more than ten million Indians during the Bengal Famine of 1770–3 brought public and parliamentary attention to bear on its doings. After receiving a seat in the House of Commons in 1780, Burke began a tireless crusade against the Company and its Governor-General, Warren Hastings, which culminated in the impeachment of Hastings on multiple charges of corruption in 1787. In a speech delivered before the House of Commons in 1783, Burke excoriates the "young men" driven to India by avaricious schemes of sudden-wealth and goes on to trace their deleterious influence at home:

> They marry into your families; they enter into your senate; they ease your estates by loans; they raise their value by demand; they cherish and protect your relations which lie heavy on your patronage; and there is scarcely a house in the kingdom that does not feel some concern and interest, that makes all reform of our eastern government appear officious and disgusting; and, on the whole, a most discouraging attempt.[47]

Burke perceived the déclassé monied interests who exploited the colonies to be equally threatening to the nation because their ill-found wealth disrupted the traditional class hierarchies. Isaac Kramnick observes, "Burke saw a conspiracy of new India money at work subverting the traditional order at home."[48] In a letter of 1787 to Sir Henry Dundas, a fellow proponent of Indian reform, Burke urged that the time was ripe to assail the faction of monied men and nip this unfolding crisis in the bud. He pleaded, "Nothing can rescue the country out of their hands but our vigorous use of the present fortunate moment, which if once lost is never to be recovered, of effectually crushing the leader and principal members of the corps."[49] Perceiving the new India money as a radical conspiracy, Burke conflated the bourgeois despoilers with Jacobin conspiracy because, in his eyes, both groups threatened the social order. At one point during the parliamentary proceedings, Burke warned the Lords that a victory for Hastings would be a victory for Jacobinism because Hastings stood "against property, rank and dignity ... against the very being of the society in which we live."[50]

Though Burke does not connect his anxiety concerning the domestic effects of empire to the imminent threat of divine retribution as Berkeley does, his belief that these effects constitute a terrible threat to the social order and moral fabric of the nation confirms Berkeley's apocalyptic view of empire. What occurs between Berkeley's *Essay* and Burke's speeches on India is a secularization of the anxiety of empire that cleaves more to the Sallustian tradition than to the tradition of Isaiah. However, with "Fears in Solitude," Coleridge reintroduces a religious framework for critiquing the terrible crimes of empire and tallying its deleterious and potentially catastrophic impact upon the nation. Yet, like Berkeley, he does so as a patriot who seeks to shepherd the nation back to the path of righteousness.

Coleridge's Transformation from Radical Republican to Religious Nationalist

In "Fears in Solitude," Coleridge expresses a religious nationalism complicated by an anxiety of empire. The poem must be understood as the culmination of a decade-long personal struggle to coordinate radical political ideals with ingrained British religious beliefs. Nicholas Roe has mapped Coleridge's political vacillations during the tumult of the 1790s in his historical study, *Wordsworth and Coleridge: The Radical Years*. Coleridge entered Jesus College, Cambridge, in 1791 a devout orthodox Anglican with liberal leanings. By 1794–5, he would find himself a Unitarian dissenter in the company of notorious radicals like William Frend, William Godwin, and John Thelwall. His further political gyrations away from this circle from 1795–8 would provide the backdrop of personal crisis that colors and informs the more immediate political crisis of "Fears in Solitude." The resolution of this crisis would entail a punctuated swing to the right, towards conservative Christian values (eventually back to Anglicanism) and mainstream national politics.

At Jesus College, Coleridge fell under the sway of William Frend, a Unitarian clergyman who espoused republican ideals and was a founding member of the Cambridge Constitutional Society. In 1793, Frend published the pamphlet *Peace & Union*, in which he warned that unless parliamentary and civil reforms were peacefully pursued, the growing schism between republicans and constitutionalists in Britain would lead to more violent clashes like the Birmingham Riots.[51] The publication came at an unpropitious moment, just as France was declaring war on Britain, and Frend was put on trial in Cambridge for attempting to incite rebellion among the lower classes. Largely through his relations with Frend, Coleridge adopted Unitarianism and embraced the politics of dissenting reformers. After a brief and impetuous stint with the King's Dragoons, he left Cambridge in 1794 to reunite with Frend and several other Cambridge dissenters in London, who were now members of the notorious London Corresponding Society. Coleridge's proximity to the Society eventually brought him into contact with John Thelwall, its persecuted founder.

Coleridge shared with Thelwall a sympathetic view of Robespierre as a well-intentioned radical provoked to violence by Britain's war of attrition, which fed traitorous plots and intrigues within France. This interpretation is conveyed in his tragedy *The Fall of Robespierre* (1794). However, what also emerges in the tragedy is a nascent critique of disinterested rationalism. Coleridge concludes that Robespierre's failure stemmed from the rigid adherence to a rationalist *telos* that sanctioned any means necessary to achieve its utopian end. He elaborates this critique in *Consciones ad Populum*, delivered during the Bristol Lectures of 1795, where he likens Robespierre to the Godwinian perfectibilitarian who is willing to sacrifice all scruples to achieve his end:

> Robespierre ... possessed a glowing ardor that still remembered the *end*, and a cool ferocity that never either overlooked, or scrupled, the *means*. What that *end*

was, is not known: that it was a wicked one, has by no means been proved. I rather think, that the distant prospect, to which he was traveling, appeared to him grand and beautiful; but that he fixed his eye on it with such intense eagerness as to neglect the foulness of the road.[52]

Coleridge's growing dissatisfaction with Godwinian rationalism would lead to the disintegration of his ill-fated utopian project in 1794. That summer, Coleridge was introduced to Robert Southey. They devised the scheme for Pantisocracy, a classless, collectivist utopian community to be built on the Susquehanna River in Pennsylvania.[53] But the scheme ultimately disintegrated as a result of burgeoning ideological differences between its founders.[54] Although Coleridge would declare himself a "compleat Necessitarian" in the vein of Hartley and Godwin in December of that year, he was nonetheless committed to a religious "Gratitudinarian" doctrine of social regeneration rooted in Christian ideals of love and sympathy rather than the disinterested reason preached by Godwin and expounded by Southey.

The year after the collapse of the Pantisocracy scheme in 1794 marked a turning point in Coleridge's personal and political life. In October 1795, he married Sara Fricker, the sister of Southey's wife, in what would become a loveless and estranged relationship. Coleridge's hasty marriage to Sara Fricker in the wake of the failure of Pantisocracy corroborates Roe's claim that "when that [Pantisocracy] impulse faltered (because of public events, and personal circumstances) we can see how emigration would grow increasingly remote, leaving disengagement and retirement as alternatives."[55] But Coleridge did not abandon the world of politics after his marriage and domestication in Nether Stowey. Rather, his activism was transformed and redirected. In the same year as his marriage, Coleridge delivered and published his controversial Bristol Lectures, in which he tackled a number of sensitive issues ranging from the ongoing war with France to the immorality of slavery and the hypocrisy of the Anglican Church.[56] These lectures also contain Coleridge's first public disavowal of Godwinism and articulation of an alternative political doctrine founded on the associative power of benevolent affection inherent in Christianity, which he believed would provide a bulwark against the tragic political errors of Robespierre and the French Revolution.[57]

In the lectures, Coleridge took particular issue with Godwin's claim in *An Enquiry Concerning Political Justice* (1793) that private affection is deleterious to society because it generates narrow self-interest, whereas disinterested reason, because it is unattached to any particular object, offers a broad foundation for the promotion of the common good. Instead, Coleridge syncretized a necessitarian and Unitarian Christian alternative elaborated from the ideas of Frend, Hartley, and Priestley. For instance, in the "Introductory Address" to *Consciones ad Populum*, Coleridge critiques Godwinian rationalism and its telos of perfectability, raising skepticism about the political efficacy of this doctrine. Using a diminutive tone, he states,

> The perfectness of future Men is indeed a benevolent tenet, and may operate on a few Visionaries, whose studious habits supply them with employment, and seclude them from temptation. But a distant prospect, which we are never to reach, will seldom quicken our footsteps, however lovely it may appear; and a Blessing, which not ourselves but *posterity* are destined to enjoy, will scarcely influence the actions of *any*—still less of the ignorant, the prejudiced, and the selfish.[58]

Coleridge was skeptical that reason could motivate people to act morally because it dismissed the benevolent affections that unite people. In his *Lectures on Revealed Religion*, he continued in this vein, sneering at the doctrine of reason for offering a "Stoical Morality which disclaims all the duties of Gratitude and domestic Affection."[59] In *Consciones* he entreats the public to practice the social gospel instead. He writes, "'Go, preach the GOSPEL to the Poor.' By its Simplicity it will meet their comprehensions, by its Benevolence soften their affections, by its Precepts it will direct their conduct, by the vastness of its Motives ensure their obedience."[60] Paramount here is the idea that scripture furnishes accessible moral precepts to the masses of uneducated poor. Christian morals will foster the benevolent affections necessary to achieve the harmony of the classes within an essentially moral social order. For this reason, he implores, "Oppression is grievous—the oppressed feel and are restless. Such things [as revolution] *may* happen. We cannot therefore inculcate on the minds of each other too often or with too great earnestness the necessity of cultivating benevolent affections."[61] Hence, Christianity could obviate the need for social revolution by providing the necessary social tonic of benevolent affection that would mitigate class antagonism.

In *Lectures on Revealed Religion*, Coleridge further argues that Christianity is the "Friend of Civil Freedom," insisting that freedom and equality are corollaries of Christianity. He cites the teachings of Jesus to explain how gratitude and affection operate to produce social harmony: "Jesus knew our nature—and that expands like the circles of a Lake—the Love of our Friends, parents and neighbours lead[s] us to love of our Country to the love of all Mankind."[62] In Coleridge's understanding, love spreads concentrically from the domestic to the national to the universal, deploying affection and gratitude to mediate relationships at an ever-grander scale. In *Consciones*, Coleridge explains how these vital benevolent affections first naturally manifest in the domestic sphere, but can be extrapolated to broader social relations. He declares, "The paternal and filial duties discipline the Heart and prepare it for the love of all Mankind. The intensity of private attachments encourages, not prevents, universal Benevolence."[63] Decisively breaking from the doctrine of disinterested reason, Coleridge extrapolates from the duty of fathers and sons to a broader set of duties, insisting that the filial love and emotional attachments first learned in the domestic sphere will give rise to patriotism and eventually to universal harmony.

In later years, after returning to the Anglican Church and in the wake of the Catholic Emancipation Bill (1829), Coleridge would officially revise these ideas, dropping the final link of universal harmony while honing the idea that religion would foment a national sodality. In *Table Talk,* while broaching the subject of the English Reformation, Coleridge's nephew records the following statement he made on 8 September 1830: "The Church ought to be a Mediator between the People and the Government—between the rich and the Poor."[64] In the same year, Coleridge produced *On the Constitution of Church and State* (1830). Nigel Leask contends that this text provides Coleridge's most trenchant argument for the necessity of a single state church as a social institution charged with the cultivation of national unity. He writes,

> Because he regarded the Church, rather than the unreformed Constitution, as "the last relic of our nationality," it was incumbent upon Coleridge to define the "twofold" nature of *enclesia* and *ecclesia,* the national and spiritual churches, as an "internal theocracy" which might moralize and cultivate the new social and political order.[65]

Coleridge believed that the "new social and political order" premised on commercial competition and self-interest threatened to erode the nation-state. But religion could preserve the imagined community required to maintain social harmony. In a letter written on the margins of a copy of *On the Constitution of Church and State*, Coleridge most succinctly expresses this point with the formula "NATION = State + Church."[66] This formula defines nationalism in terms of a conflation of religious devotion with loyalty to the state. Social harmony could thus be achieved by exploiting the concentric circles of affection that begin with religious instruction, continue through domestic attachments, and conclude with nationalism.

By 1798, Coleridge would stridently disavow his former republican politics and begin moving towards realignment with Christianity and mainstream politics. This transition is marked by two literary events, one private, one public. In a letter to his brother George dated 17 March 1798, he forcefully declares,

> I have snapped my squeaking baby-trumpet of Sedition & the fragments lie scattered in the lumber-room of Penitence. I wish to be a good man & a Christian— but I am no Whig, no Reformist, no Republican.[67]

That same month, a politically reborn Coleridge began publishing the first of several essays in *The Morning Post* and *The Courier* excoriating France and comparing it to imperial Rome, with the proviso that its empire would be infinitely briefer.[68]

A month later, Coleridge published "France: An Ode" in the *Morning Post* under the title "Recantation: An Ode." He would republish it later in a quarto by Joseph Johnson along with "Frost at Midnight" and "Fears in Solitude." As the original title suggests, the poem publicizes his recantation of the radical social aims of republicanism. It begins with an apostrophe to nature performed on a sea-cliff facing France by a vexed narrator who declares he still adores "The spirit of divinest Liberty."[69] The narrator's divided loyalties are marked by his symbolic positioning on the English side of the channel, but with a face turned towards France and the revolution. Although the poem emphasizes France's degeneration into a rapacious empire, the narrator also chastises Britain's reactionary role in joining the "dire array" of "The Monarchs marched in evil day,"[70] a reference to the plot by continental powers to re-establish the monarchy in France. Moved by Britain's treachery, the narrator hangs his head in shame and "[weeps] at Britain's name."[71] But the fact that the narrator takes responsibility for his country's wrongdoings suggests that the narrator would fain be a patriot if only Britain had acted virtuously to support the cause of Liberty. The climax of the poem comes with the troubling realization that France, provoked by reactionary intrigue (foreign and domestic) and swayed by imperial ambition, has betrayed and perverted its revolutionary ideals. With Britain and France both sullied by war and ignoble ambitions, the narrator concludes that Liberty cannot be found "in forms of human power"[72] but must instead be felt in the intangible forms of nature:

> And there I felt thee!—on that sea-cliff's verge,
>   Whose pines, scarce traveled by the breeze above,
> Had made no murmur with the distant surge!
> Yes, while I stood and gazed, my temples bare,
> And shot my being through earth, sea and air,
>   Possessing all things with intensest love,
>   O Liberty! my spirit felt thee there.[73]

The poem marks a turning point for Coleridge, who, like the narrator, has retreated back into the quiet precincts of domestic life and pious devotion (here pantheistic) as a refuge from the political fallout of the French Revolution and the disillusionment of his earlier republican convictions.

Like its companion poem, "Fears in Solitude" also marks a turning point for Coleridge. However, whereas the earlier "France: An Ode" leaves the narrator searching for liberty in the wind, "Fears in Solitude" closes with the narrator decisively leaving the precincts of nature to return back home to England, a move that symbolizes his recommitment to the nation. Nonetheless, as in "France: An Ode," Coleridge maintains a critical posture towards Britain's imperial exploits on the continent and in its colonies. As such, the poem demonstrates a complex political renegotiation in which Coleridge embraces a conditional patriotism that leaves open the right to criticize the nation, and, indeed, transmutes this right into a patriotic duty to steer the nation away from self-destructive imperial policies. Furthermore, since Coleridge expresses his anxiety about the domestic costs of empire in religious terms by interpreting the dreaded French invasion as the agent of divine retribution, the poem also demonstrates Coleridge's embrace of a patriotic Christian evangelism. Accordingly, Coleridge frames his style of critical patriotism not only as a civic responsibility, but a moral and religious one as well, since the nation must act righteously or risk the loss of its salvation.

Thanks to the work of David Fairer, we know that Coleridge's public performance of this complex political recommitment in verse was probably inspired by a parliamentary speech delivered by the Right Honourable Richard Brinsley Sheridan in the same month Coleridge wrote "Fears in Solitude."[74] The text of Sheridan's speech was widely reprinted in the London dailies, making it readily available to Coleridge during the time that he was drafting "Fears in Solitude." Sheridan had earned a reputation in Parliament as a severe critic of British imperialism and a staunch defender of the French Revolution. But the French invasion scare rekindled his patriotism. In the speech, Sheridan delivers a rousing exhortation on the need for a mass, patriotic mobilization of the citizenry in preparation for the imminent invasion, while simultaneously delivering his signature acerbic critique of British foreign policy. The central act of Sheridan's speech serves as a precedent to the mixture of patriotic call to arms and national castigation that will similarly characterize Coleridge's rhetoric in "Fears in Solitude." In his speech, Sheridan exhorts the house "to kindle the zeal, and animate the courage of the people."[75] He is confident that the citizenry will be roused to unprecedented acts of valor "as soon as one drop of English blood shall be shed by a Frenchman on English ground." He implores, "All must unite, all must go every length against them, or there are no hopes."[76] But Sheridan's patriotism is conditional, for he remains critical of Britain and its allies' role in swelling an imperialistic French army that "has grown gigantic from the efforts which the alien powers exerted to oppose its infant liberty."[77] Nonetheless, Sheridan is also careful to abjure any lingering naïve faith in the vision of a French invasion spreading *liberté*, *egalité*, and *fraternité* to the downtrodden cottagers of the British Isles. "What, then, is their object?" sneers Sheridan. "They come for what they really want: they come for ships, for commerce, for credit and for capital. Yes; they come for the sinews and the bones; for the marrow, and for the very heart's blood of Great Britain."[78] Sheridan's position is clear. They come for the sinews of empire, and Britain is largely to blame for this crisis by stoking the flames of war.

"Fears in Solitude" performs a similar process of political recantation and patriotic repositioning for a national audience, but with the superadded element of a religious revival. Like Sheridan, Coleridge will call for a mass mobilization of the citizenry to fend off the French onslaught while also blaming Britain for instigating the invasion.[79] He adds to this a religious backdrop in which France is figured as the agent of God's wrath towards a rapacious and over-proud British empire. Coleridge's rousing exhortation for a patriotic defense of a vulnerable and imperiled British nation is complicated by a biting religio-moral critique of the nation's imperial transgressions against providential will. The narrator will humbly supplicate himself before God to plead for mercy on behalf of a penitent nation, certain that catastrophe can be averted because of Britain's exclusive chosen status. The re-inscription of the nation's imperial transgressions within a providential framework of sin and redemption corresponds with Coleridge's turn to religion to negotiate his political retrenchment.

The stamp of Sheridan's speech is also evident in the poem's parallel rhetorical structure through which Coleridge negotiates a sophisticated political repositioning in the process of delivering a public address to the nation. This activity is protracted throughout the poem, but is most apparent in the poem's lyric prelude and peroration, where a sublimated confessional subtext distracts the reader from the poem's central hortatory sections. Seen in this light, "Fears in Solitude" is the obverse of its other companion poem, "Frost at Midnight," an ostensibly "domestic" conversation poem that foregrounds private considerations while sublimating the presence of significant political content.[80] While an overtly political poem, there is a significant lyrical undercurrent within "Fears in Solitude" that constitutes a nested plot within the broader theme of national mobilization to rebuff the perilous French Invasion.

Coleridge himself acknowledged the poem's generic ambiguity in a note to an autographed manuscript. He writes, "The above is, perhaps not Poetry,—but rather a sort of middle thing between Poetry and Oratory—*sermoni propriora*."[81] The Latin inscription comes from Horace and also appears as an epigraph to Coleridge's early conversation poem, "Reflections on Having Left a Place of Retirement" (1796). The phrase has various translations, but more or less refers to the poem's more appropriate status as oratorical prose. In the case of "Fears in Solitude," this prescription rests on the poem's obvious oratorical features—its address to the nation and supplication before a wrathful God—which are largely derived from the genre of religious sermon.

The upshot of Coleridge's notation has been to criticize the poem for its failure to comply with the standards of Romantic lyricism. For instance, Kelvin Everest has written that the poem's central oratorical sections are "stylistic failures" that besmirch the poem's otherwise laudable lyric sections.[82] However, these rhetorical concerns can only be maintained if the poem's two modes are treated as contradictory rather than complementary. Rather, I argue that the poem's more obvious public hortatory mode (a public reconfiguration of the Romantic conversation poem) is actually a mask for its more significant private confessional mode (formulated as the traditional Romantic lyric). In other words, the poem's generic hybridity as both political oratory and private lyric is precisely what allows the author to broach the underlying fears of dejection and isolation stemming from his radical past.[83] These modes comprise a rich dialogic whereby the narrator's provocation of the nation's incumbent rehabilitation before God serves as a foil for his own penitential rehabilitation from radical pariah to sincere patriot and pious Christian.

Given this framework, let us consider that the poem resonates with two fears: the more obvious "fears" addressed by the title are those associated with the public fear of invasion, which Coleridge, Isaiah-like, will interpret as a sign of lost salvation that requires a recommitment to the ideals of the nation's Christian faith; the less obvious "fears" stem from the poet's own personal struggle to reconfigure his political identity in the wake of a personal crisis. Paul Magnuson and Felicity James have emphasized the need to situate the poem biographically within Coleridge's vexed private life at the moment of the poem's inception.[84] Likewise, C.R. Watters has hinted that the poem's termination in Nether Stowey reflects Coleridge's "underlying mental unrest," but then assigns this unrest to "mental fears conjured up on Solitude among the hills."[85] I propose that these "mental fears" are not mere rhetorical conjurations. They make sense if the poem is read within the context of Coleridge's acute fears of and anxieties about political isolation and social ostracization in the reactionary period precipitated by the invasion scare. Rather, I agree with Paul Magnuson's claim that the poem is a form of "self-defense" and suggest that the ex-radical Coleridge is defending his patriotism by performing his political apostasy in verse.[86] The poem's occasion provides the perfect opportunity for Coleridge to rejoin the national mainstream by taking advantage of a moment of national crisis to recant his radical politics and reaffirm his commitment to God and nation. In the process, Coleridge underscores the traction of religious belief in the ideology of British nationalism.

Performing Patriotism and Penitence in "Fears in Solitude"

"Fears in Solitude" is set against the tempest of alarums and reaction stirred by the discovery of a French plot to invade the island with the alleged assistance of members of the London Corresponding Society and the United Irishmen. The reader is brought into "a green and silent spot" amid the Quantock Hills outside Nether Stowey to contemplate the nation's imminent crisis.[87] But another crisis looms—an identity crisis for Coleridge. The poem's inaugural retreat into solitary nature is an allegory for Coleridge's sense of political alienation. This sub-text is apparent in the poem's opening stanza, where he writes,

> Oh! 'tis a quiet spirit-healing nook!
> Which all, methinks, would love; but chiefly he,
> The humble man, who, in his youthful years,
> Knew just so much of folly, as had made
> His early manhood more securely wise![88]

The "humble man" here is Coleridge, who is recanting the grievous political "folly" of his "youthful years." The allusion specifically recalls Coleridge's republicanism from 1793 to 1795 at Cambridge, London, and Bristol, and how his disillusionment with these politics in the intervening years of mounting French atrocities has caused him to be humbled. Hence, the retreat into nature is also an allegory for Coleridge's retreat from republican politics.

The choice of natural settings and lyrical conventions to open a poem ostensibly about national politics seems contradictory. But it is less so if one views the dell not as an escape from the nation, but as a peculiar kind of liminal space where the natural and the national converge. In this space, love of nation is mediated by love of nature, specifically the natural spaces that exist within the national territory.[89] Likewise, the narrator's Romantic sojourn into nature catalyzes greater empathy with the nation. He reflects,

> My God! It is a melancholy thing
> For such a man, who would full fain preserve
> His soul in calmness, yet perforce must feel
> For all his human brethren—O my God!
> It weighs upon the heart, that he must think
> What uproar and what strife may now be stirring
> This way or that way o'er these silent hills—
> Invasion, and the thunder and the shout,
> And all the crash of onset; fear and rage,
> And undetermined conflict—even now,
> Even now, perchance, and in his native isle:
> Carnage and groans beneath this blessed sun![90]

Among the silent hills, the narrator can achieve a state of negative capability that allows him to feel the terror that his countrymen will soon face.

Despite these dreadful ruminations, the narrator resists the jingoistic impulse to exult in an unbounded diatribe against the nation's enemies; rather, he paints the imminent invasion in Old Testament style as the workings of God's wrath for a sinful nation guilty of irreverence, profligacy, and immorality. Acutely aware of the deity's presence in the ministry of nature, the narrator will speak to and for the nation to confess its sordid crimes:

> We have offended, Oh! my countrymen!
> We have offended very grievously,
> And been most tyrannous. From east to west
> A groan of accusation pierces Heaven!
> The wretched plead against us; multitudes
> Countless and vehement, the sons of God,
> Our brethren! Like a cloud that travels on,
> Steamed up from Cairo's swamps of pestilence,
> Even so, my countrymen! have we gone forth
> And borne to distant tribes slavery and pangs,
> And, deadlier far, our vices, whose deep taint
> With slow perdition murders the whole man,
> His body and his soul![91]

By donning the mantle of patriotism and religion, the narrator is immunized against accusations of treason and atheistic radicalism while appropriating the fearful authority of evangelical pronouncements. Adopting the inclusive "we," the narrator presumes to speak for the nation as a *bona fide* patriot and clergyman who is also complicit in the sins of the nation. The tone here is not so much polemical, which would arouse immediate retaliation, but confessional. This is, indeed, a public speech act, one in which the ministering narrator must confess the nation's litany of sins in order to redeem it before God. What are these sins? Here, Coleridge continues to propound the critique of slavery and colonial despotism he previously expounded in the Bristol Lectures. This is cited as a shameful testament to the nation's sins against the divine will, a transgression for which retribution promises to be awful. The upshot is that the nation has jeopardized its favored status with the divinity by exploiting it for the purposes of empire—to secure inordinate power and riches at the expense of morality and universal benevolence.

The stylistics of this sermonizing oration confirm Chris Jones's discovery of a possible link between Coleridge and the famous slave-trader turned Evangelist, John Newton, whose fiery sermon, "Motives to Humiliation and Praise," was published by Joseph Johnson in February 1798, only months before Johnson would publish "Fears in Solitude."[92] In the sermon, Newton compares Britons to the Israelites, declaiming their favored status before High Providence. He then goes on to catalog a list of national sins for which punishment is assured unless the elect of God choose to repent, at which point the nation will most certainly be spared. Jones contends, "Newton's treatment of contemporary evils chimed in with Coleridge's own wish to dissociate himself from political radicalism while maintaining the authority of a religious position."[93] The contours of Newton's sermon clearly match those of the poem. The poem mingles vituperative reproach with deep concern and patriotic affection, using the specter of a wrathful God to whip the nation back into shape. Michael John Kooy adds that this mixture of criticism and patriotism also suggests a line of influence to Bishop Butler's *Sermons* (1726), which Hazlitt tells us Coleridge was reading at the time that "Fears in Solitude" was written. Kooy discovers in the poem's critical patriotism the type of "disinterested patriotism" originally propounded in the *Sermons* to reconcile the pursuit of national self-interest with that of universal benevolence.[94]

From the standpoint of a disinterested patriot, the narrator can now safely enumerate the corrosive effects that a rapacious imperial policy has had for the polis:

> Meanwhile, at home,
> All individual dignity and power
> Engulfed in courts, committees, institutions,
> Associations and societies,
> A vain, speech-mouthing, speech-reporting guild,
> One benefit-club for mutual flattery,
> We have drunk up, demure as at a grace,
> Pollutions from the brimming cup of wealth;
> Contemptuous of all honourable rule,
> Yet bartering freedom and the poor man's life
> For gold, as at a market![95]

The image here is of a populace enervated, degraded, and corrupted by the soiled profits of slavery and conquest. One finds here a trenchant manifestation of the trope of luxury as the narrator meticulously diagnoses the foul corruption that spreads rancor through every major institution—from government, to civil society (reactionary and radical alike), to the press and commerce. All are implicated in the wages of sin, and all citizens are equally culpable.

If this were not enough, the nation is also accused of the ultimate transgression—blasphemy. The nation is primarily defined in religious terms as a Christian nation. But the pious institution of religion has been degraded by hypocrisy and neglect:

> The sweet words
> Of Christian promise, words that even yet
> Might stem destruction, were they wisely preached,
> Are muttered o'er by men, whose tones proclaim
> How flat and wearisome they feel their trade: ...
> Oh! blasphemous! the book of life is made
> A superstitious instrument, on which
> We gabble o'er the oaths we mean to break.[96]

4. Coleridge, Religious Nationalism and the Anxiety of Empire 143

The ministers of faith are guilty of dereliction and no longer tend to their flock. Meanwhile, the state has appropriated the garb of religion to authorize its crimes. Hypocritical oaths mask perjury while pious calls to Christian works cloak the bloody exploits of government and commerce alike. This passage alludes to ideas Coleridge first expressed in *Consciones ad Populum*, where he excoriates the "intolerable iniquity" of the nation's imperial exploits and refers to England as a nation of "practical Atheists."[97] The import of both passages is that Britain has broken its covenant with God, making its imminent collapse a self-inflicted tragedy.

Rounding off this philippic is a condemnation of overt atheism, which is allegorically and quite sarcastically depicted as the "owlet Atheism" that has boldly ventured "Forth from his dark and lonely hiding-place" to spread its false wisdom.[98] Notably, the narrator here distinguishes his critique from those boldly propounded by Godwinian rationalists, atheistic radicals, and Jacobins, self-consciously aware of how he might otherwise be lumped together with these elements as enemies of the state. No, the narrator will be a firebrand for religion, trumping those hypocrites who wield it as a convenient truncheon to bash critics of the state. Clearly, the framework of sin and retribution devised by the narrator's rhetoric leaves only one desirable solution: redemption through the nation's return to religious morals.

The narrator also attributes the current crisis to Britain's bellicose foreign policy towards France. He echoes Sheridan's claim that French imperialism was goaded by British militarism:

> Thankless too for peace
> (Peace long preserved by fleets and perilous seas),
> Secure from actual warfare, we have loved
> To swell the war-whoop, passionate for war![99]

In this acerbic passage, the narrator contravenes the conventional wisdom most poignantly articulated by Thomson that Britain's offensive naval capabilities will stave off war and guarantee prosperity. Instead, the narrator insinuates that this attitude breeds arrogance, a lack of empathy for the suffering, and a trivial complacency towards war.[100] Although the false feeling of security fostered by naval supremacy must not inexorably lead to immoral and capricious warmongering, this result is more likely than not. So Britain's intrinsically belligerent policies are cited as the ultimate source of the nation's undoing. The narrator continues:

> We, this whole people, have been clamorous
> For war and bloodshed; animating sports,
> The which we pay for as a thing to talk of,
> Spectators and not combatants! ...
> We send our mandates for the certain death

> Of thousands and ten thousands! Boys and girls,
> And women, that would groan to see a child
> Pull off an insect's leg, all read of war,
> The best amusement for our morning-meal![101]

The narrator switches to the first person plural to indicate that all citizens are implicated in the nation's crimes and in the current debacle, regardless of class or political differences. Unity is consolidated through guilt and through a shared culture of militarism that has vulgarized and brutalized the populace, turning frightening scenes of war and death into an amusing spectacle for consumption by polite society. The narrator here alludes to Britain's financing of reactionary wars on the continent, where the narrator avers that others fight and die as pusillanimous and imperious Britons stand safely aloof from the fray that their capital and intrigues have largely enabled.

Rising to a crescendo, the booming voice of the narrator shifts from condemnation to prophecy:

> Therefore, evil days
> Are coming on us, O my countrymen!
> And what if all-avenging Providence,
> Strong and retributive, should make us know
> The meaning of our words, force us to feel
> The desolation and the agony
> Of our fierce doings![102]

On the surface, the passage rings with Old Testament wrathfulness, but also with tender patriotism. For all of the sins thus listed—profligacy, greed, blasphemy, war-mongering—the nation has broken its covenant with God to spread Protestant civilization across the globe and must surely face retribution. Providence has abandoned a disobedient nation and now seeks to mete out its vengeful justice. The feared French invasion is but the agent of its will. But this outcome, although probable, is not certain, as indicated by the use of the conditional phrase "what if." The narrator has already proclaimed that earnest repentance and reformation can save the nation and restore the grace of Providence. If one teases out the Old Testament connotations of the poem, one becomes aware that the narrator is more like the stern but forgiving Isaiah than the fatalistic Jeremiah, for while the latter heaped jeremiads upon a hopeless people, the former left open the possibility of salvation. As an Isaiah figure, the narrator's excoriation of the nation must then be received as an act of love for his countrymen. He must be cruel to be kind; he must expose the corrupt soul of the nation in order to treat it with the salve of piety and penitence. If it follows his lead, it can restore the Providence that the entire structure and ideological bent of the poem registers as an essential component of what it means to be British; and, once redeemed, the British will undoubtedly repel this Philistine host from their shores.

At this point, the narrator shifts his attention back to God in order to plead for mercy on behalf of the nation:

> Spare us yet awhile,
> Father and God! O! spare us yet awhile!
> Oh! Let not English women drag their flight
> Fainting beneath the burthen of their babes,
> Of the sweet infants, that but yesterday
> Laughed at the breast![103]

This supplication is important because it deploys three central motifs of the poem—Providence, nationalism, and domesticity—that will be conflated by the poem's end. These imperiled English women and their prattling babes become a synecdoche for the nation. When Providence abandons the nation, it is this sensitive domestic core that will suffer the most.

The imagery of fainting women fleeing from their homes testifies to the bankrupt patriotism of the British men whose actions have brought upon this fate. It is to that audience that the narrator turns his attention to issue harsh rebuke and enjoin patriotic duty, connoting that the national audience consists exclusively of males in the public sphere:

> Sons, brothers, husbands, all
> Who ever gazed with fondness on the forms
> Which grew up with you round the same fire-side,
> And all who ever heard the Sabbath-bells
> Without the infidel's scorn, make yourselves pure!
> Stand forth! Be men! Repel an impious foe,
> Impious and false, a light yet cruel race,
> Who laugh away all virtue, mingling mirth
> With deeds of murder; and still promising
> Freedom, themselves too sensual to be free,
> Poison life's amities, and cheat the heart
> Of faith and quiet hope, and all that soothes
> And all that lifts the spirit![104]

This is a rallying cry for the nation to rise up and meet the challenge of the impending French onslaught. The invasion is here represented as a test by which absolution can be attained. Coleridge uses a combination of eighteenth-century and anti–Jacobin prejudices to figure the French: they are a vice-ridden "cruel race" prone to mirth and murder, while hypocritically preaching freedom. They are also an "impious foe" of Catholic idolaters now become godless atheists who "cheat the heart of faith and quiet hope." In contrast, a Briton knows only pious domestic hearths and the chime of "Sabbath-bells," insinuating that the British are the true elect. But, lest his audience forget that it is their own misdeeds that have precipitated this awful test, the narrator adds,

> And oh! may we return
> Not with a drunken triumph, but with fear.
> Repenting of the wrongs with which we stung
> So fierce a foe to frenzy![105]

This is a sobering war meant to remind the British of their impiety and wrongdoing. The reward for success will be pious humility, not prideful triumphalism. The latter would merely feed back into the circuit of imperial hubris that caused the current crisis—Britain's financing of the continental wars in pursuit of a rapacious imperialist agenda.

The fiery sermonizing that characterizes the first half of the poem is mysteriously superseded by a self-reflexive mode in which Coleridge's patriotic narrative persona proceeds to legitimate his criticism of the nation against the illegitimate criticisms made by non-patriots. But what ensues is in fact a complex psychomachia in which Coleridge is both patriot and non-patriot, legitimate critic and subversive traitor. The passage operates by conflating the dichotomy of public and private, sermon and lyric, as Coleridge entwines the nation's imperial sins with the guilt he feels from his republican past. Through this shared sense of guilt, I argue that Coleridge will attempt to negotiate a rapprochement with the nation. Following the logic of guilt, if the nation expects to be forgiven by God, then it must also be willing to forgive its penitential former subversives.

The passage begins with an anguished narrator who positions himself against those who criticize from a position of hate rather than love:

> I have told
> O Britons! O my brethren! I have told
> Most bitter truth, but without bitterness.
> Nor deem my zeal or factious or mis-timed;
> For never can true courage dwell with them,
> Who, playing tricks with conscience, dare not look
> At their own vices.[106]

Coleridge emphatically declares that he is not exploiting a moment of crisis to castigate the nation from the conventionally anti-establishmentarian position of righteous indignation, as many dissenters and republicans before him have done. Implicit in that genre, one is told, is bitterness and factious division. Rather, he approaches the nation as a humble supplicant aware of his own complicity in the crimes of the nation, and of his crimes against the nation. Indeed, it is through this act of solidarity in guilt that Coleridge symbolically reattaches himself to a nation that is struggling for unity. Coleridge deploys this associative guilt to reinvent himself as a sincere patriot and devout Christian.

This paradigm of pious patriotism offers a contending version of patriotism—one that is neither clouded by jingoistic delusions nor venomously critical. It is rooted in Christian categories of sin, expiation, and forgiveness that enable an earnest and sincere admission of national wrongdoing and a correction of errors. But Coleridge is also practicing a sort of doublespeak, whereby he implicitly confesses his own errors and proclaims his wish to return to the national fold:

> We have been too long
> Dupes of a deep delusion! Some, belike
> Groaning with restless enmity, expect
> All change from change of constituted power;
> As if a Government had been a robe,
> On which our vice and wretchedness were tagged
> Like fancy-points and fringes, with the robe
> Pulled off at a pleasure. Fondly these attach
> A radical causation to a few
> Poor drudges of chastising Providence,
> Who borrow all their hues and qualities
> From our own folly and rank wickedness,
> Which gave them birth and nursed them. Others, meanwhile,
> Dote with a mad idolatry; and all
> Who will not fall before their images,
> And yield them worship, they are enemies
> Even of their country!
> Such have I been deemed.[107]

The inclusive "we" that begins the passage seeks to heal the wounds of a nation divided, but also, and more significantly, literally reconnect Coleridge with a nation that considers him suspect for his interactions with such subversives as Frend, Godwin, and Thelwall. The use of the first person plural also conflates two sets of delusions: Coleridge's delusions of republican politics and the nation's imperial delusions. The narrator first treats the former, assailing the British radical circles, of which he was once a constituent, for seeking to achieve a reformation of society through radical changes in government and constitution *vis-à-vis* the French model. He impugns their radical critique of the state, offering an alternative etiology that locates the cause of social problems in "our own folly and rank wickedness," which also corrupts the "few Poor drudges" who promulgate this radical critique. Essentially, Coleridge is here replacing a materialist critique of society and radical politics with a moralistic critique based on original sin and a personal search for individual reformation. The latter half of the passage concerns those "Others"—a use of pronouns that signifies Coleridge's difference from them both past and present—who "dote with a mad idolatry" upon their own images. Coleridge cleverly deploys the rhetoric of anti–Catholicism to paint the sanctimonious guardians of the state as tyrannical idolaters who enforce their version of nationalism, which consists of blind loyalty and obedience to them. They label all those who rightly criticize the corrupt and imperialist policies of the state as enemies of the nation, semantically disenfranchising them of the right to speak. The contention here is that these purveyors of greed and empire should not be permitted to define what it means to be a patriot. Hence, by attacking their legitimacy, Coleridge undercuts their labeling of him as an enemy of the country.

On the contrary, in the next stanza Coleridge declares his unflinching filial love for his motherland. The proof of this patriotic devotion is putatively drawn from his upbringing among the nostalgic "heartland" of a quaint English countryside.

> But, O dear Britain! O my Mother Isle!
> Needs must thou prove a name most dear and holy
> To me, a son, a brother, and a friend,
> A husband, and a father! who revere
> All bonds of natural love, and find them all
> Within the limits of thy rocky shores.
> O native Britain! O my Mother Isle!
> How shouldst thou prove aught else but dear and holy
> To me, who from thy lakes and mountain-hills,
> Thy clouds, thy quiet dales, thy rocks and seas,
> Have drunk in all my intellectual life,
> All sweet sensations, all ennobling thoughts,
> All adoration of the God in nature,
> All lovely and all honourable things,
> Whatever makes this mortal spirit feel
> The joy and greatness of its future being?
> There lives nor form nor feeling in my soul
> Unborrowed from my country. O divine
> And beauteous island! though hast been my sole
> And most magnificent temple, in the which
> I walk with awe, and sing my stately songs,
> Loving the God that made me![108]

Several observations can be made from this passage. First, the passage is a colorful fabrication of a childhood that Coleridge borrowed whole-cloth from the experiences and nostalgic sentiments of his friend, Wordsworth. From their correspondence and poetry, one understands that Coleridge regretted the lack of time he spent as a child in this kind of idyllic natural setting. Furthermore, this edenic image of an English countryside inhabited by "God in nature" is a staple of Wordsworth's representations of Britain. This is the mythical pastoral "heartland" that his imagery conjures and resonates nationalistic feelings of domestic affection throughout his poetry.

Secondly, Coleridge is actively promoting an ethnic nationalism premised on the homogeneity of culture, language, territory, and history. By emphasizing his organic attachment to the land with phrases like "O native Britain" and "O my Mother Isle," Coleridge is venting notions of blood and soil nationalism all too common to virulently nationalist movements. He tells us, "There lives nor form nor feeling in my soul / Unborrowed from my country," defining himself in essential terms as a British nationalist. By emphasizing Britain's littoral geography with references to its "rocks and seas" and to this "beauteous island," Coleridge also insinuates the exclusivity of this territorial nationalism. In Wordsworthian fashion, Coleridge selectively represents this territory as a rustic land of "quiet dales," "lakes and mountain-hills," completely effacing the disturbingly heterogeneous and cosmopolitan urban sites of production and politics that made Britain a global power. The corollary is that a Briton is first and foremost one who can trace one's origin and sensibility back to this edenic homeland.

Finally, the passage codifies the triptych of nationalism, Providence, and domesticity that has been an immanent motif throughout the poem. If the quaint English countryside is a synecdoche for the nation, the fact that it is recalled as the putative location of the poet's formative childhood and adolescent years suggests that implicit in this nationalism is a deep reverence for sites of domesticity. Coleridge's nationalism is activated by manufactured remembrances of domestic affection, and it is formulated around the preservation of this delicate domestic core. The emphasis on domesticity explains why the nation is effectively gendered as a feminine construction—a "Mother Isle" to which the exclusively male patriot must be a son, brother, friend, husband, or even father. The chief duty of the patriot is to protect his motherland from incursions by patriots of other lands. Furthermore, in addition to being essentially domestic and feminine, the motherland is also sacred. The motherland is simultaneously a "divine / And beauteous island!" He consecrates the island, refiguring it a "most magnificent temple" in which he dwells, sings his monadic songs, and reverences God like the gentle swains of classical pastorals. This imagery is an expression of British exceptionalism, which is rooted in a firm belief in Britain's providential status. It is also a furtive sign that the narrator has never wavered in his faith that the nation will ultimately redeem itself, be forgiven, and be saved.

These utterances of a heartfelt and pious nationalism work therapeutically upon the narrator's deepest fears. Reading the title literally, these fears in solitude center on the threat of invasion. However, if one interprets this fear allegorically, then the solitude signifies not the green and pleasant hills that spatially encompass the narrator, but the psychological fear of being cast out of the national family and into the wastes of political isolation, which Coleridge acutely feels and dearly wishes to avert. Indeed, this is the deeper fear to which the poem gives vent and which its design aims to allay. For this reason, the tone of the poem switches from fear to measured hopefulness as the poem's end draws near:

> May my fears,
> My filial fears, be vain! And may the vaunts
> And menace of the vengeful enemy
> Pass like the gust, that roared and died away
> In the distant tree; which heard, and only heard
> In this low dell, bowed not the delicate grass.[109]

"Filial fears" is a polyvalent express that offers a plurality of meaning here, denoting both the fear of a patriot son for his endangered motherland and the fear of exile from the national fold. But the narrator is hopeful that both of these fears are in vain, exaggerated and amplified by the physical and psychological geography of solitude.

The narrator's return to "beloved Stowey" in the final stanza is the final chapter in Coleridge's agonistic journey from radical social pariah to orthodox patriot. The transformation is symbolically signified by the setting sun, whose "light has left the summit of the hill."[110] Coleridge's peregrination from the solitude of the hills to the familiar domestic scenes of Nether Stowey is in fact an allegory for his public renunciation of republicanism—the "folly" of his "youthful years" alluded to in the first stanza—and his return to the mainstream of national politics and religion. Both of these find their symbolic seat and expression in the domestic sphere, so it is now homeward that our sanguine narrator winds his way:

> Homeward I wind my way; and lo! Recalled
> From bodings that have well nigh wearied me,
> I find myself upon the brow, and pause
> Startled! And after lonely sojourning
> In such a quiet and surrounded nook,
> This burst of prospect, here the shadowy main,
> Dim tinted, there the mighty majesty
> Of that huge amphitheatre of rich
> And elmy fields, seems like society—
> Conversing with the mind, and giving it
> A livelier impulse and a dance of thought![111]

This is perhaps the most polysemous passage of the entire poem. The "bodings" that have "well nigh wearied" the narrator are ostensibly the fears of inva-

4. Coleridge, Religious Nationalism and the Anxiety of Empire 151

sion. To quell these fears, the narrator has retreated to the "quiet and surrounded nook" in imitation of the Romantic lyric. But this putative act of "lonely sojourning" is really a symbolic act of reconciliation with the nation. The valleys and numerous elms are metaphorically transformed into an amphitheater in which all of society has gathered to converse with the narrator. The author is here slyly alluding to the rhetorical significance of the poem as a public speech act. Coleridge explodes his familiar conversational style and the practice of Romantic interiority, appropriating their generic conventions for a generically un–Romantic political address to the nation.

Ironically, however, it is these very same conventions that the underlying meaning of the poem preserves. If one accepts that the fears in solitude expressed by the poem are personal as well as national—emanating from Coleridge's fear of being a perpetual outcast from the nation—then one understands that the poem is also generically lyrical in a Romantic sense. The secluded Romantic landscape of rolling hills and verdant trees is once again used to catalyze interiority. In this setting, Coleridge can explore his fears and anxieties of abandonment, which are homologous to the fear of the nation's abandonment by God. Both fears of abandonment can only be allayed through faith—in God's mercy and in the nation's forgiveness. Evidence of this faith can be found in the poet's courage to confess his own and the nation's sin, respectively defined in terms of radicalism and imperial hubris.

Having confessed his sins, and with faith that his fears of abandonment have been in vain, Coleridge can now return to the national fold with peace of mind. This return is allegorized as a return to the peaceful domestic sphere nested at the figural center of the nationalist imaginary. The poem has shifted its audience several times from God, to his fellow patriots, and now to the beloved denizens of Nether Stowey, among whom Coleridge has come home to rest:

> And now, beloved Stowey! I behold
> Thy church-tower, and, methinks, the four huge elms
> Clustering, which mark the mansion of my friend;
> And close behind them, hidden from my view,
> Is my own lowly cottage, where my babe
> And my babe's mother dwell in peace! With light
> And quickened footsteps thitherward I tend,
> Remembering thee, O green and silent dell!
> And grateful, that by nature's quietness
> And solitary musings, all my heart
> Is softened, and made worthy to indulge
> Love, and the thoughts that yearn for human kind.[112]

The narrator's psychological mapping of Stowey is significant in its emphasis on the coordinates of the church tower, his friend's mansion, and his home.

This is an impressionistic topography of Stowey that spatializes the concentric rings of affection necessary for personal and social regeneration. The recollection of the church tower denotes a reverence for religion and an acknowledgment of its symbolic function as the center of the community. The recollection of the friend's mansion denotes the prosperity of the nation and the brotherly affection shared by its patriotic sons. The recollection of his "lowly cottage" denotes the putative domestic bliss of mother and babe. Collectively, the rhetorical effect of this imagistic *bricolage* is to allay Coleridge's fears of exile and fulfill his wish of reconciliation by proving to the nation that he finally and organically belongs to *this* world as a Christian, compatriot, and husband—*not* to the world of London radicalism.

***

The conflation of religious and nationalist discourse that characterized seventeenth- and eighteenth-century debates over the legitimacy and practice of empire sheds light on the degree to which Britons imagined themselves to be a Christian nation. While, on the one hand, proponents cited religion as evidence of Britain's divine calling to pursue empire, on the other hand, critics used it as the basis for worried reflection and, at times, stinging invective. Coleridge's "Fears in Solitude" is part of this discourse. As the terminus of his circular political momentum during the 1790s, the poem is also a veiled attempt to seek communion with a nation that perceives him as "an enemy to his country." The blend of righteous sermonizing and patriotic effusion in the poem is calculated to remediate both situations—the perils of empire and the perils of ostracism. Both hinge on a recommitment to faith-based nationalism. In "Fears and Solitude," the Romantic contrivance of a sojourn to the "green and silent dell" sets up a meditation on empire and its excesses. But it also—and perhaps for Coleridge more importantly—catalyzes a moment of soul-searching that concludes with his literal and allegorical return to God, Family, and Nation. For Coleridge, this holy trinity is infused with "Love, and thoughts that yearn for human kind."[113] What are these thoughts but intimations of the sympathy and benevolent affection to which Coleridge programmatically attributes all social bonds. Having shed his radical pretensions, a humbled Coleridge now turns from distant schemes of Pantisocracy to the familiar scenery of Nether Stowey, where religion, patriotism, and domestic bliss all converge to nourish a native utopia.

CHAPTER 5

Patriot Women and the Future of Empire

> No patriot then the sons of freedom led
> In mountain pass devotedly to die;
> The martyr spirit of resolve was fled,
> And the high soul's unconquered buoyancy,
> And by your graves, and on your battle plains,
> Warriors! your children knelt to wear the stranger's chains.
> —Felicia Hemans[1]

> She gives life, and she leads to death; her purity is the great support of morality, and the very ground-work of society; and her profligacy enervates the courage of men, and depraves the morals of the community.
> —M. Jouy[2]

In 1828, writing about the moral influence of women on society for *The Athenaeum*, a weekly London periodical that catered to popular tastes, the prestigious French scholar and member of the French Academy, M. Jouy, conjectured, "The word female (*femina*) seems to derive its etymology from the word family (*familia*), since woman is the common centre of all families, the source of the generations of men, and the universal link of human beings."[3] Etymological accuracy notwithstanding, having asserted woman's central role in coordinating the activities of the family, the good scholar further determined that she is also the pillar of society: "Her purity is the great support of morality, and the very ground-work of society; and her profligacy enervates the courage of men, and depraves the morals of the community."[4] Were M. Jouy to have confined his commentary on women to their importance in the domestic matters of the family, one might neatly assign his beliefs to the doctrine of separate spheres that emerged in the preceding century and be done with it. However, M. Jouy's suggestion that women have a social responsibility as "the great support of morality, and the very ground-work of society" because their conduct

153

determines the "courage of men" and the "morals of the community" ascribes to women a much broader and more public role than that typically associated with the separate spheres paradigm. M. Jouy's conservative remarks about femininity suggest that Romantic-era women were expected to play a vital role in civic life precisely because their association with family and moral conduct made them uniquely situated to be a kind of moral compass for the nation.

Thanks to recent scholarship, it's now known that large numbers of Romantic-era women spoke and wrote about a variety of topics in a modern public sphere formerly believed to be off-limits to women. With the explosion of print culture enabled by social and technological developments in the eighteenth century, Paula Backscheider and Paula R. Feldman observe that women were initially sought after as contributors, and only later in the century did they begin to face resistance from male publishers, writers, and readers as markets settled and gender lines began to solidify.[5] Nonetheless, as Anne K. Mellor, and, more recently, Stephen C. Behrendt have pointed out, the Romantic period, contrary to the "big-six" paradigm that has dominated the teaching of Romanticism thus far, was astir with talented women writers who published hundreds of texts about a range of topics in a variety of genres, often with more success than their male counterparts, and frequently as conscious members of a rich community of women writers who made intertextual references to each other's work.[6] Furthermore, as Michelle Levy argues, these writers pioneered forms of collective family authorship that contrasted starkly with masculinist Romantic prescriptions about the significance of individual creativity, and, likewise, William Stafford has observed that women writers from this period do not fit into the neat generic and political categories developed around male writers.[7] Take Hannah More, for instance, who wrote conservative Christian conduct manuals for the poor and indigent, but also wrote abolitionist poems. Contrary to the separate spheres paradigm, then, women writers formed a prominent and unique part of the literary landscape in the Romantic period.

Going back to M. Jouy's remarks, one of the ways that women were able to skirt the hegemony of separate spheres and engage in national debates was by leveraging the moral authority that patriarchy often explicitly assigned to women. Mary Wollstonecraft, for instance, argues in *A Vindication of the Rights of Women* (1792) that women should receive an education and civil rights equal to men in order to perform their responsibilities as good wives and mothers, implying that without equality, women would fail to cultivate good moral character in their husbands and children, with terrible consequences for the nation as a whole.[8] Linda Colley observes that many women, some radical like Wollstonecraft, many more conservative and evangelical, engaged in civic activities in the 1790s on a similar basis of supporting their families and nation.⁹ These activities ranged from electioneering and support for the war effort to abolitionism and intemperance campaigns, leading Colley to conclude, "At one and the same time, separate sexual spheres were being increasingly prescribed in theory, yet increasingly broken through in practice."¹⁰ Women's participation in national debates and campaigns, rather than draw negative attention, often strengthened those movements. Kate Davies, for instance, has written that women's public advocacy of abolition benefitted the movement because their participation in it was interpreted as a sign of "feminine sympathy" toward the suffering of slaves, which tinctured abolitionism with a moral prerogative that transcended left and right political divisions.¹¹

James Heath, Vignette of Britannia set as the frontispiece to the *Naval Chronicle*, volumes I to VI (1799–1800). © The Trustees of the British Museum.

On the other hand, the conflation of women with domesticity also made them an apt symbol of empire because defense of the homeland served as political camouflage for expansionist wars. The iconic image of "Britannia" featured as a synecdoche for the nation in Thomson's imperial ode, "Rule, Britannia," and portrayed in many prints throughout the eighteenth and nineteenth centuries symbolizes the commonplace elision between women's domestic and imperial roles in this period. Britannia is often depicted as a comely matron dressed in classical robes, helmeted, bearing a shield, wielding a trident, and set against a nautical backdrop featuring ominous clouds of war or fleets of ships. In some illustrations she is also flanked by a lion, which symbolizes the crown. These classical, martial presentations of Britannia invoke a shared tradition of empire between Greco-Roman civilization and Britain, the former

Roman colony now become an empire in its own right. In this case, the specificity of trident and nautical setting emphasize Britain's commitment to naval supremacy and an expanding colonial empire. The comely matron, Britannia, thus functions as a powerful icon of empire in which women's domestic and maternal roles are transformed into an imperial calling to arouse and nurture the martial prowess and imperial ambition of the nation.

Women's conventional association with domesticity ironically enabled greater entrance into public debates about national policy and even matters of war and empire. On this note, Backscheider has written that since women's poetry came to be associated with morality and moral issues as a result of their identification with domesticity and "feminine virtue," female poets "perceived their writing, and were perceived themselves, as having a right to intervene in national life and its debates."[12] Likewise, Mellor writes,

> Insofar as they represented the interests of women, children, and the family, they also saw themselves as peculiarly *responsible* for defining the future direction of public policy and social reform. Their numerous and widely disseminated writings—poems, plays, novels, critical essays, political tracts—asserted both the right and the duty of women to speak *for* the nation.[13]

According to Mellor, women's assertion of their literary and political authority to speak and write about public and foreign policy dates back to the tradition of seventeenth-century female preachers, Dissenting and Quaker female prophets who were acknowledged to be the voice of Christian Virtue because of biblical precedents (e.g., Deborah, Queen Esther, Judith).[14] "Romantic women writers," she explains, "translated this religious authority into a more secular literary authority, claiming that they spoke on behalf of morality and 'right feeling' (or *true* sensibility)."[15]

And yet, women writers' participation in public debates was not without its dangers, and therefore required sophisticated forms of negotiation. Richard Polwhele's wide-ranging attack on politicized women writers in *The Unsex'd Females* (1798) lends credence to the new view of women's broad participation in the literary marketplace, but it also demonstrates the scorn faced by successful women writers, especially those who dared to write about political subjects. Polwhele attacks a variety of women writers, referring to them collectively as "A female band despising NATURE's law."[16] The title of his diatribe foregrounds his belief that these women are metaphorically "unsex'd" by what he perceives as their unnatural literary and political activities. The poem underscores Susan J. Wolfson's idea that the literary marketplace was a "hot zone" for women who espoused liberal or radical causes.[17] Marlon B. Ross has written that, for Romantic women writers, the combination of the act of writing plus the selection of political subjects to write about, especially from a liberal or radical point of view, constituted a dangerous "double dissension" that required formal and stylistic negotiation: either women could disguise their political speech in acceptably feminine modes and genres, or they could choose to feminize masculine modes of writing.[18] In a growing print culture where the status of the "literary lady" as an icon of "feminine virtue" contributed to her marketability, as Paula McDowell has observed, the viability of a woman writer's career often depended upon which strategy she selected to manage the public fallout of this transgression.[19]

This chapter will explore two ways that women writers in the Romantic period leveraged the moral authority invested in them as a result of conventional notions about femininity in order to engage in national debates about traditionally masculine topics, particularly war and empire. In the last chapter, I discussed how anxiety over the fate of empires complicated the discourse of patriotism in British literature. A century of intermittent warfare that included internal rebellions and invasion scares generated concern for the nation's well-being that eviscerated the gender line between matters of state and family matters, inviting patriot women to stake out a civic role alongside their male compatriots for or against national policies whose effects potentially impacted domestic prosperity and security. Specifically, Romantic-era women writers could speak or write about war and empire from two main positions: they could be *moral supporters* who promoted greater diligence and zeal for the war effort, framing it as a defense of domestic liberty and prosperity; or they could be *moral critics* who criticized the war effort as a betrayal of domestic and civic values that could possibly lead to moral and material ruin. Both positions claimed the mantle of patriotism—the former a conservative state patriotism that endorsed the actions of the state, the latter *counter-patriotism*, a kind of patriotism that engaged in criticism of the state based on concern for the nation.

I offer examples of each type of female patriotism in the Romantic period using Felicia Hemans's *Modern Greece* (1817) and Anna Letitia Barbauld's *Eighteen Hundred and Eleven* (1812), respectively. I read the two texts out of chronological order to first establish a baseline for feminine state patriotism before following with an example of counter-patriotism. In *Modern Greece* (1817), Felicia Hemans positively frames and endorses the western tradition of empire while acknowledging the moral and physical dangers of empire, for which she stresses the redemptive role of patriot mothers and wives whose diligence can offset the decline of empire. In *Eighteen Hundred and Eleven* (1812), Anna Letitia Barbauld criticizes the moral and material impoverishment generated by empire, projecting inevitable ruin if the nation continues on an imperial footing; yet her endorsement of cultural imperialism as a handmaiden for civilization in the Americas complicates her rejection of British imperialism and reveals the limits of counter-patriotism.

Despite their ideological differences, both authors pursue their intervention in a gendered and charged political discourse by deploying formal and narrative elements that blend the prophetic tradition with the popular techniques of modern travel writing. As Mellor has noted, women writers had adopted the prophetic mode since the seventeenth century, which made it an accessible, if not acceptable, mode for women to write about public matters. Many women writers in the Romantic period, particularly those with radical views, such as Wollstonecraft and Mary Shelley, engaged in prophecy to issue scathing criticisms of social ills with the prophet's aura of divine authority.[20] Hemans and Barbauld marshal this critical tradition to write about the future of empire and its effects on the nation from opposite perspectives, using apocalyptic imagery of a nation in ruins to warn about the possible outcomes of empire if the nation acts with too little or, alternatively, too much zeal. Furthermore, to paint these prophecies they import features of popular travel narratives, such as exotic locales, sublime prospects, and a narrator who, prophet-like, guides the reader through space and time. The result is a richly descriptive narrative in which the reader is instructed about the future of empire while traversing sublime landscapes populated by vast ruins and empty wastes. This aesthetic resembles Sarah Suleri's concept of the "Indian sublime," which she coins in reference to orientalist depictions of India—particularly those found in the speeches of Edmund Burke, which emphasize India's status as the quintessential ruin of empire upon which now rests a vast, irrational, and disorganized state of society whose inscrutability achieves the mind-boggling effect of the natural sublime.[21] However, to distinguish the use of ruins as a warning for empire-builders from the use of ruins as a rhetorical prop for Western orientalism, I refer to the former as the *ruinological sublime*.

The ruinological sublime used by Hemans and Barbauld has a long and important history in eighteenth-century political discourse. Ruins and their representation in literature could signify the permanence of tradition that held together the nation. In this vein, Laurence Goldstein has written about the pervasiveness of the "ruin sentiment" in Augustan literature, and later Romantic poetry, as a means for producing the psychological effect of "renewed loyalty to some enduring symbol of potentiality."[22] Antiquarian writing is emblematic of this mode because antiquarians interpreted congeries of ruins, relics, and other artifacts (real or forged) within a narrative of continuity and growth that naturalized and codified a cohesive and enduring national identity. On the other hand, as Anne Janowitz has suggested, ruins could produce meanings that did not fit into a nationalist framework stressing continuity and tradition.[23] The semantic volatility of the ruin-as-national symbol is evident in the many critiques of empire that deploy the ruinological sublime to emphasize the rise *and decline* of imperial nations. I have already discussed how Berkeley's *An Essay Towards Preventing the Ruin of Great Britain* concludes with an apocalyptic vision of Britain's ruins. In *Liberty: A Poem* (1735–36), James Thomson, the iconic bard of empire, also deploys the ruin motif to meditate on the causes and supports of liberty while among the vast and terrifying ruins of Rome, a reminder of the impermanence of empire. Later in the century, Edward Gibbon, in his magisterial work *The Decline and Fall of the Roman Empire* (1776), relates, "It was among the ruins of the [Roman] Capitol that I first conceived the idea of a work which has amused and exercised near twenty years of my life."[24] Similarly, in his invocation to the *Ruins of Empires* (1790), C.F. Volney recounts how his rumination on the decline and fall of empires was inspired by his travels through the "solitary ruins, holy sepulchers and silent walls" of ancient Egypt, Syria, and parts of the Ottoman Empire.[25] Hemans's and Barbauld's use of the ruinological sublime hearkens to this second tradition, where ruins are a sign of the volatility of nations that embark on an imperial path.

The ruin motif also had currency among Romantic contemporaries of Hemans and Barbauld. Tinged by revolution and the defeat of Napoleon, the Romantic period had its own edifying testaments to the impermanence and frustration of grand human designs, and the ruin offered a fitting theme for conveying these truths. Thomas McFarland, Paul de Man, Balachandra Rajan, and Marjorie Levinson have written about how Romantics transmuted the ruin motif into experiments with form that yielded the Romantic fragment poem.[26] Additionally, Bruce Haley has examined the unique features of the Romantic monument poem, in which poets sought "to restore damaged, faded, or unfamiliar figures to the status of living forms."[27] Romantic poets also seized upon images of real or imagined ruins in order to refurbish them with new meaning that emphasized the vanity of human wishes and the sober reality of mortality and mutability. In "Ozymandias" (1818), for instance, Percy Bysshe Shelley contrasts a despot's vainglorious dream of everlasting empire to the "colossal Wreck" of the monumental statue built in his image by slaves, round which now "Nothing beside remains" but the "lone and level sands."[28] And in "On Seeing the Elgin Marbles" (1817), John Keats's exposure to the renowned artifacts symbolizing the enduring grandeur of ancient Greece instead prompts a reflection on mortality and the "rude / Wasting of old time."[29] These poems make use of the ruinological sublime as a way to reveal eternal truths about the folly of personal and national ambitions from a transcendental perspective that overcomes personal and historical limitations on vision. Likewise, as this chapter demonstrates, in *Modern Greece* and *Eighteen Hundred and Eleven*, Hemans and Barbauld adopt the prophetic mode and ruinological sublime in order to transcend the momentary patriarchal constraints on women's thought and writing, and thereby enable deeper reflection on the nature of patriotism and the future of empire.

Hemans, Conservative Patriotism and the Domestication of Empire

In *Modern Greece*, a poem written in the masculine genre of the travelogue, Felicia Hemans manages the public fallout of her double dissension by disguising her gender behind an academic rigor read as masculine and propounding a conservative patriotism that endorses the pursuit of empire. The civic world of state-sponsored conservative patriotism afforded women a legitimate arena in which to participate in public debates about national politics, and Hemans was able to leverage these opportunities in her writing, which helped to broaden the role of women in public life and make her a recognized and respected model of patriotic womanhood. In *Modern Greece*, she specifically accomplishes the broadening of civic participation for women by arguing that the fall of Hellenic Greece was a result of women's failure to inculcate sufficient patriotism in the youth and men of the nation. In so doing, Hemans blurs the line between public and private spheres by underscoring the need for women to participate more broadly in the patriotic defense of the nation inside and outside the home. By attributing Greece's fall to a lack of patriotism rather than to the contradictions of empire, Hemans also disputes the view put forward by Coleridge, Gibbon, Volney, and a tradition of seventeenth- and eighteenth-century dissenting and republican texts that warned against the tragic incompatibility of nation and empire. Instead, *Modern Greece* argues for the interdependence of Western nation-making and imperialism, contending that empire can be sustained by domesticating it through the active participation of patriot women as proponents of an imperial patriotism in the public and private life of the nation.

Hemans's prodigious authorial career, extending through nineteen volumes of poetry and two dramas from the publication of *England and Spain; or, Valour and Patriotism* (1808) to the second edition of *Songs of the Affections* (1835), exhibits perhaps the most successful attempt at self-definition as a patriotic "literary lady." Indeed, her status as England's most famous female patriotic poet garnered her a place in the British canon for over a century.[30] The fact that Victorian schoolchildren were taught to rehearse patriotic lines from her poetry, particularly "Casabianca" (1826), "Homes of England" (1828), and "England's Dead" (1822), is a testament to the reach and depth of her literary fame in the nineteenth century. So successful was she at trademarking an orthodox image of femininity that she outsold almost all of her male and female competitors in the literary marketplace, and this during a period of reaction and war.[31] Her contemporary reviewers and Victorian biographers relished the delicacy and refinement of her feminine traits. The *Edinburgh Monthly Review* raved that Mrs. Hemans "never ceases to be strictly *feminine* in the whole current of her thought and feeling."³² Francis Jeffries, writing for the *Edinburgh Review*, summed up her poetry as "a fine exemplification of Female Poetry."³³ This sentiment is corroborated by her biographer, Henry F. Chorley, in his *Memorials of Mrs. Hemans* (1836), who tells us that her letters "give so fair a picture of her mind in all its *womanliness*" and approvingly cites one critic who swears that her poems "could not have been written by a man."³⁴

However, modern critics have gone a long way to debunk this feminine façade, revealing the reality of a failed marriage and absent domesticity that characterized her life. Norma Clare, for instance, explains that "the poet of domesticity, of hearth and home, had skeletons rattling by the fireside," including a father and husband's desertion, and the abandonment of her five children's welfare to her mother, sister, and brother's good will while she pursued a literary career to cover her family's expenses.³⁵ No doubt, Hemans deplored the prescriptions of femininity that consigned her to a life of financial crisis, social alienation, and distance from her children after her husband's departure pushed her into a professional literary career for economic reasons. Wolfson suggests that she managed the emotional toll of this situation by projecting her feelings into an array of female characters in her poetry who reflect the suffering endured by women as a result of the loss and isolation inflicted by the masculine world of politics and war; to compensate for the limitations and hardships they face, Hemans imbues these female characters with an almost stoical degree of heroism in the face of insurmountable suffering. Hence, Wolfson argues that Hemans's patriotic façade masked her frustration with the deplorable fate of women in a patriarchal society where the tranquility of the domestic space was constantly imperiled by political intrigue and warfare.³⁶

Hemans, neé Felicia Dorothea Browne, was born in Liverpool in 1793 to a middle-class family of six children. Her father abandoned the family in 1808, forcing them to move and propelling her into a commercial career as a poet to cover household expenses. Her marriage to Captain Hemans in 1812 yielded five children—all boys—but ended suddenly in 1818 when her husband left for Italy and never returned, leaving her pregnant with their last son and unable to cover the financial costs of her family. Destitute and poor, Hemans moved back in with her mother, older brother, and sister, who effectively raised her children while she devoted herself to full-time writing—at least until her mother's death in 1827. Of this period, Chorley writes,

> [The] peculiar circumstances of [her] position, which, by placing her in a household, as a member and not as its head, excused her from many of those small cares of domestic life, which might have either fretted away her day-dreams, and, by interruption, have made of less avail the search for knowledge to which she

bent herself with such eagerness; or, more probably still, might have imparted to her poetry more of masculine health and stamen, at the expense of some of its romance and music.[37]

To allay potential criticism of Hemans, Chorley cleverly converts Hemans's shirking of the prescribed domestic role into a positive good for the production of a feminine poetry sans the adulteration of a "masculine health" that would have been imparted to it, ironically, by the rigors and interruptions of domestic labor. This apologia points to the work of literary fabrication that went on behind Hemans's proscenium of conventional domestic femininity throughout much of her adult life. Ultimately, after a lifetime of disappointments by male providers and being early thrown into the competitive literary market to eke out a living for herself and her family, the trauma of her mother's death precipitated the onset of physical decline that eventually led to her early death at the age of 41 in 1835.

Because much of her writing came as a result of desperate financial necessity, considerations of public taste frequently impinged upon Hemans's selection of topoi and style in order to ensure commercial success. *England & Spain* (1808), her first published poem, was calculated to exploit contemporary interest in the continental war. Likewise, *The Restoration of the Works of Art to Italy* (1816), a work that sealed her literary fame, exploited popular contempt for Napoleon's plundering of Italian and Roman art. In the case of *Modern Greece* (1817), a correspondence with her publisher, John Murray, reveals that she chose the idea to contrast modern Greece to its ancient grandeur in order to exploit the nationwide interest in the recent importation of the Elgin Marbles. Yet, because of the poem's masculine academic style, she thought it circumspect to publish the poem anonymously to increase its salability.[38] Central to the poem's machinery of anonymity is its sophisticated notational apparatus, whose erudition fooled one reviewer into believing that the poem could not have been the work of a "female pen" and must certainly be the production of an ostensibly male "academical pen."[39]

The admixture of exoticism and philosophic meditation on the fate of empires presented in *Modern Greece* would have appealed to readers conditioned by grand tales of foreign adventure in strange and sublime lands, and the closing sentiment that due diligence at home can avert the decline of empire would also have aroused the admiration of mainstream patriots. Perhaps deliberately, the poem takes off from the success of Byron's *Childe Harold* in content and form. Like *Childe Harold*, it incorporates the rich features of the travelogue genre and engages the simmering debate over the Elgin Marbles. It also shares a similar stanzaic structure, notational apparatus, and episodic form. But here the similarities end. Its 101 stanzas comprise a non-chronological episodic structure with multiple rhetorical modes. It begins ostensibly in the present with a sublimely picturesque Grecian landscape colored by wild vegetation and moldering ruins. The narrator guides us through this scene by following the meandering path of a wandering *enthusiast*—ostensibly a western traveler captivated by ancient Greece. Next comes the tragic account of a Grecian émigré in the Americas that foregrounds the trauma of having lost one's homeland. From here, Hemans shifts into a specious historicity, narrating the fall of classical Greece (and conflating this with the decline of the Byzantine Empire) on the very morning "When Asia poured / Her fierce fanatics to Byzantium's wall."[40] Hemans then turns back to the present to magnify the contrast between past glory and present ruin. The poem then concludes by shifting into prophecy, reclaiming Greek heritage (manifested in the expropriation of the Elgin Marbles) for an emergent British imperium and striking a potentially jarring final note with a disturbing vision of Britain's future ruins that is reminiscent of Volney's sentiment in the *Ruins*, where the narrator witnesses the ruination of past civilizations and ponders whether one day a traveler like himself might also sit silently amidst the ruins of Europe and "weep in solitude over the ashes of their inhabitants, and the memory of their former greatness."[41] However, contrary to Volney's assertion of the disastrous folly of empire, Hemans suggests that a strong domestic sphere can beat back the moral and physical decadence that leads to decline.

For Hemans, interest in the fate of empires may have been spurred by a childhood fascination with ruins. Peter W. Trinder tells us that she spent much of her childhood lingering and reading among the ruins of Conway Castle.[42] Her visits to Conway Castle in search of inspiration as she read resembles the narrative of *Modern Greece*, where a wandering enthusiast seeks similar inspiration by traversing the sublime tombs and monuments of modern Greece—"the ruin Time and Fate have wrought."[43] It is a "Realm of sad beauty," she writes,

> A shrine
> That Fancy visits with Devotion's zeal,
> To catch high thoughts and impulses divine
> And all the glow of soul enthusiasts feel
> Amidst the tombs of heroes.[44]

Hemans's early fascination with ruins may have prompted her to read more about the history of empires, which, more often than not, ended in ruin. Indeed, the notes to *Modern Greece* are freighted with citations of Gibbon's *Decline and Fall*, and the themes and motifs present in the poem clearly betray a line of influence. Trinder has found evidence to suggest that Gibbon's *Decline* was one of her favorite books, and that Gibbon's awesome and sublime vision of Rome's final moments before the fall inspired Hemans to write the poem

Alaric in Italy as well.⁴⁵ Moreover, Chorley reveals that Volney's *Ruins* was also quite influential for the young poet. He cites a correspondence with Bishop Heber in which Hemans mentions her abandonment of a plan to write a critique of the origins of religion along the lines of Volney's *Ruins* "to trace out the symbolical meaning, by which the popular faiths of every land are linked together."⁴⁶ Daniel White has revealed that this poem was probably the unfinished *Superstition and Revelation* (1820), a twenty-eight stanza poem in which Hemans argues that Christianity is the root of all religions, and that all current religions are adulterations of Christianity.⁴⁷

The theme of ruin and the aesthetic of the ruinological sublime are central to the ideology of colonialism and empire embedded in *Modern Greece*. By narrating Greece through the aesthetic of the ruinological sublime, Hemans succeeds in orientalizing *Modern Greece*, symbolically opening it up to Western exploitation, for which the importation of the Elgin Marbles stood as a sign. Therefore, she presents modern Greece as a vast wilderness of "savage cliffs and solitudes"⁴⁸ so that its territories can be imaginatively evacuated for European colonial acquisition. Through a clever temporal disjuncture that posits a radical and unmediated cultural dislocation between past and present, Hemans is able to reconcile this orientalized image of *Modern Greece* with a concomitant Hellenic revival that contrarily depicts Greece as the cradle of Western civilization. As the narrative goes, Greece *was* part and provenance of the constellation of western civilization, a fact to which its ruins testify. But now, one is told, these ruins litter a territory only sparsely populated by another culture, dubiously "Greek," but bearing no connection to the past inhabitants of the land. In fact, the only thing these cultures share in common is a geographic coordinate. Interestingly, Greece's geographical location, on the metaphoric borderline between East (Levant) and West (Europe), sustains such a condition of categorical confusion. These factors fertilize the orientalist imaginary in which *Modern Greece* is transformed into a sublime sepulcher of tombs, ruins, and silent plains where all is "silence round, and solitude, and death."⁴⁹

Hemans imagines the modern Greeks to be a debased "second race" who "inherit but their name" and for whom

> No patriot feeling binds them to the soil,
> Whose tombs and shrines their fathers have not rear'd,
> Their glance is cold indifference, and their toil
> But to destroy what ages have revered.⁵⁰

The specter of cultural miscegenation is duly exorcized by insisting that this "second race" is really the progeny of an invading Muslim "Crescent horde" from

> Regions, to intellect a desert space,
> A wild without a fountain or a flower,
> Where towers Oppression 'midst the deepening glooms.'[51]

The vast chasm separating this "second race" from the ancient Hellenes is glibly denoted by the use of the modifier "modern" in the title *Modern Greece*. The phrase, ironically, is an oxymoron, because one is led to believe, in fact, that there is nothing really modern about them.[52] Instead, they appear wholly the production of an expansionist, despotic, and conventionally oriental culture that has plundered and destroyed the ancient glories of Hellenic Greece; exterminated or exiled its people; annexed its territories to the landscape of the oriental sublime; and, tragically for the "civilized" West, extended the purview of its pre-modern regime of barbarism to include the sacred Hellenic origins of Western culture itself.[53]

This narrative tour-de-force legitimates intervention by Western forces, who are figured as the proper heirs and descendants of that "nobler race" now displaced by a "second race" which lacks the intellect and sensibility to appreciate the Grecian legacy. Gibbon offers a possible source for this passage in his citation of Petrarch's astonishment at the "supine indifference" of the modern Romans towards the stupendous monuments and ruins of ancient Rome, and who marvels that a "stranger of the Rhone was more conversant with these antiquities than the nobles and natives of the metropolis."[54] Gibbon viewed himself as just such a stranger, characterizing himself as a "devout pilgrim from the remote and once savage countries of the North" who has now returned to the cradle of western civilization to pay homage and resurrect its glories.[55]

Hemans proposes that if the "savage" natives cannot appreciate the relics and ruins of a fallen empire, then it behooves the "civilized" nations to send their own archeological teams to recover this history for the presumed benefit of humanity. True to the kind of modern orientalism described by Edward Said, Hemans's *Modern Greece* posits that Hellenic Greece's ruins can be metaphorically read, appreciated, and understood only by an enthusiast from the West.[56] The colonial expropriator is here figured in the seemingly innocuous guise of the wandering enthusiast. Like Gibbon, Hemans offers us a pilgrimmatic figure—a "wandering son of other lands"—possessed of a Byronesque Romantic sensibility. The narrator, who functions as a guide and chronicler, describes the wandering enthusiast who traverses the vast solitudes and sublime ruins of *Modern Greece* as one

> Whose enthusiast mind
> Each muse of ancient days hath deep imbued
> With lofty lore, and all his thoughts refined
> In the calm school of silent solitude.[57]

This is the quintessential Wordsworthian traveler "fostered alike by beauty and by fear," who exhibits a penchant for introspection and a profound sensitivity to one's natural surroundings. This traveler is distinguished from the modern Greek in every way that matters. In fact, the only character similar in disposition and sensibility to the peripatetic protagonist is the figure of the exiled Greek, who is also portrayed as possessing a Romantic demeanor as he traverses the North America wilds.

The traveling Romantic enthusiast operates within the narrative in a manner similar to that of Mary Louise Pratt's "sentimental narrator" of contemporary travel narratives who feigns innocence and vulnerability while performing the interior exploration of native lands slated for expropriation, exploitation, and colonization.[58] In this sense, the restless Romantic enthusiast is also an imperialist agent, culturally expropriating Grecian territory and artifacts based on a presumed commonality of sensibility and shared historical experience of imperial and civilizational *grandezza*. When one considers this in conjunction with the fact that Hemans's text also comes equipped with a panoply of ethnographic and topographical notes that subject Greece to a scrupulous investigation by Western academics, one can begin to see the various layers of cultural appropriation that operate within the text. Ultimately, Hemans poem displaces and deterritorializes the modern Greeks, offering instead a genealogy in which the modern Briton, who is presented as the Romantic antithesis of the savage modern Greek, becomes the legitimate heir to Hellenic Greece. Nowhere is this more apparent than in the mirroring of the modern Briton in the Romantic figure of the exiled Greek.

The British cooptation of a Grecian national heritage is further impelled by the act of mourning over its demise. Tricia Lootens has explored the complicity of mourning with nation-building in Hemans's poems. Heroes' graves bind national folk communities, and the work of the female poet is to memorialize these graves and thus impress them into the national imaginary as sentimental signposts of a shared national experience of loss.[59] In addition, as in the case of "England's Dead," these graves are often found spread across the empire, thus working to assimilate settler communities into a nationalist framework and thereby further legitimate expansionary imperialist polices.[60] In *Modern Greece*, then, one discovers the psychological annexation of Greece to a "Greater" Britain through the sentimental act of mourning for a supposedly long dead people whose territory remains a vast sepulcher which only the British Romantic subject, as cultural heir to Grecian antiquity, is properly equipped to appreciate.

Hemans's choice of narratology is remarkable because it raises the gendered politics of the travelogue genre. Hemans's decision to publish the poem anonymously suggests a profound sensitivity to the gendered exclusivity of the travel narrative with its rigorous academic style and apotheosis of masculine mobility and independence.[61] To make it accessible to women authors writing within a discourse of patriotic inclusion, she finds it expedient to tamper with the conventions of the genre by retrofitting it with an overtly patriotic rhetoric and value, insinuating that she understood full well the consequences of unmitigated generic transgression. By resituating this generic form within the discursive horizon of patriotic texts, Hemans was quite deliberately fashioning a strategy whereby a "female pen" could experiment with a conventionally masculine genre without fear of reprisal.

The narratological structure of the poem elaborates this strategy. Unlike Byron, who eventually outs himself as the protagonist of his travel narrative *Childe Harold*, Hemans cannot claim firsthand knowledge of Greece and must instead operate behind the invented persona of a Romantic enthusiast. This ploy bespeaks Hemans's awareness of the severe limitations placed on women's geographical mobility in the early nineteenth century. In light of this, Byron's hasty denunciation of the poem as "good for nothing; written by some one who has never been there" comes off as a callously insensitive remark that carelessly overlooks the reality of immobility faced by middle-class women like Hemans.[62] One way around this sad reality is to construct a protagonist that is recognizably a male Romantic while developing a narrator who is altogether disembodied (and thereby degendered), existing outside of space-time like Volney's Genius, and who is thus able to traverse time and reconstruct the minutia of historical events. Of course, this historical imaginary is largely enabled by Britain's privileged role as Queen of the seas: Britain's powerful navy and colonial infrastructure provide the unique vantage point from which Hemans can project her piercing and acquisitive vision of *Modern Greece*.

Hemans's narrator can rather effortlessly distill the national essence and history of a bygone people largely by virtue of the statuary and architecture whose ruins litter the landscape. In the tradition of eighteenth-century ruinology, these fragments of art are mined for their unique expression of national identity. In the text, Hemans proffers the Athenian city-state as a synecdoche for Greece itself. And Athens is rendered knowable through an investigation of the ruins of the Parthenon, which Hemans calls "the purest model of Athenian taste,"[63] locating in a nation's art its peculiar sensibility. She also subscribes to the eighteenth-century fascination with the nationalist role of the bardic artist when she hails Greece as the "fair land of Phidias,"[64] the renowned sculptor and architect who oversaw the building of the Parthenon and personally sculpted the statue of Athena (or Minerva in the Roman lexicon), which is stationed in its central shrine.

Yet, Hemans modifies this tradition by outfitting the study of ruins with a capacity for augury. At will, her narrator can recount the events that transpired during the "closing night of that imperial race."[65] Furthermore, by the agency of the creative imagination, the narrator can also conjure up vivid imagery of a pre-lapsarian Greece, recovering the splendid vistas of a once glorious Athens from the ruins of time:

> Again renewed by Thought's creative spells,
> In all her pomp thy city, Theseus! Towers:
> Within, around, the light of glory dwells
> On art's fair fabrics, wisdom's holy bowers.
> There marble fanes in finished grace ascend,
> The pencil's world of life and beauty glows,
> Shrines, pillars, porticoes, in grandeur blend,
> Rich with the trophies of barbaric foes; ...
> Athens! Thus fair the dream of thee appears,
> As Fancy's eye pervades the veiling cloud of years.[66]

By meditating upon the nation's ruins, the narrator is able to precipitate a spell of imaginative reconstruction whereby imperial Athens is delivered from decay and presented at the height of its *grandezza*.

Interestingly, the Parthenon, which occupies a special place in the text's discursive topography, is a site that conflates Athenian nationalism *and* imperialism. Hemans uses the semantic value of this site to place the British Empire within an imperial tradition dating back to the roots of Western culture in Hellenic Greece and its imperial ambitions. At the time of its construction, Athens was pursuing an overt policy of imperial expansion. Sophia Psarra has pointed out that the processional frieze depicted along the metopes and pediments of the structure tie the nation's present imperial exploits to a history of actual (but also mythical) warfare that consolidated an Athenian nation.[67] This history is symbolically co-opted by Britain through the expropriation of the Elgin Marbles, which are quite literally fragments of this mythology because they are fragments of the Parthenon's processional frieze. Thus, continues Hemans's narrator:

> Who may grieve that, rescued from their hands,
> Spoilers of excellence and foes to art,
> Thy relics, Athens! Borne to other lands,
> Claim homage still to thee from every heart?[68]

To paraphrase, better that Britain, heir to the legacy of Western civilization, recover these fragments than that they be lost to the ignorance and obscurity of an orientalized and debased "second race" whose only claim to them is that they happen to be squatting upon the lands once occupied by a "nobler race" of ancient Greeks. Since, "In those fragments ... the soul of Athens lives," the narrator declaims, "These [fragments] were destined to a noble lot ... to light another land, the quenchless ray that soon shall gloriously expand."[69] Hemans proposes that art, as the embodiment of national sensibility, can act as a conduit of culture. This notion was not unique to Hemans since, as Guari Viswanathan has revealed, British literature was being utilized in India and elsewhere in the same way, as a technology to interpellate Indian subjects with a uniquely British sensibility, and thus produce compliant colonial subjects under the ruse of spreading civilization.[70] In this instance, however, art becomes the vehicle for passing the torch of empire from one nation to the next, thus quickening the birth of another great civilization. Britain, one is told, "hast [the] power to be what Athens e'er hath been."[71] To realize this grand imperial destiny, Hemans argues that the nation must first cultivate its own native art—"treasures oft unprized, unknown"—instead of prizing foreign "gems far less rich than those, thus precious, and thus lost."[72]

In the passages that follow, Hemans enters a prophetic mode in which she imagines possible future scenarios for the British Empire. Imitating Gibbon and Volney, the narrative shifts into the future, where a post-lapsarian Britain, its empire long since expired, lies in ruins. Yet, like Greece, whose Elgin Marbles inspired the poem, one is assured that Britain can have an everlasting life-after-death in the preserved fragments of its art and architecture, which can serve to activate the next turning of the imperial gyre:

> So, should dark ages o'er thy glory sweep,
> Should thine e'er be as now are Grecian plains,
> Nations unborn shall track thine own blue deep
> To hail thy shore, to worship thy remains;
> Thy mighty monuments with reverence trace.
> And cry, "This ancient soil hath nursed a glorious race!"[73]

Hemans's vision of Britain's future ruins as a kind of Mecca reverently visited by "Nations unborn" is calculated to avoid outraging the censors of political propriety by suggesting that the ruinous course of empire augments rather than diminishes the prestige of this "glorious race." The use of the modal verb "should" in the passage above is even more interesting, for its conditionality suggests that this apocalyptic vision is not inexorable, and that, therefore, the pursuit of empire need not lead to ruin as maintained by the Sallustian and biblical traditions described in the previous chapter.

Accordingly, Hemans attributes the cause of Greece's demise not to some inevitable contradiction between liberty and empire, but to a lack of diligence and patriotic devotion that, like the terrible vision of Britain's awful fate, could have been prevented:

> Ye slept, O heroes! Chief ones of the earth!
> High demigods of ancient days! Ye slept: ...
> No patriot then the sons of freedom led
> In mountain pass devotedly to die;

> The martyr spirit of resolve was fled,
> And the high soul's unconquered buoyancy,
> And by your graves, and on your battle plains,
> Warriors! your children knelt to wear the stranger's chains.[74]

Unlike the boy in "Casabianca" who loyally, if foolhardily, remains upon the burning deck out of filial affection and patriotic zeal, the sons of Greece shrank from their duty as patriots, and, subsequently, a once-mighty nation fell. At the center of this narrative is a re-inscription of the vital role of the domestic sphere in cultivating the proper degree of patriotism among the sons of the nation. "O, where were then thy sons" exclaims the narrator as the morning of Greece's fall unfolds.[75] Compared to the British child in "Casabianca" who stands steadfast in the face of mortal danger, the conduct of these derelict Grecian sons reveals not only a failure of collective courage, but also a failure of the domestic sphere to cultivate such courage. The subtext here therefore points to the vital role and presence of women in the service of patriotism. Put glibly, the nation is only as strong as its women, whose central role in raising patriots shores up the strength of the nation and its empire.

Another clue to Hemans's conflation of public and private spheres can be found in the way she deploys Minerva, the patron goddess of Athens, as a symbol of the life (and death) of the nation. Kevin Eubanks has argued that Hemans's reference to Minerva in the poem is a symbolic affront to the modern notion of separate spheres.[76] Indeed, Minerva represents the merger of feminine and masculine traits in her combination of fertility, wisdom, and martial prowess, thus functioning as a figure that combines the public and private spheres in a circle of common patriotic duty. In the text, Hemans uses Minerva metonymically by addressing Greece as "Minerva's land." She also uses the image of "Minerva's rent veil" as a symbol of Greece's fall.[77] The tattered veil variously signifies the cultural and spiritual decline of the nation; the pillaging of the nation's most cherished sites—in this case the temple of Minerva within the Parthenon; and the literal and metaphorical rape of the nation, resulting in the extinction of a people and the procreation of an utterly distinct "second race." Given Hemans's speculation that Greece fell because of a lack of patriotism ("Ye slept, O Heroes!"), I suggest that the figure of Minerva symbolizes her belief in a pre-ordained role for women in civic discourse as the moral supports of patriotism, and that the tragic image of "Minerva's rent veil" portrays what happens when this role is neglected, curbed, or prohibited. By placing the blame for Greece's fall upon the failure of its heroes to stand steadfast against its enemies, Hemans both eschews the established wisdom that liberty and empire are in contradiction, and emphasizes the vital role played by patriot women to, in the words of M. Jouy, swell the "courage of men."

Greece's fate serves as a particularly germane lesson for Britain, whose fate is left undetermined in the poem. The parallels are striking: Britain is a modern nation that views itself as the heir of the Hellenic Western tradition; it is similarly inclined toward empire-building; and it also sports a patron goddess—Britannia—who commingles feminine delicacy with a masculine aptitude for war. If the poem has a moral, it is that Britons can avert the tragedy that befell their Grecian ancestors, symbolized by the image of "Minerva's rent veil" and all the many forms of violence and violation it implies, if British women, Britannia-like, are ready and willing to serve alongside their warrior men as the moral and physical supports of the circle of family, nation, and empire. In so doing, such committed patriot women will achieve the domestication of imperial values necessary to ensure that Britons will not only equal the achievements of their legendary ancestors, but likely surpass them.

Ultimately, *Modern Greece*, like Berkeley's *Essay*, does issue a warning to Britons, but not one consonant with Gibbon, Volney, or the tradition of pastoral and abolitionist poetry, which railed against the corruptions of luxury wrought by unrestrained greed and imperial ambition. Reminiscent of Berkeley's rhetoric of concern and redemption, Hemans conjures a vision of ruins in order to warn Britons not to pursue too vigorously the ideology of separate spheres, which, when too rigid, can foreclose the essential public role played by women in the patriotic instruction of youth and the promotion of patriotism in civic discourse. Through the very act of authoring *Modern Greece*, Hemans underscores the public participation of women in the patriotic defense of the nation and its empire, suggesting that only they, from their unique position as moral authorities who straddle the public and private spheres, can circumvent the decline of the imperial nation-state by cultivating the domestic affections in the service of patriotism.

Barbauld, Counter-Patriotism and the Cycle of Empire

By arguing for a widening of the sphere of female public participation based on the vital role women can play in the inculcation of patriotism and the defense of empire, Hemans adopts a broadened, but orthodox patriotism. To the extent that she offers criticism of the nation, it is firmly compassed by the existing value structure and goals of the nation, and thereby limited to a call for a more significant role for women as actors in the unfolding drama of British imperialism. On the other hand, Anna Letitia Barbauld's equally apocalyptic poem, *Eighteen Hundred and Eleven*, offers a rebuttal to conservative patriotism that leverages morality and the prophet's vision to criticize what she perceives as the self-destructive pursuit of empire. From this critical perspective, which I have called *counter-patriotism*, Barbauld, like Coleridge before her, demonstrates that patriotic affection for the nation can reside as much in honest criticism as in fulsome praise. Barbauld's politics in the poem are patriotic rather than seditious—as some conservative critics branded it, or internationalist—as radical progressives might be wont to view it, because it seeks to serve the nation by condemning policies inconsistent with its professed values and does not challenge the categorical significance of the nation as a framework for identity. But perhaps the most salient evidence of her devotion to the nation is her frank endorsement of cultural imperialism as a positive effect of empire that spreads civilization to new parts of the world, an idea that ultimately realigns Barbauld with her conservative counterparts. This last feature of Barbauld's politics reveals the ideological limits of counter-patriotism, which, though oppositional, is still complicit with nationalism by upholding the belief in the supremacy of the nation.

Barbauld's unorthodox political thought was inspired early on and germinated into a unique admixture of radical and conservative strains evident throughout her prodigious writing career from the 1760s to the 1810s. Born in 1743, Anna Letitia Aikin, later Barbauld, was raised in the progressive milieu of the Warrington Academy, where her father, Dr. John Aikin, was a tutor and theologian. In the dissenting Warrington Academy's atmosphere of what Janowitz calls "free familiar conversation,"[78] Ms. Aikin freely participated in debates about politics and religion from a young age. Angela Keane suggests that this early exposure to discursive freedom helped shape her sense of the domestic *as* public.[79] At Warrington, her intellectual development was also shaped by the dissenting rationalism of its members, such as Joseph Priestley, who is briefly mentioned in *Eighteen Hundred and Eleven* as one of the notables of British culture. After publishing her first collection of poetry, *Poems* (1772), she married her husband-to-be, Rochemont Barbauld, whom she met at the Academy, and they settled in Palgrave, Suffolk, where they jointly ran a Dissenting academy for boys while she published several educational tracts, including *Hymns in Prose for Children* (1781). Later, during the heady years of the early 1790s, Barbauld became a member of the Johnson circle of liberal Dissenters who promoted religious tolerance, an enlightened position on gender, the abolition of slavery, and enthusiasm for the French Revolution.

Although Barbauld insisted that both men and women should develop and exercise their rational and moral facilities, her conception of gender equality appears to be circumscribed by prevailing notions of femininity. For instance, Barbauld turned down an offer from Elizabeth Montagu to help found an academy for young women because, as Janowitz writes, she decided "the best way for a woman to acquire knowledge is from conversation with a father or brother," a position that is congruent with the manner of education she received at Warrington.[80] Her poetry also reveals the limitations of her feminist politics. In "To a Lady, with some painted Flowers," published in *Poems* (1773), she compares women to flowers "sweet, and gay, and delicate," arguing that, like flowers, the primary function of women is "to please."[81] Perhaps for this concession to orthodoxy she is only gently abused by Polwhele in *The Unsex'd Females*. Although he lists Barbauld among the "female band despising NATURE's law," he compares her favorably to Wollstonecraft in a footnote to the poem:

> But though Mrs. B. has lately published several political tracts which, if not discreditable to her talents and virtues, can by no means add to her reputation, yet, I am sure, she must reprobate, with me, the alarming eccentricities of Miss Wollstonecraft.[82]

Wollstonecraft had been publicly contemptuous of the "ignoble comparison" made in "To a Lady," which prompted Barbauld to respond in kind with her poem "The Rights of Woman" (1793), where she satirizes egalitarian feminists, presenting them as man-haters who seek to "Make treacherous Man thy subject, not thy friend," and concludes with the rather un-feminist position that "separate rights are lost in mutual love."[83]

While not as radical as Wollstonecraft in her feminism, Barbauld supported republican causes and took an outspoken position as a critic of the slave trade and the Test and Corporation Acts. These activities earned her the scorn of Horace Walpole, who dubbed her the "virago Barbauld" and a "disciple of Paine."[84] Indeed, her literary works of the 1790s established her reputation as a republican poet. Among them are the *Address to the Opposers of the Repeal* (1790), which trumpets the cause of religious toleration while merging it with support for the egalitarianism of the French Revolution; antislavery invectives like the *Epistle to William Wilberforce* (1791); and reformist tracts like *Civic Sermons to the People* (1790–3) and *Sins of Government, Sins of the Nation* (1793) that critique the government. In these literary endeavors, she had the full support of her publisher, Joseph Johnson, whose circle of intellectuals in the 1780s and 90s included notable Dissenters and Republicans uplifted by the revolutionary spirit of the French Revolution. Yet, like Wordsworth and Coleridge, she soon grew disillusioned with the revolution and distanced herself from republican circles. However, she continued to propound the causes of democratic reform, abolition, and the denunciation of imperialism. In the midst of an economic crisis prompted by Britain's self-interested participation in the Napoleonic Wars and on the eve of another war, the War of 1812 in which Britain would invade the United States, Barbauld published perhaps her most radical instance of counter-patriotism yet, *Eighteen Hundred and Eleven*, a visionary poem with a far-ranging critique of war, slavery, and empire that solidified her notoriety among critics and virtually ended her professional career as a writer.

In *Eighteen Hundred and Eleven*, Barbauld assumes a counter-patriotic stance to warn her compatriots that expansionary wars reap destruction at home as well as abroad. She is critical of the fact that Britain "feeds the fierce strife"[85] of war, depicting the tragic consequences of British militarism on the continent in a sequence of awful vignettes featuring stolen harvests, widowed mothers, streams of blood, and a countryside dotted by corpses. She also addresses the domestic perils of war and warns, "Thou who has shared the guilt must share the woe."[86] Barbauld was aware of the fact that the Napoleonic Wars had nearly collapsed Britain's economy in 1810, prompting many of her contemporaries to challenge the conventional wisdom that war and empire bring security and prosperity. The poem reflects her opinion that the hardships faced by the nation are a direct result of the gross disjunction between its peaceful domestic values and its belligerent foreign policy.[87]

Accordingly, she disagrees with "flatterers" who perceive Britain as "An island Queen amidst thy subject seas" that can "sport in wars, while danger keeps aloof."[88] The allusion here is to James Thomson's flattering poem-become-anthem, "Rule, Britannia" (1740), in which he associates security and prosperity with Britain's ability to "rule the waves."[89] Barbauld asserts the opposite, affirming that the "baseless wealth" engendered by war "dissolves in air away."[90] War leads to an ironic reversal of colonialism as wealth now flows away from Britain toward its colonies in the West:

> Yes, thou must droop; thy Midas dream is o'er;
> The golden tide of Commerce leaves thy shore,
> Leaves thee to prove the alternate ills that haunt
> Enfeebling Luxury and ghastly Want.[91]

Her emphasis on the contrast between "Enfeebling Luxury and ghastly Want"[92] suggests the moral and material bankruptcy of empire, which produces on the one hand the technological wonders of "summer ices" and "winter rose" enjoyed by high society, on the other hand a "mass of misery" as poverty and social inequality increase.[93] In this respect, Barbauld's pairing of luxury with enfeeblement situates the poem within the eighteenth-century debate about the dangers of over-refinement, which shone a critical light on the domestic dangers posed by slavery, war, and empire.[94] Furthermore, her belief that this state of affairs is evidence of a "sickness, only of the soul"[95] insinuates a fundamental problem that requires radical change.[96]

Yet, Barbauld does not limit her critique to present woes. Instead, she moves into a visionary mode and strikes an oracular pose to prophesy the inevitable ruin that will be wrought by empire. Daniel P. Watkins has argued for a reassessment of Barbauld's *Poems* (1773, 1792) as a primary example of Romantic women writers' rich contribution to the tradition of British visionary poetics since Milton, and *Eighteen Hundred and Eleven* may be adduced as further evidence of Barbauld's contribution to this tradition.[97] Like Coleridge in "Fears in Solitude" (1798), she portends the coming of "evil days," but this time the agent of retribution is not Britain's rival, France, but its Western colonies.[98] Accordingly, she describes "the tempest blackening in the distant West," an allusion to the escalations that led to the War of 1812.[99] "The worm is in thy core," writes Barbauld, because "Arts, arms and wealth destroy the fruits they bring."[100] The trinity of arts/science, arms/techne, and wealth/capital, she warns, both sustains and destroys civilizations by spurring them on to the dead end of empire. Consequently, Barbauld imagines a future era in which "Europe sit[s] in dust as Asia now" and "gothic night" again sets over an English landscape now reduced to the sublime spectacle of "gray ruin and mouldering stone."[101]

Unlike her seventeenth- and eighteenth-century predecessors, Barbauld's donning of the prophet's robe did not succeed in neutralizing the political fallout of her act of double dissension. John Aikin, who considered the poem "the finest production of [Barbauld's] genius," also predicted that, "its view of present & vatication of future evils will not please those *patriots* who think their country just in all her projects, & inexhaustible in her resources."[102] Aikin was correct, of course. While the *New British Lady's Magazine* defended the poem for issuing a welcome, if unpopular, call for "a counter-spirit of peace, reason, and religion,"[103] most reviews of the poem struck an outraged tone and followed Polwhele's gender-policing tactics by criticizing Barbauld's audacity in daring to take a publicly critical stance towards national policies. For instance, John Wilson Croker's stinging denouncement of the poem in the *Quarterly Review* was as much motivated by the poet's break with the gendered decorum of *belle lettres* as by the slant of its message, writing that she should "desist from satire, which indeed is satire on herself alone," and entreating her to stop writing "party pamphlets in verse.[104] The crux of Croker's criticism is that Barbauld broke from the unspoken gendered conventions of writing by experimenting with the masculine genres of political satire and party polemic.[105] John Montgomery in a review of the poem for the *Eclectic Review* shared a similar disposition, finding that "the whole tone of it is in a most extraordinary degree unkindly and unpatriotic—we had almost said unfilial."[106] Attacking a poem for being unpatriotic was common enough in a period characterized by war and paranoia of subversives. But labeling a poem "unkindly" and "unfilial" would have been at best irrelevant and at worst ludicrous *if* the author had been male. With a female author, the result was otherwise. Accusations of "unkindly" and "unfilial" behavior were a virtual indictment of unladylike behavior for a woman writer, and such indiscretions would surely have aroused both shock and contempt from readers. Even Barbauld's friend and confidant Henry Crabbe Robinson opined that she had overreached by engaging in "a sort of arrogant determining of the fate of nations without any authentication by sagacious remark of the right even to guess at the probable issue," expressing his frank wish that "she had not written it."[107] In other words, rather than legitimate her critique of the nation, Robinson believed that Barbauld's use of prophecy to convey such an extreme vision of the nation's demise was a political liability because she was not qualified to make such a prognostication.

If Barbauld's attempt to save the nation from itself by prophesying its demise drew the ire of critics, these same critics largely overlooked the fact that the bulk of what she professes in the poem is a rather orthodox view of empire that celebrates the achievements of British culture and endorses the tutelary role it plays in spreading civilization to its colonies. The better part of the poem conveys this message by developing a westward theory of the progress of civilization and empire that celebrates the less violent—but equally dominating—practices of cultural imperialism. Barbauld uses the looming War of 1812 ("The tempest blackening in the distant West") as an indication of this process. It portends the impending ruin of the nation and transfer of cultural hegemony to the west. However, in her eulogy to Britain, she emphasizes that, contra rivals like the Ottoman Empire, British culture will live on by quickening the rise of new civilizations across its former colonies:

> Not like the dim cold Crescent shalt thou fade
> Thy debt to Science and the Muse unpaid;
> Thine are the laws surrounding states revere,
> Thine the full harvest of the mental year,
> Thine the bright stars in Glory's sky that shine,
> And arts that make it life to live are thine.
> If westward streams the light that leaves thy shores,
> Still from thy lamp the streaming radiance pours.[108]

Barbauld's characterization of Islam and the Ottoman Empire as a "dim cold Crescent" reinforces the orientalist view that Islamic culture is moribund. Interestingly, Barbauld also orientalizes the West by depicting it in the ruins of "gothic night." But she contrasts the faded glory of the Middle-east with the immortal fecundity of British civilization, whose cultural legacy will continue to uplift the primitive Americas through a transfer of advanced laws, science, art, and reason even after it lies in ruins. She assures one that "westward streams the light that leaves thy shores," spreading enlightenment throughout the Americas from "Niagara's fall" in the temperate north to "the spreading Platan's tent-like shade" in the tropical south.[109]

In this narrative, British imperialism is portrayed as a benevolent system that spreads civilization. Imperialism remakes the peoples of the Western hemisphere in the image of middle-class Britons, replete with empirical modes of thought, a Romantic sensibility, and a taste for British literature. She selects the canon for this Anglophone New World from a stable of living and dead British philosophers, bards, dramatists, painters, scholars, and scientists, many of whom were close acquaintances, such as Priestley.[110] This benign view of cultural imperialism is an example of what Uday Singh Mehta has called "liberal imperialism." According to Mehta, liberal imperialism derives from Enlightenment theories of stadial development, the belief that societies progress in certain stages, and thus subaltern groups (especially children, women, slaves, uneducated whites, and indigenous peoples) must achieve an "anthropological minimum," or minimum level of social development, before they are eligible for national sovereignty or the rights of citizenship granted by a liberal democracy.[111] The ideology of liberal imperialism is another version of colonialism, based not on military conquest but on raising the subaltern to the status of the "civilized" through education, missions, and other means. Barbauld describes this process using the biological metaphor of planting to suggest that the British Empire lovingly nurtures its "seedlings" in the colonies: "Nations beyond the Appalachian hills / Thy hand has planted and thy spirit fills."[112] The benign processes of cultural imperialism bring these seedlings to maturity:

> Soon as their gradual progress shall impart
> The finer sense of morals and of art,
> Thy stores of knowledge the new states shall know,
> And think thy thoughts, and with thy fancy glow.[113]

Barbauld distances the processes of colonial domination from the overt military violence of the Napoleonic Wars by portraying indigenous peoples as willing students of British culture. In this conceit, she imagines regular pilgrimages to the British Isles undertaken by young enthusiasts from the Americas:

> Yet then the ingenuous youth whom Fancy fires
> With pictured glories of illustrious sires,
> With duteous zeal their pilgrimage shall take
> From the Blue Mountains, or Ontario's Lake,
> With fond adoring steps to press the sod
> By statesmen, sages, poets, heroes trod.[114]

Barbauld's characterization of the pilgrim as an "ingenuous youth" normalizes the colonial relationship by equating it with the natural process of education, refinement, and maturity. The pilgrimage emulates the grand tours of Europe undertaken by British aristocrats and gentry as a rite of passage to manhood. In Barbauld's apocalyptic future, Britain has faded, but its former colonies in the West have achieved the anthropological minimum of Western civilization by mimicking its culture. Homi K. Bhabha has written that mimicry is "one of the most elusive and effective strategies of colonial power and knowledge."[115] In this case, the young pilgrim seeks to become a simulacrum of the mature European "man of feeling" who has long since vanished, but whose trace lives on in mimicry. As in *Modern Greece*, the pilgrim, a neo–Romantic, mimics the man of feeling by seeking inspiration among the picturesque vistas of the Lake District and the sublime ruins of London. The latter is a sort of Mecca that he approaches "with throbbing bosom," pausing along his way to appreciate such fabled glories as "the ponderous mass of Johnson's form" and "Howard's sainted feet."[116] What the ruins of Greece and Rome once were to the civilized Britons, Barbauld predicts the ruins of London will become to its former colonies, beginning a new chapter in Western civilization. Thus, Barbauld is critical of empire, but uncritical of cultural imperialism.

Of course, Barbauld's ideas about the benevolence of cultural imperialism were not original in her day, but rather confirmed the orthodox view that empire was a sort of paternal responsibility—Kipling's "white man's burden"—to civilize "backwards" peoples. In the same vein, her theory of the westward progress of empire also had notable precedents. For instance, her speculation that the mantle of empire flows westward echoes the writings of the minister George Berkeley, who formulated his own theory of a westward-flowing arc of civilization seventy years earlier in "Verses on the Prospect of Planting Arts and Learning in America" (1752): "Westward the Course of Empire takes its Way."[117] Berkeley allegorizes progress as a "Muse" that travels from East to West, presaging Barbauld's description of a westward-traveling "Genius" of progress:

> The Muse, disgusted at an Age and Clime,
> Barren of every glorious Theme,
> In distant Lands now waits a better Time,
> Producing Subjects worthy of Fame.[118]

Berkeley also preempts Barbauld's use of a planting metaphor, as the title of his poem suggests, to describe how colonialism serves as a vehicle for the westward migration of civilization.

Edward Gibbon's *The Decline and Fall of the Roman Empire* (1776) and C.F. Volney's the *Ruins of Empires* (1790) also establish precedents for Barbauld's narrative of empire. For instance, Volney's narrative invokes a "Genius of the tombs and ruins" that can decipher the lessons of history:

> I will invoke from the bosom of the tombs the spirit which once in Asia gave splendor to states, and glory to nations; I will ask of the ashes of legislators, *by what secret causes do empires rise and fall; from what sources spring the prosperity*

5. Patriot Women and the Future of Empire   179

and misfortunes of nations; on what principles can the peace of society, and the happiness of man be established?[119]

A ghostly Genius rises from the ruins and proceeds to narrate a universal tale about the rise of civilizations, the cupidity that induces them to become empires, and the internal corruption that precipitates a terminal decline. After narrating the fall of the Western Roman Empire, Gibbon arrives at a similar conclusion:

> The decline of Rome was the natural and inevitable result of immoderate greatness. Prosperity ripened the principles of decay; the causes of destruction multiplied with the extent of conquest; and as soon as time or accident had removed the artificial supports, the stupendous fabric yielded to the pressure of its own weight.[120]

As in the writings of these contemporaries, the conceit of an omniscient Genius, the idea that history is cyclical, and the notion that empires inevitably collapse of their own internal corruption appear in Barbauld's narrative of history.

Despite these similarities, however, Barbauld departs from her predecessors in innovative ways. For one thing, her Genius functions less as a guide than as an animating impulse of history, much like the Hegelian notion of a Spirit that presides over a teleology of progress:

> There walks a Spirit o'er the peopled earth,
> Secret his progress is, unknown his birth;
> Moody and viewless as the changing wind,
> No force arrests his foot, no chains can bind;
> Where'er he turns, the human brute awakes,
> And, roused to better life, his sordid hut forsakes:
> He thinks, he reasons, glows with purer fires,
> Feels finer wants, and burns with new desires.[121]

While her tale of development leading from primitiveness to modern refinement is consonant with the stadial and teleological theories of Scottish Enlightenment thinkers like Adam Ferguson and Adam Smith, the resemblance ends when Barbauld explains that the *telos* of civilization is not modern capitalism, but the ruins of empire:

> The Genius now forsakes the favoured shore,
> And hates, capricious, what he loved before;
> Then empires fall to dust, then arts decay,
> And wasted realms enfeebled despots sway.[122]

The most significant innovation, though, is Barbauld's use of a novel adaptation of *translatio imperii* to qualify the parabolic cycles of rise and decline. The term *translatio imperii* literally means "transfer of power" and refers to the ceremony developed in imperial Rome and continued during the Holy Roman Empire in which power succeeded to the next Caesar. In Barbauld's narrative, what is transferred is not state power but the imperial hegemon, with cultural imperialism acting as a sort of midwife to ensure that former colonies mature into powerful empires. Through the conceit of the Genius's westward progress, Barbauld traces an epic historical metanarrative that pans from East to West as the fall of one empire quickens the rise of another: Babylon falls as Egypt rises, Egypt falls as Persia rises, Persia falls as Greece rises, Greece falls as Carthage rises, Carthage falls as Rome rises, Rome falls as the Norse, Baltic, Celtic, and Gothic nations of Northern Europe rise. The British Empire emerges from among these contenders, only to fall and give way to the Americas. The pilgrimage motif is an allegory for the ancient ceremony of *translatio imperii* in which the would-be Caesar would return to the capitol in order to lay claim to his crown. Likewise, the young civilization, here figured as a devout pilgrim, must legitimate its claim to hegemony by returning to the previous seat of power in order to demonstrate through mimicry an unbroken line of ascension from one empire to the next. In other words, the empire is dead; long live the empire.

Despite her endorsement of cultural imperialism, it's worth noting that Barbauld's metanarrative has a positive corollary: it posits a radical parallelism between East and West that jettisons orientalist theories about the essential and absolute difference between the two. Edward Said describes orientalism as "a style of thought based upon an ontological and epistemological distinction made between 'the Orient' and (most of the time) 'the Occident.'"[123] Barbauld's metanarrative, however, emphasizes sameness rather than difference by selectively including parts of the Orient (Babylon, Egypt, Persia, and Carthage) in her narrative of rise and decline alongside central actors in the Western tradition (Greece, Rome, and Northern Europe). Though the East is further along this trajectory than the West, they share a similar pattern of development from savagery to empire and decline. While Barbauld still depicts the East in orientalist fashion as an alien site of decadence, despotism, and ruin, she presents a new paradigm in which such typically orientalist depictions of the East function as premonitions of the "gothic night" that awaits the British Empire, and, indeed, all empires, regardless of cultural provenance.

Overall, Barbauld's *Eighteen Hundred and Eleven* is an interesting example of how women could and did join their male peers by writing as counter-patriots openly critical of the state. Unlike their male peers, it also demonstrates the vicious censure that women could expect for their double-dissension, the cutting edge of which was a pronounced attack on their feminine virtues. But what is perhaps most significant about this case of counter-patriotism is the fact that it ultimately demonstrates the ideological limits of counter-patriotism, which, as a form of nationalism, is still indebted to the values and beliefs of the nation. Though counter-patriots ostensibly sought to protect these values from the forces of greed and corruption, this inclination could play into the narrative of cultural imperialism, as evident in Barbauld's case, because both ideologies make a similar claim about the worth of national culture and its potential benefit to others.

Yet, one mystery remains. The triumphal tone of Barbauld's final line jars with her assurance that empire must ultimately fail. "Thy world, Columbus, shall be free,"[124] writes Barbauld, but the reader knows better. If her prophetic vision about the cycle of empire is correct, the American states, once remade in the image of their British colonizers, will also begin to tread the well-worn path of empire and decline that brings with it the domestic woes of poverty and tyranny. Subsequently, pilgrims, though of another kind, will once again seek its shores.

***

Modern Greece and *Eighteen Hundred and Eleven* are but two examples of the ways that Romantic women writers staked out public positions on matters of state and attempted to manage the public fallout of intervening in a masculine discourse with various degrees of success. In this case, Hemans and Barbauld, through the use of prophecy, both express anxiety about the future of empire, but they resolve these anxieties in different ways—one by holding out the possibility of redemption through a re-commitment to the patriotic defense of the nation and its empire spearheaded by patriot women, the other by shining a critical light on the self-destructive practices of war and empire, yet promising that the cultural seed planted through imperialism is a benefit to the colonies and will give the dying nation a kind of second life. Though informed by conflicting versions of patriotism—conservative and counter-cultural—these ruminations on the future of empire ultimately share a partisan commitment to the nation that drives each poet to preserve it from moral corruption and the ruins of empire. As patriot women, then, both Hemans and Barbauld confirm M. Jouy's belief that women have a vital public role to play as "the great support of morality, and the very ground-work of society."

Conclusion: William Blake's Prophecies and the Limits of Nationalism

> When shall Jerusalem return & overspread all the Nations?
> —William Blake[1]

A major premise of this study has been that nationalism was a political phenomenon that gripped poets and their critics as much as it did statesmen and critics of the state. From bardic criticism, to the English ethnicism and class politics of Wordsworth's bardic poetics, to Coleridge's Protestant nationalism, to the anthems of empire produced by Felicia Hemans and the cultural imperialism propagated by Anna Letitia Barbauld, I have essayed to trace some of the ways that poetry in general and Romantic poetry in particular contributed to the growth of British nationalism over the two centuries following the first Act of Union in 1707. In all of this, I have maintained that British nationalism was an artificial construction conjured out of a will to unification driven largely by English internal colonialism and the interests of economic elites, whose control of the state ensured that Britain would develop a modern industrial capitalist economy and pursue an empire of trade and colonies to sustain it. From the eighteenth century on, vernacular literature—demanded by a rising literate middle class, made affordable by changes in print technology and copyright law, made available in the new literary marketplace, and promulgated by bardic critics and educators—operated as a convenient medium for incubating state nationalism and disseminating it to the general populace, where it sometimes gained traction and took on its own initiatives, either for conservative or radical ends.

To conclude this study here, however, wrongly suggests that nationalism was a monolithic phenomenon among the Romantics. The examples of counter-patriotism by Coleridge and Barbauld in this study at least make clear that a vibrant counter-discourse to state-authorized nationalism existed among the Romantics. While some appropriated the trappings of patriotism to wage campaigns critical of the state, others went further by challenging the narrow constraints of nationalism in favor of internationalism. For instance, Lord Byron's extremely popular *Childe Harold* (1812–8), which expresses ardent support for Greek, Italian, and Albanian independence against the machinations of Ottoman, British, and French imperialism, demonstrates that internationalist politics had a following in Romantic-era Britain. The spirit of internationalism also pervades the works of Percy Bysshe Shelley: consider the Golden-Age vision of world peace and liberation presented in *Prometheus Unbound* (1820). Of course, Shelley's most salient expression of internationalism, and perhaps the most affirmative statement of a poet's international role, arrives at the conclusion to the *Defence* (1821), where he famously proclaims, "Poets are the unacknowledged legislators of the world."[2]

Such examples demonstrate that the spirit of internationalism was always-already present in the age of nationalism, existing in creative tension with nationalist values and politics. During the Romantic period, internationalism offered a utopian alternative to national one-sidedness, jingoism, and war by imagining a global community premised on peace, justice, and harmony. The utopian element of this vision is important because it suggests why and how Romantic poets were able to transcend the powerful political horizon of nationalism. The philosopher Paul Ricoeur remarks that, while one cannot critique ideology by stepping outside it, one can critique it from within by constructing a utopia against which to compare and judge it:

> This is my conviction: the only way to get out of the circularity in which ideologies engulf us is to assume a utopia, declare it, and judge an ideology on this basis. Because the absolute onlooker is impossible, then it is someone within the process itself who takes the responsibility for judgment.[3]

Ricoeur's concept of utopia as an internal process of critique applies as much to nationalism as to its opposite, internationalism. In contrast to the centuries of monarchic and aristocratic despotism, the powerful themes of national unity and civic duty imagined and expressed in British political movements, literature, and art from the eighteenth century on must have had an almost utopian ring. Yet, the conflicted reality of internal colonialism, class struggle, and imperialism also belied the utopian airs of nationalist politics and culture. By imagining utopia in the form of internationalism, Romantic poets thus were able to "get out of the circularity" of nationalist ideology and critique it from within, thereby laying bare its unexplored assumptions, moral hazards, and political limits.

I conclude this study contrapuntally with a case study in Romantic internationalism focusing on William Blake's continental prophecies—*America* (1793), *Europe* (1794), and *The Song of Los* (1795)—which offer the most sustained example of the utopian desire for egalitarian internationalism in the Romantic period. Influenced by the radical antinomianism of the English Civil War and the democratic impulse of the American and French Revolutions, by the 1790s Blake was already breaking the "mind-forg'd manacles"[4] of nationalism, religion, and empire. This is most evident in the continental prophecies, where Blake narrates a sequence of visions featuring uprisings that radiate from the American colonies to the imperial centers in Europe, and then reverberate back out again to Asia and Africa. Just as the utopian desire of the millenarian impulse propelled revolutionaries during the English Civil War, Blake channels the millenarian impulse to envision a global revolution that sweeps away national borders and distinctions, replacing the global system of imperialism with an international community that restores the pre-lapsarian order of peace, freedom, and equality.

Curiously, Blake's internationalist politics were overlooked in the early reception of his poetry, which was marred by misunderstanding and misinterpretation. He was disregarded as a wild-eyed, detached, and inscrutable mystic by his contemporaries. But nineteenth-century bardic critics re-evaluated Blake's contribution to English poetry and re-invented him as an English nationalist. This feat was in large part accomplished through a surface reading of the "Jerusalem" epigraph to *Milton* (1804), which critics took as a frank expression of English patriotism. Thereafter, the epitaph was set to patriotic music and anthologized in compulsory school readers, consolidating a nationalist re-appropriation of the once-ignored poet. By the early twentieth century, the nationalist view of Blake was so established that the scholar Esmé Wingfield-Stratford, in a work historicizing English patriotism, comfortably asserted, "Blake thinks and writes in terms of patriotism."[5] Like his predecessors, Wingfield-Stratford interpreted Blake's appropriation of the English millenarian tradition and terms such as "Albion"—the earliest Gaelic name for the island of Britain—as incontrovertible evidence of the poet's support for English nationalism. "From the beginning to the end of his career," he writes, "[Blake] adored his country with the deep religious fervour of the Hebrew, and with the laughing ardour of the Greek."[6] Going further, Wingfield-Stratford even speculates that *Milton* provides clear evidence of Blake's enthusiasm for the British Empire because "Jerusalem is to be the emanation of Albion, and is to overspread the whole earth."[7]

Since David Erdman's groundbreaking study, *Blake: Prophet Against Empire* (1954), however, this view of Blake as an ardent nationalist and proponent of empire has been debunked. Erdman revolutionized the field of Blake scholarship by historicizing Blake's poetry within the revolutionary ferment in England following the American and French Revolutions, producing a new image of the poet as someone deeply engaged with contemporary events and radical culture. A.L. Morton's *The Everlasting Gospel* (1958) further radicalized the critical understanding of Blake by tracing his ideas back to the radical religious ferment of seventeenth-century England with its volatile combination of millenarianism and egalitarian politics. Spurred by these critical reassessments of Blake's life and work, more recent scholarship on Black has continued to probe his radical roots and legacy. Jackie DiSalvo's *War of Titans* elucidates Blake's radical critique and appropriation of religion, while John Mee's *Dangerous Enthusiasm* historicizes Blake's connection to radical Christianity in the 1790s. Stewart Crehan's *Blake in Context* provides a class analysis that attributes the "spirit of revolt" in Blake's work to his social condition as a member of an artisanal class at odds with industrial capitalism and the new bourgeois ruling class. Saree Makdisi's *Romantic Imperialism* and *William Blake and the Impossible History of the 1790s* foreground Blake's anti-imperialist and internationalist politics. Christopher Z. Hobson's *The Chained Boy* shifts attention to Blake's figuration of revolutionary desire in Orc, while his *Blake and Homosexuality* brings to focus Blake's revolutionary ideas about sexuality. Several books specifically address Blake's complex and antagonistic relationship with nationalism, including Jason Whittaker's *William Blake and the Myths of Britain*, Julia M. Wright's *Blake, Nationalism, and the Politics of Alienation*, and the compilation *Blake, Nation and Empire* edited by Steve Clark and David Worrall.[8] The new picture of Blake that emerges from this scholarship is of a poet, prophet, and artist who critically appropriated elements of national mythology and religion to further a radically subversive agenda.

    Taking off from the new picture of Blake that emerges from the work of these scholars, this conclusion specifically examines Blake's prophecies in order to drill down and identify several ways that he develops and promotes an internationalist, anti-imperialist, and egalitarian poetics. First, he orients each prophecy toward continents (America, Europe, Asia, and Africa) rather than individual nation-states. Although each nation must wage revolution against its own particular tyrants, they are depicted as collectively comprising a single global system of domination and oppression, and the revolution negates the form of the nation-state as it establishes a new international order of peace, justice, and cooperation. Second, Blake eschews the linear theories of national development propounded by nationalists and embedded in liberal economics and racist discourse. Instead, he reinstates an eschatological and circular Christian narrative of paradise, fall, and redemption, but on an international scale. Third, in accordance with this space-time axis, he interprets the events of the American and French Revolutions as the opening salvos of a global uprising that will bring about a new Golden Age, the "Jerusalem" to which he refers in the epigraph to *Milton*. And yet, if this vision is inspired by the tradition of Christian millenarianism, it is also at odds with the professed values and mythos of official Christianity, presenting the Satanic Orc as the standard-bearer of the egalitarian, international revolution, while the Jehovah-like Urizen and his minions in church and state frantically attempt to squelch the revolution. This pattern of flipping binaries continues in his treatment of colonialism, class, patriarchy, and sexuality, revealing Western civilization to be intellectually, morally, and spiritually bankrupt. Ultimately, in Blake's vision, the global revolution sweeps away divisive distinctions such as East and West, nationalism, class, religion, race, gender, and sexuality, restoring the primitive egalitarianism of a single, global, pre-lapsarian society.

To dramatize this epic saga of global proportions, Blake fashions a unique mythological system that subsumes various cultural streams.[9] There are several main characters in this saga. The figure of Urizen represents reason and moral law, which have ruled over humanity for millennia. He is associated with domestic tyranny—in the form of religious and secular law—and the tyranny of empire. In *The Song of Los*, Urizen is clearly associated with Jehovah, who hands down moral law to mankind. But his association elsewhere in the prophecies with the sun, sky, light, civilization, lightning, mind, old-age, and holy word/books, reveal him to be a composite of the patriarchal sky-gods (Horus, Mithridates, Zeus, Jehovah, Odin, etc.) of several major religions. Albion, the spiritual emanation of Britain, oversees Urizen's empire, explicitly linking empire to the themes of domination and oppression rather than civilization and enlightenment. Challenging Urizen is Orc, an allegorical figure for revolutionary egalitarianism and freedom. In *America* and *The Song of Los*, Orc is depicted as physically and metaphorically chained by force and jealousy, which aligns him both with Prometheus and Satan. Orc is also associated with rebellion, fire, youth, the subterranean, darkness, the lower half of the body, hedonism, and sexual desire, which, like Urizen, make him a composite of deities, demons, and devils from several religions (Set, Prometheus, Dionysus, Hades, Satan, Loki). This mythology reveals how Blake reverses the polarity of good and evil, portraying Urizen, who sits on his throne in the empyreal heavens, as a usurper and tyrant who has upset the balance of power. On the other hand, the demonic red Orc, an archetypal fallen angel who resists Urizen's tyranny and is punished for it, forwards the cause of human liberation.

The prophecies weave actual historical events into a visionary tapestry that documents the ultimate liberation of humanity. Accordingly, they begin with *America*, which recounts the first stage in the overthrow of Urizen's reign as Albion loses its thirteen colonies to a revolution precipitated by the return of Orc. Inverting the civilization paradigm, the British Empire serves as a proxy for Urizen's oppressive empire of reason and moral law on earth. Deep in his prison-cave, Orc has burst the iron rivets that bind him, signifying the unleashing of revolutionary desire and the beginning of the American Revolution. Urthona, Orc's jailor and Urizen's daughter, succumbs to Orc's lustful grip and has a portent of his revolutionary destiny:

> I know thee, I have found thee, & I will not let thee go;
> Thou art the image of God who dwells in darkness of Africa;
> And thou art fall'n to give me life in regions of dark death.
> On my American plains I feel the struggling afflictions
> Endur'd by roots that writhe their arms into the nether deep:
> I see a serpent in Canada, who courts me to his love;
> In Mexico an Eagle, and a Lion in Peru;
> I see a Whale in the South-sea, drinking my soul away.
> O what limb rending pains I feel. They fire & my frost
> Mingle in howling pains, in furrows by thy lightnings rent;
> This is eternal death; and this the torment long foretold.[10]

Urthona bewails America's artificial division by various powers, which are represented by animal forms (serpent, eagle, lion, and whale). Orc's return implicitly spells the defeat of these powers and the reunification of the "American plains." Orc's association with "the darkness of Africa" suggests that the least civilized places, according to modern European paradigms, are in fact the most enlightened because they are the least subjugated by Urizen's system, whose power is most acute in Europe. Symbolizing Blake's overturning of the mind/body dichotomy, Orc's sensual embrace frees Urthona from the mind-controlling grip of Urizen's propaganda and converts her to the revolutionary cause.

In line with Blake's reversal of conventional polarities, when the American Revolution erupts, he does not attribute it to liberalism or republican ideals, concepts entangled with Urizenic reason and the hegemonic imperial narratives of progress and civilization, but to the reincarnation of the Satanic principle of rebellion and unbounded revolutionary energy embodied by Orc. Albion's draconic Guardian illustrates this by describing Washington, Paine, and Warren as the "rebel form that rent the ancient / Heavens; Eternal Viper self-renew'd."[11] Orc is denounced as Satan himself, the "Blasphemous Demon, Antichrist, hater of Dignities."[12]

These epithets do not deter Albion's angels—its colonial governors—from falling sway to Orc's magnetic power; they soon become "fallen angels" by joining the rebellion to break the metaphorical and material iron chain that stretches across the Atlantic from the imperial center in London to the American colonies. The revolt of Albion's Angels is followed by a current of egalitarian desire that sweeps back even into the heart of empire itself, in London where "the millions sent up a howl of anguish and threw off their hammerd mail, / And cast their swords & spears to earth, & stood a naked multitude."[13] From the uprising of American colonials, to the defection of the governors, to the support shown by ordinary Britons, the Orcish revolution demonstrates both the righteousness of the revolutionary cause and the tenuous nature of national loyalty.

The ultimate success of the revolution is marked above all by the fall of Urizenic constraints on sexuality enforced by church and state:

> The doors of marriage are open, and the Priests in rustling scales
> Rush into reptile coverts, hiding from the fires of Orc,
> That play around the golden roofs in wreaths of fierce desire,
> Leaving the females naked and glowing with the lusts of youth.[14]

But it is also marked by the globalization of the revolutionary spirit as the "Demons light" turns next to Europe. The spread of the revolution ultimately portends the end of Urizen's global empire: "For Empire is no more, and now the Lion & Wolf shall cease."[15]

In *Europe*, Blake reveals that Urizen's tyranny of reason and moral law is strongest at the center of empire, thus unmasking the European Enlightenment as another form of ideological darkness. Indeed, in *The Song of Los*, Orc is described as departing from "European darkness,"[16] ironically reversing the polarity of colonial ideology. Europe is depicted as thoroughly controlled by a conspiracy of government, state religion, patriarchy, commercial interests, and false Newtonian science. Here, Urizen's tyranny is nearly complete, having lasted for eighteen hundred years and concomitant with the rise of Christianity:

> Then was the serpent temple form'd, image of infinite
> Shut up in finite revolutions, and man became an Angel;
> Heaven a might circle turning; God a tyrant crown'd.[17]

The moral suasion of state religion binds Europe in an iron cage of discipline and repression whose tenets are revealed in a sermon:

> Go! Tell the Human race that Woman's love is Sin!
> That an Eternal life awaits the worms of sixty winters
> In an allegorical abode where existence hath never come:
> Forbid all Joy, & from her childhood shall the little female
> Spreads nets in every secret path.[18]

The repression of women is most acute because their sexuality, if left unrestrained, can topple the patrilineal system of property and inheritance enshrined in Europe's class system.

In a type of visionary wish-fulfillment, Blake sends the revolution first to Albion, where Orc mounts an assault against the core institutions of this system, its "Churches, Palaces, and Towers."[19] With its Angels immolated and the Guardian of state crumbling, Urizen comes to Albion's aid baring the holy books of empire, a clear reference to the Bible and missionizing, and readying the "trump of the last doom,"[20] a reference to the seven trumpets in Revelation that signal the Last Judgment. However, Orc reveals that Revelation, the final act in the Bible, is also the final trump in a doctrine of myths and lies used to quell resistance to the system. As this last desperate gambit fails to staunch Orc's revolutionary flames, Newtonian science comes to the aid of religion, demonstrating Blake's contention that empiricism is yet another form of false consciousness. Blake disputes the Newtonian theory of sensory perception, which holds that only "Five windows light the cavern'd Man,"[21] but also the Cartesian theory of time-space and individuated subjectivity that subtends this position. Newton ultimately fails to squelch the revolution. Albion is freed from Urizen's tyranny as "the night of holy shadows / And human solitude is past,"[22] signifying the end of false religion and science, respectively. As with the liberation of America, the success of the revolution is marked by the loosening of the chains of sexual repression. The Orcish revolution turns next to "the vineyards of red France" where "appear'd the light of his fury."[23]

The Song of Los provides an overview of Blake's theory of the fall and vision of an eventual redemption. The narrative is recounted by Los, the mythic bard-like creator of humanity, whose being defies myths of distinct national origin and stresses the common origin of all nations. The first part, "Africa," takes place in the cradle of humanity and describes the fateful events leading up to the fall. Upturning convention, Blake traces the fall of humanity not to the temptations of the serpent in Paradise, but to the handing down of God's law to the nations. This marks the beginning of Urizen's usurpation of power, which creates an oppressive imbalance that places reason over desire, mind over body, control over freedom. Blake traces the major religious, political and philosophic systems of Western and Eastern traditions to this fateful event, revealing that they form a global system of oppression.

Urizen's usurpation requires the repression of Orc, who represents the qualities of equality, freedom, and sensuality suppressed by the Urizenic order. Blake uses the Promethean image of Orc howling on Mount Atlas "chain'd down with the Chain of Jealousy"[24] to symbolize the inner repression and imbalance generated by the fall. To contain Orc's influence, the guardians and beneficiaries of Urizenic civilization variously portray Orc as an evil demon or devil. This allows them to proscribe the values associated with him, which, if allowed to spread, could unleash a tide of revolutionary ferment that would destroy their order. In addition, churches, hospitals, castles, and palaces—the spatial coordinates of power—have been built to police and contain any outbursts of Orcish revolutionary energy. They operate "Like nets & gins & traps to catch the joys of Eternity."[25]

Trapped in the finitude of the shackled mind, peering out in despair through the windows of the five senses, Blake describes how the human body and the body politic are hopelessly bound and prostrate before the will of Urizen, whose empire extends across the earth:

> Clouds roll heavy upon the Alps round Rousseau & Voltaire:
> And on the mountains of Lebanon round the deceased Gods
> Of Asia; & on the desarts of Africa round the Fallen Angels
> The Guardian Prince of Albion burns in his nightly tent.[26]

But the thick, rolling clouds above Europe rise from the flames of revolution, which soon will blow towards Africa and Asia as well.

In the second part of the song, Blake depicts the spreading of the revolution from West to East as Orc departs from "European darkness"[27] to fan the flames of revolutionary desire in Asia. The "Kings of Asia" scramble to their posts in defense of the Urizenic order, but the traditional controls of law and religion are unable to contain the outbreak of Orc's "thought-creating fire."[28] The "allegoric riches,"[29] a biting reference to the religious superstitions that promise riches in Heaven in exchange for obedience on Earth, lose their grip over the minds of the poor as they begin to join the conflagration. Urizen must intervene directly to save his empire. The fact that he departs from his throne in Europe symbolizes the colonial system of power, which extends from European capitals to their subjugated colonies across the globe. Just as in the West, however, Urizen is unable to staunch the flames of revolution. His "Books of brass iron & gold / Melted over the land as he flew,"[30] symbolizing the breaking of the mental shackles of religious and secular law. Defeated, Urizen returns weeping to the "woven darkness above,"[31] a paradoxical allusion to the heavens that belies its false enlightenment. Conversely, Blake describes the advent of true enlightenment on Earth as the liberation of Asia completes the global revolution. The revolution once again brings with it the removal of sexual prohibitions as "all flesh naked stands."[32] But the ultimate victory of the revolution is marked by the laying to rest of the Christian bogeymen of Sin and Death, which leaves behind a grave that "swells with wild desire."[33] In the finale to his vision of global revolution, Blake alludes to Golden-Age imagery to signify the restoration of a pre-lapsarian paradise:

> And milk & blood & glandous wine
> In rivers rush & shout & dance,
> On mountain, dale and plain.[34]

Far from the jingoistic ascriptions made by bardic critics, the continental prophecies reveal Blake to be a forward-thinking radical visionary who anticipated the egalitarian internationalism that would gain prominence a century later. Ironically, this vision recurs most poignantly in *Milton*, the very text erroneously interpreted by Wingfield-Stratford and other bardic critics as incontrovertible evidence of Blake's allegiance to jingoistic nationalism and empire. In *Milton*, Blake wonders, "When shall Jerusalem return & overspread all the Nations."[35] With the revolutionary millenarian backdrop of the earlier prophecies firmly in place, the radical import of this query becomes clear: "Jerusalem" is not a slogan for British nationalism and imperialism, but a metaphor for a utopian social order premised on egalitarian internationalism.

***

Throughout this study, I have argued that the structure of feeling of Romantic poetry propagated nationalism, which was the dominant form of political and cultural affiliation in the two centuries following the first Act of Union. Bardic critics aided and abetted this process by reimagining the inspired, solitary poet as a national bard and *vox populi*. Yet, the continental prophecies highlight the existence of a subtle, but profound counter-discourse to nationalism and empire in the Romantic period. Blake and the other Romantic poets who espoused a utopian vision of internationalism or championed counter-patriotism in their poetry demonstrate that nationalism was neither monolithic nor as ideal as its adherents made it out to be. The nationalist belief in an imagined community premised on longstanding ethnic ties and held together with the virtuous bond of citizenship and patriotic duty obscured the reality of internal conflict, inequality, and oppression, and gave ideological cover to war and conquest. While the ideals of internationalism would not come to political fruition for another century, these Romantic visionaries at least were able to see beyond nationalism and imagine alternatives. In so doing, they complicated prevailing notions about nationalism and helped to establish a basis for later critiques.

Chapter Notes

Introduction

1. Samuel Taylor Coleridge, "Fears in Solitude," in *Samuel Taylor Coleridge: The Complete Poems*, ed. William Keach (New York: Penguin Classics, 1997), lines 154–5. All poetry citations for the rest of the study refer to line numbers unless otherwise indicated.
2. M.H. Abrams, *Natural Supernaturalism: Tradition and Revolution in Romantic Literature* (New York: W.W. Norton, 1973), 14.
3. Coleridge, "Fears in Solitude," *Complete Poems*, 154.
4. Wordsworth, Preface, in *Lyrical Ballads*, ed. R.L. Brett and A.R. Jones, 2d ed. (New York: Routledge, 1991), 241, 255.
5. Marilyn Butler's essay "Romanticism in England" categorizes expressions of nationalism in English literature from the country movement to the late Romantics. Peter Ackroyd's *Albion: The Origins of the English Imagination* is also worth mentioning because he observes some English characteristics of British Romanticism. Furthermore, there are important studies of literary nationalism in England prior to the formation of Great Britain that provide helpful background material for this study. For instance, Richard Helgerson's *Forms of Nationhood: The Elizabethan Writing of England* relies on the historical work of G.R. Elton (see *The Tudor Revolution in Government: Administrative Changes in the Reign of Henry VIII*) to argue that a generation of English vernacular poets, all born between 1551 and 1564, were the first to cultivate English nationalism. Conversely, Gillian E. Brennan's *Patriotism, Power and Print: National Consciousness in Tudor England* takes issue with Elton's work and challenges Helgerson's claim to an early modern nationalism consciously identified with the state, contending that the Elizabethan monarchy was apprehensive toward patriotism because it was a spur for anti-monarchic nationalism rather than a prop for a supposed early modern nation-state. On this note, Brennan relates that the term "patriot" was associated with liberal or radical criticism of the court throughout the eighteenth century, and it wasn't until popular reaction to the French Revolution that the word finally came to have the conservative connotation of loyalty to the state. See Marilyn Butler, "Romanticism in England," in *Romanticism in National Context*, ed. Roy Porter and Mikulas Teich (New York: Cambridge University Press, 1988), 37–67; Peter Ackroyd, *Albion: The Origins of the English Imagination* (Norwell, MA: Anchor Press, 2004), 447–53; Richard Helgerson, *Forms of Nationhood: The Elizabethan Writing of England* (Chicago: University of Chicago Press, 1995); and Gillian E. Brennan, *Patriotism, Power and Print: National Consciousness in Tudor England* (Pittsburgh: Duquesne University Press, 2003).
6. Katie Trumpener, *Bardic Nationalism* (Princeton: Princeton University Press, 1996), 6.
7. Anne Frey, *British State Romanticism: Authorship, Agency, and Bureaucratic Nationalism* (Palo Alto: Stanford University Press, 2009), 12.
8. David Aram Kaiser, *Romanticism, Aesthetics, and Nationalism* (New York: Cambridge University Press, 1999), 3.
9. Yoon Sun Lee, *Nationalism and Irony: Burke, Scott, Carlyle* (New York: Oxford University Press, 2004), 6.
10. Suvir Kaul, *Poems of Nations, Anthems of Empire: English Verse in the Long Eighteenth Century* (Charlottesville: University of Virginia Press, 2000), 132, emphasis original.
11. Anthony D. Smith, *Ethnic Origins of Nations* (Malden, MA: Blackwell, 1999), 13.
12. Ernest Renan, "What Is a Nation?" in

Becoming National: A Reader, ed. Geoff Eley and Ronald Grigor Suny (New York: Oxford University Press, 1996), 43, 45.

13. Benedict Anderson, *Imagined Communities* (New York: Verso, 1991), 5–7.

14. See Michel Foucault's *Security, Territory, Population: Lectures at the Collège de France, 1977–1978*, ed. Michel Senellart, trans. Graham Burchell (New York: Palgrave Macmillan, 2004).

15. Homi K. Bhabha, *Nation and Narration* (New York: Routledge, 1990), 1, 3.

16. Linda Colley, *Britons: Forging the Nation, 1707–1837* (New Haven: Yale University Press, 1992), 5. A distinguishing feature of Colley's argument is that British nationalism sprang from popular sentiment rather than from state intervention. She writes, "It would be wrong, then, to interpret the growth of British national consciousness in this period in terms of a new cultural and political uniformity being resolutely imposed on the peripheries of the island by its center" (373). Many critics have taken issue with this bottom-up view of the provenance of British nationalism. For instance, Anne Frey critiques Colley's contention that national identity arose among the populace, demonstrating instead that her coordinates (anti–Gallicanism, anti–Catholicism, and colonialism) had corresponding state agencies (the Anglican Church, the courts, and the East-India Company) that propagated loyalty to the state. Laurence Brockliss, David Eastwood, and Michael John warn not to "confuse a patriot rhetoric of Britishness, forged or deployed in wartime, with a pervasive or persistent sense of Britishness as a primary or normative identity" and suggest that Parliament held together a heterogeneous nation by providing "a political framework through which differences could be accommodated or contested." J.E. Cookson contends that the outlook of militias was local rather than national, and that economic opportunism rather than patriotism motivated the poor to volunteer for military service. While I join with others in challenging Colley's paradigm because it minimizes the nurturing and, at times, overt role played by the British state apparatus in promoting nationalism, this criticism does not invalidate her nuanced explanation of how the dynamics of British imperialism to a large degree fostered a sense of British nationalism in the public. Frey, *British State Romanticism*, 11; Laurence Brockliss, David Eastwood, and Michael John, "From Dynastic Union to European State: The European Experience," in *A Union of Multiple Identities: The British Isles, c. 1750–c. 1850*, ed. Laurence Brockliss and David Eastwood (Manchester: Manchester University Press, 1997), 193, 195; and J.E. Cookson, *The British Armed Nation, 1793–1815* (New York: Clarendon Press, 1997), 9.

17. Colley, *Britons*, 5.

18. Tom Nairn, among others, has investigated the post–World War II phenomenon of the cultural dissolution of "Britishness" and the resurgence of Scottish and Welsh counter-nationalism. In *The Break-up of Britain: Crisis and Neo-Nationalism*, Nairn suggests that Britain's imperial decline after World War II generated a crisis of identity, exacerbating the ethnic fractures that had always lain just beneath the surface of British society during its imperial heyday. He explains that the rise of the EU as an alternate formation to a British nation-state has provided a viable political alternative for counter-nationalist sentiment within Britain. Tom Nairn, *The Break-up of Britain: Crisis and Neo-Nationalism*, 2d ed. (London: Verso, 1981). See also Tom Nairn, *After Britain: New Labour and the Return of Scotland* (London: Granta Books, 2000); Raphael Samuel, ed., *Patriotism: The Making and Unmaking of British Identity*, 3 vols. (London: Routledge, 1989); Peter Hitchens, *The Abolition of Britain: From Winston Churchill to Princess Diana* (San Francisco: Encounter Books, 2000); and Andrew Marr, *The Day Britain Died* (London: Profile Books, 2000), later turned into a BBC documentary. For a survey of this literature, see also Stuart Ward's "The End of Empire and the Fate of Britishness" in *History, Nationhood and the Question of Britain*, ed. Helen Brocklehurst and Robert Phillips (New York: Palgrave Macmillan, 2004).

19. Jean Roemer in his 1888 study of the English language, *Origins of the English People and of the English Language* (New York: D. Appleton, 1888) speculates that the word originates from the Iberian Peninsula and was later transferred to the Greeks by Punic mariners. This origin of the word concurs with recent scientific studies that demonstrate a strong genetic link between the Celtic-descended populations of modern Scotland, Wales, and Ireland and the Iberian-descended populations of Spain, Portugal, and parts of France. See Bryan Sykes, *Blood of the Isles: Exploring the Genetic Roots of Our Tribal History* (New York: Bantam Press, 2006) and Stephen Oppenheimer, *The Origins of the British: A Genetic Detective Story: The Surprising Roots of the English, Irish, Scottish, and Welsh* (New York: Carroll & Graf, 2006) for compelling evidence that supports this genetic link.

20. Cited in "Briton," Oxford English Dictionary, accessed June 21, 2013, http://www.oed.com.lib2.bmcc.cuny.edu/view/Entry/23468?redirectedFrom=briton#eid.

21. Michael Hechter, *Internal Colonialism:*

The Celtic Fringe in British National Development, 1536–1966 (London: Routledge, 1975), 8–11.

22. Krishan Kumar, *The Making of English National Identity* (Cambridge: Cambridge University Press, 2003), 1.

23. Ibid., 35.

24. Porter, "'Who Talks of My Nation?' The Role of Wales, Scotland, and Ireland in Constructing 'Englishness,'" in *Imagined States: Nationalism, Utopia and Longing in Oral Cultures*, ed. Luisa Del Giudice and Gerald Porter (Logan: Utah State University Press, 2001), 102. There are many studies of English nationalism not mentioned here. They include Anthony Easthope's *Englishness and National Culture* (New York: Routledge, 1999), which begins with the hypothesis that "the English tradition is essentially *empiricist*" (ix, emphasis original); Paul Langford's *Englishness Identified: Manners and Characters, 1650–1850* (New York: Oxford University Press, 2000), which categorically describes several identifying characteristics of Englishness—Energy, Candor, Decency, Taciturnity, Reserve, and Eccentricity; Kathleen Wilson's *The Island Race: Englishness, Empire and Gender in the Eighteenth Century* (New York: Routledge, 2003), which challenges the notion that "British" and "English" can be conceived in such discrete categories because Britain's growing empire greatly affected English perceptions of themselves (15–6); and Gerald Newman's *The Rise of English Nationalism: A Cultural History, 1740–1830*, rev. ed. (New York: St. Martin's Press, 1997).

25. Thomas F. Bonnell, *The Most Disreputable Trade: Publishing the Classics of English Poetry, 1765–1810* (New York: Oxford University Press, 2008), 7.

26. Ibid., 1.

27. John Brewer, *The Pleasures of the Imagination: English Culture in the Eighteenth Century* (New York: Farrar, Straus and Giroux, 1997), xvi–xvii.

28. Terry Eagleton, *The Ideology of the Aesthetic* (Malden, MA: Blackwell, 1990), 28. The German philosopher Alexander Baumgarten coined the term "aesthetics" in the 1750s to describe the affective qualities of the mind; afterwards, a proliferation of aesthetic theories followed that attempted to map subjectivity onto space with categories like the sublime, beautiful, picturesque, and oriental. However, the pleasure-pain principle in John Locke's *An Essay Concerning Human Understanding* (1690) and the discourse on the pleasures of the imagination in Joseph Addison and Richard Steele's *Spectator* (1712, nos. 411–21) and Mark Akenside's essay "The Pleasures of the Imagination" (1744) had already begun to investigate qualities that would later be categorized as "aesthetic."

29. Thomas Carlyle, *On Heroes, Hero-Worship and the Heroic in History*, ed. Carl Niemeyer (Lincoln: University of Nebraska Press, 1966), 114.

30. Trumpener's *Bardic Nationalism* explores the relevance of Scott's novels for national culture. Other notable studies of Scott and nationalism include Alyson Bardsley's "In and Around the Borders of the Nation in Scott's Guy Mannering," *Nineteenth-Century Contexts* 24, no. 4 (2002): 397–415; Andrew Lincoln's "Walter Scott and the Birth of the Nation," *Romanticism: The Journal of Romantic Culture and Criticism* 8, no. 1 (2002): 1–17; Charlotte Sussman's "The Emptiness at the Heart of Midlothian: Nation, Narration, and Population," *Eighteenth-Century Fiction* 15, no. 1 (2002): 103–26; Craig Cairns's "Scott's Staging of the Nation," *Studies in Romanticism* 40, no. 1 (2001): 13–28; Carolyn F. Austin's "Home and Nation in the Heart of Midlothian," *SEL: Studies in English Literature, 1500–1900* 40, no. 4 (2000): 621–34; and Yoon Sun Lee's "A Divided Inheritance: Scott's Antiquarian Novel and the British Nation" *ELH* 64, no. 2 (1997): 537–67. A broader study of the impact of novelistic prose upon British culture and subjectivity can be found in two classic and seminal studies: Ian Watt's *The Rise of the Novel* (repr. Berkeley: University of California Press, 2001) and Michael McKeon's *The Origins of the English Novel, 1600–1740* (repr. Baltimore: Johns Hopkins University Press, 2002).

31. Mark Rose acknowledges the seminal role of Romantic ideas about authorhood in the invention of copyright: "Copyright is founded on the concept of the unique individual who creates something original and is entitled to reap a profit from those labors. Until recently, the dominant modes of aesthetic thinking have shared the romantic and individualistic assumptions inscribed in copyright." Mark Rose, *Authors and Owners: The Invention of Copyright* (Cambridge: Harvard University Press, 1993), 2.

32. Karl Marx and Frederick Engels, *The Communist Manifesto*, introd. Eric Hobsbawm (New York: Verso, 2001), 37.

33. Theodor W. Adorno, "Lyric Poetry and Society," in *Critical Theory and Society: A Reader*, ed. Stephen Eric Bronner and Douglas MacKay Kellner (New York: Routledge, 1989), 56.

34. Matthew Arnold, "The Study of Poetry," in *The Complete Prose Works*, ed. R.H. Super (Ann Arbor: University of Michigan Press, 1973), 9:161–2.

35. John Stuart Mill, *Autobiography* (1873; New York: Penguin, 1989), 121.

36. Thomas Percy, *Reliques of Ancient English Poetry*, ed. Henry B. Wheatley (1765; New York: Dover, 1966), 1:346.
37. William Wordsworth, Preface, in *Lyrical Ballads*, ed. R.L. Brett and A.R. Jones, 2d ed. (New York: Routledge, 1991), 255.
38. Raymond Williams, *Marxism and Literature* (New York: Oxford University Press, 1977), 132.
39. The former are dealt with later in the chapter. In regard to urban planning, Romantic conceptions of nature are clearly evident in the "Garden City" designs of Ebenezer Howard. His designs became the basis for the modern suburbs, which were first built in Victorian England as a panacea for working-class people looking to escape from the alienation and muck of city life. The Garden City model has influenced suburban developments, city housing projects, and intentional communities for over a century.
40. Jerome McGann, *The Romantic Ideology: A Critical Investigation* (Chicago: University of Chicago Press, 1983), 1.
41. Ian Reid, *Wordsworth and the Formation of English Studies* (Burlington, VT: Ashgate, 2004), 43. Interestingly, Reid demonstrates that the same utilitarian impulse against which Wordsworth railed is also present in the poet's own writing, *The Prelude*. On this note, Reid cites Clifford H. Siskin, who has called *The Prelude* "the most famous resume in English literary history," and Thomas Pfau, who observes that *The Prelude* commodified the interiority of the middle-class subject. Reid, *Wordsworth*, 45. See also Clifford H. Siskin's "Wordsworth's Prescriptions: Romanticism and Professional Power," in *The Romantics and Us*, ed. Gene W. Ruoff (New Brunswick, NJ: Rutgers University Press, 1990), 303–21, and Thomas Pfau's *Wordsworth's Profession: Form, Class, and the Logic of Early Romantic Cultural Production* (Palo Alto: Stanford University Press, 1997).
42. Stephen Potter, *The Muse in Chains: A Study in Education* (London: Jonathan Cape, 1937), 135.
43. Alan Richardson, *Literature, Education, and Romanticism: Reading as Social Practice, 1780–1832* (New York: Cambridge University Press, 1994), xiii.
44. William St. Clair, *The Reading Nation in the Romantic Period* (New York: Cambridge University Press, 2004), 424.
45. Ibid., 422.
46. Ibid., 429.
47. Ian Michael, *The Teaching of English: From the Sixteenth Century to 1870* (Cambridge: Cambridge University Press, 1987), 236.
48. Fredric Jameson, *The Political Unconscious: Narrative as a Socially Symbolic Act* (Ithaca: Cornell University Press, 1982), 76.
49. Karl Marx, Preface to *A Contribution to the Critique of Political Economy*, ed. Maurice Dobb, trans. S.W. Ryazanskaya (London: Lawrence & Wishart, 1970), 21.

Chapter 1

1. Carlyle, *On Heroes*, 114.
2. Matthew Arnold, "Wordsworth," *Complete Prose*, 11: 54.
3. Lord Byron, "English Bards and Scotch Reviewers," in *Byron*, ed. Jerome J. McGann (1809; New York: Oxford University Press, 1986), 1:64.
4. Ibid., ll.340–1.
5. Maureen McLane, *Balladeering, Minstrelsy, and the Making of British Romantic Poetry* (Cambridge: Cambridge University Press, 2008), 5.
6. Arnold, "Function of Criticism at the Present Time," *Complete Prose*, 3:261.
7. Margaret Mathieson, *The Preachers of Culture: A Study of English and Its Teachers* (Totowa, NJ: Rowman && Littlefield, 1975), 11; Terry Eagleton, *Literary Theory: An Introduction*, 2d ed. (Minneapolis: University of Minnesota Press, 1996), 21.
8. Bernard Bergonzi, *Exploding English: Criticism, Theory, Culture* (New York: Clarendon Press, 1990), 28; Chris Baldick, *The Social Mission of English Criticism, 1848–1932* (New York: Oxford University Press, 1983), 16.
9. D.J. Palmer, *The Rise of English Studies* (New York: Oxford University Press, 1965), 29–40.
10. Brian Doyle, *English and Englishness* (New York: Routledge, 1989), 20.
11. Franklin E. Court, *Institutionalizing English Literature: The Culture and Politics of Literary Study, 1750–1900* (Palo Alto: Stanford University Press, 1992), 17.
12. Patrick Parrinder, *Authors and Authority: A Study of English Literary Criticism and its Relation to Culture, 1750–1900* (Boston: Routledge, 1977), 7.
13. See especially the first chapter of Robert Crawford's *Devolving English Literature* (New York: Clarendon Press, 1992); Franklin E. Court's *Institutionalizing English Literature*; Thomas P. Miller's *The Formation of College English: Rhetoric and Belles Lettres in the British Cultural Provinces*. (Pittsburgh: University of Pittsburgh Press, 1997); and the essays collected in *The Scottish Invention of English Literature*, ed. Robert Craw-

ford (New York: Cambridge University Press, 1998).

14. Court, *Institutionalizing*, 17–24.

15. For instance, Court notes that Thomas Dale, who was appointed the first professor of English language and literature at University College, London, in 1828, was a practicing minister who explicitly used literature to inculcate Christian values. Furthermore, he notes that David Masson, who took over as English Chair at University College, London, in 1852, was a racial philologist who taught English language and literature from the perspective of propagating a racialized nationalism. Court, *Institutionalizing*, 59–67, 132.

16. Robert Phillipson, *Linguistic Imperialism* (New York: Oxford University Press, 1992), 109. A useful critique of Phillipson's passage on Defoe is offered in Alastair Pennycook, *English and the Discourses of Colonialism* (New York: Routledge, 1998), 10–6.

17. Gauri Viswanathan, *Masks of Conquest: Literary Study and British Rule in India* (New York: Columbia University Press, 1989), 3.

18. Court, *Institutionalizing*, 136.

19. Eric J. Hobsbawm, *The Age of Revolution* (1962; New York: Vintage, 1996), 256.

20. For instance, the list includes notable works by Joseph Addison (1712), Francis Hutcheson (1725), David Hume (1757), Edmund Burke (1757), Alexander Gerard (1759), Lord Kames (1762), and Archibald Alison (1790).

21. According to Parrinder, eighteenth-century editions of Shakespeare's works were compiled by Rowe (1709), Pope (1725), Theobald (1735), Hanmer (1744), Warburton (1747), Johnson (1765), Capell (1768), Steevens (1773), and Malone (1790). Parrinder, *Authors and Authority*, 7.

22. Brewer, *Pleasures*, 473–83.

23. Eric J. Hobsbawm and Terence Ranger, eds., *The Invention of Tradition* (Cambridge: Cambridge University Press, 1992), 1, 4.

24. Arnold, "The Study of Poetry," *Complete Prose*, 9:161.

25. See Smith, *Ethnic Origins of Nations*.

26. See Hechter, *Internal Colonialism*, 8–11.

27. Stuart Piggott, *Ancient Britons and the Antiquarian Imagination: Ideas from the Renaissance to the Regency* (New York: Thames & Hudson, 1989), 140.

28. Ibid., 54. The popularity of flood narratives intensified with the work of Athanasius Kircher, a counter–Reformation scholar who in 1675 published a quasi-historical treatise on the flood, the Ark, and post-diluvian events (54). Piggott cites excerpts from contemporaries including Sir Walter Raleigh, Nathanael Carpenter, Sir Thomas Browne, Aylett Sammes, and Henry Rowlands to show how widespread was the belief in peopling by transplantation (61). While this originary myth fed speculations about how the ancient Britons were descended from the sons and grandsons of Noah, Japhet and Gomer, it was also used by these and other authors to justify colonial transplants in the Americas. The story goes that all lands to the west of the Biblical lands were peopled by Noah's Ark, including the Americas. The relative barbarity and primitiveness of the ancient Britons and indigenous Americans alike supported the belief in a "Westward degeneracy" of civilization (63). Following this ideology, the state of indigenous Americans could shed insight on the life of ancient Britons. Furthermore, modern Britons were obliged to spread their advanced civilization to their more primitive brethren to the west. The idea that Britons are descendants of the original Israelites informs the national myth that Britons are New Israelites inhabiting a New Jerusalem (73–85). The profound ramifications of this concept for British national identity will be explored in subsequent chapters on Providentialism.

29. Ibid., 36.

30. Ibid., 124–5.

31. The *Reliques* went through three editions in ten years (1765, 1767, 1775). A fourth edition appeared in 1794.

32. Despite accusations of forgery by Joseph Ritson and later antiquarians, Percy maintained that most of the 180 pieces collected in the *Reliques* were drawn from an MS folio that he recovered at an early age from his friend, Humphrey Pitt. A memorandum he wrote on the cover of the folio dated Nov. 7, 1769, relates the humorous tale of how he saved the MS from destruction: "This very curious old manuscript, in its present mutilated state, but unbound and sadly torn, &c., I rescued from destruction, and begged at the hands of my worthy friend Humphrey Pitt, Esq., then living at Shiffnal, in Shropshire, afterwards of Priorslee, near that town; who died very lately at Bath (viz., in summer 1769). I saw it lying dirty on the floor, under a Bureau in ye Parlour: being used by the maids to light the fire." Percy, qtd. in "General Introduction," *Reliques*, lxxxi-ii. However, subsequent scholarship has revealed that only 45 pieces came from the folio, and many of these were revised by Percy. The rest were extracted from other collections, including the Pepys Library's collection of broadside ballads and the *Collection of Old Ballads* (1723) attributed to Ambrose Philips. For editing decisions, Percy relied on correspondents like Sir

David Dalrymple (Lord Hailes), who himself contributed several of his own poems to the *Reliques*. Troubled by Percy's scholarship, Joseph Ritson published *Ancient Songs and Ballads from the Reign of King Henry the Second to the Revolution* (1790). The collection begins with an introductory essay, "Observations on the Ancient English Minstrels," in which he questions the authenticity of many ballads in the collection and contradicts many of Percy's claims concerning the history of English minstrelsy. This rivalry precipitates in the "Advertisement" to the first edition, which alludes to the dubious authenticity of Percy's selections: "The reader must not expect to find, among the pieces here preserved, either the interesting fable, or the romantic wildness of a late elegant publication [*Reliques*]. But, in whatever light they may exhibit the lyric powers of our ancient Bards, they will at least have the recommendation of evident and indisputable authenticity: the sources from which they have been derived will be faithfully referred to, and are, in general, public and accessible." Ritson was of the modern school of textual scholarship that preferred to present texts in their original, unedited format rather than artfully composing a single text from several variants, as Percy did. Ritson also faulted Percy for including and passing on imitation pieces as authentic relics. The extent of Ritson's disdain for Percy's scholarship can be measured by the stinging allusion to Percy implied in the conclusion to his essay, in which he hopes that the MS folio will one day be published in its original form by "an editor who prefers truth to hypothesis, and the genuine remains of the minstrel-poets, however mutilated or rude, to the indulgence of his own poetical vein, however fluent or refined" (xxxiii). The original MS folio was eventually published in three volumes as *Bishop Percy's Folio Manuscript: Ballads and Romances* (1868). Francis James Child published the definitive collection of 305 authentic English and Scottish ballads and their American variants in the ten-volume *The English and Scottish Popular Ballads* (1882–1898). Like Ritson, his approached stressed textual accuracy above aesthetic considerations, so he presented pieces with all their variants intact rather than compiling a single copy-text from several variants, as Percy did. While Percy's reputation among scholars has been much impugned since Ritson's criticisms, Nick Groom's recent study *The Making of Percy's* Reliques reopens the historical debate on Percy's scholarship by pointing out the difficulties Percy encountered while editing the *Reliques*, which included the lack of a reasonable copy-text, anonymous or unclear authors, and contradictory sources. For these reasons, Groom argues, "Percy himself was stuck between editing and authorship." Nick Groom, *The Making of Percy's* Reliques (Oxford: Clarendon Press, 1999), 13, 9.

33. In his brief Autobiography—included in John Gibson Lockhart's *Life of Sir Walter Scott* (1837–38)—Scott relates: "To read and remember was in this instance the same thing, and henceforth I overwhelmed my school-fellows, and all who would hearken to me, with tragic recitations from the Ballads of Bishop Percy. The first time, too, I could scrape a few shillings together ... I bought unto myself a copy of these beloved volumes; nor do I believe I ever read a book half so frequently, or with half the enthusiasm." Scott, qtd. in Alan Bold, *The Ballad*, The Critical Idiom (New York: Methuen, 1979), 41:9.

34. Sir Walter Scott, *Minstrelsy of the Scottish Border*, ed. T.F. Henderson (1802; repr. Detroit: Singing Tree Press, 1968), 1:38.

35. William Wordsworth, "Essay Supplementary to the Preface," in *The Prose Works of William Wordsworth*, ed. W.J.B. Owen and Jane Worthington Smyser (Oxford: Clarendon, 1974), 3:78.

36. As a point of clarification, the essay here mentioned appears in the appendix to the Dover edition used for this study. The 1966 Dover edition is a reproduction of the Swan, Sonneschein, Lebas, & Lowrey edition of 1886.

37. Percy, *Reliques*, 1:346.
38. Ibid.
39. Ibid., 1:346–7.
40. Ibid., 1:351.
41. Ibid., 1:347.
42. Scott, *Minstrelsy*, 1:18, 3.
43. Ibid., 1:8.
44. Ibid., 1:5.
45. Ibid., 1:6.
46. Ibid., 1:5.
47. Thomas Gray, "The Bard," in *Thomas Gray*, ed. Robert L. Mack (London: J.M. Dent, 1996), 3:3.148.
48. Maureen McLane, "Ballads and Bards: British Romantic Orality," *Modern Philology* 98, no. 3 (2001): 425.
49. Terence A. Hoagwood, *From Song to Print: Romantic Pseudo-Songs* (New York: Palgrave Macmillan, 2010), 6.
50. Erik Simpson, *Literary Minstrelsy, 1770–1830* (New York: Palgrave Macmillan, 2008), 1.
51. See Michael Gamer, *Romanticism and the Gothic: Genre, Reception, and Canon Formation* (New York: Cambridge University Press, 2000).
52. Steve Newman, *Ballad Collection, Lyric, and the Canon: The Call of the Popular from Restoration to the New Criticism* (Philadelphia: University of Pennsylvania Press, 2007), 1.

53. From a review of Thomas Campbell's *Specimens of the British Poets: With Biographical and Critical Notices, and an Essay on English Poetry*, 7 vols. (London: John Murray, 1819) in the *Edinburgh Review* (March 1819), reprinted in Francis Jeffrey, *Contributions to the Edinburgh Review*, 2d ed. (London: Longman, Brown, Green, and Longmans, 1846), 2:9.

54. Richard Hurd, *Letters on Chivalry and Romance* (1762; New York: Garland, 1971), 54.

55. Qtd. in Donald H. Reiman, ed., *The Romantics Reviewed: Contemporary Reviews of British Romantic Writers* (New York: Garland, 1972), 2:511; Ibid., 2:699; Ibid., 1:338.

56. Ibid., 1:65–6 and 2:784.

57. Ibid., 1:131.

58. Ibid., 1:338 and 2:760.

59. Coleridge, "To William Wordsworth," *Complete Poems*, 49.

60. Arnold, "The Study of Poetry," *Complete Prose*, 9:168.

61. Hurd, *Letters*, 76.

62. Campbell, *Specimens*, 1:15–6.

63. Carlyle, *On Heroes*, 114.

64. Arnold, Preface to *The Poems of Wordsworth*, *Complete Prose*, 9:55.

65. Arnold, "The Study of Poetry," *Complete Prose*, 9:161.

66. Pierre Bourdieu, *Language and Symbolic Power*, ed. John B. Thompson, trans. Gino Raymond and Matthew Adamson (Cambridge: Harvard University Press, 1991), 50, emphasis original.

67. Noah Webster, *American Dictionary*, qtd. in Albert C. Baugh and Thomas Cable, *A History of the English Language*, 5th ed. (Upper Saddle River, NJ: Prentice Hall, 2002), 347.

68. Samuel Johnson, *A Dictionary of the English Language* (London: Knapton, Longman, Hitch, Hawes, Millar, and Dodsley, 1755), 1:xvi.

69. Samuel Johnson, "Life of Milton," in *Lives of the English Poets*, ed. George Birkbeck Hill (1781; repr. New York: Octagon, 1967), 1:xvi.

70. Jack Lynch, *Becoming Shakespeare: The Unlikely Afterlife That Turned a Provincial Playwright into the Bard* (New York: Walker, 2007), 8. Don-John Dugas takes issue with the idea that the critics produced the tastes and opinions that turned Shakespeare into a national poet. Rather, he begins with the quite valid point that "performance had a far greater impact on the formation of taste in late-seventeenth-century England than either print or criticism." Don-John Dugas, *Marketing the Bard: Shakespeare in Performance and Print, 1660–1740* (Columbia: University of Missouri Press, 2006), 2. While I agree with Dugas's methodology, which views market forces as primary over scholarship in regards to the revival of Shakespeare's reputation, I don't think these two forces need be in contradiction. As Dugas points out, Shakespeare's plays were often revived and adapted for the stage after 1660 because they made money for theatre owners; however, most theatre goers—even intellectuals like Samuel Pepys—rarely asked or cared who the author was, but instead selected plays based on the actors or genre, much like today's modern audience (7–8). I suggest that this commercial transformation of taste in favor of Shakespeare is what prompted the conversion from stage to print and the subsequent critical reception of Shakespeare by name as the great benefactor of British drama. In other words, in a commodity system these two processes—consumption and criticism—are not always antithetical, as say the distinction between popular and high art, but rather can, in the case of Shakespeare, work in harmony to sort and select national poets.

71. John Dryden, "Essay," in *Dryden*, ed. Keith Walker, The Oxford Authors (New York: Oxford University Press, 1987), 110.

72. Samuel Johnson, "Preface to Shakespeare," in *The Works of Samuel Johnson* (New Haven: Yale University Press, 1958–2012), 7:90.

73. Ibid., 7:70.

74. Ibid.

75. Ibid., 7:62.

76. Ibid., 7:88 and 7:86.

77. Ibid.

78. Ibid., 7:88.

79. Ibid., 7:71–5.

80. Ibid., 7:81.

81. Ibid., 7:82.

82. Ibid., 7:83.

83. William Hazlitt, *The Spirit of the Age, or, Contemporary Portraits*, ed. Harold Bloom (1825; New York: Chelsea House, 1983), 47.

84. Ibid., 1–9.

85. Ibid., 151.

86. Ibid., 152.

87. Ibid.

88. Ibid., 153.

89. Ibid., 151.

90. Qtd. in Reiman, *Romantics Reviewed*, 2:415, emphasis original.

91. Ibid., 2:792–3.

92. Ibid., 2:845.

93. Ibid., 2:816.

94. Ibid., 2:612.

95. Hazlitt, *Spirit of the Age*, 152. On this point, Hazlitt contrasts Wordsworth to Shakespeare, whom he positively regards as "the least of an egotist of any body in the world" because of the negative capability expressed in his ability to draw life-like characters (160). Hazlitt expounds

his critique of Romantic egotism and consequent dramatic failure in his essay "Shakespeare" (1818): "The great fault of a modern school of poetry is, that it is an experiment to reduce poetry to a mere effusion of natural sensibility; or what is worse, to divest it both of imaginary splendor and human passion, to surround the meanest objects with the morbid feelings and devouring egotism of the writers' own minds" (331). Conversely, he praises Shakespeare's negative capability: "Each of his characters is as much itself, and as absolutely independent of the rest, as well as of the author, as if they were living persons, not fictions of the mind. The poet may be said, for the time, to identify himself with the character he wishes to represent, and to pass from one to another, like the same soul successively animating different bodies" (328).

96. Ibid., 163, 164.
97. Ibid., 155.
98. Ibid., 164.
99. William Hazlitt, "My First Acquaintance with the Poets," in *Selected Writings*, ed. Jon Cook (New York: Oxford, 1998), 224.
100. Ibid., 223.
101. Hazlitt, *Spirit of the Age*, 151.
102. Ibid.
103. Ibid., 154.
104. Ibid., 155.
105. Ibid., 156.
106. Carlyle, *On Heroes*, 1.
107. Ibid., 78.
108. Ibid., 80.
109. William Wordsworth, *The Prelude: 1799, 1805, 1850*, ed. Jonathan Wordsworth, M.H. Abrams, and Stephen Gill (New York: W.W. Norton, 1979), 7.302.
110. Carlyle, *On Heroes*, 105, emphasis original, and Wordsworth, "Tintern Abbey," *Complete Poems*, 50.
111. Carlyle, *On Heroes*, 114.
112. Ibid.
113. Ibid., 110.
114. Ibid., 114.
115. Ibid., 113.
116. In the introduction to *The Popular Education of France* (1861), entitled "Democracy," *Complete Prose*, vol. 2, Arnold defends the liberal idea of state-sponsored popular education against parochial and private education. He does the same in "Education and the State," *Complete Prose*, vol. 4, a series of two letters he wrote to the Pall Mall Gazette in 1865 expressing his disapproval of the Revised Code, which decreased funding for state schools.
117. Arnold, "A Guide to English Literature," *Complete Prose*, 8:238.
118. Arnold, "The Literary Influence of Academies," *Complete Prose*, 3:241.
119. Arnold, "On the Modern Element in Literature," *Complete Prose*, 1:20–2.
120. Ibid., 1:34, emphasis original.
121. Arnold, "The Function of Criticism at the Present Time," *Complete Prose*, 3:269.
122. Ibid., 3:267.
123. Ibid., and 3:262–3.
124. Ibid., 3:263.
125. Ibid., 3:262.
126. Ibid., 3:267.
127. Ibid., 3:261, emphasis mine.
128. Ibid., 3:283, emphasis original.
129. Ibid., 3:261.
130. Ibid., 3:263.
131. Arnold writes, "But, after all the criticism I am really concerned with,—criticism which alone can much help us for the future, the criticism which, through-out Europe, is at the present day meant, when so much stress is laid on the importance of criticism and the critical spirit,—is a criticism which regards Europe as being, for intellectual and spiritual purposes, one great confederation, bound to a joint action and working to a common result; and whose members have, for their proper outfit, a knowledge of Greek, Roman, and Eastern antiquity, and of one another. Special, local, and temporary advantages being put out of account, that modern nation will in the intellectual and spiritual sphere make most progress, which most thoroughly carries out this programme." Ibid., 3:284. This statement is consistent with Arnold's promulgation of comparative literature and European cosmopolitanism.
132. Ibid., 3:261.
133. Arnold, "The Study of Poetry," *Complete Prose*, 9:161.
134. Ibid., 9:175.
135. Arnold, "Milton," *Complete Prose*, 11:332 and 11:333.
136. Arnold, *The Poems of Wordsworth*, in *Complete Prose*, 9:55.
137. Richard Ohmann, *English in America: A Radical View of the Profession*, rev. ed. (Middletown, CT: Wesleyan University Press, 1996), xiii-lii, 66–91.
138. Ralph Waldo Emerson, "The American Scholar," in *The Essential Writings of Ralph Waldo Emerson*, ed. Brooks Atkinson (New York: Modern Library, 2000), 59.
139. Scholes records that the first endowed chair in English literature at an American university was created in 1804 with the Professorship of Oratory and Belles Lettres at Brown University. Graff explains that the shift to an elective system at Harvard in 1884 under the auspices of incom-

ing President Charles W. Eliot marked the rapid decline of classical studies as students overwhelmingly demanded courses in English literature; it also shifted priorities away from the traditional skills of rhetoric and oratory, which were suited to the pulpit, and towards composition and literature, which were suited to more modern, commercial and civic applications. Interestingly, Graff observes that Eliot's motivation for implementing the elective system was the desire to prepare a new cadre of national leaders. Despite an earlier start by private institutions, however, Penn State University, a public land-grant institution, was the first to appoint a Professor of American Literature with the hiring of Fred Lewis Pattee in 1894. Robert Scholes, *The Rise and Fall of English: Reconstructing English as a Discipline* (New Haven, CT: Yale University Press, 1998), 4; Gerald Graff, *Professing Literature: An Institutional History* (Chicago: University of Chicago Press, 1987), 10–11, 130.

Chapter 2

1. Wordsworth, Preface (1802), *Lyrical Ballads*, 255. All future references to the Preface are to the 1802 version. From here on, all citations from the "Advertisement," Preface, "Appendix on Poetic Diction," and the poems of *Lyrical Ballads* refer to *Lyrical Ballads*, ed. R.L. Brett and A.R. Jones, 2d ed. (New York: Routledge, 1991); all citations from other prose works by Wordsworth refer to *The Prose Works of William Wordsworth*, ed. W.J.B. Owen and Jane Worthington Smyser, 3 vols. (Oxford: Clarendon, 1974); all citations from *The Prelude* are from the 1805 edition unless otherwise stated and refer to *The Prelude: 1799, 1805, 1850*, ed. Jonathan Wordsworth, M.H. Abrams, and Stephen Gill (New York: W.W. Norton, 1979); and all citations from other poems by Wordsworth refer to *The Major Works*, ed. Stephen Gill (New York: Oxford, 2000) unless otherwise stated.

2. *European Magazine*, qtd. in Reiman, *Romantics Reviewed*, 2:511.

3. Coleridge, "To William Wordsworth," *Complete Poems*, 47.

4. Wordsworth, "Advertisement," 7.

5. From *European Magazine* (1819), *New European Magazine* (1822), *Monthly Repository* (1835), and *Eclectic Review* (1842), qtd. in Reiman, *Romantics Reviewed*, 2:511, 2:784, 2:699, and 1:401, respectively.

6. Hazlitt, *Spirit of the Age*, 151, and Arnold, "Wordsworth," *Complete Prose*, 11:54.

7. Kathryn Sutherland has argued that Wordsworth is indebted to Percy in two ways: "One is to the more vigorous and simple modes of expression made available by the ballad revival; the other is to Percy's description of the descent and character of the native English poet." Kathryn Sutherland, "The Native Poet: The Influence of Percy's Minstrel from Beattie to Wordsworth," *Review of English Studies* NS 33, no. 132 (1982): 414–5. Karl Kroeber's *Romantic Narrative Art* (Madison: University Wisconsin Press, 1960) examines the impact of the *Reliques* on several authors, including Wordsworth. See also Ted Olson, "Thomas Percy's Role in the Rise of Romanticism and in the Emergence of Modern Ballad Scholarship," *Publications of the Mississippi Philological Association* (1994): 120–5, which argues for a reassessment of Percy's contribution to European Romanticism and ballad scholarship.

8. Wordsworth, "Essay Supplementary to the Preface," 3:78.

9. Wordsworth, Preface, 318.

10. Percy, *Reliques*, 346.

11. Several studies have explored on the relationship between mapping, geography, and conceptions of the nation in Wordsworth's topographical writing. Michael Wiley in *Romantic Geography: Wordsworth and Anglo-European Spaces* (New York: St. Martin's, 1998) argues that Wordsworth is a "geographical poet" because his utopian conceptions of nature, solitude, and imagination are part of the complex mapping of an alternative geography that critiques British institutional landscapes and offers new strategies for realizing revolutionary hopes. Ron Broglio, writing about Wordsworth's Black Comb poems written in 1811 after a trip to the famous site where Captain William Mudge surveyed the southern extremity of Cumberland in 1807 and 1808 for the first ever national Ordnance Survey of Britain, argues that "cartography provides a visible cipher for nationalism." Ron Broglio, "Mapping British Earth and Sky," *The Wordsworth Circle* 33, no. 2 (Spring 2002): 70. James M. Garrett interprets Wordsworth's use of the "prospect view" in the Black Comb and 1816 commemorative poems as a mechanism for seeing beyond local affiliations to a broader national community. He writes, "The 'prospect view,' the novel, and the newspaper participate in the project of national formation by creating the sense of space and time needed to imagine a coherent community that transcends the local—that is, that transcends a community that an individual can see." He goes on to complicate this reading by tracing Wordsworth's fear that a "totalized vision of the nation ... would risk loss of perception of the

local." James M. Garrett, "Surveying and Writing the Nation: Wordsworth's Black Comb and 1816 Commemorative Poems," in *REAL: Yearbook of Research in English and American Literature*, ed. Brook Thomas, Literature and the Nation 14 (Tübingen, Germany: Gunter Narr Verlag Tübingen, 1998), 77. Garrett's book-length study, *Wordsworth and the Writing of the Nation*, continues to pursue these themes in Wordsworth's writing, particularly in his poetry after 1815. Garrett uses Anderson's conception of the census, map, and museum as institutions of national invention to organize his study into the different modalities that Wordsworth uses to write his own story and that of the nation. What emerges is a depiction of the middle-aged poet as "a figure solicitous not just for his public identity as a poet but also for the purported identity of the nation." James M. Garrett, *Wordsworth and the Writing of the Nation* (Aldershot, UK: Ashgate, 2008), 8. Nahoko Miyamoto argues that Wordsworth places Grasmere at the center of national discourse, removing London and Windsor to the periphery. See Nahoko Miyamoto, "Wordsworth and Romantic Geography" (paper presented at the Graduate Student Conference in Romanticism, Emory University, Atlanta, April 12, 1996). Andrew Hazucha argues that Wordsworth's "subtle linking of foreigners with non-native plant species, and his distaste for both, suggest how thoroughly Wordsworth's nationalistic temper suffused his aesthetic pronouncement's about the Lake District's natural charms." Andrew Hazucha, "Neither Deep nor Shallow but National: Eco-Nationalism in Wordsworth's *Guide to the Lakes*," *Isle: Interdisciplinary Studies in Literature and Environment* 9, no. 2 (2002): 63. Benjamin Kim uses the *Guide to the Lakes* to illustrate how Wordsworth's theory of the sublime is "dissociated from a universal reason and instead tied to a national sensibility." Benjamin Kim, "Generating a National Sublime: Wordsworth's *The River Duddon* and *The Guide to the Lakes*," *Studies in Romanticism* 45 (Spring 2006): 52. On this subject, see also Christoph Bode, "Putting the Lake District on the (Mental) Map: William Wordsworth's *Guide to the Lakes*," *Journal for the Study of British Cultures* 4, nos. 1–2 (1997): 95–111. On the nationalism of Wordsworth's *Ecclesiastical Sonnets*, Jonathan Bate suggests, "It was not until the reading of Milton's sonnets in 1802 that Wordsworth found a medium in which to write directly about contemporary history and national identity." Conversely, Bate prefers to emphasize *Lyrical Ballads*' "private form" and notes a contrast between the "historical tales of battles and heroes" that typify nationalist-sounding ballads and the more mundane tone of Wordsworth's "seemingly inconsequential [ballad] narratives about idiot boys and old men digging at roots." Jonathan Bate, "Inventing Region and Nation: Wordsworth's Sonnets," *Swansea Review* (1994): 3.

12. The earliest major study on the influence of the popular folk ballad on Wordsworth is by Charles W. Stork, "The Influence of the Popular Ballad on Wordsworth and Coleridge," *PMLA* 29 (Fall 1914): 299–326. This was followed by a more extensive study by Paul G. Brewster, "The Influence of the Popular Ballad on Wordsworth's Poetry," *Studies in Poetry* 35 (October 1938): 588–618. Several decades later, Mary Jacobus's *Tradition and Experiment in Wordsworth's Lyrical Ballads (1798)* (Oxford: Clarendon, 1976) identified many ballad sources and analogs for Wordsworth's poetry, and Judith W. Page's "Style and Rhetorical Intention in Wordsworth's *Lyrical Ballads*," *Philological Quarterly* 62, no. 3 (1983) explored Wordsworth's intention to renovate English poetry by returning it to its folk origins in the ballad. More recent studies that address the relationship between Wordsworth and popular balladry include Richard Gravil's *Wordsworth's Bardic Vocation, 1787–1842* (New York: Palgrave Macmillan, 2003), Erik Simpson's *Literary Minstrelsy*, Maureen McLane's *Balladeering, Minstrelsy, and the Making of British Romantic Poetry*, and Steve Newman's *Ballad Collection, Lyric, and the Canon*. For studies on the influence of the broadside ballad on Wordsworth see especially F.W. Bateson, *Wordsworth: A Reinterpretation* (London: Longmans, 1956); Vivian de Sola Pinto, *The Common Muse* (London: Chatto & Windus, 1957); Albert B. Friedman, *The Ballad Revival: Studies in the Influence of Popular on Sophisticated Poetry* (Chicago: University of Chicago Press, 1961); Charles Ryskamp, "Wordsworth's *Lyrical Ballads* in Their Time," in *From Sensibility to Romanticism: Essays Presented to Frederick A. Pottle*, ed. Frederick W. Hilles and Harold Bloom (New York: Oxford University Press, 1965), 357–72; Carl R. Woodring, *Wordsworth* (Boston: Houghton Mifflin, 1965); G. Malcolm Laws, Jr., *The British Literary Ballad: A Study in Poetic Imitation* (Carbondale: Southern Illinois University Press, 1972); and Linda Venis, "The Problem of Broadside Balladry's Influence on the *Lyrical Ballads*," *SEL* 24 (1984): 617–32.

13. Gravil presents Wordsworth as a poet enmeshed in the antiquarian interests of his day and writes that there is "sublimation in Wordsworth's *oeuvre* of the antiquarian impulse that raged in the latter part of the eighteenth century." Gravil, *Wordsworth's Bardic Vocation*, 1. The

book ranges from early works like "Salisbury Plain" (1795) to later works like the *Ecclesiastical Sonnets* (1822) in order to illustrate Wordsworth's preoccupation with the ancient Welsh and British bards like Urien, Aneirin, Mryddin, and Taliesin. For instance, Gravil demonstrates that Wordsworth, Coleridge, and Southey drew upon the work of the Welsh antiquarian and self-styled bard, Iolo Morganwg (neé Edward Williams, 1747–1826). According to Gravil, Morganwg presented Coleridge a copy of his work, *Poems Lyric and Pastoral*, sometime between 1797–1798. Morganwg's poetic manifesto can be reduced to the following ancient Welsh triad, "*The three primary and indispensable requisites* of POETIC GENIUS *are, an* EYE THAT CAN SEE NATURE, *a* HEART THAT CAN FEEL NATURE, *and a* RESOLUTION THAT DARES FOLLOW NATURE" (44, emphasis original). We can clearly see the imprint of these ideas on the *esprit* of *Lyrical Ballads* and Wordsworth's later career.

14. Ibid., 8, emphasis original. For Gravil's reading of *Lyrical Ballads*, see Chapter 5 of *Wordsworth's Bardic Vocation*, "A Defence of the People, Part 2: 'The Pathos of Humanity,'" 92–114.

15. Trumpener, *Bardic Nationalism*, xi.

16. Ibid., 6.

17. William Wordsworth, *Guide to the Lakes*, ed. Ernest de Selincourt, 5th ed. (New York: Oxford University Press, 1984), 67–8.

18. Samuel Taylor Coleridge, *Biographia Literaria*, ed. James Engell and W. Jackson Bate, The Collected Works of Samuel Taylor Coleridge 7, Bollingen Series LXXV (Princeton: Princeton University Press, 1983), 2.14.6.

19. Ibid.

20. Wordsworth, "Advertisement," 7.

21. Ibid.

22. Wordsworth, Preface, 242, 243.

23. A review by Robert Southey in *The Critical Review*, 2nd Series (October 1798), qtd. in Wordsworth and Coleridge, *Lyrical Ballads*, 322.

24. A review by Dr. Charles Burney in *The Monthly Review* (June 1799), qtd. in Wordsworth and Coleridge, *Lyrical Ballads*, 324, emphasis original.

25. A review attributed to the Rev. Francis Wrangham in *British Critic* (October 1799), qtd. in Wordsworth and Coleridge, *Lyrical Ballads*, 327. The reference here is most likely to Erasmus Darwin's botanical treatise in verse, the *Zoönomia* (1794–6). In many ways, it epitomizes the grosser elements of eighteenth-century poetic diction with its turgid and florid style.

26. Wendell Harris writes that "1832 saw perhaps the first review other than J.G.M. Moultrie's 1820 essay hidden away in the *Etonian* praising Wordsworth for that for which he wished to be praised with almost no admixture of detraction." Wendell Harris, "Romantic Bard and Victorian Commentators: The Meaning and Significance of Meaning and Significance," *Victorian Poetry* 24, no. 4 (1986): 456. Echoing Wordsworth's complaint about the "pre-established codes of decision," Harris attributes the stinginess of reviewers to the fact that "most of this commentary either incontinently rushes to evaluate Wordsworth's poetry in terms of certain stated or unstated criteria, or analyzes it relative to some external structure of thought" (457–8). Harris's source for the reviews is N.S. Bauer's annotated *William Wordsworth: A Reference Guide to British Criticism, 1793–1899* (Boston: Twayne, 1978).

27. Wordsworth, "Essay Supplementary," 3:70.

28. Wordsworth, "It is not to be thought of that the Flood," 11–13.

29. Wordsworth, Preface, 242.

30. St. Clair, *Reading Nation*, 661. St. Clair notes that at a price of 5 or 6 shillings, the first edition sold 500 copies, the two volumes of the second edition sold 750 and 1000 copies, respectively, and the third edition sold 500 copies.

31. Ibid., 633, 653.

32. Michael, *Teaching of English*, 224–36.

33. Jonathan Bate, *Romantic Ecology: Wordsworth and the Environmental Tradition* (New York: Routledge, 1991), 113.

34. Wordsworth, Preface, 255.

35. Ibid., 241.

36. Ibid., 251.

37. Ibid., 261, 245–6.

38. Nigel Leask, "Burns, Wordsworth and the Politics of Vernacular Poetry," in *Land, Nation and Culture, 1740–1840: Thinking the Republic of Taste*, ed. Peter de Bolla, Nigel Leask, and David Simpson (New York: Palgrave Macmillan, 2005), 214.

39. David Simpson, *Wordsworth's Historical Imagination: The Poetry of Displacement* (New York: Methuen, 1987), 102–4.

40. Ibid., 103, 106.

41. Olivia Smith, *The Politics of Language, 1791–1819* (New York: Oxford University Press, 1984), 224.

42. Susan Manly, *Language, Custom, and Nation in the 1790s: Locke, Tooke, Wordsworth, Edgeworth* (Aldershot, UK: Ashgate, 2007), 105.

43. Wordsworth, "Essay Supplementary," 3:78.

44. Wordsworth, "Appendix," 318.

45. Ibid.

46. Ibid., 318–9.

47. Simpson, *Wordsworth's Historical Imagination*, 64.

48. Wordsworth, Preface, 249.
49. Coleridge, for instance, criticized the language of "The Thorn," a poetic experiment that Wordsworth admits "is not supposed to be spoken in the author's own person: the character of the loquacious narrator will sufficiently shew itself in the course of the story." Wordsworth, "Advertisement," 8. Coleridge rejoins, "But in a poem, still more in a lyric poem ... it is not possible to imitate truly a dull and garrulous discourser, without repeating the effects of dullness and garrulity." Coleridge, *Biographia Literaria*, 2.17:49. Coleridge particularly took issue with the following lines: "I've measured it from side to side: / 'Tis three feet long, and two feet wide." Wordsworth, "The Thorn," 32–3.
50. Wordsworth, Preface, 269.
51. For a concise review of the origin, style, and content of the ballad, see Bold, *The Ballad*.
52. Wordsworth, Preface, 252.
53. There are several studies on the implications of Wordsworth's use of common or plain language and its link to the ballads. Judith W. Page argues that "by returning to folk origins, Wordsworth begins his project to renovate English poetry with a form that predates the influence of French Neoclassicism on English taste." Page, "Style and Rhetorical Intention," 293. G. Malcolm Laws, Jr., suggests that Wordsworth's precedent for common diction is the broadside ballad rather than the popular folk ballads. He argues that Wordsworth's simple language is "the real language of men as that language was used in the broadsides," and that by using this language Wordsworth intentionally avoids "the artificialities of eighteenth-century poetic diction." Laws, *The British Literary Ballad*, 100. Concerned strictly with the power of plain English, or what he calls the "low register," David Rosen suggests that plain English has power because it is associated with truthfulness. He writes, "Plain English is itself the locus for several competing and probably incompatible ambitions that Wordsworth has for his work: to record the natural world faithfully, to speak with authority on national issues, to convey moments of uncanny but possibly meaningless power." Rosen's larger argument is that the Romantic turn to plain English continues through Modernism. David Rosen, *Power, Plain English and the Rise of Modern Poetry* (New Haven: Yale University Press, 2006), 1–2, 8.
54. Some ballad historians support the "communalist theory" of ballad origins, which holds that the popular ballads sprang from the collective and spontaneous song-making of common peasants. One finds this theory, for instance, in the Introduction to Francis B. Gummere's *Old English Ballads* (Boston: Ginn & Co., 1897). This theory serves to distinguish the spontaneous collective production of popular ballads from the production of broadside ballads, which is the work of individual minstrels or songwriters usually intended for sale or performance in the city. However, there is a debate among ballad scholars as to the viability of the "communalist theory," with some adhering to an "individualist theory" that attributes initial production to an individual, with the community playing a secondary role in the selection of variants and oral transmission. Cecil J. Sharp endorses this theory in *English Folk Song: Some Conclusions* (London: Simpkin & Co., 1907). Thomas Percy's ballad history is also premised on the individualist theory of origination.
55. Wordsworth, Preface, 258.
56. Ibid., 261.
57. The ascription of political, moral and social significance to the sensations of pleasure and pain was common among eighteenth-century philosophers who sought to locate in the senses a greater understanding of the mechanisms of behavior. Locke and Hume elaborated pleasure principles to help account for human behavior. See John Locke's *An Essay on Human Understanding* (1690) and David Hume's *An Enquiry Concerning Human Understanding* (1748).
58. Wordsworth, Preface, 246, 256. Gerald N. Izenberg explains the desire to portray oneself as qualitatively different from others as a Romantic reaction to the quantifying rationality of the Enlightenment that provided everyone with equal rights at the price of uniformity. He writes, "Now the individual that had thus become independent also wished to distinguish himself from other individuals. The important point no longer was the fact that he was a free individual as such, but that he was this specific, irreplaceable given individual.... The new individualism might be called qualitative, in contrast with the quantitative individualism of the eighteenth-century." Gerald N. Izenberg, *Impossible Individuality: Romanticism, Revolution, and the Origins of Modern Selfhood, 1787–1802* (Princeton: Princeton University Press, 1992), 4.
59. Wordsworth, Preface, 261.
60. Quintilian, *Institutio Oratoria*, 2.7:15, emphasis mine. Qtd. in Wordsworth and Coleridge, *Lyrical Ballads*, 124. The original Latin reads, "Pectus enim id est quod disertos facit, & vis mentis; ideoque imperitis quoquo, si modo sint aliquo affectu concitati, verba non desunt."
61. Wordsworth, Preface, 246.
62. Ibid., 261.

63. Ibid., 247–8.
64. Adorno, "Lyric Poetry and Society," *Critical Theory*, 155–71.
65. Wordsworth, Preface, 244.
66. Ibid., 245.
67. Coleridge, *Biographia Literaria*, 2:45; see also 2:40–57.
68. Wordsworth, *Guide to the Lakes*, 67–8.
69. Lore Metzger, *One Foot In Eden: Modes of Pastoral in Romantic Poetry* (Chapel Hill: University of North Carolina Press, 1986), xiv.
70. Annabel Patterson, *Pastoral and Ideology: Virgil to Valery* (Berkeley: University of California Press, 1987), 269.
71. Raymond Williams, *The Country and the City* (New York: Oxford University Press, 1975), 127–41.
72. Aira Kemiläinen, "Romanticist and Realistic Elements in Nationalist Thinking in the 19th Century," *History of European Ideas* 16, nos. 1–3 (1993): 309.
73. According to William A. Wilson, "Romantic nationalism is, by definition, a folklore movement." He writes, "The folk revival moved German literature away from the rationalism and cosmopolitanism of the Enlightenment ... and based it on the irrational and creative force of the people." William A. Wilson, "Herder, Folklore and Romantic Nationalism," *Journal of Popular Culture* 6 (1978): 832, 829.
74. Herder writes, "Every [nationality] carries within itself the standard of its own perfection, which can in no way be compared with that of others." Qtd. in Wilson, "Herder," 822. Wilson's citations of Herder are from the main collection of his works, *Sämmtliche Werke*, ed. Bernard Suphan, 33 vols. (1877–1913; repr. Hildesheim, Germany: Georg Olms, 1967–8). Subsequent references to Herder will refer both to citations in Wilson and to the corresponding volume and page numbers in the Suphan edition. This passage is from Suphan 14:227.
75. Herder writes, "Oceans, mountain chains, and rivers are the most natural boundaries not only of lands, but also of peoples, customs, languages, and empires; and even in the greatest revolutions of human affairs they have been the guiding lines and the limits of world history." Qtd. in Wilson, "Herder," 822; Suphan, *Sämmtliche Werke*, 13:37–8. See also Charles de Secondat Montesquieu, *De l'Esprit des Lois* (1748).
76. Giambattista Vico argued that Homer was not a real person but a composite of the Grecian people, and thus was a construction of their unique cultural expression. See Giambattista Vico, *Scienza Nuova* (1725), trans. Thomas G. Bergin and Max H. Fixch as *The New Science of Giambattista Vico* (Ithaca: Cornell University Press, 1968).
77. Qtd. in Wilson, "Herder," 825; Suphan, *Sämmtliche Werke*, 18:137.
78. Qtd. in Wilson, "Herder," 826; Suphan, *Sämmtliche Werke*, 9:532, 3:29, and 9:530.
79. See Herder's *Volksleider* (1778–9).
80. I'm thinking specifically of Heinrich Heine's "Die Lorelei," a German national treasure that incorporates ballad meter and folklore.
81. Donna Landry, *The Invention of the Countryside: Hunting, Walking and Ecology in English Literature, 1671–1831* (New York: Palgrave, 2001), 1.
82. Gerald MacLean, Donna Landry, and Joseph P. Ward, eds. *The Country and the City Revisited: England and the Politics of Culture, 1550–1850* (Cambridge: Cambridge University Press, 1999), 5.
83. For a comprehensive analysis and catalog of eighteenth-century social caricatures, see George Paston's *Social Caricature in the Eighteenth Century* (1905; repr. New York: Benjamin Blom, 1968).
84. Wordsworth, *Prelude* (1805), 7.158.
85. Ibid., 7.572–3.
86. Ibid., 7.689, 691–2.
87. Thomas West, *A Guide to the Lakes* (London: Richardson & Urquhart, 1778), 4.
88. The title page of the *Fortnight's Ramble* gives the author as "by a Rambler." Budworth subsequently changed his surname to Palmer.
89. Joseph Budworth, *Fortnight's Ramble to the Lakes in Westmoreland, Lancashire, and Cumberland* (London: Hookham & Carpenter, 1792), 223–4, 226–7.
90. Ibid., 227.
91. Wordsworth, *Guide to the Lakes*, 67–8, emphasis original.
92. Wordsworth, *Convention of Cintra*, 1: 238.
93. Wordsworth's reversal of center (London/Windsor) and periphery (rural countryside) is also the subject of Nahoko Miyamoto's "Wordsworth and Romantic Geography."
94. Wordsworth, *Prelude*, 2.31–3.
95. Wordsworth, Preface, 249.
96. Ibid. Wordsworth's characterization of the gothic as somehow foreign and alien is inaccurate: the earliest gothic romance is attributed to a fellow Englishman, Horace Walpole, who published *The Castle of Otranto* in 1764. Walpole initially tried to pass it off as an extant medieval manuscript, but admitted the hoax by the second edition. After Walpole, the literary gothic lapsed in England and inspired the works of German

Romantics, including the sensationally popular folk ballads of Gottfried August Bürger. Their popularity soon reached England and rekindled the craze for gothic novels, which were lucratively supplied by Ann Radcliffe and Matthew "Monk" Lewis. It is against these native "imitators" of the gothic that Wordsworth rails. For more on the origin and development of the gothic romance, see David H. Richter, *The Progress of Romance: Literary Historiography and the Gothic Novel* (Columbus: Ohio State University Press, 1996). Furthermore, see Michael Gamer's *Romanticism and the Gothic* for more on how there is, in actuality, a dialogic between "high" Romanticism and "low" Gothicism.

97. Ibid.

98. From Wordsworth's unpublished note written in 1842 for a manuscript of the poem "Thoughts Suggested the Day Following on the Banks of the Nith, Near the Poet's Residence." Cited in William Wordsworth, *The Fenwick Notes of William Wordsworth*, ed. Jared Curtis (Penrith, UK: Humanities-Ebooks, 2007), 345, n.128.

99. Wordsworth's reaction to cosmopolitan scenes of London city life is entirely consistent with Aira Kemiläinen's definition of Romantic nationalism as specifically a "reaction against 18th-century Cosmopolitanism" that used folksongs, folklore, customs, and national poetry to define an essential national identity. Kemiläinen, "Romanticist and Realistic Elements," 309.

100. Brewer, *The Pleasures of the Imagination*, xxi.

101. Ibid., xxii.

102. Charles Norton Coe argues that Wordsworth's interest in primitivism was nourished and informed by the travel books that he read. See Charles Norton Coe, *Wordsworth and the Literature of Travel* (New York: Bookman Associates, 1953), 43.

103. Stephen Parrish attributes Wordsworth's construction of an English pastoral golden age to his childhood memories in the English countryside. He writes, "If we think of the pastoral as a form which embodies nostalgic memories of an imagined golden age, of the idealized purity and nobility of a time and a race uncorrupted by civilization, we can find equivalent memories in Wordsworth. His idealization of the common rural people of Cumberland and Westmoreland—it caused some surprise among contemporaries who knew the peasantry better than he did—arose out of the deep impression made on his boyhood sensibilities by the solitary figures he met in his native hills." Stephen M. Parrish, "'Michael' and the Pastoral Ballad," in *Bicentenary Wordsworth Studies: In Memory of John Alban Finch*, ed. Jonathan Wordsworth (Ithaca: Cornell University Press, 1970), 60.

104. Wordsworth, "Last of the Flock," 71–4.

105. Wordsworth, *Prelude*, 8.393–4.

106. One can contextualize the coeval rise of aesthetic discourse and travel literature within a century of European and colonial wars that conditioned the rising British middle class to spend its discretionary wealth and leisure on domestic tours and summer estates in the country. More specifically, the forced assimilation of the Scottish border region following the last Jacobite rebellion (1745–6) and the accelerated enclosure of lands, which expedited the relocation of the traditional peasantry to newly developed urban worksites like Manchester, prepared the countryside for tourism and gentrification. These social and political developments find literary correlatives in texts like Burke's *A Philosophical Enquiry into the Origins of Our Ideas of the Sublime and Beautiful* (1759), which marks the growth of interest in topographical aesthetics, and in the vibrant and prodigious travel guides of the 1770s. This genre includes Thomas Gray's *Journal in the Lakes* (written 1769, published 1775); W. Hutchinson's *Excursion to the Lakes in Westmoreland and Cumberland* (1773); Thomas Pennant's *A Tour in Scotland* (1774–6); Arthur Young's *A Six Months' Tour through the North of England* (1778); Thomas West's *A Guide to the Lakes* (1778); William Gilpin's *Three Essays on Picturesque Beauty* (1786); James Clarke's *A Survey of the Lakes* (1789); John Housman's *A descriptive Tour and Guide to the Lakes* (1800); and Wordsworth's very own *Guide to the Lakes* (1811).

107. Wordsworth, "The Brothers, A Pastoral Poem," 216–19.

108. Ibid., 312–3.

109. Ibid., 309–10.

110. Ibid., 39, 311.

111. Ibid., 306.

112. Ibid., 41–3.

113. Ibid., 359.

114. Stephen Parrish writes about this in "'Michael' and the Pastoral Ballad," where he discusses Wordsworth's experimentation with the pastoral ballad in *Lyrical Ballads*. He provides a facsimile of the *Chirstabel Notebook* manuscript at the end of his essay. For more on this subject see also his chapter "The Ballad as Pastoral" in *The Art of the Lyrical Ballads* (Cambridge: Harvard University Press, 1973), 149–87.

115. Wordsworth, "Michael," 79, 40. This place is now the location of The Forest Side, a converted manor house serving as a popular inn just outside Grasmere. The ruins of Michael's fold

are believed to be just above The Forest Side on the slopes of Greenhead Gill.

116. Ibid., 246–7.
117. Ibid., 250, 267, 447.
118. Ibid., 451–6.
119. Ibid., 466, 475, 482.
120. Ibid., 37–9.
121. Wordsworth, "Heart-leap Well," 134, 64.
122. Wordsworth, "Lucy Gray," 60.
123. Wordsworth, "We Are Seven," 5. Arthur K. Moore offers a non–Christian explanation for the little girl's superstitious folk attitude. He writes, "The attitude of the child, as reported by Wordsworth, suggests the survival of non–Christian belief in continued existence within the grave, though the poet may not have been aware of this possibility." Arthur K. Moore, "A Folk Attitude in Wordsworth's 'We Are Seven,'" *Review of English Studies* 23 (1947): 260.
124. Wordsworth, "Advertisement," 8.
125. Wordsworth, "The Idiot Boy," 436.
126. Gottfried August Bürger, *Lenore*, trans. Dante Gabriel Rosetti (London: Ellis & Elvey, 1900), 89–90.
127. Wordsworth, "The Mad Mother," 80.
128. Timothy Fulford, "Fallen Ladies and Cruel Mothers: Ballad Singers and Ballad Heroines in the Eighteenth Century," *The Eighteenth Century* 47, nos. 2–3 (2006): 321. Fulford locates this motif, for instance, in Southey's "The Complaints of the Poor," which appeared in the *Morning Post* (June 1798).
129. Jacobus, *Tradition and Experiment*, 241. These themes are also present in two contemporary English works, John Langhorne's *Country Justice* (3 vols., 1774–77) and Richard Merry's *Pains of Memory* (1796).
130. Wordsworth, "The Thorn," 252–3.
131. Wordsworth, qtd. in Jacobus, *Tradition and Experiment*, 240–1.
132. Dorothy Wordsworth, *The Grasmere and Alfoxden Journals*, ed. Pamela Woof (New York: Oxford University Press, 2002), 149
133. Fulford, "Fallen Ladies and Cruel Mothers," 323. Fulford also suggests that some of Southey's concurrent ballads on forlorn and forsaken women were influenced by "The Cruel Mother."
134. Ibid., 329, n.38. A reprint of the poem can be found in Pepys, *Pepys Ballads*, 5:4.
135. David Herd, *Ancient and Modern Scottish Songs, Heroic Ballads, etc.*, (1776; Edinburgh: Scottish Academic Press, 1973), 2:237.
136. Fulford, "Fallen Ladies and Cruel Mothers," 323. Fulford attributes this knowledge of the dating and derivation of the poem to a private correspondence with Duncan Wu (329, n.39).

137. Wordsworth, qtd. in Helen Darbishire, *The Poet Wordsworth*, Clark Lectures (Oxford: Clarendon, 1949), 37–8. Darbishire admits to finding the transcription in an "early notebook." But she mistakenly attributes Herd's *Ancient and Modern Scottish Songs* to "*Hurd*," perhaps confusing David Herd for the Bishop Richard Hurd, author of another contemporary piece of antiquarianism, the *Letters on Chivalry and Romance* (1762).
138. The original by Bürger is titled "Des Pfarres Tochter von Taubenhain."
139. Jacobus, *Tradition and Experiment*, 243.
140. Ibid.
141. Anderson, *Imagined Communities*, 163–4.
142. Fiona Stafford, *Local Attachments: The Province of Poetry* (New York: Oxford University Press, 2010), 104. See Stafford's chapter "Local Attachments and Adequate Poetry" (96–134) for a more complete understanding of her critique of Wordsworth's poetry of place. In the introduction to the book, she links the rise of local attachments and provincial poetry in the Romantic period to eighteenth-century empiricism, which, because it substituted the value of personal experience for universal axioms, laid the foundation for challenging Neoclassical poetry, grounded as it was in Platonic ideal forms, by turning to a poetics rooted in local truths (21–26).
143. Arguing against most narratives of Wordsworth's middle-age and late poetry, Garrett contends, "Wordsworth's turn or return to the local was not a retreat from the politics of the nation, but a conscious attempt to redefine the nation along the lines of the local." Garrett, *Wordsworth and the Writing of the Nation*, 10.
144. See David Hartley, *Observations on Man, His Frame, His Duty, and His Expectations*, 2 vols. (1749; Gainesville: Scholars' Facsimiles & Reprints, 1966).
145. Wordsworth, Preface, 272.
146. Anthony D. Smith, *Myths and Memories of the Nation* (New York: Oxford University Press, 1999), 16.
147. Garrett, *Wordsworth and the Writing of the Nation*, 11.
148. Marlon B. Ross, "Romancing the Nation-State: The Poetics of Romantic Nationalism," in *Macropolitics of Nineteenth-Century Literature: Nationalism, Exoticism, Imperialism*, ed. Jonathan Arac and Harriet Ritvo (Philadelphia: University of Pennsylvania Press, 1991), 58, emphasis original.
149. Wordsworth, *Complete Poetical Works*, 54.
150. In 1244, the Scots threatened to invade England and King Henry III responded by fortifying the border region. Meanwhile, the English

Barons, led by the French-born Simon de Montfort, mounted a rebellion against the monarchy. They demanded an assertion of Magna Carta and greater baronial power. Henry's forces were defeated at the Battle of Lewes in 1264, and he was taken prisoner. Montfort's rebellion was eventually defeated at the Battle of Evesham in 1265, and vicious reprisals followed. The baronial rebellion was the closest England came to complete abolition of the monarchy until the Commonwealth of 1649–60. Certainly, for Wordsworth this period in English history resonated with the events of the French Revolution, which initially began as an uprising of the aristocracy against centralized monarchy from 1787–1788. The unintended murder of Baron Herbert by Marmaduke, his servant and would-be son-in-law, also alludes to King Henry's subjugation by the barons.

151. Wordsworth, *Guide to the Lakes*, 106.
152. Ibid., 91–2.
153. I am punning the phrase "national prospect" here to mean both something physical and something imagined.
154. See Barbara T. Gates, "Wordsworth's Use of Oral History," *Folklore* 85 (1974): 254–67 for more instances of local oral history that appear in Wordworth's poems and writings, and in Dorothy's journals.
155. Janowitz concludes her reading of *The Prelude* by emphasizing its peculiar merger of self and nation in and through nature: "The mutual making of nation and self is the climax of the poem. The reparative action of the Imagination and of its nationalist function are inseparable: here in native geography, the country answers the poets, for here 'had Nature lodged / The soul, the imagination of the whole' (1805, 13:64–5). To speak of nature is to speak of the nation: the fragments cohere into a whole, the ruin is repaired, and as the nation moves through each person, so each person moves through the nation." Anne Janowitz, *England's Ruins: Poetic Purpose and the National Landscape* (Cambridge, MA: Blackwell, 1990), 144.
156. Wordsworth, "Lines, Written with a Slate-pencil upon a Stone," 6, 1.
157. Wordsworth, "Lines, left upon a Seat in a Yew-tree," 12–13.
158. Wordsworth, "Tintern Abbey," 1–4.
159. Wordsworth, "Poems on the Naming of Places," 217.
160. Wordsworth, "It Was an April Morning," 47.
161. Wordsworth, "To Joanna," 28, 82, 30, 85.
162. Wordsworth, "A narrow girdle of rough stones and crags," 80.
163. Wordsworth, "To M.H.," 15, 23. The poem was written in December 1799, and the two married on October 4, 1802.

Chapter 3

1. Wordsworth, "Salisbury Plain," 541–5.
2. Wordsworth, "The Female Vagrant," 267–70.
3. Arnold, "Culture and Anarchy," *Complete Prose*, 5:112–13.
4. Wordsworth, *A Letter to the Bishop of Llandaff*, 3:43. Wordsworth wrote the letter in defense of the regicide and the ongoing French Revolution, against which the Anglican Bishop cast public aspersions. Britain's declaration of war with France earlier that year caused many proponents of the revolution to muzzle their support, and Wordsworth was no exception. The letter was never sent, but the manuscript still provides an invaluable source of evidence for Wordsworth's radical state of mind in this period.
5. The phrase "green language" is the title of a chapter devoted to Wordsworth's nature poetry in Raymond Williams's *The Country and the City*.
6. Wordsworth, "The Female Vagrant," 261.
7. Christopher Caudwell, *Illusion and Reality: A Study of the Sources of Poetry* (1937; repr. New York: International, 1963), 89–90, 93.
8. Gary Kelly, "The Limits of Genre and the Institution of Literature: Romanticism between Fact and Fiction," in *Romantic Revolutions: Criticism and Theory*, ed. Kenneth R. Johnston, et al. (Bloomington: Indiana University Press, 1990), 158. The bulk of Kelly's essay is concerned with how the Romantic revolution assimilated and qualified the existing genres of prose fiction to its new regime of literature. He argues that Romanticism replaced the two dominant modes of literature—literature as "a humanist institution of 'polite learning'" that served court culture and literature as "an Enlightenment institution of demystification and social criticism" that served middle-class culture—with a new mode that absorbed the extant oral and written traditions of language and refashioned them to represent and serve the interests of the middle class (158).
9. The following works come to mind: Jerome J. McGann, *The Romantic Ideology: A Critical Investigation* (Chicago: University of Chicago Press, 1983); Clifford H. Siskin, *The Historicity of Romantic Discourse* (New York: Oxford University Press, 1988); James K. Chandler, *Wordsworth's Second Nature: A Study of the Poetry and Politics* (Chicago: University of Chicago Press, 1984) and *England in 1819: The Politics of Literary Culture and the Case of Romantic His-*

toricism (Chicago: University of Chicago Press, 1998); Marjorie Levinson, *Wordsworth's Great Period Poems: Four Essays* (New York: Cambridge University Press, 1986); David Simpson, *Wordsworth's Historical Imagination*; Alan Liu, *Wordsworth: A Sense of History* (Palo Alto: Stanford University Press, 1989); Nicholas Roe, *Wordsworth and Coleridge: The Radical Years* (Oxford: Clarendon Press, 1990) and *The Politics of Nature: Wordsworth and Some Contemporaries*, 2d ed. (New York: Palgrave, 2002); Timothy Fulford and Peter J. Kitson, eds., *Romanticism and Colonialism: Writing and Empire, 1780–1830* (New York: Cambridge University Press, 1998); Timothy Fulford, *Romantic Indians: Native Americans, British Literature, and Transatlantic Culture, 1756–1830* (New York: Oxford University Press, 2006); and Peter J. Kitson, *Romantic Literature, Race and Colonial Encounter* (New York: Palgrave Macmillan, 2007).

10. McGann, *Romantic Ideology*, 1.

11. Ibid. Clifford H. Siskin's *The Historicity of Romantic Discourse*, Jonathan Arac's *Critical Genealogies: Historical Situations for Postmodern Literary Studies* (New York: Columbia University Press, 1987), and David Riede's *Oracles and Hierophants: Constructions of Romantic Authority* (Ithaca: Cornell University Press, 1991) also deal with the influence of the Romantic ideology on Romantic studies.

12. Jonathan Bate suggests that the Romantic tradition is consonant with an ecological viewpoint and that Wordsworth in particular exists in an "historical continuity of a tradition of environmental consciousness." Bate, *Romantic Ecology*, 9. Similarly, Karl Kroeber writes that the Romantics "were neither seekers after an unattainable transcendence nor anxiety-ridden prophets of nihilism but rather forerunners of a new biological materialist understanding of humanity's place in the natural cosmos." Karl Kroeber, *Ecological Literary Criticism: Romantic Imagining and the Biology of Mind* (New York: Columbia University Press, 1994), 2. James C. McKusick adds that the "new holistic paradigm" of the English Romanticism "offered a conceptual and ideological basis for American environmentalism." He concludes that the romantics were "the first full-fledged ecological writers in the Western literary tradition." James C. McKusick, *Green Writing: Romanticism and Ecology* (New York: St. Martin's, 2000), 11, 19. On the other hand, Timothy Morton has critiqued the ecocritical perspective by arguing that it valorizes a concept of Romantic "Nature" that is in fact "an arbitrary rhetorical construct, empty of independent, genuine existence behind or beyond the texts we create about it." In this sense, Morton treats Romantic "Nature" as part of the Romantic ideology that Romanticists uncritically accept. Tim Morton, *Ecology without Nature: Rethinking Environmental Aesthetics* (Cambridge: Harvard University Press, 2007), 22.

13. Michael Löwy and Robert Sayre, *Romanticism Against the Tide of Modernity* (Durham: Duke University Press, 2001), 1–56.

14. V.G. Kiernan, "Wordsworth and the People," in *Poets, Politics and the People*, ed. Harvey J. Kaye (New York: Verso, 1989), 96–128.

15. Ernst Fischer, *The Necessity of Art: A Marxist Approach*, trans. Anna Bostock (New York: Penguin, 1963), 52.

16. Eagleton, *Literary Theory*, 17.

17. Hobsbawm, *Age of Revolution*, 259.

18. Williams, *Country and the City*, 61.

19. Ibid., 132.

20. Ibid., 130.

21. Raymond Williams, *Culture and Society: 1780–1950* (repr. New York: Columbia University Press, 1983), 30.

22. Ibid.

23. Anne Janowitz, *Lyric and Labour in the Romantic Tradition* (New York: Cambridge University Press, 1998), 13, emphasis original.

24. Arnold, "Culture and Anarchy," *Complete Prose*, 5:112–3.

25. Qtd. in Mathieson, *Preachers of Culture*, 74.

26. Edward P. Thompson, *The Making of the English Working Class* (1963; repr. New York: Vintage Books, 1966), 194.

27. G.D.H. Cole, *A Short History of the British Working-Class Movement, 1789–1947* (London: George Allen & Unwin, 1952), 15.

28. Peter Linebaugh explains the process by which "the forms of exploitation pertaining to capitalist relations caused or modified the forms of criminal activity." Dispossession and unemployment created a huge surplus labor pool that subsisted by petty theft, beggary, and vagabondage, each of which became criminalized. At the Old Bailey courthouse in London, small property-holders regularly served as jurors in trials that sentenced working-class criminals to lengthy prison terms, removal to the colonies, or public execution. Linebaugh relates that a handful of men were hanged at Tyburn Tree every six weeks merely as "examples" for the rest, until it was finally decommissioned in 1783 in response to public outrage. Peter Linebaugh, *The London Hanged: Crime and Civil Society in the Eighteenth Century* (New York: Cambridge, 1992), xxi, 74.

29. Thompson, *Making of the English Working Class*, 198–9.

30. Friedrich Engels, *The Condition of the*

Working Class in England (1845; New York: Penguin, 1987), 62.

31. Duncan Wu, *Wordsworth: An Inner Life* (Malden, MA: Blackwell, 2004), 1.

32. Mary Moorman, *William Wordsworth: A Biography* (Oxford: Clarendon Press, 1957–65), 1:88.

33. Wordsworth, *Prelude*, 7.424–7.

34. Wordsworth, "An Evening Walk," 244–6.

35. Wordsworth narrates the story of this trip in Book Nine of *The Prelude*. Gone to Orleans ostensibly to learn French, he has an affair with Annette Vallon, who subsequently entices him to move to her family home in Blois. It's there in the Loire valley that Wordsworth meets and befriends Michel Beaupuy, a royal guard and member of the republican "Friends of the Constitution."

36. Wordsworth, *Prelude*, 9.519–20.

37. Ibid., 9.521–6.

38. Ibid., 9.123–6.

39. In addition to his exposure to the radical cauldron of the French Revolution, Wordsworth's class politics may have been influenced by Thomas Paine's *Rights of Man* (1790), Part Two of which focuses on economic rights by addressing the problem of poverty in England with liberal solutions that call for progressive taxation and social security.

40. Nicholas Roe explains that Wordsworth's reading of Godwin's *An Enquiry Concerning Political Justice* (1793) in 1794 motivated him to travel to London in 1795, where he met and corresponded directly with Godwin, Thelwall, and their associates in the London Corresponding Society, but that Wordsworth left this circle shortly thereafter, most likely over a philosophical falling out. Roe, *Wordsworth and Coleridge*, 176–7. The nature of this falling out is disputed by Edward P. Thompson. For more on this subject, see Roe's chapter "'A Light Bequeathed': Coleridge, Thelwall, Wordsworth, Godwin" in *Wordsworth and Coleridge*, 145–98, and Edward P. Thompson's chapter "Wordsworth's Crisis" in *The Romantics: England in a Revolutionary Age* (New York: New Press, 1997), 75–95. Roe further suggests that Wordsworth's interaction with Godwin influenced the publication of the *Philanthropist*, an oppositional journal that first appeared shortly after his trip to London. Roe and Thompson disagree over how much of the writing in the *Philanthropist* is creditable to Wordsworth, with Thompson taking the position that Wordsworth not only helped edit but also wrote substantial portions of the text (79).

41. It must be noted that Alfred Cobban has also discussed how the failure of the French Revolution leads Wordsworth closer to nationalism, though he stresses the elements of Burkean traditionalism in this nationalist turn. See his chapter "Wordsworth and Nationality" in *Edmund Burke and the Revolt Against the Eighteenth Century: A Study of the Political and Social Thinking of Burke, Wordsworth, Coleridge and Southey*, 2d ed. (London: George Allen & Unwin, 1962).

42. Wordsworth, "England! The time is come when thou shouldst wean," 11–14.

43. Wordsworth, "Composed in the Valley, near Dover, On the Day of Landing," 12–13.

44. Wordsworth, "September 1802," 13.

45. Wordsworth, *Convention of Cintra*, 1:280.

46. Ibid., 1:305.

47. Ibid., 1:323.

48. Ibid., 1:328.

49. Kenneth R. Johnston, "Wordsworth's Revolutions, 1793–1798," in *Revolution and English Romanticism: Politics and Rhetoric*, ed. Keith Hanley and Raman Selden (New York: St. Martin's, 1990), 171.

50. Contra Johnston, Edward P. Thompson maintains that Wordsworth remained an "'odious democrat'" until after the Peace of Amiens, and that the tension between "boundless political aspirations—for liberty, reason, *égalité*, perfectibility—and a peculiarly harsh and unregenerate reality" stimulated the creative impulse behind *Lyrical Ballads*, which subsequently waned in the following years as he became more conservative. Thompson, *The Romantics*, 94, 37. Carl R. Woodring puts forward a similar argument in *Politics in English Romantic Poetry* (Cambridge: Harvard University Press, 1970). Lore Metzger also takes a different position, arguing that the shift to radical aesthetics does not entail an abandonment of radical politics, but is instead a salutary adaptation of essentially revolutionary aims to a repressive political climate. Metzger writes that Wordsworth's "underlying commitment is to achieve reform through aesthetic imperatives and to bring about ... the social results of the French Revolution without a revolution." Lore Metzger, "Ideology: The Poetics of Schiller and Wordsworth," in *Sensibility in Transformation: Creative Resistance to Sentiment from the Augustans to the Romantics*, ed. Syndy McMillen Conger (Madison, NJ: Fairleigh Dickinson, 1990), 173. It is difficult to assess the veracity of this perennial claim, particularly in light of Wordsworth's vacillating allegiance to the French Revolution during the period of his formal experimentation.

51. Williams, *Country and the City*, 96.

52. Morton, *Ecology Without Nature*, 22.

53. Chandler, *Wordsworth's Second Nature*, xviii.

54. Wordsworth, Preface, 245.
55. Saree Makdisi, *Romantic Imperialism: Universal Empire and the Culture of Modernity* (New York: Cambridge University Press, 1998), 46, see also 23–69.
56. Ibid., 68.
57. György Lukács, *History and Class Consciousness: Studies in Marxist Dialectics*, trans. Rodney Livingstone (1923; Cambridge: MIT Press, 1999), 93.
58. György Lukács, "Realism in the Balance," in *Aesthetics and Politics: The Key Texts of the Classic Debate Within German Marxism*, ed. Fredric Jameson (New York: Verso, 1977), 36–7. "Realism in the Balance" was first published in *Das Wort* in 1938 as a rejoinder to Ernst Bloch's "Discussing Expressionism," in which Bloch defends Expressionism against accusations of reactionary politics by Lukács and his adherents. In "Realism in the Balance," Lukács explicates his critique of modernism and the *avant-garde* as the decadent outgrowth of the imperialist era and defends the vitality of social realism for progressive and Popular Front politics. For Lukács, realism is synonymous with popular art, which he conceives in conventionally nationalist terms as a genuine expression of the people.
59. Lukács, *History and Class Consciousness*, 89.
60. György Lukács, "The Ideology of Modernism," in *Marxist Literary Theory: A Reader*, ed. Terry Eagleton and Drew Milne (Oxford: Blackford, 2000), 150.
61. Lukács, *History and Class Consciousness*, 200.
62. Ibid., 157–8.
63. Wordsworth, *Prelude*, 7.601–2.
64. Ibid., 7.612–5.
65. Ibid., 7.616–20.
66. Ibid., 7.622–3.
67. Ibid., 7.624–5.
68. Ibid., 7.692.
69. Ibid., 7.696, 7.703–5, and 7.741.
70. "The Solitary Reaper" was first published in *Poems, in Two Volumes* (1807). A note included in *Poems* tells us: "This poem was suggested by a beautiful sentence in a MS. [manuscript] Tour in Scotland written by a friend, the last line being taken from it *verbatim*." The manuscript became Thomas Wilkinson's *Tours to the British Mountains* (1824), and the "beautiful sentence" is "Passed a female who was reaping alone: she sung in Erse as she bended over her sickle; the sweetest human voice I ever heard: her strains were tenderly melancholy, and felt delicious, long after they were heard no more." Thomas Wilkinson, *Tours to the British Mountains* (London: Taylor & Hessey, 1824), 12. Both Wordsworth and Wilkinson stress the feeling of beauty associated with the song, rather than the song itself. We know from Dorothy's memories of their 1803 Scottish tour that the poem was limned on 5 November 1803. See Dorothy Wordsworth, *Recollections of a Tour Made in Scotland* (1803; New Haven: Yale University Press, 1997).
71. Wordsworth, "Solitary Reaper," 25–32.
72. Keats coined the "egotistical sublime" in a letter to Richard Woodhouse, 27 October 1818. He writes, "As to the poetical Character itself … that sort distinguished from the Wordsworthian or egotistical sublime … it has no self—it is everything and nothing—It has no character … the camelion Poet … is the most unpoetical of anything in existence; because he has no Identity—he is continually in for—and filling some other Body." John Keats, *Selected Letters,* ed. Robert Gittings, revised John Mee (New York: Oxford, 2002), 147–8.
73. In a letter to George and Tom Keats, 21, 27 December 1817, Keats describes "negative capability" as a state of total anti-self-consciousness "when man is capable of being in uncertainties, Mysteries, doubts, without any irritable reaching after fact & reason." Keats, *Selected Letters*, 41–2. For Keats, Shakespeare is the premier "camelion Poet" who most approaches the ego-less state of "negative capability" in his uncanny ability to insert himself into myriad subject positions, social contexts, and eras. Patricia Ball describes the "egotistical and chameleon creative effort" as "the two poles of the Romantic imagination." Patricia M. Ball, *The Central Self: A Study in Romantic and Victorian Imagination* (London: Athlone, 1968), 2. Theresa M. Kelley takes issue with the description of the Wordsworthian sublime as "egotistical." She argues, "For most of his career Wordsworth was at least as suspicious of the sublime as Keats and Hazlitt were because, like them, he recognized that sublime transcendence might become little more than sublime egotism." She evokes Burkean and Tory values to explain how the "Wordsworthian beautiful opposes the willful self-aggrandizement of the revolutionary or Satanic sublime, advocating instead communicability and a sense of known limits in art as well as society." Theresa M. Kelley, *Wordsworth's Revisionary Aesthetics* (New York: Cambridge University Press, 1988), 2, 3.
74. Hazlitt, *Spirit of the Age*, 152.
75. Wordsworth, Preface, 246.
76. This point obviates Kurt Heinzelman's premise that Wordsworth is searching for a "more-than-pastoral" solution to the problem of authentic representation and acknowledgement of the

laborer's voice intrinsic to the traditional pastoral mode, against which Wordsworth offers a georgic alternative. Kurt Heinzelman, "The Uneducated Imagination: Romantic Representations of Labor," in *At the Limits of Romanticism: Essays in Cultural, Feminist, and Materialist Criticism*, ed. Mary A. Favret and Nicola J. Watson (Bloomington: Indiana University Press, 1994), 107–10.

77. On this subject, Metzger writes, "His [Wordsworth's] emphasis on feeling plays a crucial role both in revolutionizing poetics and in displacing political issues." She continues, "In restating the nature of his experimental poetics for the full-fledged preface of 1800, Wordsworth deemphasizes the social nature of his experiment and elaborates the notions of subjective sensation and aesthetic pleasure.... He proposes to trace in his poems the laws governing the association of ideas in a state of excitement. And thus he severs his poetics from the historical moment." Metzger concludes that with Wordsworth one finds an "unacknowledged ideology that promotes a hierarchy of feeling that masks his complicity with a repressive and exploitative socioeconomic system." Metzger, "Ideology," 183, 185, 191.

78. Gary Harrison, *Wordsworth's Vagrant Muse: Poetry, Poverty, and Power* (Detroit: Wayne State University Press, 1994), 17–8.

79. Ibid., 29.
80. Ibid.
81. Ibid., 75.
82. Wordsworth, "Goody Blake and Harry Gill," 17–20.
83. Ibid., 21–4.
84. Ibid., 1–8.
85. Ibid., 57–8.
86. Ibid., 96.
87. Ibid., 99–100.
88. Wordsworth, "Simon Lee," 1–2. David Simpson provides evidence that suggests the poem is autobiographical. In the spring of 1798, when the poem is presumed to have been written, the Wordsworths were living as tenants at Alfoxden House in Somersetshire, a manor that had once belonged to the Squire of Alfoxden. Simon Lee is probably based on Christopher Tricky, who lived with his wife at the dog pound just outside the grounds of the house. The Wordsworths had quietly retreated to the countryside amidst what Simpson terms the "national paranoia" brought on by the threat of a French Invasion earlier that year. Simpson, *Wordsworth's Historical Imagination*, 150.

89. Wordsworth, "Simon Lee," 50.
90. Ibid., 25–32.
91. Ibid., 65–8.
92. Ibid., 73–6.
93. Ibid., 87–8.
94. Ibid., 89–92.
95. Ibid., 95–6.
96. Celeste Langan, *Romantic Vagrancy: Wordsworth and the Simulation of Freedom* (Cambridge: Cambridge University Press, 1995), 19.
97. Wordsworth, "Old Cumberland Beggar," 180, 179.
98. Ibid., 184–9, emphasis original.
99. Langan, *Romantic Vagrancy*, 17.
100. Wordsworth, note to "Old Cumberland Beggar," 205.
101. Philip Connell, *Romanticism, Economics and the Question of 'Culture'* (Oxford: Oxford University Press, 2001), 21.
102. Chandler, *Wordsworth's Second Nature*, 87.
103. Wordsworth, "Old Cumberland Beggar," 22–4.
104. Ibid., 44–53, emphasis original.
105. Ibid., 69–70.
106. See Wordsworth, "Postscript to *Yarrow Revisited and Other Poems* (1835)," *Prose Works*, 3:240–59.
107. Wordsworth, "Old Cumberland Beggar," 79–87.
108. Ibid., 114–24.
109. Wordsworth, "Lines Written in Early Spring," 1–4.
110. Ibid., 5–8.
111. Ibid., 22.
112. Ibid., 19–20.
113. Ibid., 23–4.
114. Wordsworth, "Tables Turned," 1, 15–6.
115. Ibid., 21–4.
116. Ibid., 26–7.
117. Ibid., 29–32.
118. Wordsworth, "Tintern Abbey," 1–4.
119. Marjorie Levinson, *Wordsworth's Great Period Poems*, 37–8.
120. Ibid., 55.
121. Ibid., 32.
122. Ibid.
123. Ibid., 57.
124. Thomas McFarland, *William Wordsworth: Intensity and Achievement* (Oxford: Clarendon Press, 1992), 6.
125. Ibid., 9, italics original.
126. Ibid., 17.
127. Roe, *The Politics of Nature*, 180.
128. Ibid., 173–4.
129. Ibid., 177–8.
130. Wordsworth, "Sublime and the Beautiful," 2:357.
131. Ibid., 2:359.
132. Ibid., 2:354.
133. Wordsworth, "Tintern Abbey," 59.

134. Ibid., 26–7.
135. Ibid., 30.
136. Ibid., 37. See also Thomas McFarland, *Romanticism and the Forms of Ruin: Wordsworth, Coleridge, and Modalities of Fragmentation* (Princeton: Princeton University Press, 1981), 29.
137. Wordsworth, "Tintern Abbey," 37–49.
138. Ibid., 123–4.

Chapter 4

1. James Thomson, "Ode: Rule, Britannia," *Poetical Works*, ed. J. Logie Robertson (repr. New York: Oxford University Press, 1965), 1–6, emphasis original.
2. Coleridge, "Fears in Solitude," 72–8. All references to "Fears in Solitude" are to *The Complete Poems*, ed. Keach.
3. Christopher Lake Moody, "Review of 'Fears in Solitude,'" *Monthly Review* (May 1799), qtd. in Reiman, ed., *Romantics Reviewed*, 2:710.
4. Anon., *Analytical Review* (Dec. 1798), 590–592. Qtd. in Reiman, ed., *Romantics Reviewed*, 1:11.
5. Thompson, *The Romantics*, 46.
6. *Monthly Mirror* (Jan. 1799), 36–7. Qtd. in Reiman, ed., *Romantics Reviewed*, 2:686.
7. *Analytical Review* (Dec. 1798), 590–2. Qtd. in Reiman, ed., *Romantics Reviewed*, 1:11.
8. *New Annual Register* (1799), 309–10. Qtd. in Reiman, ed., *Romantics Reviewed*, 2:779.
9. Moody, *Monthly Review* (May 1799), 43–7. Qtd. in Reiman, ed., *Romantics Reviewed*, 2:710.
10. I have in mind, respectively, Kelvin Everest's *Coleridge's Secret Ministry: The Context of the Conversation Poems 1795–1798* (New York: Barnes & Noble, 1979); John Gatta, Jr.'s "Coleridge's 'Fears in Solitude' and the Prospect of Social Redemption," *Cithara: Essays in the Judeo-Christian Tradition* 26, no. 1 (November 1986): 36–43; and Alan Vardy's "Fears in Solitude, 1848," *Coleridge Bulletin* 22 (2003): 32–8.
11. As Charles De Paolo has noted, this providential historical framework is the source of Coleridge's main disagreement with Gibbon. Coleridge contributed sporadically to the controversial reaction to Gibbon's historiography; his commentary is scattered over the period from 1795 to 1833. Charles De Paolo, "Coleridge and Gibbon's Controversy over *The Decline and Fall of the Roman Empire*," *CLIO: A Journal of Literature, History, and the Philosophy of History* 20, no. 1 (Fall 1990): 13. Coleridge vehemently disputed the Enlightenment historiography intrinsic to Gibbon's method, which stemmed from Lockean empiricism and Humean skepticism, because it implicitly attributed the barbarism of the Dark Ages to the hegemony of Christianity. De Paolo sums up the disagreement: "Specifically, Coleridge rejected Gibbon's thesis that Christianity was part of the barbaric invasion that had destroyed ancient culture and that introduced the Dark Ages" (14). On the contrary, Coleridge believed that "the advent of Christianity had actually synthesized the best features of Hebrew, of Greek, and of Roman culture, fulfilling the providentially-ordained development of Western Civilization—a view Gibbon had lamented as 'the triumph of barbarism and religion'" (14–5).
12. Coleridge, *Table Talk*. Qtd. in Harold Orel, *English Romantic Poets and the Enlightenment* (Oxford: Oxford University Press, 1973), 61.
13. Paul W.L. Arthur has also shed light on Coleridge's countenancing of British imperialism, which he argues has been downplayed in Romantic Studies by ignoring Coleridge's abundant political prose. Arthur states, "The traditional emphasis upon Coleridge as poet of fantasy, supernaturalism and of the primary imagination, has all but blocked out his other major public role—that of enthusiastic supporter of political issues of the day including the politics of empire." Paul W.L. Arthur, "From Politics to Pleasure: Coleridge and Romantic Imperialism," *SPAN* 45 (October 1997): 73. Iain Robertson Scott argues that Coleridge, Wordsworth, and Southey supported Britain's bellicose reaction to the French Revolution on the grounds that the nation was "truly committed to spreading liberty and morality throughout Europe." Iain Robertson Scott, "'Things As They Are': The Literary Response to the French Revolution, 1789–1815," in *Britain and the French Revolution, 1789–1815*, ed. H.T. Dickinson (London: Macmillan, 1989), 242. On Coleridge's sympathetic turn in favor of empire, Timothy Fulford argues that Coleridge's trip to Malta from 1804 to 1805, when it was a British colony, was instrumental for this transition. He found the island's Catholic populace to be benighted and deplorable, viewing Catholicism as a deleterious creed analogous to Islam, Hinduism, and polytheistic paganism. Fulford avers that this prejudice confirmed his faith in "the superiority of national cultures based on Protestantism" and convinced him that "the empire was a historic and civilizing mission." Timothy Fulford, "Catholicism and Polytheism: Britain's Colonies and Coleridge's Politics," *Romanticism* 5 (1999): 233. His subsequent adoration of Sir Alexander Ball, Britain's first Civil Commissioner of Malta, resulted from a growing ardor for the

brand of paternal colonialism practiced by this stalwart agent of empire.

14. S.B. Greenfield and D.G. Calder, *A New Critical History of Old English Literature* (New York: New York University Press, 1986), 58.

15. Piggott, *Ancient Britons*, 54–86. Piggott cites a number of antiquarian texts from this period that lend credibility to the idea of a Noachian westward plantation of Europe, including Sir Walter Raleigh's *History of the World* (1614), Nathanael Carpenter's *Geography Delineated forth in two books* (1625), Sir Thomas Browne's *Pseudodoxia* (1658), Aylett Sammes's *Britannia Antiqua Illustrata* (1676), and Henry Rowland's *Mona Antiqua Restaurata* (1723).

16. The idea of a plantation-driven westward theory of civilization resonates with the other major theory of origin for the Britons, that propounded by Geoffrey of Monmouth in the twelfth-century *Historia Regum Britanniae*, where he credits Brutus, the descendant of the Trojan hero and founder of Rome, Aeneas, with founding the Britons. This theory traces a mythical lineage from ancient Greece to the Roman Empire to the ancient Britons and their descendants in the British Empire, thereby establishing a historical pattern for the westward course of civilization by means of colonization.

17. There is a methodological distinction between these author's treatments of the subject that deserves mention. Whereas Weber believed that the ideology of Protestantism determined the rise of capitalism, Tawney used a Marxist schema in which the economic base of early capitalism determined Protestantism, which formed part of the ideological superstructure that rationalized capitalist class relations.

18. Max Weber, *The Protestant Work Ethic and the Spirit of Capitalism*, trans. Talcott Parsons (1905; New York: Charles Scribner's Sons, 1958), 80.

19. R.H. Tawney, *Religion and the Rise of Capitalism* (1926; New Brunswick, NJ: Transaction, 2000), 230, 246.

20. Before turning it into a popular air, Thomson originally included the poem in *Alfred*, a masque co-written with David Mallet about King Alfred the Great, the legendary English king. This suggests the degree to which English nationalism forms the sub-structure of British nationalism.

21. Suvir Kaul highlights the eighteenth-century poet's privileged role in the articulation of this program: "'Rule, Britannia!' ... is testimonial to the fact that poets in the long eighteenth century imagined poetry to be a unique and privileged literary form for the enunciation of a puissant (and plastic) vocabulary of nation, particularly one appropriate to a Britain proving itself ... great at home and abroad." Kaul, *Poems of Nations*, 5.

22. Thomson, "Rule, Britannia," 1, 4, 5.

23. Ibid., 6.

24. Rudyard Kipling, "The White Man's Burden," in *Poetry of the Victorian Period*, ed. Jerome Hamilton Buckley and George Benjamin Woods, 3d ed. (New York: HarperCollins, 1965), 33–40.

25. The Old Testament Book of Isaiah holds out the comforting hope of Israel's redemption:

Comfort ye, comfort ye my people, saith your God.

Speak ye comfortably to Jerusalem, and cry unto her, that her warfare is accomplished, that her iniquity is pardoned: for she hath received of the LORD'S hand double for all her sins [Isaiah 40:1–2, King James Version].

Conversely, the Book of Jeremiah is unequivocal in its apocalyptic fatalism:

But this thing commanded I them, saying, Obey my voice, and I will be your God, and ye shall be my people: and walk ye in all the ways that I have commanded you, that it may be well unto you.

But they hearkened not, nor inclined their ear, but walked in the counsels *and* in the imagination of their evil heart, and went backward, and not forward.

Since the day that your fathers came forth out of the land of Egypt unto this day I have even sent unto you all my servants the prophets, daily rising up early and sending *them*:

Yet they hearkened not unto me, nor inclined their ear, but hardened their neck: they did worse than their fathers.

Therefore thou shalt speak all these words unto them; but they will not hearken to thee: thou shalt also call unto them; but they will not answer thee.

But thou shalt say unto them, This is a nation that obeyeth not the voice of the LORD their God, nor receiveth correction: truth is perished, and is cut off from their mouth.

Cut off thine hair, *O Jerusalem*, and cast *it* away, and take up a lamentation on high places; for the LORD hath rejected and forsaken the generation of his wrath [Jeremiah 7:23–9, emphasis original, KJV].

26. David Armitage, *The Ideological Origins of the British Empire*, Ideas in Context 59 (repr. New York: Cambridge University Press, 2004), 125–45.

27. Ibid., 136.

28. Ibid., 135. Armitage cites Marchamont Nedham's numerous editorials printed between 1651 and 1652 in the *Mercurius Politicus*, and later revised and reprinted as *The Excellencie of a Free Statee* in 1656, as evidence of how Sallustian and Machiavellian narratives provided a ready-made rhetoric for addressing the declension from Protector to Dictator.

29. For more on Milton's reading of Sallust, see Nicholas von Maltzahn, *Milton's History of Britain: Republican Historiography in the English Revolution* (Oxford: Oxford University Press, 1991), 75–7, and Martin Dzelzainis, "Milton's Classical Republicanism," in *Milton and Republicanism*, ed. David Armitage, Armand Himy and Quentin Skinner (New York: Cambridge University Press, 1995), 22–4.

30. John Milton, "The Readie and Easie Way," in *The Riverside Milton*, ed. Roy Flannigan (New York: Houghton Mifflin, 1998), 1148.

31. Kaul, *Poems of Nations*, 143.

32. So numerous and catastrophic were the era's bizarre "bubble" schemes that Parliament had to pass a Bubble Act in 1720 requiring all joint-stock companies to secure a Royal Charter. The controversial practice of speculation in eighteenth-century Britain generated much public debate and dialogue, as did the contingent practices of printing paper money and issuing public credit. In *The Spectator* No. 3, Addison turns his wit on these practices in a parodic vision that exposes the chimerical fortunes of speculation. He imagines a visit to the Bank of England, inside which he spies a prodigious heap of money bags. Soon, his initial observation is disabused: "There was as great a Change in the Hill of Mony Bags and the Heaps of Mony, the former shrinking, and falling into so many empty Bags, that I now found not above a tenth part of them had been filled with Mony. The rest that took up the same Space, and made the same Figure as the bags that were really filled with Mony, had been blown up with Air, and called into my Memory the Bags full of Wind, which Homer tells us his Hero received as a present from Aeolus. The great Heaps of Gold on either side the Throne now appeared to be only Heaps of Paper, or little Piles of notched Sticks, bound up together in Bundles, like Bath-Faggots." Joseph Addison, "March 3, 1711," in *The Spectator*, ed. Donald F. Bond (Oxford: Clarendon, 1965), 1:14.

33. George Berkeley, *An Essay Towards Preventing the Ruin of Great Britain*, in *The Works of George Berkeley Bishop of Cloyne*, ed. A.A. Luce and T.E. Jessop (repr. Camden, NJ: Nelson, 1964), 6:71.

34. Ibid.

35. Ibid.

36. Ibid., 6:79.

37. Shaftesbury's *Characteristicks* (1714) recapitulates the medieval Christianized Aristotelian ethos that private virtue grounded in charity and *oikos* (civic duty) fosters public good. The values and sensibility of the aristocracy were rooted in the classical doctrine of "virtu," which bases freedom and civility on the ownership of land, the existence of rank, and the social ethics of *noblesse oblige*. Throughout the eighteenth century, this position was championed by landed Tory aristocrats over and against an emergent bourgeois culture driven by self-interest and monetary reward. Published in the same year, Mandeville's *Fable of the Bees* assails these institutions. A Dutch native raised in a commercial society where the state facilitated private mercantile and colonial pursuits, Mandeville is in many respects the mouthpiece for a monied bourgeois elite who were waging a cultural revolution against an entrenched European aristocracy. J.G.A. Pocock's "The Mobility of Property and the Rise of Eighteenth-Century Sociology," in *Virtue, Commerce, and History: Essays on Political Thought and History, Chiefly in the Eighteenth Century*, J.G.A. Pocock (Cambridge: Cambridge University Press, 1985), 103–23 provides a valuable study of the class tension between the landed and monied classes.

38. Berkeley, "Essay Towards Preventing the Ruin of Great Britain," *Works*, 6:74–5.

39. Ibid., 6:74.

40. Ibid., 6:85.

41. Ibid., 6:79.

42. Ibid., 6:85.

43. David Hume, "Of Simplicity and Refinement in Writing," in *Essays: Moral, Political, and Literary*, ed. Eugene F. Miller. (1742; Indianapolis: Liberty Fund, 1987), 196. Hume explains how cultural refinement, swelled with age and imperial growth, led to decadence and degeneracy in the classical world, marking a cyclical pattern of rise and decline that applies also to contemporary Europe. He writes, "It was thus the ASIATIC eloquence degenerated so much from the ATTIC: It was thus the age of CLAUDIUS and NERO became so much inferior to that of AUGUSTUS in taste and genius: And perhaps there are, at present, some symptoms of a like degeneracy of taste, in FRANCE as well as in ENGLAND" (196).

44. Edward Gibbon, *The Decline and Fall of the Roman Empire*, Everyman's Library 95 (New York: Alfred A. Knopf, 1993–4), 4:119. The full passage reads:

> The decline of Rome was the natural and inevitable result of immoderate greatness. Prosperity ripened the principles of

decay; the causes of destruction multiplied with the extent of conquest; and as soon as time or accident had removed the artificial supports, the stupendous fabric yielded to the pressure of its own weight.

It comes from Gibbon's "General Observations on the Fall of the Roman Empire in the West" (1781), an essay appended to the end of Chapter 38 of *The Decline*, just before he commences a history of the Eastern Roman Empire. Although intended to summarize the major vectors of the Western Roman Empire's rise and decline, it is self-consciously addressed to a British public that is presumed to be unmindful of its own approaching imperial zenith and the cautious lessons to be learned from Rome's experience.

45. C.F. Volney, *Ruins or Meditations on the Revolutions of Empires and the Law of Nature*, 1890 ed. (Whitefish, MT: Kessinger, 2004), 32. Written over several years, from 1784 to 1791, Volney's *Ruins* would prove to be a prescient text in light of the French Revolution. Volney opines, "New revolutions will agitate nations and empires; powerful thrones will again be overturned, and terrible catastrophes will again teach mankind that the laws of nature and the precepts of wisdom and truth cannot be infringed with impunity" (41). The book was published in England as two separate texts: *The Ruins* in 1791 and *The Law of Nature* in 1793.

46. William Cowper, *The Task*, in *The Poetical Works of William Cowper*, ed. H.S. Milford. 4th ed. (New York: Oxford, 1950), 1.22, 1.39–43, 1.686–8.

47. D.B. Horn and Mary Ransome, eds., *English Historical Documents, 1714–1783* (London: Eyre and Spottiswoode, 1957), 821–2.

48. Isaac Kramnick, *The Rage of Edmund Burke: Portrait of An Ambivalent Conservative* (New York: Basic Books, 1977), 130.

49. Qtd. in Kramnick, *Rage of Edmund Burke*, 131. See the entire letter "Burke to Henry Dundas" (25 March 1787) printed in Burke, *The Correspondence of Edmund Burke* (Chicago: University of Chicago Press, 1958–71), 5:314.

50. Qtd. in Kramnick, *Rage of Edmund Burke*, 133. Uday Singh Mehta corroborates Burke's view of the social instability perpetrated by wealthy British nabobs returning home from India: "The colonies, and especially India, had become a place where men and boys of humble and dislocated roots went not just to make a fortune but also to 'acquire British society.' Having destroyed the nobility and gentry in India, plucked the rice and salt from the Bengali peasant, they return to England with the monetary and social profits of that endeavor and insinuate their mercenary logic into the historically sanctioned estates that anchor British society. They make money the medium of social and political circulation and order; they buy power and social standing and, in doing so, subvert what for Burke are the traditional and historically appropriate foundations of each. They are, in this sense, like the Jacobins." Uday Singh Mehta, *Empire and Liberalism: A Study in Nineteenth-Century British Liberal Thought* (Chicago: University of Chicago Press, 1999), 173.

51. In 1791, the Birmingham Constitutional Society was attacked by a "church and king" mob for celebrating the second anniversary of the storming of the Bastille. The most famous victim of this mob violence was Joseph Priestley, an outspoken proponent of Unitarianism and the French Revolution who was forced into exile after his estate was destroyed.

52. Samuel Taylor Coleridge, "Consciones ad Populum," in *The Collected Works of Samuel Taylor Coleridge*, ed. Kathleen Coburn, Bollingen Series LXXV (Princeton: Princeton University Press, 1969), 1:35, emphasis original.

53. Robert Sayre argues that the Pantisocracy scheme evidences Coleridge's nostalgia for a return to the social relations of primitive rural communism, this time at a higher level of development. He cites Coleridge's early anti-property politics as just one example of his broader theory that Romanticism is opposed to modernity, is inherently anti-capitalist, and harbors a nostalgia for pre-capitalist social formations. Robert Sayre, "The Young Coleridge: Romantic Utopianism and the French Revolution," *Studies in Romanticism* 28, no. 3 (Fall 1989): 411.

54. Roe tells us that the scheme attracted at least 38 individuals, including Sara Fricker, Coleridge's soon-to-be wife. Nicholas Roe, "Pantisocracy and the Myth of the Poet," in *Romanticism and Millenarianism*, ed. Timothy Fulford (New York: Palgrave, 2007), 94.

55. Roe, *Wordsworth and Coleridge*, 98.

56. Billing himself a learned graduate of Jesus College, Coleridge secured several venues throughout Bristol to deliver a series of eleven lectures on various subjects. These included three lectures on contemporary politics and morality published collectively in December of 1795 as *Conciones ad Populum, Or Addresses to the People*. Included in this collection is a revised version of *A Moral and Political Lecture* and *On the Present War*. Other lectures published separately include *The Plot Discovered*, an attack on the Two Bills introduced by the Pitt administration to suppress seditious publications and limit the right of public assembly (eventually passed in 1796 as the Two

Acts); a *Lecture on the Slave-Trade* excoriating the immorality and viciousness of this practice and endorsing abolition; and six *Lectures on Revealed Religion, Its Corruptions and Political Views*, which exposed the corruptness of established Christianity while maintaining that true Christian morality sustained freedom and equality. This set him against the grain of rationalist thinkers who conflated all religions with superstition and tyranny. Notably, in these lectures and continued in his periodical publication, *The Watchman* (March–May 1796), Coleridge developed an argument for the moral necessity of private property, a decided rupture from his collectivist Pantisocratic scheme. Coleridge further developed his defense of property-based politics in a later periodical publication, *The Friend* (June 1809–March 1810). For more on Coleridge's evolving views on morality, private property, and the state, see John Morrow, *Coleridge's Political Thought: Property, Morality, and the Limits of Traditional Discourse* (New York: St. Martin's, 1990).

57. Edward P. Thompson characterizes Coleridge as "a sort of little Bristol Thelwall" for the daringly radical content of these lectures. Thompson, *The Romantics*, 46.

58. Coleridge, "Consciones ad Populum," *Collected Works* 1:44, emphasis original.

59. Coleridge, "Lectures on Revealed Religion," *Collected Works*, 1:163.

60. Coleridge, "Consciones ad Populum," *Collected Works*, 1:44.

61. Ibid., 1:48, emphasis original.

62. Coleridge, "Lectures on Revealed Religion," *Collected Works*, 1:163.

63. Coleridge, "Consciones ad Populum," *Collected Works*, 1:46.

64. Coleridge, "Table Talk" (8 September 1830), *Collected Works*, 14:188.

65. Nigel Leask, *The Politics of Imagination in Coleridge's Critical Thought* (New York: St. Martin's, 1988), 210, emphasis original.

66. Coleridge, "On the Constitution of Church and State," *Collected Works*, 10:233–4. The letter from Coleridge to the Rev. James Gillman appeared in the margins of a second edition copy of 1830. The full transcript can be found in the *Collected Works*, 10:233–4, Appendix E. Julie A. Carson makes reference to the same marginalia to explain Coleridge's conceptualization of the relationship between imagination and nation. Julie A. Carson, *In the Theatre of Romanticism: Coleridge, Nationalism, Women*, Cambridge Studies in Romanticism 5 (New York: Cambridge University Press, 1994), 45.

67. Samuel Taylor Coleridge, *Collected Letters of Samuel Taylor Coleridge*, ed. E.L. Griggs (Oxford: Oxford University Press, 1956), 1:397–8.

68. Stephen Cheeke traces Coleridge's rhetorical usage of historical parallelism on the subject of France through several essay contributions to *The Morning Post* and *The Courier*, the earliest appearing on 8 March 1798, just weeks before writing "Fears in Solitude." This parallelism was very common among contemporary political pundits who were well versed in Gibbon's historiography of Rome. Notably, Cheeke argues that Coleridge's method was aimed at discrediting the analogy with Rome by offering forensic details "in which the closer the comparisons became, the weaker France's position seemed." Stephen Cheeke, "The Sword 'Which eats into itself': Romanticism, Napoleon and the Romantic Parallel," *Romanticism: The Journal of Romantic Culture & Criticism* 10, no. 2 (2004): 212. The import of these expostulations was to undermine exaggerated claims of a nascent French imperium, which I suggest creates a discursive space for "Fears in Solitude," where the narrator, bolstered by the certitude of a degenerate and declining France, can seriously consider a French defeat.

69. Coleridge, "France," *Collected Works*, 21.

70. Ibid., 30.

71. Ibid., 42.

72. Ibid., 92.

73. Ibid., 99–105.

74. See the transcript of Richard B. Sheridan's "Traitorous Correspondence, and Preparation for Invasion" (26 April 1798) in Richard B. Sheridan, *The Speeches of the Right Honourable Richard Brinsley Sheridan. With a Sketch of His Life*, ed. A Constitutional Friend, vol. 3 (1842; repr. New York: Russell & Russell, 1969). Credit must be given to David Fairer for unearthing this speech and astutely discerning its timely influence on Coleridge's "Fears in Solitude." In a seminal paper "'Patriot Rage and Indignation High': The Voice of Sheridan in 'Fears in Solitude'" delivered at the Coleridge Summer Conference 2004, Fairer argued that "the public voice of 'Fears in Solitude' responds to that of Sheridan, who at the critical moment when a French attack was thought to be imminent called on Britons to unite in the nation's defence." David Fairer, "'Patriot Rage and Indignation High': The Voice of Sheridan in 'Fears in Solitude,'" paper presented at the Coleridge Summer Conference, Cannington, UK, Summer 2004.

75. Sheridan, *Speeches*, 3:240–1.

76. Ibid., 3:242 and 3:247.

77. Ibid., 3:243.

78. Ibid., 3:245.

79. Coleridge had publicly begun to espouse the position that Britain was responsible for French atrocities years earlier in 1795 when, in a lecture "On the Present War" published in *Consciones ad Populum*, he declared, "Lastly, in this inventory of guilt as the immediate and peculiar effect of the present War, and justly attributable to our Ministry, we must place the excesses of the French, their massacres and blasphemies, all their crimes and all their distresses. This effect the War produced by a two-fold operation of terror:— First, on the people of France, secondly, on their Rulers." Coleridge, "Consciones ad Populum," *Collected Works*, 72. Earlier in the text, he avers that there was no serious attempt by the British to negotiate peace and thus avert war; hence, Coleridge, like Sheridan, largely attributes hostilities with France and the terror within France to British foreign policy. However, Paul W.L. Arthur cites Coleridge's Essay XIV from *The Friend* (1809) to make the opposite point, that Coleridge exonerates Britain of any wrongdoing in its prosecution of war against France. Arthur, "From Politics to Pleasure," 82. In Essay XIV, Coleridge inveighs against French despotism and paints Britain as wholly innocent and benign. This act of political revisionism is consistent with my argument thus far, ergo that Coleridge was gradually sliding to the right during the period of strife with Napoleonic France. As in "Fears in Solitude," he used his writings to publicly refashion himself.

80. Both Paul Magnuson in "The Politics of 'Frost at Midnight,'" *Wordsworth Circle* 22 (1991): 3–11 and Judith Thompson in "An Autumnal Blast, A Killing Frost: Coleridge's Poetic Conversation with John Thelwall," *Studies in Romanticism* 36 (Fall 1997): 427–56 have discussed how this and other conversational poems should be read as coded engagements with the political furor of the period, particularly in terms of Coleridge's agonistic struggle with poetic reinvention as he retreats from his radical political stance of the early 1790s.

81. Samuel Taylor Coleridge, *The Poetical Works of Samuel Taylor Coleridge*, ed. E.H. Coleridge (Oxford: Oxford University Press, 1912), 1:257, emphasis original.

82. Everest, *Coleridge's Secret Ministry*, 270.

83. My illumination of the poem's deeply private and confessional conversational sub-text effectively develops and substantiates Carl R. Woodring's claim that the poem is "a representative Romantic poem" for its "approach through subjective mood to public theme." Carl R. Woodring, *Politics in the Poetry of Coleridge* (Madison: University of Wisconsin Press, 1961), 193. This "subjective mode" is a sign of the poem's sublimated confessional mode.

84. In *Reading Public Romanticism* (Princeton: Princeton University Press, 1998), Paul Magnuson explores how the poem is in dialog with Coleridge's other work and with that of Wordsworth, while in "Coleridge and the Fears of Friendship, 1798," *The Coleridge Bulletin* NS 24 (Winter 2004): 11–8, Felicity James places the poem in the context of Coleridge's unspoken fears and anxieties over his disintegrating private relationships in 1797–8, particularly with Charles Lamb and Charles Lloyd.

85. C.R. Watters, "A Distant 'Boum' Among the Hills: Some Notes on Coleridge's 'Fears in Solitude' (1798)," *The Charles Lamb Bulletin* 59 (July 1987): 94–5.

86. Paul Magnuson, "The Shaping of 'Fears in Solitude,'" in *Coleridge's Theory of Imagination Today*, ed. Christine Gallant (New York: AMS Press, 1989), 199.

87. Coleridge, "Fears in Solitude," 1.

88. Ibid., 12–6.

89. Michael Simpson has theorized the connection between nationalism and Romanticism by suggesting that the Romantic formulation that love of nature leads to love of mankind is mediated by the love of nation; the nation is the pivot between nature and culture. Michael Simpson, "The Morning (Post) After: Apocalypse and Bathos in Coleridge's 'Fears in Solitude,'" in *Romanticism and Millenarianism*, 76.

90. Coleridge, "Fears in Solitude," 29–40.

91. Ibid., 41–53.

92. Chris Jones, "John Newton and Coleridge's 'Fears in Solitude,'" *Notes and Queries* 41, no. 3 (September 1994): 339–41. Jones speculates on a variety of possible contexts in which Coleridge may have met Newton or been exposed to his work. These include indirect transmission of Newton's works through Dorothy Wordsworth; discovery of certain tracts during his own antislavery research; an introduction by Charles Lamb, whose office was near Newton's church; or an encounter facilitated by their shared familiarity with the Wedgwoods.

93. Ibid., 339.

94. Michael John Kooy, "Disinterested Patriotism: Bishop Butler, Hazlitt and Coleridge's Quarto Pamphlet of 1798," *The Coleridge Bulletin* 21 (2003): 55–65.

95. Coleridge, "Fears in Solitude," 53–63.

96. Ibid., 63–7, 70–3.

97. Coleridge, "Consciounes ad Populum," *Collected Works*, 1:58.

98. Coleridge, "Fears in Solitude," 81.

99. Ibid., 86–9.

100. Simon Bainbridge has examined the broad response of British poetry to the wars raging throughout the late-eighteenth and early-nineteenth centuries. He reads the import of this passage in terms of "a national failure of imagination and feeling," whereby he interprets the feared invasion to be a byproduct of Britain's comfortable distance from the scenes of actual warfare, which, as I suggest, bred an almost complacent attitude towards the warmongering policies of state. Simon Bainbridge, *British Poetry and the Revolutionary and Napoleonic Wars: Visions of Conflict* (New York: Oxford University Press, 2003), 68.
101. Coleridge, "Fears in Solitude," 93-9, 103-7.
102. Ibid., 122-8.
103. Ibid., 129-34.
104. Ibid., 134-46.
105. Ibid., 150-4.
106. Ibid., 154-9.
107. Ibid., 159-75.
108. Ibid., 176-97.
109. Ibid., 197-202.
110. Ibid., 31.
111. Ibid., 210-20.
112. Ibid., 221-32.
113. Ibid., 32.

Chapter 5

1. Felicia Hemans, *Modern Greece*, in *Felicia Hemans: Selected Poems, Letters, Reception Materials*, ed. Susan J. Wolfson (Princeton: Princeton University Press, 2000), stanza XLII. All references to *Modern Greece* are to *Felicia Hemans*, ed. Wolfson.
2. M. Jouy, "Untitled," *The Athenaeum*, March 4, 1828, 177.
3. Jouy, "Untitled," *The Athenaeum*, 177.
4. Ibid.
5. See Paula Backscheider, *Eighteenth-Century Women Poets and Their Poetry: Inventing Agency, Inventing Genre* (Baltimore: Johns Hopkins University Press, 2005), 3-4, and Paula R. Feldman, ed., introduction to *British Women Poets of the Romantic Era: An Anthology* (Baltimore: Johns Hopkins University Press, 1997).
6. See the introductions to Anne K. Mellor, *Mothers of the Nation: Women's Political Writing in England, 1780-1830* (Bloomington: Indiana University Press, 2000) and Stephen C. Behrendt, *British Women Poets and the Romantic Writing Community* (Baltimore: Johns Hopkins University Press, 2009).
7. See Michelle Levy, *Family Authorship and Romantic Print Culture* (New York: Palgrave Macmillan, 2008) and William Stafford, *English Feminists and Their Opponents in the 1790s: Unsex'd and Proper Females* (Manchester: Manchester University Press, 2002).
8. Mary Wollstonecraft, *A Vindication of the Rights of Women* (1792; Amherst, NY: Prometheus, 1989), 189.
9. See Colley, *Britons*, Chapter 6.
10. Ibid., 250.
11. Kate Davies, "A Moral Purchase: Femininity, Commerce, and Abolition, 1788-1792," in *Women, Writing and the Public Sphere, 1700-1830*, ed. Elizabeth Eger, Charlotte Grant, and Cliona O. Gallchoir (Cambridge: Cambridge University Press, 2001), 133-59.
12. Backscheider, *Eighteenth-Century Women Poets*, 8.
13. Mellor, *Mothers of the Nation*, 9, emphasis original.
14. Ibid., 9-10. See also Mellor's essay "The Female Poet and the Poetess: Two Traditions of British Women's Poetry, 1780-1830," *Studies in Romanticism* 36 (Summer 1997): 261-76.
15. Ibid., 10, emphasis original.
16. Richard Polwhele, "The Unsex'd Females: A Poem," in *The Feminist Controversy in England, 1788-1810*, ed. Gina Luria, Garland Series (New York: Garland, 1974), 12.
17. Susan J. Wolfson, *Borderlines: The Shiftings of Gender in British Romanticism* (Palo Alto: Stanford University Press, 2006), 15.
18. Marlon B. Ross, "Configurations of Feminine Reform: The Woman Writer and the Tradition of Dissent," in *Re-visioning Romanticism: British Women Writers, 1776-1837*, ed. Carol Shiner Wilson and Joel Haefner (Philadelphia: University of Pennsylvania Press, 1994), 95.
19. See Paula McDowell, "Consuming Women: The Life of the 'Literary Lady' as Popular Culture in Eighteenth-Century England," *Genre* 26 (1993): 219-52.
20. In *A Vindication of the Rights of Woman*, Mary Wollstonecraft surreptitiously dons the prophet's robes. She writes, "It is difficult for us purblind mortals to say to what height human discoveries and improvements may arrive when the gloom of despotism subsides, which makes us stumble at every step; but, when morality shall be settled on a more solid basis, then, without being gifted with a prophetic spirit, I will venture to predict that woman will be either the friend or slave of man." Wollstonecraft, *Vindication*, 44. Mary Wollstonecraft Shelley's *Frankenstein* (1818) is a prophetic text of a different kind. Lacking her mother's optimism for scientific discoveries and improvement schemes, the book warns of the dan-

gers posed by the promethean over-reaching of unbridled scientific experimentation. *The Last Man* (1826) continues in this darkly sci-fi vein by prophesying the extinction of humanity via a mysterious plague sometime in the twenty-first century. Written prior to 1822, *Valperga* (1823) and *Matilda* (published posthumously in 1959) foreshadow Percy Shelley's drowning death in 1822 by portraying the drowning deaths of central characters. The resemblance is especially startling in *Valperga*, where the fictional Countess Euthanasia, an ardent Italian republican, drowns off the Italian coast while fleeing from her captors, eerily mirroring the fate of Percy Shelley, also an ardent republican, who drowned off the Italian coast en route to his home in Livorno. Mary Shelley herself referred to these peculiar coincidences as instances of prophecy in a letter to Maria Gisborne dated 3 May 1823. She writes, "Is not the catastrophe [in *Valperga*] strangely prophetic [?] But it seems to me that in what I have hitherto written I have done nothing but prophecy what has arrived to. *Matilda* foretells even many small circumstances most truly—& the whole of it is a monument of what now is." Mary Wollstonecraft Shelley, *Letters*, ed. Betty T. Bennett (Baltimore: Johns Hopkins University Press, 1980), 1:336. For more on Mary Wollstonecraft Shelley and the prophetic tradition see Betty T. Bennett and Stuart Curran, eds., *Mary Shelley in Her Times* (Baltimore: Johns Hopkins University Press, 2000).

21. Sarah Suleri, *The Rhetoric of English India* (Chicago: University of Chicago Press, 1992), 28. Burke deploys the "Indian sublime" in his "Speech on Mr. Fox's East India Bill" to convey the futility of mapping and classifying India according to Western categories and under Western forms of governance: "All this vast mass [of India], composed of so many orders and classes of men, is again infinitely diversified by manners, by religion, by hereditary employment, through all their possible combinations. This renders the handling of India a matter in an high degree critical and delicate. But, oh, it has been handled very rudely indeed!" Qtd. in Suleri, *Rhetoric of English India*, 27. For more on Suleri's concept of the "Indian sublime," see Chapter 2 of *The Rhetoric of English India*, "Burke and the Indian Sublime."

22. Laurence Goldstein, *Ruins and Empire: The Evolution of a Theme in Augustan and Romantic Literature* (Pittsburgh: University of Pittsburgh Press, 1977), 8.

23. Janowitz, *England's Ruins*, 3.

24. Gibbon, *Decline and Fall*, 6:642–3.

25. Volney, *Ruins*, 1–3.

26. The conversation on the Romantic fragment poem had several notable episodes in the 1980s. Thomas McFarland treats the Romantic fragment poem as emblematic of a dominant cultural theme characterized by the "diasparactive" triad of incompleteness, fragmentation, and ruin. This theme is not mediated by social and political history, yet manifests in Romantic literature as the expression of longing and melancholy that culminates in a pervasive *sentiment des ruines*. McFarland, *Romanticism and the Forms of Ruin*, 5–7, 15. Contrastingly, in his study of Shelley's *Triumph of Life*, Paul de Man argues that one must resist the urge to seek semantic closure for the Romantic fragment poem by arbitrarily settling its meaning within a pre-determined historical or semantic order, a process that he calls "monumentalization." Paul de Man, *The Rhetoric of Romanticism* (New York: Columbia University Press, 1984), 121. Likewise, Balachandra Rajan also argues for leaving the fragmentary poem unfinished because its rejection of closure throws into relief pervasive confrontations that underlie its meaning. He writes, "The form of the unfinished is the form of the poem as it is and not some larger form in which the poem participates and to which we are persuaded to annex it." Balachandra Rajan, *The Form of the Unfinished: English Poetics from Spenser to Pound* (Princeton: Princeton University Press, 1985), 3–4, 4–5. Rajan stresses that the unfinished poem differs from a true ruin, which invites semantic completion because its fragmentary form was once complete. Hence, the form of the unfinished poem is not fragmentary, but complete in itself and must be read this way rather then placed within an artificial organizational field supplied by scholars. Approaching the subject from a New Historical perspective, Marjorie Levinson disputes McFarland's essentializing tendency by arguing for a historically nuanced reading of the fragment poem that disentangles the history of its composition, publication, and reception from the signification produced by the early nineteenth-century literary milieu and the legacy of Romantic ideology influencing modern critical discourse. Marjorie Levinson, *The Romantic Fragment Poem: A Critique of a Form* (Chapel Hill: University of North Carolina Press, 1986), 8.

27. Bruce Haley, *Living Forms: Romantics and the Monumental Figure* (Albany: State University of New York Press, 2003), 5.

28. Percy Bysshe Shelley, "Ozymandias," in *Shelley's Poetry and Prose: Authoritative Texts and Criticism*, ed. Donald H. Reiman and Sharon B. Powers (New York: W.W. Norton, 1977), 13, 12, 14.

29. John Keats, "On Seeing the Elgin Marbles," in *Complete Poems*, ed. Jack Stillinger (Cambridge: Belknap, 1982), 12–13.

30. See also Tricia Lootens's discussion of Hemans's American reception as a transatlantic patriotic poet in "Hemans and her American Heirs: Nineteenth-Century Women's Poetry and National Identity," in *Women's Poetry, Late Romantic to Late Victorian: Gender and Genre, 1830–1900*, ed. Isobel Armstong and Virginia Blain (New York: St. Martin's, 1999), 243–60.

31. With the exception of Scott and Byron, Hemans generated more revenue by the sale of the multiple editions of her works than any other Romantic contemporary. Paula R. Feldman documents this phenomenon in "The Poet and the Profits: Felicia Hemans and the Literary Marketplace," in *Women's Poetry, Late Romantic to Late Victorian: Gender and Genre, 1830–1900*, ed. Isobel Armstrong and Virginia Blain (New York: St. Martin's, 1999) 71–101.

32. *The Edinburgh Monthly Review* (April 1820), 373–83. Qtd. in Wolfson, ed., *Felicia Hemans*, 531, emphasis original.

33. *The Edinburgh Review* (October 1829) 32–47. Qtd. in Wolfson, ed., *Felicia Hemans*, 551.

34. Henry F. Chorley, *Memorials of Mrs. Hemans* (New York: Saunders & Otley), 1836, 1:112–13, emphasis original.

35. Norma Clarke, *Ambitious Heights: Writing, Friendship, Love—The Jewsbury Sisters, Felicia Hemans, and Jane Welsh Carlyle* (New York: Routledge, 1990), 45–8.

36. Susan J. Wolfson, "'Domestic Affections' and 'the Spear of Minerva': Felicia Hemans and the Dilemma of Gender," in *Re-Visioning Romanticism*, 128–66.

37. Chorley, *Memorials*, 1:35–6.

38. See the *Letter to John Murray* (26 February 1817), qtd. in Wolfson, ed., *Felicia Hemans*, 480–1. These marbles—scavenged from the ruins of the Parthenon and imported to London by Lord Elgin in 1804, and eventually sold to the British government in 1816—are featured in Keats's self-reflexive poem, *On Seeing the Elgin Marbles* (1817). But they were also the subject of a popular furor over their rightful ownership involving Byron when he, in Part II of *Childe Harold* (1812), explicitly deplores their theft. Interestingly, contemporary reviewers believed *Modern Greece* to have been written by Byron despite the fact that the poem clearly weighs-in in favor of this expropriation of Grecian art. See the July 1817 review of *Modern Greece* in the *British Lady's Magazine*. See also Susan J. Wolfson's study of Hemans's relationship with Byron and his poetry in "Hemans and the Romance of Byron," in *Felicia Hemans: Reimagining Poetry in the Nineteenth Century*, edited by Nanora Sweet and Julie Melnyk (New York: Palgrave, 2001), 155–80.

39. See *The British Review and London Critical Journal* (June 1820), 299–310, qtd. in Wolfson, ed., *Felicia Hemans*, 532.

40. Hemans, *Modern Greece*, XXXVI.

41. Volney, *Ruins*, 8.

42. Peter W. Trinder, *Mrs. Hemans* (Cardiff: University of Wales Press, 1984), 11.

43. Hemans, *Modern Greece*, XXX.

44. Ibid., XXI.

45. Trinder, *Mrs. Hemans*, 24–5.

46. Chorley, *Memorials*, 1:46–7.

47. Daniel E. White, "'Mysterious Sanctity': Sectarianism and Syncretism from Volney to Hemans," *European Romantic Review* 15, no. 2 (2004): 269–76.

48. Hemans, *Modern Greece*, XLIX.

49. Ibid., XXXII.

50. Ibid., LXXXVII.

51. Ibid., XXXV.

52. In a letter to John Murray (4 September 1917), Byron, bristled by this wordplay, indignantly retorts, "Besides, why '*modern*?' You may say *modern Greeks*, but surely *Greece* itself is rather more ancient than ever it was." Qtd. in Wolfson, ed., *Felicia Hemans*, 536, emphasis original.

53. Saree Makdisi makes a similar argument about Shelley's description of the East in the poem "Alastor." Makdisi argues that Shelley discursively depopulates and reduces to ruins the entirety of the Eastern territories in order to enable a reframing of the East as a pre-modern space situated within a historical continuum that leads teleologically to Western European civilization. See his chapter "Beyond the Realm of Dreams: Byron, Shelley, and the East" in *Romantic Imperialism* (122–153).

54. Gibbon, *Decline and Fall*, 2:638.

55. Ibid., 2:641–2.

56. Hemans is here operating within the mode of modern orientalism. Edward W. Said explains that the modern orientalist performs a vital function for imperialism by discursively mastering and dominating those peoples and regions under its scrutiny. According to Said, the practice of "discovering" the East operates within a modern paradigm of orientalism that figures the East as backwards and essentially knowable because it occupies a past stage in Western development. Said explains that this paradigm is contrary to classical orientalism, which figures the East as exotic, essentially different from the West, and therefore inscrutable. Edward W. Said, *Orientalism* (New York: Vintage, 1978), 120–3. Byron's treatment of Greece and the Levant in *Childe Harold* adheres closer to the latter mode.

57. Hemans, *Modern Greece*, III.

58. In *Imperial Eyes*, Mary Louise Pratt offers

Mungo Park's *Travels in the Interior Districts of Africa* (1816) as a text that exemplifies the central traits of a "sentimental narrator." The "sentimental narrator" is defined as experiential, innocent, passive, and imperiled by natives, thereby deflecting any claim to imperial ambitions, when, in fact, this narrator is performing the necessary task of collecting data on unexplored territories. The narrator also inverts imperial reality by presenting soon-to-be conquered natives as dangerous aggressors while depicting the imperialist West as fundamentally benign, inquisitive, and innocent. Mary Louise Pratt, *Imperial Eyes: Travel Writing and Transculturation* (New York: Routledge, 1992), 69–85.

59. Tricia Lootens, "Hemans and Home: Victorianism, Feminine 'Internal Enemies,' and the Domestication of National Identity," *PMLA* 109, no. 2 (1994): 247.

60. Stuart Ward contends that sameness, not alterity, is the primary force that consolidated a cohesive British identity by psychologically binding Britain with its white settler communities across the globe. Stuart Ward, "The End of Empire and the Fate of Britishness," 245. Accepting this, their globally scattered graves also work to engrave a British presence upon disparate and far-flung regions of the globe, symbolically annexing these territories to a British Commonwealth.

61. See the *Letter to John Murray* (26 February 1817). Qtd. in Wolfson, ed., *Felicia Hemans*, 480–1.

62. See *Byron's Letter to John Murray* (4 September 1817). Qtd. in Wolfson, ed., *Felicia Hemans*, 536.

63. Hemans, *Modern Greece*, LXXIV.
64. Ibid., I.
65. Ibid., XXXVII.
66. Ibid., LXXII-III.

67. See Sophia Psarra, "The Parthenon and the Erechtheion: The Architectural Formation of Place, Politics and Myth," *The Journal of Architecture* 9 (Spring 2004): 77–104. Psarra's study focuses on two adjacent structures that stand upon the Acropolis: the Parthenon and the Erechtheion. The former roots present imperial exploits in the nation's past, thereby granting it legitimacy, while the latter anchors an ancient religion and mythology in the present, granting continuity to the nation's culture.

68. Hemans, *Modern Greece*, LXXXVIII.
69. Ibid., XCI., XCVII.

70. Gauri Viswanathan pursues this theme at length in *Masks of Conquest*.

71. Hemans, *Modern Greece*, XCIX.

72. Ibid., C. Here, Hemans takes up the cause of the native arts movement, following in the footsteps of Blake, Wordsworth, and numerous other British poets and painters. For more on this, see also Morris Eaves, *The Counter-Arts Conspiracy: Art and Industry in the Age of Blake* (Ithaca: Cornell University Press, 1992).

73. Ibid., CI.
74. Ibid., XLII.
75. Ibid., XXXIX.

76. Kevin Eubanks, "Minerva's Veil: Hemans, Critics, and the Construction of Gender," *European Romantic Review* 8, no. 4 (1997): 345.

77. Hemans, *Modern Greece*, LXXXVI, LXXXI.

78. Anne Janowitz, "Amiable and Radical Sociability: Anna Barbauld's 'Free Familiar Conversation,'" in *Romantic Sociability: Social Networks and Literary Culture in Britain, 1770–1840*, ed. Gillian Russell and Clara Tuite (Cambridge: Cambridge University Press, 2002), 62.

79. Angela Keane, "The Market, the Public and the Female Author: Anna Laetitia Barbauld's Gift Economy," *Romanticism: The Journal of Romantic Culture and Criticism* 8, no. 2 (2002): 165.

80. Janowitz, "Amiable and Radical Sociability," 66.

81. Barbauld, Anna Letitia, "To a Lady," in *Poems of Anna Letitia Barbauld*, ed. William McCarthy and Elizabeth Kraft (University of Georgia Press, 1994), 3, 18.

82. Polwhele, *The Unsex'd Females*, 6, 17.
83. Barbauld, "Rights of Woman," 19, 30.

84. Horace Walpole to Charlotte Berry, "Strawberry Hill, Dec. 20, 1790, very late at night," in *The Letters of Horace Walpole*, ed. The Earl of Orford, 6 vols. (London: Richard Bentley, 1840), 6:384; Horace Walpole to Charlotte Berry, "Strawberry Hill, July 26, 1791," *Letters*, 6:449.

85. Barbauld, *Eighteen Hundred and Eleven*, 4. All references to the poem are to *Poems of Anna Letitia Barbauld*, ed. McCarthy and Kraft.

86. Ibid., 46.

87. Josephine McDonagh, "Barbauld's Domestic Economy," *Essays and Studies* 51 (1998): 75.

88. Barbauld, *Eighteen Hundred and Eleven*, 40, 43.

89. Thomson, "Rule, Britannia," 5.

90. Barbauld, *Eighteen Hundred and Eleven*, 53.

91. Ibid., 61–4.
92. Ibid., 64.
93. Ibid., 306, 320.

94. Diego Saglia has also discussed this aspect of the poem. See "The Dangers of Over-Refinement: The Language of Luxury in Romantic Poetry By Women, 1793–1811," *Studies in Romanticism* 38, no. 4 (1999): 643.

95. Barbauld, *Eighteen Hundred and Eleven*, 52.

96. Maggie Favretti has arrived at a similar conclusion. See "The Politics of Vision: Anna Barbauld's 'Eighteen Hundred and Eleven,'" in *Women's Poetry in the Enlightenment: The Making of a Canon, 1730-1820*, ed. Isobel Armstrong and Virginia Blain (New York: St. Martin's, 1999), 104.

97. Daniel P. Watkins, *Anna Letitia Barbauld and Eighteenth-Century Visionary Poetics* (Baltimore: Johns Hopkins University Press, 2012), 28–33.

98. Barbauld, *Eighteen Hundred and Eleven*, 58.

99. Ibid., 60.

100. Ibid., 314, 315. Penny Bradshaw has written that this statement contains a nascent critique of the Enlightenment in which Barbauld expresses her view that there is a contradiction between what the Enlightenment promises and what it delivers. Penny Bradshaw, "Gendering the Enlightenment: Conflicting Images of Progress in the Poetry of Anna Laetitia Barbauld," *Women's Writing* 5, no. 3 (1998): 354.

101. Barbauld, *Eighteen Hundred and Eleven*, 121–6.

102. Letter to James Montgomery (29 February 1812), qtd. in McCarthy and Kraft, *Poems*, 309, emphasis original.

103. This magazine is singular in its qualified defense of the poem: "Her theme is serious; and some may think her strains too melancholy, and her visions of her country's future fate too gloomy. Be they so. Too much of excitement to the slaughter of our species, by flattering views of false glory, has England now received, to leave in the minds, even of the most martial among us, any apprehension of a counter-spirit of peace, reason, and religion." Qtd. in McCarthy and Kraft, *Poems*, 310. The date of the review is 1815—after the Battle of Waterloo—which McCarthy & Kraft suggest explains its cautiously approbative posture (310).

104. *The Quarterly Review* (1812), 309. Qtd. in William Keach, "A Regency Prophecy and the End of Anna Barbauld's Career," *Studies in Romanticism* 33 (1994): 570.

105. McCarthy and Kraft corroborate Croker's taxonomic categorization of the poem, stating that it is "in part a Juvenalian, or 'tragical,' satire." They adduce contemporary reviews to support this position: the *Universal Magazine* perceived its affinity with Johnson's satire, *London*, and the *Anti-Jacobin Review* declared the poem "a miserable travestie" of Goldsmith's *Deserted Village*. McCarthy and Kraft, *Poems*, 310.

106. Qtd. in McCarthy and Kraft, *Poems*, 310.

107. Qtd. in Penny Bradshaw, "Dystopian Futures: Time-Travel and Millenarian Visions in the Poetry of Anna Barbauld and Charlotte Smith," *Romanticism on the Net: An Electronic Journal Devoted to Romantic Studies* 21 (February 2001): 9, http://users.ox.ac.uk/~scat0385/21bradshaw.html.

108. Barbauld, *Eighteen Hundred and Eleven*, 73–80.

109. Ibid., 96, 91.

110. Deirdre Coleman argues that Priestley's inclusion in this line up suggests Barbauld's desire to achieve reconciliation with this exiled friend, scientist, and fellow Dissenter who was made a pariah even among his own circle of Dissenters in the wake of the Birmingham riots, which were attributed to his inflammatory public agitation. She writes, "The poem is a powerful statement of Barbauld's solidarity with her old friend." Deirdre Coleman, "Firebrands, Letters and Flowers: Mrs. Barbauld and the Priestleys," in *Romantic Sociability*, 101. If so, Priestley's inclusion intimates how self-conscious Barbauld was of her own dissenting counter-patriotism. Nicholas Birns has also discussed the allusions to Priestley in the poem. See Nicholas Birns, "'Thy World Columbus!': Barbauld and Global Space, 1803, '1811,' 1812, 2003," *European Romantic Review* 16, no. 5 (2005): 552.

111. Mehta, *Empire and Liberalism*, 51–2.

112. Barbauld, *Eighteen Hundred and Eleven*, 83–4.

113. Ibid., 85–8.

114. Ibid., 127–32.

115. Homi K. Bhabha, *The Location of Culture* (New York: Routledge, 1994), 85.

116. Barbauld, *Eighteen Hundred and Eleven*, 177, 185–6.

117. Berkeley, "Verses on the Prospect of Planting Arts and Learning in America," *Works*, 7:21. Although revised and first published in the *Miscellany* (1752), the poem was originally penned in a letter to Lord Percival, London, dated 10 February 1726, under the title *America or the Muse's Refuge: A Prophecy*.

118. Berkeley, "Verses," 13–6.

119. Volney, *Ruins*, 13, emphasis original.

120. Gibbon, *Decline and Fall*, 4:119.

121. Barbauld, *Eighteen Hundred and Eleven*, 215–22.

122. Ibid., 241–4.

123. Said, *Orientalism*, 2.

124. Barbauld, *Eighteen Hundred and Eleven*, 334.

Conclusion

1. William Blake, *Milton*, in *The Complete Poetry and Prose of William Blake*, ed. David V. Erdman, rev. ed. (New York: Anchor, 1988), 100. For the rest of the chapter, all references to Blake's poetry are to this edition and refer to page numbers rather than lines.

2. Shelley, *Defence, Shelley's Poetry and Prose*, 508.

3. Paul Ricoeur, *Lectures on Ideology and Utopia*, ed. George H. Taylor (New York: Columbia University Press, 1986), 172–3.

4. Blake, "London," 8.

5. Esmé Wingfield-Stratford, *The History of English Patriotism* (New York: John Lace, 1913), 1:613.

6. Ibid., 1:602.

7. Ibid., 1:613. Blake's unfortunate inscription within an English nationalist discourse is discussed.

8. In the Introduction to *Blake, Nation and Empire* (New York: Palgrave Macmillan, 2006), 1–19, Steve Clark and David Worrall suggest that Blake's removal of the "Jerusalem" epigraph from later editions of *Milton* may have been in response to a common nationalist misreading of the poem. The compilation includes relevant essays by Makdisi ("Immortal Joy: William Blake and the Cultural Politics of Empire," 20–39) and Jason Whittaker ("The Matter of Britain: Blake, Milton and the Ancient Britons," 186–200). Also pertinent is Julia M. Wright's "Greek and Latin Slaves of the Sword: Rejecting the Imperial Nation in Blake's *Milton*" collected in *Milton and the Imperial Vision*, ed. Balachandra Rajan and Elizabeth Sauer (Pittsburgh: Duquesne University Press, 1999), 255–72.

9. For a thorough explanation of Blake's mythological system, see Northrop Frye's *Fearful Symmetry: A Study of William Blake* (1947; repr. Boston: Beacon Press, 1962).

10. Blake, *America*, 52.
11. Ibid., 54.
12. Ibid., 53.
13. Ibid., 57.
14. Ibid.
15. Ibid., 57, 53.
16. Blake, *Song of Los*, 69.
17. Blake, *Europe*, 63.
18. Ibid., 62.
19. Ibid., 64.
20. Ibid.
21. Ibid., 60.
22. Ibid., 65.
23. Ibid., 66.
24. Blake, *Song of Los*, 67.
25. Ibid.
26. Ibid., 68.
27. Ibid., 69.
28. Ibid., 68.
29. Ibid.
30. Ibid., 69.
31. Ibid.
32. Ibid.
33. Ibid.
34. Ibid., 69–70.
35. Blake, *Milton*, 100.

Bibliography

Abrams, M.H. *Natural Supernaturalism: Tradition and Revolution in Romantic Literature*. New York: W.W. Norton, 1973.

Ackroyd, Peter. *Albion: The Origins of the English Imagination*. New York: Doubleday, 2003.

Addison, Joseph. *The Spectator*. 1711. Edited and with introduction by Donald F. Bond. 5 vols. Oxford: Clarendon, 1965.

Adorno, Theodor W. "Lyric Poetry and Society." In *Critical Theory and Society: A Reader*, edited by Stephen Eric Bronner and Douglas MacKay Kellner, 155–71. New York: Routledge, 1989.

Akenside, Mark. *The Poetical Works of Mark Akenside*. Edited by Robin Dix. Madison, NJ: Fairleigh Dickinson, 1996.

Anderson, Benedict. *Imagined Communities*. New York: Verso, 1991.

Arac, Jonathan. *Critical Genealogies: Historical Situations for Postmodern Literary Studies*. New York: Columbia University Press, 1987.

Arac, Jonathan, and Harriet Ritvo, eds. *Macropolitics of Nineteenth-Century Literature: Nationalism, Exoticism, Imperialism*. Philadelphia: University of Pennsylvania Press, 1991.

Armitage, David. *The Ideological Origins of the British Empire*. Ideas in Context 59. 2000. Reprint, New York: Cambridge University Press, 2004.

Armitage, David, Armand Himy, and Quentin Skinner, eds. *Milton and Republicanism*. Ideas in Context. New York: Cambridge University Press, 1998.

Armstrong, Isobel, and Virginia Blain, eds. *Women's Poetry in the Enlightenment: The Making of a Canon, 1730–1820*. New York: St. Martin's, 1999.

———, and ———. *Women's Poetry, Late Romantic to Late Victorian: Gender and Genre, 1830–1900*. New York: St. Martin's, 1999.

Arnold, Matthew. *The Complete Prose Works*. Edited by R.H. Super. 11 vols. Ann Arbor: University of Michigan Press, 1960–77.

Arthur, Paul W.L. "From Politics to Pleasure: Coleridge and Romantic Imperialism." *SPAN* 45 (October 1997): 73–87.

Austin, Carolyn F. "Home and Nation in the Heart of Midlothian." *SEL: Studies in English Literature, 1500–1900* 40, no. 4 (2000): 621–34.

Backscheider, Paula R. *Eighteenth-Century Women Poets and Their Poetry: Inventing Agency, Inventing Genre*. Baltimore: Johns Hopkins University Press, 2005.

Bainbridge, Simon. *British Poetry and the Revolutionary and Napoleonic Wars: Visions of Conflict*. New York: Oxford University Press, 2003.

Baldick, Chris. *The Social Mission of English Criticism, 1848–1932*. New York: Oxford University Press, 1983.

Ball, Patricia M. *The Central Self: A Study in Romantic and Victorian Imagination*. London: Athlone, 1968.

Barbauld, Anna Letitia. *Poems of Anna Letitia Barbauld*, edited by William McCarthy and Elizabeth Kraft. Athens: University of Georgia Press, 1994.

Barczewski, Stephanie L. *Myth and National Identity in Nineteenth Century Britain: The Legends of King Arthur and Robin Hood*. New York: Oxford University Press, 2000.

Bardsley, Alyson. "In and Around the Borders of the Nation in Scott's Guy Mannering." *Nineteenth-Century Contexts* 24, no. 4 (2002): 397–415.

Bate, Jonathan. "Inventing Region and Nation: Wordsworth's Sonnets." *Swansea Review* (1994): 2–22.

_____. *Romantic Ecology: Wordsworth and the Environmental Tradition*. New York: Routledge, 1991.

Bateson, F.W. *Wordsworth: A Reinterpretation*. London: Longmans, 1956.

Bauer, N.S. *William Wordsworth: A Reference Guide to British Criticism, 1793–1899*. Boston: Twayne, 1978.

Baugh, Albert C., and Thomas Cable. *A History of the English Language*, 5th ed. Upper Saddle River, NJ: Prentice Hall, 2002.

Behrendt, Stephen C. *British Women Poets and the Romantic Writing Community*. Baltimore: Johns Hopkins University Press, 2009.

Bennett, Betty T., ed. *The Letters of Mary Shelley*. 3 vols. Baltimore: Johns Hopkins University Press, 1980–8.

Bennett, Betty T., and Stuart Curran, eds. *Mary Shelley in Her Times*. Baltimore: Johns Hopkins University Press, 2000.

Bergonzi, Bernard. *Exploding English: Criticism, Theory, Culture*. New York: Clarendon Press, 1990.

Berkeley, George. *The Works of George Berkeley Bishop of Cloyne*. Edited by A.A. Luce and T.E. Jessop. 7 vols. Reprint, Camden, NJ: Nelson, 1964.

Bhabha, Homi K. *The Location of Culture*. New York: Routledge, 1994.

_____, ed. *Nation and Narration*. New York: Routledge, 1990.

Birns, Nicholas. "'Thy World Columbus!' Barbauld and Global Space, 1803, '1811,' 1812, 2003." *European Romantic Review* 16, no. 5 (2005): 545–62.

Blake, William. *The Complete Poetry and Prose of William Blake*. Edited by David V. Erdman, rev. ed. New York: Anchor, 1988.

Bode, Christoph. "Putting the Lake District on the (Mental) Map: William Wordsworth's *Guide to the Lakes.*" *Journal for the Study of British Cultures* 4, nos. 1–2 (1997): 95–111.

Bold, Alan. *The Ballad*. The Critical Idiom. Vol. 41. New York: Methuen, 1979.

Bonnell, Thomas F. *The Most Disreputable Trade: Publishing the Classics of English Poetry, 1765–1810*. New York: Oxford University Press, 2008.

Bourdieu, Pierre. *Language and Symbolic Power*. Edited by John B. Thompson. Translated by Gino Raymond and Matthew Adamson. Cambridge: Harvard University Press, 1991.

Bradshaw, Penny. "Dystopian Futures: Time-Travel and Millenarian Visions in the Poetry of Anna Barbauld and Charlotte Smith." *Romanticism on the Net: An Electronic Journal Devoted to Romantic Studies* 21 (February 2001). http://users.ox.ac.uk/~scat0385/21bradshaw.html.

_____. "Gendering the Enlightenment: Conflicting Images of Progress in the Poetry of Anna Laetitia Barbauld." *Women's Writing* 5, no. 3 (1998): 353–71.

Brennan, Gillian E. *Patriotism, Power and Print: National Consciousness in Tudor England*. Pittsburgh: Duquesne University Press, 2003.

Breuilly, John. *Nationalism and the State*, 2d ed. Chicago: University of Chicago Press, 1993.

Brewer, John. *The Pleasures of the Imagination: English Culture in the Eighteenth Century*. New York: Farrar, Straus and Giroux, 1997.

Brewster, Paul G. "The Influence of the Popular Ballad on Wordsworth's Poetry." *Studies in Poetry* 35 (October 1938): 588–618.

Brocklehurst, Helen, and Robert Phillips, eds. *History, Nationhood, and the Question of Britain*. New York: Palgrave Macmillan, 2004.

Brockliss, Laurence, David Eastwood, and Michael John. "From Dynastic Union to European State: The European Experience." In *A Union of Multiple Identities: The British Isles, c. 1750–c. 1850*, edited by Laurence Brockliss and David East-

wood. Manchester: Manchester University Press, 1997.
Broglio, Ron. "Mapping British Earth and Sky." *The Wordsworth Circle* 33, no. 2 (Spring 2002): 70–6.
Bronner, Stephen Eric, and Douglas MacKay, eds. *Critical Theory and Society: A Reader*. New York: Routledge, 1989.
Budworth, Joseph. *Fortnight's Ramble to the Lakes in Westmoreland, Lancashire, and Cumberland*. London: Hookham & Carpenter, 1792.
Bürger, Gottfried August. *Lenore*. Translated by Dante Gabriel Rosetti. London: Ellis & Elvey, 1900.
Burke, Edmund. *The Correspondence of Edmund Burke*. 9 vols. Chicago: University of Chicago Press, 1958–71.
———. *A Philosophical Enquiry into the Origins of Our Ideas of the Sublime and Beautiful*. Edited by James T. Boulton. Notre Dame: University Notre Dame Press, 1968.
Butler, Marilyn. "Romanticism in England." In *Romanticism in National Context*, edited by Roy Porter and Mikulas Teich, 37–67. New York: Cambridge University Press, 1988.
Byron, George Gordon Lord. *Byron*. Edited by Jerome J. McGann. New York: Oxford University Press, 1986.
Cairns, Craig. "Scott's Staging of the Nation." *Studies in Romanticism* 40, no. 1 (2001): 13–28.
Campbell, Thomas. *Specimens of the British Poets: With Biographical and Critical Notices, and an Essay on English Poetry*. 7 vols. London: John Murray, 1819.
Carlyle, Thomas. *On Heroes, Hero-Worship and the Heroic in History*. Edited by Carl Niemeyer. Lincoln: University of Nebraska Press, 1966.
Carson, Julie A. *In the Theatre of Romanticism: Coleridge, Nationalism, Women*. Cambridge Studies in Romanticism 5. New York: Cambridge University Press, 1994.
Caudwell, Christopher. *Illusion and Reality: A Study of the Sources of Poetry*. 1937. Reprint, New York: International, 1963.
Chandler, James K. *England in 1819: The Politics of Literary Culture and the Case of Romantic Historicism*. Chicago: University of Chicago Press, 1998.
———. *Wordsworth's Second Nature: A Study of the Poetry and Politics*. Chicago: University of Chicago Press, 1984.
Cheeke, Stephen. "The Sword 'Which eats into itself': Romanticism, Napoleon and the Romantic Parallel." *Romanticism: The Journal of Romantic Culture & Criticism* 10, no. 2 (2004): 209–27.
Child, Francis James. *The English and Scottish Popular Ballads*. 10 vols. 1882–98. Reprint, New York: Dover, 1965.
Chorley, Henry F. *Memorials of Mrs. Hemans*. 2 vols. New York: Saunders & Otley, 1836.
Clark, Steve, and David Worrall, eds. *Blake, Nation and Empire*. New York: Palgrave Macmillan, 2006.
Clarke, Norma. *Ambitious Heights: Writing, Friendship, Love—The Jewsbury Sisters, Felicia Hemans, and Jane Welsh Carlyle*. New York: Routledge, 1990.
Cobban, Alfred. *Edmund Burke and the Revolt Against the Eighteenth Century: A Study of the Political and Social Thinking of Burke, Wordsworth, Coleridge and Southey*, 2d ed. London: George Allen & Unwin, 1962.
Coe, Charles Norton. *Wordsworth and the Literature of Travel*. New York: Bookman Associates, 1953.
Cole, G.D.H. *A Short History of the British Working-Class Movement, 1789–1947*. London: George Allen & Unwin, 1952.
Coleman, Deirdre. "Firebrands, Letters and Flowers: Mrs. Barbauld and the Priestleys." In *Romantic Sociability: Social Networks and Literary Culture in Britain, 1770–1840*, edited by Gillian Russell and Clara Tuite, 82–103. Cambridge: Cambridge University Press, 2002.
Coleridge, Samuel Taylor. *Biographia Literaria*. Edited by James Engell and W. Jackson Bate. The Collected Works of Samuel Taylor Coleridge 7. Bollingen Series LXXV. Princeton, NJ: Princeton University Press, 1983.
———. *The Collected Letters of Samuel Taylor Coleridge*. Edited by E.L. Griggs. 6 vols. Oxford: Oxford University Press, 1956.

———. *The Collected Works of Samuel Taylor Coleridge*. Edited by Kathleen Coburn. 16 vols. Bollingen Series LXXV. Princeton, NJ: Princeton University Press, 1969.

———. *The Complete Poems*. Edited by William Keach. New York: Penguin, 1997.

———. *The Poetical Works of Samuel Taylor Coleridge*. Edited by E.H. Coleridge. 2 vols. Oxford: Oxford University Press, 1912.

Colley, Linda. *Britons: Forging the Nation, 1707–1837*. New Haven: Yale University Press, 1992.

Conger, Syndy McMillen, ed. *Sensibility in Transformation: Creative Resistance to Sentiment from the Augustans to the Romantics*. Madison, NJ: Fairleigh Dickinson, 1990.

Connell, Philip. *Romanticism, Economics and the Question of 'Culture.'* New York: Oxford University Press, 2001.

Cookson, J.E. *The British Armed Nation, 1793–1815*. New York: Clarendon Press, 1997.

Court, Franklin E. *Institutionalizing English Literature: The Culture and Politics of Literary Study, 1750–1900*. Palo Alto: Stanford University Press, 1992.

Cowper, William. *The Poetical Works of William Cowper*, 4th ed. Edited by H.S. Milford. New York: Oxford, 1950.

Crawford, Robert. *Devolving English Literature*. New York: Clarendon Press, 1992.

———, ed. *The Scottish Invention of English Literature*. New York: Cambridge University Press, 1998.

Crehan, Stewart. *Blake in Context*. Atlantic Highlands, NJ: Humanities Press, 1984.

Darbishire, Helen. *The Poet Wordsworth*. Clark Lectures. Oxford: Clarendon Press, 1949.

Davies, Kate. "A Moral Purchase: Femininity, Commerce, and Abolition, 1788–1792." In *Women, Writing and the Public Sphere, 1700–1830*, edited by Elizabeth Eger, Charlotte Grant, and Cliona O. Gallchoir, 133–59. Cambridge: Cambridge University Press, 2001.

Davis, Leith. *Acts of Union: Scotland and the Literary Negotiation of the British Nation, 1707–1830*. Stanford: Stanford University Press, 1998.

de Bolla, Peter, Nigel Leask, and David Simpson, eds. *Land, Nation and Culture, 1740–1840: Thinking the Republic of Taste*. New York: Palgrave Macmillan, 2005.

de Man, Paul. *The Rhetoric of Romanticism*. New York: Columbia University Press, 1984.

De Paolo, Charles. "Coleridge and Gibbon's Controversy over *The Decline and Fall of the Roman Empire*." *CLIO: A Journal of Literature, History, and the Philosophy of History* 20, no. 1 (Fall 1990): 13–22.

de Sola Pinto, Vivian. *The Common Muse*. London: Chatto & Windus, 1957.

Del Giudice, Luisa, and Gerald Porter, eds. *Imagined States: Nationalism, Utopia and Longing in Oral Cultures*. Logan: Utah State University Press, 2001.

Defoe, Daniel. *Robinson Crusoe*. 1719. New York: W.W. Norton, 1994.

Dickinson, H.T., ed. *Britain and the French Revolution, 1789–1815*. London: Macmillan, 1989.

DiSalvo, Jackie. *War of Titans: Blake's Critique of Milton and the Politics of Religion*. Pittsburgh: University of Pittsburgh Press, 1983.

Doyle, Brian. *English and Englishness*. New York: Routledge, 1989.

Dryden, John. *Dryden*. Edited by Keith Walker. The Oxford Authors. New York: Oxford University Press, 1987.

Dugas, Don-John. *Marketing the Bard: Shakespeare in Performance and Print, 1660–1740*. Columbia: University of Missouri Press, 2006.

Dzelzainis, Martin. "Milton's Classical Republicanism." In *Milton and Republicanism*, edited by David Armitage, Armand Himy and Quentin Skinner, 3–24. Cambridge: Cambridge University Press, 1995.

Eagleton, Terry. *The Ideology of the Aesthetic*. Malden, MA: Blackwell, 1990.

———. *Literary Theory: An Introduction*, 2d ed. Minneapolis: University of Minnesota Press, 1996.

Easthope, Antony. *Englishness and National Culture*. New York: Routledge, 1999.

Eaves, Morris. *The Counter-Arts Conspiracy: Art and Industry in the Age of Blake*. Ithaca: Cornell University Press, 1992.

Eley, Geoff and Ronald Grigor Suny, eds. *Becoming National: A Reader*. New York: Oxford University Press, 1996.

Ellis, George. *Specimens of the Early English Poets*. London: Edwards, 1790.

Elton, G.R. *The Tudor Revolution in Government: Administrative Changes in the Reign of Henry VIII*. New York: Cambridge University Press, 1953.

Engels, Friedrich. *The Condition of the Working Class in England*. New York: Penguin, 1987.

Erdman, David. *Blake: Prophet Against Empire*. 3d ed. New York: Dover, 1977.

Emerson, Ralph Waldo. "The American Scholar." In *The Essential Writings of Ralph Waldo Emerson*, edited by Brooks Atkinson and introduced by Mary Oliver, 43–59. New York: Modern Library, 2000.

Eubanks, Kevin. "Minerva's Veil: Hemans, Critics, and the Construction of Gender." *European Romantic Review* 8, no. 4 (1997): 341–59.

Everest, Kelvin. *Coleridge's Secret Ministry: The Context of the Conversation Poems 1795–1798*. New York: Barnes & Noble, 1979.

Fairer, David. "'Patriot Rage and Indignation High': The voice of Sheridan in 'Fears in Solitude.'" Paper presented at the Coleridge Summer Conference, Cannington, UK, Summer 2004.

Favretti, Maggie. "The Politics of Vision: Anna Barbauld's 'Eighteen Hundred and Eleven.'" In *Women's Poetry in the Enlightenment: The Making of a Canon, 1730–1820*, edited by Isobel Armstrong and Virginia Blain, 99–110. New York: St. Martin's, 1999.

Feldman, Paula R. "The Poet and the Profits: Felicia Hemans and the Literary Marketplace." In *Women's Poetry, Late Romantic to Late Victorian: Gender and Genre, 1830–1900*, edited by Isobel Armstrong and Virginia Blain, 71–101. New York: St. Martin's, 1999.

_____, ed. *British Women Poets of the Romantic Era: An Anthology*. Baltimore: Johns Hopkins University Press, 1997.

Fischer, Ernst. *The Necessity of Art: A Marxist Approach*. Translated by Anna Bostock. New York: Penguin, 1963.

Foucault, Michel. *Security, Territory, Population: Lectures at the Collège de France, 1977–1978*. Edited by Michel Senellart. Translated by Graham Burchell. New York: Palgrave Macmillan, 2004.

Frey, Anne. *British State Romanticism: Authorship, Agency, and Bureaucratic Nationalism*. Palo Alto: Stanford University Press, 2009.

Friedman, Albert B. *The Ballad Revival: Studies in the Influence of Popular on Sophisticated Poetry*. Chicago: University of Chicago Press, 1961.

Frye, Northrop. *Fearful Symmetry: A Study of William Blake*. 1947. Reprint, Boston: Beacon Press, 1962.

Fulford, Timothy. "Catholicism and Polytheism: Britain's Colonies and Coleridge's Politics." *Romanticism* 5 (1999): 232–53.

_____. "Fallen Ladies and Cruel Mothers: Ballad Singers and Ballad Heroines in the Eighteenth Century." *The Eighteenth Century* 47, nos. 2–3 (2006): 309–29.

_____. *Romantic Indians: Native Americans, British Literature, and Transatlantic Culture, 1756–1830*. New York: Oxford University Press, 2006.

_____, ed. *Romanticism and Millenarianism*. New York: Palgrave, 2002.

Fulford, Timothy, and Peter J. Kitson, eds. *Romanticism and Colonialism: Writing and Empire, 1780–1830*. New York: Cambridge University Press, 1998.

Gamer, Michael. *Romanticism and the Gothic: Genre, Reception, and Canon Formation*. Cambridge: Cambridge University Press, 2000.

Garrett, James M. "Surveying and Writing the Nation: Wordsworth's Black Comb and 1816 Commemorative Poems." In *REAL: Yearbook of Research in English and American Literature*, edited by Brook Thomas, 77–109. Literature and the Nation 14. Tübingen, Germany: Gunter Narr Verlag Tübingen, 1998.

_____. *Wordsworth and the Writing of the Nation*. Aldershot, UK: Ashgate, 2008.

Gates, Barbara T. "Wordsworth's Use of Oral History." *Folklore* 85 (1974): 254–67.

Gatta, John, Jr. "Coleridge's 'Fears in Solitude' and the Prospect of Social Redemption." *Cithara: Essays in the Judeo-Christian Tradition* 26, no. 1 (November 1986): 36–43.

Gellner, Ernest. *Nations and Nationalism.* Ithaca: Cornell University Press, 1983.

Gibbon, Edward. *The Decline and Fall of the Roman Empire.* Introduced by Hugh Trevor-Roper. 6 vols. Everyman's Library 95. New York: Alfred A. Knopf, 1993–94.

Gill, Stephen, ed. *The Major Works*, by William Wordsworth. New York: Oxford University Press, 2000.

Gilpin, William. *Three Essays on Picturesque Beauty; on Picturesque Travel; and on Sketching Landscape: To Which is Added a Poem, on Landscape Painting*, 2d ed. 1786. Reprint, Westmead, UK: Gregg International, 1972.

Godwin, William. *An Enquiry Concerning Political Justice.* 1793. New York: Penguin, 1985.

Goldstein, Laurence. *Ruins and Empire: The Evolution of a Theme in Augustan and Romantic Literature.* Pittsburgh: University of Pittsburgh Press, 1977.

Graff, Gerald. *Professing Literature: An Institutional History.* Chicago: University of Chicago Press, 1987.

Gravil, Richard. *Wordsworth's Bardic Vocation, 1787–1842.* New York: Palgrave Macmillan, 2003.

Gray, Thomas. *Thomas Gray.* Edited by Robert L. Mack. London: J.M. Dent, 1996.

Greenfield, S.B., and D.G. Calder. *A New Critical History of Old English Literature.* New York: New York University Press, 1986.

Groom, Nick. *The Making of Percy's Reliques.* Oxford: Clarendon Press, 1999.

Gummere, Francis Barton. *Old English Ballads.* Boston: Ginn & Co., 1897.

Hales, John W., and Frederick J. Furnivall. *Bishop Percy's Folio Manuscript: Ballads and Romances.* Edited by Leslie Shepard. 3 vols. Detroit: Singing Tree Press, 1968.

Haley, Bruce. *Living Forms: Romantics and the Monumental Figure.* Albany: State University of New York Press, 2003.

Hanley, Keith, and Raman Selden, eds. *Revolution and English Romanticism: Politics and Rhetoric.* New York: St. Martin's, 1990.

Harris, Wendell. "Romantic Bard and Victorian Commentators: The Meaning and Significance of Meaning and Significance." *Victorian Poetry* 24, no. 4 (1986): 455–69.

Harrison, Gary. *Wordsworth's Vagrant Muse: Poetry, Poverty, and Power.* Detroit: Wayne State University Press, 1994.

Hartley, David. *Observations on Man, His Frame, His Duty, and His Expectations.* 2 vols. Gainesville: Scholars' Facsimiles & Reprints, 1966.

Hazlitt, William. *Selected Writings.* Edited by Jon Cook. New York: Oxford, 1998.

_____. *The Spirit of the Age, or, Contemporary Portraits.* Edited by Harold Bloom. New York: Chelsea House, 1983.

Hazucha, Andrew. "Neither Deep nor Shallow but National: Eco-Nationalism in Wordsworth's *Guide to the Lakes.*" *Isle: Interdisciplinary Studies in Literature and Environment* 9, no. 2 (2002): 61–73.

Hechter, Michael. *Internal Colonialism: The Celtic Fringe in British National Development, 1536–1966.* London: Routledge, 1975.

Heinzelman, Kurt. "The Uneducated Imagination: Romantic Representations of Labor." In *At the Limits of Romanticism: Essays in Cultural, Feminist, and Materialist Criticism*, edited by Mary A. Favret and Nicola J. Watson, 101–24. Bloomington: Indiana University Press, 1994.

Helgerson, Richard. *Forms of Nationhood: The Elizabethan Writing of England.* Chicago: University of Chicago Press, 1994.

Hemans, Felicia. *Felicia Hemans: Selected Poems, Letters, Reception Materials.* Edited and introduced by Susan J. Wolfson. Princeton, NJ: Princeton University Press, 2000.

Herd, David. *Ancient and Modern Scottish Songs, Heroic Ballads, etc.*, new ed. 1776. 2 vols. Edinburgh: Scottish Academic Press, 1973.

Herder, Johann Gottfried. *Sämmtliche Werke.* Edited by Bernhard Suphan. 33 vols. 1877–1913. Reprint, Hildesheim, Germany: Georg Olms, 1967–8.

Hilles, Frederick W., and Harold Bloom, eds. *From Sensibility to Romanticism: Essays Presented to Frederick A. Pottle*. New York: Oxford University Press, 1965.

Hitchens, Peter. *The Abolition of Britain: From Winston Churchill to Princess Diana*. San Francisco: Encounter Books, 2000.

Hoagwood, Terence A. *From Song to Print: Romantic Pseudo-Songs*. New York: Palgrave Macmillan, 2010.

Hobsbawm, Eric J. *The Age of Revolution*. 1962. Reprint, New York: Vintage, 1996.

———. *Nations and Nationalism Since 1780: Programme, Myth, Reality*. Cambridge: Cambridge University Press, 1990.

Hobsbawm, Eric J., and Terence Ranger, eds. *The Invention of Tradition*. Cambridge: Cambridge University Press, 1992.

Hobson, Christopher Z. *Blake and Homosexuality*. New York: Palgrave, 2000.

———. *The Chained Boy: Orc and Blake's Idea of Revolution*. Lewisburg, NJ: Bucknell University Press, 1999.

Horn, D.B., and Mary Ransome, eds. *English Historical Documents, 1714–1783*. London: Eyre and Spottiswoode, 1957.

Hume, David. *Essays: Moral, Political, and Literary*, rev. ed. Edited by Eugene F. Miller. 1742. Indianapolis: Liberty Fund, 1987.

———. *An Inquiry Concerning Human Understanding*. Edited by Charles W. Hendel. New York: Bobbs-Merrill, 1955.

Hurd, Richard. *Letters on Chivalry and Romance*. 1762. New York: Garland, 1971.

Izenberg, Gerald N. *Impossible Individuality: Romanticism, Revolution, and the Origins of Modern Selfhood, 1787–1802*. Princeton, NJ: Princeton University Press, 1992.

Jacobus, Mary. *Tradition and Experiment in Wordsworth's Lyrical Ballads (1798)*. Oxford: Clarendon Press, 1976.

James, Felicity. "Coleridge and the Fears of Friendship, 1798." *The Coleridge Bulletin* NS 24 (Winter 2004): 11–8.

Jameson, Fredric. *The Political Unconscious: Narrative as a Socially Symbolic Act*. Ithaca: Cornell University Press, 1982.

———, ed. *Aesthetics and Politics: The Key Texts of the Classic Debate Within German Marxism*. New York: Verso, 1977.

Janowitz, Anne. "Amiable and Radical Sociability: Anna Barbauld's 'Free Familiar Conversation.'" In *Romantic Sociability: Social Networks and Literary Culture in Britain, 1770–1840*, edited by Gillian Russell and Clara Tuite, 62–81. Cambridge: Cambridge University Press, 2002.

———. *England's Ruins: Poetic Purpose and the National Landscape*. Cambridge, MA: Blackwell, 1990.

———. *Lyric and Labour in the Romantic Tradition*. Cambridge: Cambridge University Press, 1998.

Jeffrey, Francis. *Contributions to the Edinburgh Review*, 2d ed. 3 vols. London: Longman, Brown, Green, and Longmans, 1846.

Johnson, Samuel. *A Dictionary of the English Language*. 2 vols. London: Knapton, Longman, Hitch, Hawes, Millar, and Dodsley, 1755.

———. *Lives of the English Poets*. Edited by George Birkbeck Hill. 3 vols. Reprint, New York: Octagon, 1967.

———. *The Works of Samuel Johnson*. 23 vols. New Haven: Yale University Press, 1958–2012.

Johnston, Kenneth R. "Wordsworth's Revolutions, 1793–1798." In *Revolution and English Romanticism: Politics and Rhetoric*, edited by Keith Hanley and Raman Selden, 169–204. New York: St. Martin's, 1990.

Johnston, Kenneth R., Gilbert Chaitin, Karen Hanson, and Herbert Marks, eds. *Romantic Revolutions: Criticism and Theory*. Bloomington: Indiana University Press, 1990.

Jones, Chris. "John Newton and Coleridge's 'Fears in Solitude.'" *Notes and Queries* 41, no. 3 (September 1994): 339–41.

Jouy, M. "Moral Condition and Influence of Women in Society." *The Athenaeum*, March 4, 1828.

Kaiser, David Aram. *Romanticism, Aesthetics, and Nationalism*. Cambridge: Cambridge University Press, 1999.

Kant, Immanuel. *Critique of Judgment*. Translated by James Creed Meredith. Oxford: Clarendon Press, 1952.

Kaul, Suvir. *Poems of Nations, Anthems of Empire: English Verse in the Long Eigh-

teenth Century. Charlottesville: University of Virginia Press, 2000.
Kaye, Harvey J., ed. *Poets, Politics and the People.* New York: Verso, 1989.
Keach, William. "A Regency Prophecy and the End of Anna Barbauld's Career." *Studies in Romanticism* 33 (1994): 569–77.
Keane, Angela. "The Market, the Public and the Female Author: Anna Laetitia Barbauld's Gift Economy." *Romanticism: The Journal of Romantic Culture and Criticism* 8, no. 2 (2002): 161–78.
Keats, John. *Complete Poems.* Edited by Jack Stillinger. Cambridge: Belknap, 1982.
_____. *Selected Letters.* Edited by Robert Gittings. Revised by John Mee. New York: Oxford, 2002.
Kelly, Gary. "The Limits of Genre and the Institution of Literature: Romanticism between Fact and Fiction." In *Romantic Revolutions: Criticism and Theory*, edited by Kenneth R. Johnston, Gilbert Chaitin, Karen Hanson, and Herbert Marks, 158–75. Bloomington: Indiana University Press, 1990.
Kelley, Theresa M. *Wordsworth's Revisionary Aesthetics.* Cambridge: Cambridge University Press, 1988.
Kemiläinen, Aira. "Romanticist and Realistic Elements in Nationalist Thinking in the 19th Century." *History of European Ideas* 16, nos. 1–3 (1993): 307–14.
Kiernan, V.G. "Wordsworth and the People." In *Poets, Politics and the People*, edited by Harvey J. Kaye, 96–128. New York: Verso, 1989.
Kim, Benjamin. "Generating a National Sublime: Wordsworth's *The River Duddon* and *The Guide to the Lakes*." *Studies in Romanticism* 45 (Spring 2006): 49–75.
Kipling, Rudyard. "The White Man's Burden." 1899. In *Poetry of the Victorian Period*, 3d ed. Edited by Jerome Hamilton Buckley and George Benjamin Woods. New York: HarperCollins, 1965.
Kitson, Peter J. *Romantic Literature, Race and Colonial Encounter.* New York: Palgrave Macmillan, 2007.
Kooy, Michael John. "Disinterested Patriotism: Bishop Butler, Hazlitt and Coleridge's Quarto Pamphlet of 1798." *The Coleridge Bulletin* 21 (2003): 55–65.
Kramnick, Isaac. *The Rage of Edmund Burke: Portrait of An Ambivalent Conservative.* New York: Basic Books, 1977.
Kroeber, Karl. *Ecological Literary Criticism: Romantic Imagining and the Biology of Mind.* New York: Columbia University Press, 1994.
_____. *Romantic Narrative Art.* Madison: University Wisconsin Press, 1960.
Kumar, Krishan. *The Making of English National Identity.* Cambridge: Cambridge University Press, 2003.
Landry, Donna. *The Invention of the Countryside: Hunting, Walking and Ecology in English Literature, 1671–1831.* New York: Palgrave, 2001.
Langan, Celeste. *Romantic Vagrancy: Wordsworth and the Simulation of Freedom.* Cambridge: Cambridge University Press, 1995.
Langford, Paul. *Englishness Identified: Manners and Character, 1650–1850.* New York: Oxford University Press, 2000.
Laws, G. Malcolm, Jr. *The British Literary Ballad: A Study in Poetic Imitation.* Carbondale: Southern Illinois University Press, 1972.
Leask, Nigel. "Burns, Wordsworth and the Politics of Vernacular Poetry." In *Land, Nation and Culture, 1740–1840: Thinking the Republic of Taste*, edited by Peter de Bolla, Nigel Leask, and David Simpson, 202–22. New York: Palgrave Macmillan, 2005.
_____. *The Politics of Imagination in Coleridge's Critical Thought.* New York: St. Martin's, 1988.
Lee, Yoon Sun. "A Divided Inheritance: Scott's Antiquarian Novel and the British Nation." *ELH* 64, no. 2 (1997): 537–67.
_____. *Nationalism and Irony: Burke, Scott, Carlyle.* New York: Oxford University Press, 2004.
Levinson, Marjorie. *The Romantic Fragment Poem: A Critique of a Form.* Chapel Hill: University of North Carolina Press, 1986.
_____. *Wordsworth's Great Period Poems: Four Essays.* Cambridge: Cambridge University Press, 1986.
Levy, Michelle. *Family Authorship and Romantic Print Culture.* New York: Palgrave Macmillan, 2008.

Lincoln, Andrew. "Walter Scott and the Birth of the Nation." *Romanticism: The Journal of Romantic Culture and Criticism* 8, no. 1 (2002): 1–17.

Linebaugh, Peter. *The London Hanged: Crime and Civil Society in the Eighteenth Century*. Cambridge: Cambridge University Press, 1992.

Liu, Alan. *Wordsworth: A Sense of History*. Palo Alto: Stanford University Press, 1989.

Locke, John. *An Essay Concerning Human Understanding*. Edited by Peter H. Nidditch. New York: Oxford University Press, 1979.

Lootens, Tricia. "Hemans and Her American Heirs: Nineteenth-Century Women's Poetry and National Identity." In *Women's Poetry, Late Romantic to Late Victorian: Gender and Genre, 1830–1900*, edited by Isobel Armstong and Virginia Blain, 243–60. New York: St. Martin's, 1999.

———. "Hemans and Home: Victorianism, Feminine 'Internal Enemies,' and the Domestication of National Identity." *PMLA* 109, no. 2 (1994): 238–53.

Löwy, Michael, and Robert Sayre. *Romanticism Against the Tide of Modernity*. Durham: Duke University Press, 2001.

Lukács, György. *History and Class Consciousness: Studies in Marxist Dialectics*. Translated by Rodney Livingstone. Cambridge: MIT Press, 1999.

———. "The Ideology of Modernism." In *Marxist Literary Theory: A Reader*, edited by Terry Eagleton and Drew Milne, 141–62. Oxford: Blackford, 2000.

———. "Realism in the Balance." In *Aesthetics and Politics: The Key Texts of the Classic Debate Within German Marxism*, edited by Fredric Jameson, 28–59. New York: Verso, 1977.

Lynch, Jack. *Becoming Shakespeare: The Unlikely Afterlife That Turned a Provincial Playwright into the Bard*. New York: Walker, 2007.

Mack, Robert L., ed. *Thomas Gray*. London: J.M. Dent, 1996.

MacLean, Gerald, Donna Landry, and Joseph P. Ward, eds. *The Country and the City Revisited: England and the Politics of Culture, 1550–1850*. Cambridge: Cambridge University Press, 1999.

Magnuson, Paul. "The Politics of Frost at Midnight." *Wordsworth Circle* 22 (1991): 3–11.

———. *Reading Public Romanticism*. Princeton, NJ: Princeton University Press, 1998.

———. "The Shaping of 'Fears in Solitude.'" In *Coleridge's Theory of Imagination Today*, edited by Christine Gallant, 197–210. New York: AMS Press, 1989.

Makdisi, Saree. "Immortal Joy: William Blake and the Cultural Politics of Empire." In *Blake, Nation and Empire*, edited by Steve Clark and David Worrall, 20–39. New York: Palgrave Macmillan, 2006.

———. *Romantic Imperialism: Universal Empire and the Culture of Modernity*. New York: Cambridge University Press, 1998.

———. *William Blake and the Impossible History of the 1790s*. Chicago: University of Chicago Press, 2003.

Mandeville, Bernard. *The Fable of the Bees*. Edited by F.B. Kaye. 2 vols. Indianapolis: Liberty Fund, 1988.

Manly, Susan. *Language, Custom, and Nation in the 1790s: Locke, Tooke, Wordsworth, Edgeworth*. Aldershot, UK: Ashgate, 2007.

Marr, Andrew. *The Day Britain Died*. London: Profile Books, 2000.

Marx, Karl. *A Contribution to the Critique of Political Economy*. Edited by Maurice Dobb. Translated by S.W. Ryazanskaya. London: Lawrence and Wishart, 1970.

Marx, Karl, and Frederick Engels. *The Communist Manifesto*. Introduced by Eric J. Hobsbawm. Reprint. New York: Verso, 2001.

Mathieson, Margaret. *The Preachers of Culture: A Study of English and Its Teachers*. Totowa, NJ: Rowman & Littlefield, 1975.

McCarthy, William and Elizabeth Kraft, eds. *The Poems of Anna Letitia Barbauld*. Athens: University of Georgia Press, 1994.

McDonagh, Josephine. "Barbauld's Domestic Economy." *Essays and Studies* 51 (1998): 62–77.

McDowell, Paula. "Consuming Women:

The Life of the 'Literary Lady' as Popular Culture in Eighteenth-Century England." *Genre* 26 (1993): 219–52.

McFarland, Thomas. *Romanticism and the Forms of Ruin: Wordsworth, Coleridge, and Modalities of Fragmentation*. Princeton, NJ: Princeton University Press, 1981.

———. *William Wordsworth: Intensity and Achievement*. Oxford: Clarendon Press, 1992.

McGann, Jerome J. *The Romantic Ideology: A Critical Investigation*. Chicago: University of Chicago Press, 1983.

———, ed. *Byron*. New York: Oxford University Press, 1986.

McKeon, Michael. *The Origins of the English Novel, 1600–1740*. Reprint, Baltimore: Johns Hopkins University Press, 2002.

McKusick, James C. *Green Writing: Romanticism and Ecology*. New York: St. Martin's, 2000.

McLane, Maureen. *Balladeering, Minstrelsy, and the Making of British Romantic Poetry*. Cambridge: Cambridge University Press, 2008.

———. "Ballads and Bards: British Romantic Orality." *Modern Philology* 98, no. 3 (2001): 423–43.

Mee, John. *Dangerous Enthusiasm: William Blake and the Cultural Radicalism of the 1790s*. Reprint. Oxford: Clarendon Press, 2002.

Mehta, Uday Singh. *Empire and Liberalism: A Study in Nineteenth-Century British Liberal Thought*. Chicago: University of Chicago Press, 1999.

Mellor, Anne K. "The Female Poet and the Poetess: Two Traditions of British Women's Poetry, 1780–1830." *Studies in Romanticism* 36 (Summer 1997): 261–76.

———. *Mothers of the Nation: Women's Political Writing in England, 1780–1830*. Bloomington: Indiana University Press, 2000.

Metzger, Lore. "Ideology: The Poetics of Schiller and Wordsworth." In *Sensibility in Transformation: Creative Resistance to Sentiment from the Augustans to the Romantics*, edited by Syndy McMillen Conger, 172–94. Madison, NJ: Fairleigh Dickinson University Press, 1990.

———. *One Foot In Eden: Modes of Pastoral in Romantic Poetry*. Chapel Hill: University of North Carolina Press, 1986.

Michael, Ian. *The Teaching of English: From the Sixteenth Century to 1870*. Cambridge: Cambridge University Press, 1987.

Mill, John Stuart. *Autobiography*. 1873. New York: Penguin, 1989.

Miller, Thomas P. *The Formation of College English: Rhetoric and Belles Lettres in the British Cultural Provinces*. Pittsburgh: University of Pittsburgh Press, 1997.

Milton, John. *The Riverside Milton*. Edited by Roy Flannigan. New York: Houghton Mifflin, 1998.

Miyamoto, Nahoko. "Wordsworth and Romantic Geography." Paper presented at the Graduate Student Conference in Romanticism, Emory University, Atlanta, April 12, 1996. http://prometheus.cc.emory.edu/panels/2A/N.Miyamoto.html.

Montesquieu, Charles de Secondat. *Spirit of the Laws*. Edited by Anne M. Cohler, Basia Carolyn Miller, and Harold Samuel Stone. Cambridge Texts in the History of Political Thought. Cambridge: Cambridge University Press, 1989.

Moore, Arthur K. "A Folk Attitude in Wordsworth's 'We Are Seven.'" *Review of English Studies* 23 (1947): 260–2.

Moorman, Mary. *William Wordsworth: A Biography*. 2 vols. Oxford: Clarendon Press, 1957–65.

Morrow, John. *Coleridge's Political Thought: Property, Morality and the Limits of Traditional Discourse*. New York: St. Martin's, 1990.

Morton, A.L. *The Everlasting Gospel: A Study in the Sources of William Blake*. London: Lawrence and Wishart, 1958.

Morton, Timothy. *Ecology Without Nature: Rethinking Environmental Aesthetics*. Cambridge: Harvard University Press, 2007.

Nairn, Tom. *After Britain: New Labour and the Return of Scotland*. London: Granta Books, 2000.

———. *The Break-up of Britain: Crisis and Neo-Nationalism*, 2d ed. London: Verso, 1981.

Newman, Gerald. *The Rise of English Nationalism: A Cultural History, 1740–1830*, rev. ed. New York: St. Martin's Press, 1997.

Newman, Steve. *Ballad Collection, Lyric, and the Canon: The Call of the Popular from Restoration to the New Criticism.* Philadelphia: University of Pennsylvania Press, 2007.

Ohmann, Richard. *English in America: A Radical View of the Profession*, rev. ed. Middletown, CT: Wesleyan University Press, 1996.

Olson, Ted. "Thomas Percy's Role in the Rise of Romanticism and in the Emergence of Modern Ballad Scholarship." *Publications of the Mississippi Philological Association* (1994): 120–5.

Oppenheimer, Stephen. *The Origins of the British: A Genetic Detective Story: The Surprising Roots of the English, Irish, Scottish, and Welsh*. New York: Carroll & Graf, 2006.

Orel, Harold. *English Romantic Poets and the Enlightenment.* Oxford: Oxford University Press, 1973.

Owen, W.J.B., and Jane Worthington Smyser, eds. *The Prose Works of William Wordsworth*. 3 vols. Oxford: Clarendon, 1974.

Oxford English Dictionary. "Briton." Accessed June 21, 2013. http://www.oed.com.lib2.bmcc.cuny.edu/view/Entry/23468?redirectedFrom=briton#eid.

Page, Judith W. "Style and Rhetorical Intention in Wordsworth's *Lyrical Ballads*." *Philological Quarterly* 62, no. 3 (1983): 293–313.

Paine, Thomas. *Rights of Man*. Introduced by Eric Foner. Reprint, New York: Penguin, 1985.

Palmer, D.J. *The Rise of English Studies.* New York: Oxford University Press, 1965.

Parrinder, Patrick. *Authors and Authority: A Study of English Literary Criticism and its Relation to Culture, 1750–1900.* Boston: Routledge, 1977.

Parrish, Stephen M. *The Art of the Lyrical Ballads.* Cambridge: Harvard University Press, 1973.

———. "'Michael' and the Pastoral Ballad." In *Bicentenary Wordsworth Studies: In Memory of John Alban Finch*, edited by Jonathan Wordsworth, 50–75. Ithaca: Cornell University Press, 1970.

Paston, George. *Social Caricature in the Eighteenth Century.* 1905. Reprint, New York: Benjamin Blom, 1968.

Patterson, Annabel. *Pastoral and Ideology: Virgil to Valery.* Berkeley: University of California Press, 1987.

Pennycook, Alastair. *English and the Discourses of Colonialism.* New York: Routledge, 1998.

Percy, Thomas. *Reliques of Ancient English Poetry.* Edited by Henry B. Wheatley. 3 vols. New York: Dover, 1966.

Pepys, Samuel. *The Pepys Ballads.* Edited by Hyder Edward Rollins. 8 vols. Cambridge: Harvard University Press, 1929–31.

Pfau, Thomas. *Wordsworth's Profession: Form, Class, and the Logic of Early Romantic Cultural Production.* Palo Alto: Stanford University Press, 1997.

Phillipson, Robert. *Linguistic Imperialism.* New York: Oxford University Press, 1992.

Piggott, Stuart. *Ancient Britons and the Antiquarian Imagination: Ideas from the Renaissance to the Regency.* New York: Thames & Hudson, 1989.

Pocock, J.G.A. "The Mobility of Property and the Rise of Eighteenth-Century Sociology." In *Virtue, Commerce, and History: Essays on Political Thought and History, Chiefly in the Eighteenth Century*, edited by J.G.A. Pocock, 103–23. Cambridge: Cambridge University Press, 1985.

Polwhele, Richard. "The Unsex'd Females: A Poem." In *The Feminist Controversy in England, 1788–1810*, edited by Gina Luria. Garland Series. New York: Garland, 1974.

Porter, Gerald. "'Who Talks of My Nation?' The Role of Wales, Scotland, and Ireland in Constructing 'Englishness.'" In *Imagined States: Nationalism, Utopia and Longing in Oral Cultures*, edited by Luisa Del Giudice and Gerald Porter, 101–35. Logan: Utah State University Press, 2001.

Porter, Roy, and Mikulas Teich, eds. *Romanticism in National Context.* Cambridge: Cambridge University Press, 1988.

Potter, Stephen. *The Muse in Chains: A Study in Education*. London: Jonathan Cape, 1937.

Pratt, Mary Louise. *Imperial Eyes: Travel Writing and Transculturation*. New York: Routledge, 1992.

Psarra, Sophia. "The Parthenon and the Erechtheion: The Architectural Formation of Place, Politics and Myth." *The Journal of Architecture* 9 (Spring 2004): 77–104.

Rajan, Balachandra. *The Form of the Unfinished: English Poetics from Spenser to Pound*. Princeton, NJ: Princeton University Press, 1985.

Rajan, Balachandra, and Elizabeth Sauer, eds. *Milton and the Imperial Vision*. Pittsburgh: Duquesne University Press, 1999.

Reid, Ian. *Wordsworth and the Formation of English Studies*. Burlington, VT: Ashgate, 2004.

Reiman, Donald H., ed. *The Romantics Reviewed: Contemporary Reviews of British Romantic Writers*. 9 vols. New York: Garland, 1972.

Renan, Ernest. "What is a Nation?" In *Becoming National: A Reader*, edited by Geoff Eley and Ronald Grigor Suny, 42–55. New York: Oxford University Press, 1996.

Richardson, Alan. *Literature, Education, and Romanticism: Reading as Social Practice, 1780–1832*. Cambridge: Cambridge University Press, 1994.

Richter, David H. *The Progress of Romance: Literary Historiography and the Gothic Novel*. Columbus: Ohio State University Press, 1996.

Ricoeur, Paul. *Lectures on Ideology and Utopia*. Edited by George H. Taylor. New York: Columbia University Press, 1986.

Riede, David. *Oracles and Hierophants: Constructions of Romantic Authority*. Ithaca: Cornell University Press, 1991.

Ritson, Joseph. *Ancient Songs and Ballads from the Reign of King Henry the Second to the Revolution*, 3d ed. Edited by W. Carew Hazlitt. Detroit: Singing Tree Press, 1968.

Robertson, J. Logie, ed. *Poetical Works*, by James Thomson. Reprint, New York: Oxford University Press, 1965.

Roe, Nicholas. "Pantisocracy and the Myth of the Poet." In *Romanticism and Millenarianism*, edited by Timothy Fulford, 87–102. New York: Palgrave, 2007.

———. *The Politics of Nature: Wordsworth and Some Contemporaries*. 2d ed. New York: Palgrave, 2002.

———. *Wordsworth and Coleridge: The Radical Years*. Oxford: Clarendon Press, 1990.

Rose, Mark. *Authors and Owners: The Invention of Copyright*. Cambridge: Harvard University Press, 1993.

Rosen, David. *Power, Plain English and the Rise of Modern Poetry*. New Haven: Yale University Press, 2006.

Ross, Marlon B. "Configurations of Feminine Reform: The Woman Writer and the Tradition of Dissent." In *Re-visioning Romanticism: British Women Writers, 1776–1837*, edited by Carol Shiner Wilson and Joel Haefner, 91–110. Philadelphia: University of Pennsylvania Press, 1994.

———. "Romancing the Nation-State: The Poetics of Romantic Nationalism." In *Macropolitics of Nineteenth-Century Literature: Nationalism, Exoticism, Imperialism*, edited by Jonathan Arac and Harriet Ritvo, 56–85. Philadelphia: University of Pennsylvania Press, 1991.

Roemer, Jean. *Origins of the English People and of the English Language*. New York: D. Appleton, 1888.

Ruoff, Gene W., ed. *The Romantics and Us*. New Brunswick, NJ: Rutgers University Press, 1990.

Ryskamp, Charles. "Wordsworth's *Lyrical Ballads* in Their Time." In *From Sensibility to Romanticism: Essays Presented to Frederick A. Pottle*, edited by Frederick W. Hilles and Harold Bloom, 357–72. New York: Oxford University Press, 1965.

Said, Edward W. *Orientalism*. New York: Vintage, 1978.

St. Clair, William. *The Reading Nation in the Romantic Period*. Cambridge: Cambridge University Press, 2004.

Saglia, Diego. "The Dangers of Over-Refinement: The Language of Luxury in Romantic Poetry By Women, 1793–1811." *Studies in Romanticism* 38, no. 4 (1999): 641–72.

Samuel, Raphael, ed. *Patriotism: The Making and Unmaking of British National Identity*. 3 vols. London: Routledge, 1989.

Sayre, Robert. "The Young Coleridge: Romantic Utopianism and the French Revolution." *Studies in Romanticism* 28, no. 3 (Fall 1989): 397–415.

Scholes, Robert. *The Rise and Fall of English: Reconstructing English as a Discipline*. New Haven: Yale University Press, 1998.

Scott, Iain Robertson. "'Things As They Are': The Literary Response to the French Revolution, 1789–1815." In *Britain and the French Revolution, 1789–1815*, edited by H.T. Dickinson, 229–51. London: Macmillan, 1989.

Scott, Sir Walter. *Minstrelsy of the Scottish Border*. Edited by T.F. Henderson. 4 vols. Reprint, Detroit: Singing Tree Press, 1968.

Shaftesbury, Anthony, Third Earl of. *Characteristicks of Men, Manners, Opinions, Times*. Foreword by Douglas Den Uyl. 3 vols. Indianapolis: Liberty Fund, 2001.

Sharp, Cecil James. *English Folk Song: Some Conclusions*. London: Simpkin & Co., 1907.

Shelley, Mary Wollstonecraft. *Letters*. Edited by Betty T. Bennett. 3 vols. Baltimore: Johns Hopkins University Press, 1980.

Shelley, Percy Bysshe. *Shelley's Poetry and Prose: Authoritative Texts and Criticism*. Edited by Donald H. Reiman and Sharon B. Powers. New York: W.W. Norton, 1977.

Sheridan, Richard B. *The Speeches of the Right Honourable Richard Brinsley Sheridan. With a Sketch of His Life*. Edited by A Constitutional Friend. 3 vols. 1842. Reprint, New York: Russell & Russell, 1969.

Simpson, David. *Wordsworth's Historical Imagination: The Poetry of Displacement*. New York: Methuen, 1987.

Simpson, Erik. *Literary Minstrelsy, 1770–1830*. New York: Palgrave Macmillan, 2008.

Simpson, Michael. "The Morning (Post) After: Apocalypse and Bathos in Coleridge's 'Fears in Solitude.'" In *Romanticism and Millenarianism*, edited by Timothy Fulford, 71–86. New York: Palgrave, 2002.

Siskin, Clifford H. *The Historicity of Romantic Discourse*. New York: Oxford University Press, 1988.

———. "Wordsworth's Prescriptions: Romanticism and Professional Power." In *The Romantics and Us*, edited by Gene W. Ruoff, 303–21. New Brunswick, NJ: Rutgers University Press, 1990.

Smith, Anthony D. *Ethnic Origins of Nations*. Reprint, Malden, MA: Blackwell, 1999.

———. *Myths and Memories of the Nation*. New York: Oxford University Press, 1999.

Smith, Olivia. *The Politics of Language, 1791–1819*. New York: Oxford University Press, 1984.

Stafford, Fiona. *Local Attachments: The Province of Poetry*. New York: Oxford, 2010.

Stafford, William. *English Feminists and Their Opponents in the 1790s: Unsex'd and Proper Females*. Manchester: Manchester University Press, 2002.

Stork, Charles W. "The Influence of the Popular Ballad on Wordsworth and Coleridge." *PMLA* 29 (Fall 1914): 299–326.

Suleri, Sarah. *The Rhetoric of English India*. Chicago: University of Chicago Press, 1992.

Super, R.H., ed. *The Complete Prose Works*, by Matthew Arnold. 11 vols. Ann Arbor: University of Michigan Press, 1960–77.

Suphan, Bernhard, ed. *Sämmtliche Werke*, by Johann Gottfried Herder. 1877–1913. 33 vols. Reprint, Hildesheim, Germany: Georg Olms, 1967–8.

Sussman, Charlotte. "The Emptiness at the Heart of Midlothian: Nation, Narration, and Population." *Eighteenth-Century Fiction* 15, no. 1 (2002): 103–26.

Sutherland, Kathryn. "The Native Poet: The Influence of Percy's Minstrel from Beattie to Wordsworth." *Review of English Studies* NS 33, no. 132 (1982): 414–33.

Sweet, Nanora, and Julie Melnyk, eds. *Felicia Hemans: Reimagining Poetry in the*

Nineteenth Century. New York: Palgrave, 2001.

Sykes, Brian. *Blood of the Isles: Exploring the Genetic Roots of Our Tribal History*. New York: Bantam, 2006.

Tawney, R.H. *Religion and the Rise of Capitalism*. 1926. Reprint, New Brunswick, NJ: Transaction, 2000.

Thompson, Edward P. *The Making of the English Working Class*. 1963. Reprint, New York: Vintage, 1966.

———. *The Romantics: England in a Revolutionary Age*. New York: New Press, 1997.

Thompson, Judith. "An Autumnal Blast, A Killing Frost: Coleridge's Poetic Conversation with John Thelwall." *Studies in Romanticism* 36 (Fall 1997): 427–56.

Thomson, James. *Poetical Works*. Edited by J. Logie Robertson. Reprint, New York: Oxford University Press, 1965.

Trinder, Peter W. *Mrs. Hemans*. Cardiff: University of Wales Press, 1984.

Trumpener, Katie. *Bardic Nationalism: The Romantic Novel and the British Empire*. Princeton, NJ: Princeton University Press, 1997.

Vardy, Alan. "Fears in Solitude, 1848." *Coleridge Bulletin* 22 (2003): 32–8.

Venis, Linda. "The Problem of Broadside Balladry's Influence on the *Lyrical Ballads*." *SEL* 24 (1984): 617–32.

Vico, Giambattista. *The New Science of Giambattista Vico*. Trans. Thomas G. Bergin and Max H. Fixch. Ithaca: Cornell University Press, 1968.

Viswanathan, Gauri. *Masks of Conquest: Literary Study and British Rule in India*. New York: Columbia University Press, 1989.

Volney, C.F. *Ruins or Meditations on the Revolutions of Empires and the Law of Nature*. 1890 ed. Whitefish, MT: Kessinger, 2004.

von Maltzahn, Nicholas. *Milton's History of Britain: Republican Historiography in the English Revolution*. Oxford: Oxford University Press, 1991.

Walpole, Horace. *The Letters of Horace Walpole*. Edited by The Earl of Orford. 6 vols. London: Richard Bentley, 1840.

Ward, Stuart. "The End of Empire and the Fate of Britishness." In *History, Nationhood and the Question of Britain*, edited by Helen Brocklehurst and Robert Phillips, 242–58. New York: Palgrave Macmillan, 2004.

———, ed. *British Culture and the End of Empire*. Manchester: Manchester University Press, 2001.

Warton, Thomas. *The History of English Poetry from the Twelfth to the Close of the Sixteenth Century*. Edited by W. Carew Hazlitt. 4 vols. Reprint. New York: Haskell House, 1970.

Watkins, Daniel P. *Anna Letitia Barbauld and Eighteenth-Century Visionary Poetics*. Baltimore: Johns Hopkins University Press, 2012.

Watt, Ian. *The Rise of the Novel*. Reprint, Berkeley: University of California Press, 2001.

Watters, C.R. "A Distant 'Boum' Among the Hills: Some Notes on Coleridge's 'Fears in Solitude' (1798)." *The Charles Lamb Bulletin* 59 (July 1987): 85–96.

Weber, Max. *The Protestant Work Ethic and the Spirit of Capitalism*. Translated by Talcott Parsons. New York: Charles Scribner's Sons, 1958.

West, Thomas. *A Guide to the Lakes*. London: Richardson & Urquhart, 1778.

Wheatley, Henry B., ed. *Reliques of Ancient English Poetry*, by Thomas Percy. 3 vols. New York: Dover, 1966.

White, Daniel E. "'Mysterious Sanctity': Sectarianism and Syncretism from Volney to Hemans." *European Romantic Review* 15, no. 2 (2004): 269–76.

Whittaker, Jason. "The Matter of Britain: Blake, Milton and the Ancient Britons." In *Blake, Nation and Empire*, edited by Steve Clark and David Worrall, 186–200. New York: Palgrave MacMillan, 2006.

———. *William Blake and the Myths of Britain*. New York: St. Martin's Press, 1999.

Wiley, Michael. *Romantic Geography: Wordsworth and Anglo-European Spaces*. New York: St. Martin's, 1998.

Wilkinson, Thomas. *Tours to the British Mountains*. London: Taylor & Hessey, 1824.

Williams, Raymond. *The Country and the*

City. New York: Oxford University Press, 1975.
———. *Culture and Society: 1780–1950*. Reprint, New York: Columbia University Press, 1983.
———. *Marxism and Literature*. New York: Oxford University Press, 1977.
Wilson, Carol Shiner, and Joel Haefner, eds. *Re-Visioning Romanticism: British Women Writers, 1776–1837*. Philadelphia: University of Pennsylvania Press, 1994
Wilson, Kathleen. *The Island Race: Englishness, Empire, and Gender in the Eighteenth Century*. New York: Routledge, 2003.
Wilson, William A. "Herder, Folklore and Romantic Nationalism." *Journal of Popular Culture* 6 (1978): 819–35.
Wingfield-Stratford, Esmé. *The History of English Patriotism*. 2 vols. New York: John Lace, 1913.
Wolfson, Susan J. *Borderlines: The Shiftings of Gender in British Romanticism*. Palo Alto, CA: Stanford University Press, 2006.
———. "'Domestic Affections' and 'the Spear of Minerva': Felicia Hemans and the Dilemma of Gender." In *Re-Visioning Romanticism: British Women Writers, 1776–1837*, edited by Carol Shiner Wilson and Joel Haefner, 128–66. Philadelphia: University of Pennsylvania Press, 1994.
———. "Hemans and the Romance of Byron." In *Felicia Hemans: Reimagining Poetry in the Nineteenth Century*, edited by Nanora Sweet and Julie Melnyk, 155–80. New York: Palgrave, 2001.
———, ed. and introd. *Felicia Hemans: Selected Poems, Letters, Reception Materials*. Princeton, NJ: Princeton University Press, 2000.
Wollstonecraft, Mary. *A Vindication of the Rights of Women*. Amherst, NY: Prometheus, 1989.
Woodring, Carl R. *Politics in English Romantic Poetry*. Cambridge: Harvard University Press, 1970.
———. *Politics in the Poetry of Coleridge*. Madison: University of Wisconsin Press, 1961.
———. *Wordsworth*. Boston: Houghton Mifflin, 1965.
Wordsworth, Dorothy. *The Grasmere and Alfoxden Journals*. Edited by Pamela Woof. New York: Oxford University Press, 2002.
———. *Recollections of a Tour Made in Scotland*. New Haven: Yale University Press, 1997.
Wordsworth, Jonathan, ed. *Bicentenary Wordsworth Studies: In Memory of John Alban Finch*, Ithaca: Cornell University Press, 1970.
Wordsworth, Jonathan, M.H. Abrams, and Stephen Gill, eds. *The Prelude: 1799, 1805, 1850*. New York: W.W. Norton, 1979.
Wordsworth, William. *Complete Poetical Works*. Introduced by John Morley. New York: Thomas Y. Crowell, 1892.
———. *The Fenwick Notes of William Wordsworth: A Revised Electronic Edition*. Edited by Jared Curtis. Rev. ed. Penrith, UK: Humanities-Ebooks, 2007.
———. *Guide to the Lakes*, 5th ed. Edited by Ernest de Selincourt. New York: Oxford University Press, 1984.
———. *The Major Works*. Edited by Stephen Gill. New York: Oxford, 2000.
———. *The Prelude: 1799, 1805, 1850*. Edited by Jonathan Wordsworth, M.H. Abrams, and Stephen Gill. New York: W.W. Norton, 1979.
———. *The Prose Works of William Wordsworth*. Edited by W.J.B. Owen and Jane Worthington Smyser. 3 vols. Oxford: Clarendon Press, 1974.
Wordsworth, William, and Samuel Taylor Coleridge. *Lyrical Ballads*, 2d ed. Edited by R.L. Brett and A.R. Jones. New York: Routledge, 1991.
Wright, Julia M. *Blake, Nationalism, and the Politics of Alienation*. Athens: Ohio University Press, 2004.
———. "Greek and Latin Slaves of the Sword: Rejecting the Imperial Nation in Blake's *Milton*." In *Milton and the Imperial Vision*, edited by Balachandra Rajan and Elizabeth Sauer, 255–72. Pittsburgh: Duquesne University Press, 1999.
———. *Ireland, India, and Nationalism in Nineteenth-Century Literature*. Cambridge: Cambridge University Press, 2007.
Wu, Duncan. *Wordsworth: An Inner Life*. Malden, MA: Blackwell, 2004.

Index

Abrams, M.H. 3, 193n2, 200n109, 201n1
Ackroyd, Peter 193n5
Act of Union (1707) 1, 9, 10, 18, 19, 22, 23, 25, 49, 182, 191
Addison, Joseph 195n28, 197n20, 215n32
Adorno, Theodor 12, 63, 195n33, 205n64
Africa 96, 184–85, 187, 189–90, 222n58
Albion 17, 19, 184, 186–87, 189–90, 193n5
Alfoxden 40, 80, 94, 96, 207n132, 212n88
alterity 16, 104, 222
America 15, 44, 48, 50–1, 84, 95, 125, 128, 157, 163, 166, 176, 178, 180–1, 187–89, 197n28, 198n32, 200n137, 201n139, 202n11, 209n9, 221n30, 223n117
American Revolution 95, 184–5, 187–88
Anderson, Benedict 7, 8, 81, 194n13, 202n11, 207n141
Anglophone 51, 177
Anglo-Saxons 48
antiquarian 4, 11, 16, 19–21, 23–26, 29–39, 45, 52–54, 58, 60, 86, 123, 158, 195n30, 197n27, 202 n13, 203n13, 214n15
architecture 26, 167, 169
Armitage, David 126, 214n26, 215n28
Arnold, Matthew 13, 14, 16, 19, 21, 24, 31, 33, 34, 35, 38, 44–49, 51, 52, 73, 88, 92, 116, 195n34, 196n2, 197n24, 199n60, 199n64, 199n65, 200n116, 200n117, 200n118, 200n119, 200n121, 200n131, 200n133, 200n135, 200n136, 201n6, 208n3, 209n24
Asia 163, 175, 178, 184, 185, 190, 215n43
Athena 168
The Athenaeum 153, 219n2, 219n3
Athens 46, 167–70

Babylon 180
Bachscheider, Paula R. 154, 156, 219n5, 219n12

ballad 1, 5, 11, 16, 19–22, 26, 29–33, 38, 54, 60, 62, 76, 78–81, 83, 86, 197–98n32, 198n33, 198n48, 198n52, 201n7, 202n11, 202n12, 204n51, 204n53, 204n54, 205n80, 206n96, 206n103, 206n114, 207n128, 207n133, 207n134, 207n135; *see also* Wordsworth, William, *Lyrical Ballads*
Barbauld, Anna Letitia 1, 4, 14, 17, 157–59, 171–83, 222n78, 222n79, 222n81, 222n83, 222n85, 222n87, 222n88, 222n90, 223n95, 223n96, 223n97, 223n98, 223n100, 223n101, 223n104, 223n107, 223n108, 223n110, 223n112, 223n116, 223n121, 223n124
bard 1, 3–6, 11, 13, 15–17, 19–20, 25–33, 36–38, 43, 45, 52, 58, 60–63, 198n32, 203n13
bardic criticism 1, 3, 4–6, 11, 13, 15–17, 19–51
bardic poetics 16, 52–87, 89, 90, 98, 182
Bate, Jonathan 57, 91, 202n11, 203n33, 209n12
Beattie, James 30, 201n7
beau monde 67, 70
Behrendt, Stephen 154, 219n6
Berkeley George 127–31, 159, 171, 178, 215n33, 215n38, 223n117, 223n118
Bhabha, Homi 8, 178, 194n15, 223n115
The Bible 15, 25, 59, 189; Old Testament 122–23, 126–27, 141, 144, 214n25
Blake, William 4, 7, 15, 17, 182–91, 222n72, 224n1, 224n4, 224n7, 224n8, 224n9, 224n10, 224n16, 224n17, 224n24, 224n35
Boitard, L.P. 67
Bold, Alan 198n33, 204n51
Bonnell, Thomas F. 10, 195n25
Bourdieu, Pierre 35, 199n66
Bourgeoisie 12, 16, 28, 83, 90–93, 99–101, 119, 131, 215n37
Brennan, Gillian 193n5

Breuilly, John 8
Brewer, John 11, 73, 195*n*27, 197*n*22, 206*n*100
Bristol 56, 120, 140, 216*n*56, 217*n*57
Britain 8–10, 22–25, 194*n*16–18, 195*n*24, 195*n*28, 214*n*20, 22*n*60
Britannia 9, 10, 25, 155–6, 171, 174
British Empire 5, 6, 8–10, 16–17, 22, 34–35, 42–44, 48–49, 51, 54, 57, 67, 71, 76, 136–39, 213*n*13, 214*n*16; anxiety of 120–131; religion and 120–131; women and 155–181
Briton 3, 6, 8–13, 20, 23, 25–26, 28, 39, 49, 50, 67, 70–71, 82, 84, 86, 120–26, 130, 141, 144–46, 149, 152, 166, 171, 177–78, 188, 194*n*20, 197*n*28, 214*n*16, 217*n*74, 224*n*8; *see also* Colley, Linda; Piggott, Stuart
Broglio, Ron 201*n*11
Budworth, Joseph 71, 205*n*88, 205*n*89
Bürger, Gottfried August 79, 81, 207*n*126
Burke, Edmund 47, 59, 69, 83, 98, 117, 130–31, 158, 193*n*9, 197*n*20, 206*n*106, 210*n*41, 211*n*73, 216*n*48, 216*n*49, 216*n*50, 220*n*21
Burns, Robert 57, 59, 82
Butler, Marilyn 193*n*5
Byron, George Gordon Lord 15, 17, 19, 33, 162, 165, 167, 183, 196*n*3, 221*n*31, 221*n*38, 221*n*52, 221*n*53, 221*n*56, 222*n*62

Calvinism 124
Campbell, Thomas 34, 49, 199*n*53, 199*n*62
capitalism 7, 12, 21, 58, 74, 75, 79, 83, 90–92, 98–101, 105, 107, 112–13, 119, 124, 179, 182, 185, 209*n*28, 214*n*17, 214*n*18, 216*n*53
Carlyle, Thomas 11, 19, 24, 34, 35, 38, 42–44, 45, 48–49, 195*n*29, 196*n*1, 199*n*63, 200*n*106, 200*n*110, 200*n*111
Catholic 9–10, 21, 43, 124, 135, 145, 148, 194*n*16, 213*n*13
Caudwell, Christopher 90, 208*n*7
Celts 9, 27, 124, 180, 194*n*19, 195*n*21
census 7, 81, 202*n*11
Chandler, James K. 98, 109, 208*n*9, 210*n*53, 212*n*102
Chatterton, Thomas 30
Chaucer, Geoffrey 24, 35, 45, 48
Chepstow Castle 116
Child, Francis James 198*n*32
Chorley, Henry F. 161–62, 164, 221*n*34, 221*n*37, 221*n*46
class-consciousness 16, 18, 88–119
Coleridge, Samuel Taylor 1, 3–4, 6, 15–18, 30, 33, 38, 40, 52, 54, 61, 64, 82, 96, 120–52, 160, 171, 173, 175, 182, 183, 193*n*1, 193*n*3, 199*n*59, 201*n*3, 202*n*12, 203*n*13, 203*n*18, 203*n*23, 203*n*24, 203*n*25, 204*n*49, 204*n*60, 205*n*67, 209*n*9, 210*n*40, 210*n*41, 213–19; *Biographia Literaria* 54, 64, 203*n*18, 204*n*49, 205*n*67; Bristol Lectures 122, 132–33, 141, 216*n*56, 217*n*56, 217*n*57; "Fears in Solitude" 3, 4, 16, 120–23, 131–32, 136–52, 175, 193*n*3, 213*n*2, 213*n*3, 213*n*10, 217*n*68, 217*n*74, 218*n*79, 218*n*85, 218*n*86, 218*n*87, 218*n*89, 218*n*90, 218*n*92, 218*n*95, 218*n*98, 219*n*101; "France: An Ode" 136; "Frost at Midnight" 136, 138, 218*n*80; *On the Constitution of Church and State* 135, 217*n*66; Pantisocracy 133, 152, 216*n*53
Colley, Linda 8–10, 121, 154–55, 194*n*16, 194*n*17, 219*n*9
colonialism 9–10, 12, 15–16, 23–24, 50, 77, 81, 122–24, 141, 156, 164–69, 174, 177–78, 182–83, 187–90, 194*n*16, 197*n*28, 206*n*106, 214*n*13, 215*n*37
Combination Act 94
commonwealth 54, 64, 71–72
Conway Castle 163
copyright 10, 12, 23, 182, 195*n*31
Corresponding Societies 94, 132, 140, 210*n*40; Corresponding Societies Act 94
counter-patriotism 4, 17, 18, 157, 171, 173–75, 180–81, 183, 191, 223*n*110
countryside 94, 115, 119, 148–49, 174, 205*n*93, 206*n*106, 212*n*88
Court, Franklin E. 196*n*11, 196*n*13, 197*n*14, 197*n*15, 197*n*18
Cowper, William 56, 130, 216*n*46
Crehan, Stewart 185
Cromwell, Oliver 126–27
Cumberland 75, 90, 201*n*11, 206*n*103

Davis, Leith 1, 5, 20
Defoe, Daniel 22, 197*n*16
DiSalvo, Jackie 185
dissenter 19, 132, 146, 172–73, 223*n*110
Dryden, John 12, 19, 35–36, 199*n*71

Eagleton, Terry 11, 91, 195*n*28, 196*n*7, 209*n*16, 211*n*60
Edinburgh Review 39, 160–61, 199*n*53, 221*n*33
Egypt 96, 125–26, 159, 180, 214*n*25
Elgin Marbles 159, 162–4, 168–69, 220*n*29, 221*n*38
Ellis, George 32
Emerson, Ralph Waldo 50–51, 200*n*138
enclosure 64, 93–94, 115, 206*n*106
Engels, Friedrich 94, 195*n*32, 209*n*30
England 3, 5, 8–10, 15–16, 17, 19, 21, 24, 27,

34, 36, 38, 41, 46, 48–49, 51, 53–54, 57, 59, 63–72, 73–75, 83–84, 86–87, 89, 92, 94, 96, 99, 103, 122–24, 135, 137, 143, 145, 148–49, 160, 175, 182, 184–85, 193n5, 194n19, 195n24, 198n32, 202n12, 204n53, 206n103, 207–08n150, 210n39, 215n43, 224n7; Civil War 25, 116, 122, 127, 184
English studies 5, 13–15, 20–25, 31–32, 44–45, 49–51, 92, 196n41, 196n7–13, 197n15, 200–01n139
Enlightenment 7, 21, 29, 61, 64–65, 73, 125, 177, 179, 188, 204n58, 205n73, 208n8, 213n11, 223n100
Erdman, David 184, 224n1
ethnie 7, 9, 10, 15–16, 23–24, 53–54, 87
ethnoscape 82–83, 85
Europe 16, 27, 46–48, 50–51, 79, 86, 97, 123, 163–64, 175, 177- 80, 184–190, 194n16, 214n15, 215n37
Evangelism 137, 141, 154
Everest, Kelvin 122, 138, 218n82
exploitation 89–90, 94–95, 98–99, 104, 164, 166, 209n28

Fairer, David 137, 217n74
Feldman, Paula R. 154, 219n5, 221n31
Feminism 51, 91, 173
feudalism 90, 107–08
folk 30–31, 53–54, 57, 64, 67, 71–80, 86, 106, 166, 202n12, 204n53–54, 207n123
folklore 22, 26, 65, 83–84, 205n73, 205n79, 206n99, 208n154; *see also* ballad
Foucault, Michel 8, 194n14
France 64, 89, 95–96, 115–17, 132–38, 143, 175, 189, 208n4, 215n43, 217n68, 218n79; French imperialism 121–22, 137–40, 143–47, 183, 212n88, 217n68, 217n74; French Revolution 39, 46, 64, 72, 91–97, 133, 136, 172–73, 184–85, 193n5, 208n150, 208n4, 213n13, 216n45, 216n51, 216n53, 218n79; Frenchified 67; Gallicanism 9, 15, 16, 194n16
Frey, Anne 2, 6, 20, 193n7, 194n16
Fricker, Sarah 133, 216n54
Frye, Northrop 224n9
Fulford, Timothy 79–81, 207n128, 207n133, 207n136, 209n9, 213n13, 216n54

Gallic Wars 25
Gamer, Michael 21, 30, 198n51, 206n96
Garrett, James M. 5, 82, 202n11, 207n143, 207n147
Gellner, Ernest 8
Germany 6, 22, 27, 28, 39, 46, 50, 61, 65, 72, 97, 170, 195n28, 205n73, 205n80

Gibbon, Edward 122, 130, 159–71, 178–79, 213n11, 215–16n44, 217n68, 220n24, 221n54, 223n120
Gilpin, William 206n106
Godwin, William 89, 96, 120, 132–33, 143, 147, 210n40
Goldstein, Laurence 158, 220n22
Gothic 19–20, 26–27, 30, 33, 54, 72, 81, 175–76, 180
Graff, Gerald 50, 200–01n139
Grasmere 71–72, 77, 85, 94, 202n11, 206n115, 207n132
Gravil, Richard 1, 5, 21, 53, 202n12–13, 203n13–14
Gray, Thomas 30, 43, 54, 63, 198n47, 206n106
Greco-Roman 32, 47, 48, 155
Greece 46, 96, 160–71, 178, 180, 214n16
Grimm, J.H. 65, 69–70
Groom, Nick 198n32

Harrison, Gary 105–06, 212n78
Harrison, J. 9
Hartley, David 82, 133, 207n144
Hastings, Warren 130–31
Hazlitt, William 24, 34–35, 38–42, 45, 48–49, 52, 103–04, 142, 199n83, 199n95, 200n99, 200n101, 201n6, 211n73–74, 218n94
Hechter, Michael 9, 24, 194n21, 197n26
Hegel, G.W.F. 179
Helgerson, Richard 193n5
Hellenism 160, 164–66, 168, 171
Hemans, Felicia 1, 4, 15, 17, 153, 157–71, 181, 182, 219n1, 221–22n30–77
Herd, David 80, 207n135
Herder, Johann Gottfried 22, 65, 71, 73, 82, 205n73–75, 205n77–79
Hoagwood, Terence A. 5, 21, 30, 198n49
Hobsbawm, Eric J. 8, 22–23, 91, 195n32, 197n19, 197n23, 209n17
Hobson, Christopher 185
Hogarth, William 69
Hume, David 130, 197n20, 204n57, 213n11, 215n43
Hurd, Richard 32–33, 199n54, 199n61, 207n137

India 1, 5, 22, 70, 96, 130–31, 158, 169, 194n16, 197n17, 216n50, 220n21
Industrial Revolution 91, 93
internal colonialism *see* Hechter, Michael
internationalism 4, 7, 172, 183–86, 191
Ireland 3, 5, 8, 12, 51, 54, 57, 140, 194n19, 195n24

Isaiah 126, 131, 139, 144, 214*n*25
Islam 164, 176, 213*n*13

Jacobin 131, 143, 145, 216*n*50
Jacobus, Mary 80–81, 202*n*12, 207*n*129, 207*n*131, 207*n*139
James I 9, 59
Jameson, Fredric 15, 196*n*48, 211*n*58
Janowitz, Anne 85, 92, 158, 172, 208*n*155, 209*n*23, 220*n*23, 222*n*78, 222*n*80
Jeffrey, Francis 32, 39, 199*n*53
Jeremiah 126, 144, 214*n*25
Johnson, Samuel 16, 24, 32, 34–38, 48, 56, 61, 136, 141, 172–73, 178, 199*n*68–69, 199*n*72, 223*n*105
Johnston, Kenneth R. 97, 208*n*8, 210*n*49–50
Jouy, M. 153–54, 170, 181, 219*n*2–3

Kaiser, David Aram 2, 6, 193*n*8
Kant, Immanuel 118
Kaul, Suvir 6, 20, 127, 193*n*10, 214*n*21, 215*n*31
Keats, John 48, 103–04, 159, 211*n*72–73, 220*n*29, 221*n*38
Kelley, Theresa M. 211*n*73
Kelly, Gary 90, 208*n*8
Kiernan, V.G. 91, 209*n*14
Kipling, Rudyard 125–26, 178, 214*n*24
Kooy, Michael John 142, 218*n*94
Kroeber, Karl 201*n*7, 209*n*12
Kumar, Krishan 9, 195*n*22

Lake District 12, 41, 53, 57, 64, 70–71, 75, 77–78, 82, 84, 86, 98–99, 103, 178, 202*n*11
Landry, Donna 67, 205*n*81–82
Langan, Celeste 108–09, 212*n*96, 212*n*99
Leask, Nigel 59, 135, 203*n*38, 217*n*65
Lee, Yoon Sun 6, 193*n*9, 195*n*30
Levinson, Marjorie 115–17, 159, 209*n*9, 212*n*119, 220*n*26
Levy, Michelle 154, 219*n*7
Linebaugh, Peter 209*n*28
Liu, Alan 209*n*9
Locke, John 195, 204*n*57
Lootens, Tricia 166, 221*n*30, 222*n*59
Löwy, Michael 91, 209*n*13
Lukács, György 93, 99–100, 211*n*57–61
luxury 123, 127, 129, 142, 171, 174, 222*n*94
Lynch, Jack 36, 199*n*70

Machiavelli, Niccolò 126, 146, 215*n*28
Macpherson, James 29, 65
Magnuson, Paul 139, 218*n*80, 218*n*84, 218*n*86

Makdisi, Saree 20, 99, 185, 211*n*55, 221*n*53
Malthus, Thomas 109
Mandeville, Bernard 129, 215*n*37
Manly, Susan 59, 74, 203*n*42
Marx, Karl 17, 90, 100, 195*n*32, 196*n*49, 214*n*17
Mathieson, Margaret 196*n*7, 209*n*25
McCarthy, William 222*n*81, 222*n*85, 223*n*102–03, 223*n*105–06
McDowell, Paula 157, 219*n*19
McFarland, Thomas 116, 118, 159, 212*n*124, 213*n*136, 220*n*26
McGann, Jerome 13, 90–92, 116, 196*n*40, 196*ch*1*n*3, 208*n*9, 209*n*10
McKusick, James C. 91, 209*n*12
McLane, Maureen 1, 5, 21, 30, 196*n*5, 198*n*48, 202*n*12
Mee, John 185, 211*n*72
Mehta, Uday Singh 177, 216*n*50, 223*n*111
Mellor, Anne K. 154, 156, 158, 219*n*6, 219*n*13–14
Metzger, Lore 64, 205*n*69, 210*n*50, 212*n*77
Michael, Ian 15, 56, 196*n*47
Mill, John Stuart 13, 73, 195*n*35
millenarianism 17, 122, 125, 127, 184–86, 191, 216*n*54, 218*n*89, 223*n*107
Milton, John 23, 33, 35–36, 44, 48–49, 56, 72, 116, 126–27, 175, 184, 186, 191, 202*n*11, 215*n*29–30, 224*n*8
Minerva 167, 170–71
minstrel 1, 5, 26–30, 54, 60, 204*n*54
Monmouth, Geoffrey of 25, 214*n*16
Monthly Review 33, 55, 160, 203*n*24, 213*n*3, 213*n*6, 213*n*9
Moorman, Mary 94, 210*n*32
More, Hannah 154
Morton, A.L. 185
Morton, Timothy 98, 209*n*12, 210*n*52
Moses 125

Nairn, Tom 9, 194*n*18
Napoleon 72, 123, 159, 162, 173–74, 177, 218*n*79
nationalism 7–15, 193–195*n*5–30; canon and 10–15, 19–25; census and 7, 81, 202*n*11; gender and 149, 153–59; geography and 81, 149–50, 201–02*n*11, 208*n*155; mapping and 7, 81–82, 86, 201–02*n*11
nature 90–91, 98–101, 103, 112–19, 136–37, 140–41, 196*n*39, 201*n*11, 203*n*13, 208*n*155, 209*n*12, 218*n*89
Neoclassicism 11, 19, 54, 62, 97, 204*n*53, 207*n*142
Nether Stowey 120, 133, 139–40, 150–53
New Critics 50

Index

"Newbolt Report" 92
Newman, Gerald 195n24
Newman, Steve 5, 21, 30, 198n52, 202n12
Noah 25, 35, 123–24, 197n28, 214n15
Norman 27–28, 45, 123

Ohmann, Richard 50, 200n137
Ottoman Empire 159, 176, 183

Paine, Thomas 173, 187, 210n39
Palmer, D.J. 196n9
Park, Mungo 222n58
Parthenon 167–70, 221n38, 222n67
Paston, George 205n83
pastoral 16, 41, 53–54, 57, 64–65, 71–77, 86, 89, 97–98, 105, 115, 117, 119, 149, 206n103, 206n114, 211–12n76
patriarchy 154, 186, 188
Patterson, Annabel 64, 205n70
Peninsular War 96
Pennycook, Alastair 197n16
Percy, Thomas 11, 13, 17, 26–32, 36, 45, 51, 53, 60, 65, 196n36, 197–98n32, 198n33, 198n37, 201n7, 201n10, 204n54
Persia 129, 180
Pfau, Thomas 196n41
picturesque 105, 116–19, 195n28
Piggott, Stuart 25–26, 197n27, 214n15
Pocock, J.G.A. 215n37
Polwhele, Richard 156, 173, 175, 219n16, 222n82
Porter, Gerald 10, 195n24
Porter, Roy 193n5
Pratt, Mary Louise 166, 221–22n58
Priestley, Joseph 133, 172, 177, 216n51, 223n110
Protestant 9, 15, 16, 24, 59, 121, 144, 182, 214n17–18
Puritanism 25, 69, 123–24, 127–28

Quantock Hill 80
Quintilian 62, 204n60

Rajan, Balachandra 159, 220n26, 224n8
Reformation 47, 135, 197n28
Reid, Ian 14, 196n41
reification 4, 16, 23, 87, 90, 92–93, 99–119
Reiman, Donald H. 199n55, 199n90, 201n2, 201n5, 213n3–4, 213n6–9, 220n28
Renaissance 25, 32, 47
Renan, Ernest 7–8, 193n12
Richardson, Alan 14, 196n43
Richter, David H. 206n96
Ricoeur, Paul 183, 224n3
Ritson, Joseph 197–98n32

River Wye 114–19
Robespierre, Maximilien 132–33
Roe, Nicholas 98, 116–19, 132–33, 209n9, 210n40, 212n127, 216n54–55
Rome 126, 136, 159, 163, 165, 178–80, 214n16, 215–16n44, 217n68
Rose, Mark 195n31
Ross, Marlon 83, 156, 207n148, 219n18
ruinological sublime 158–59, 164
ruins 76, 78, 83–85, 107, 157–59, 163–71, 174–81, 206n115, 208n155, 220n26, 221n38, 221n53

Saglia, Diego 222n94
Said, Edward W. 165, 180, 221n56, 221n123
St. Clair, William 14–15, 196n44, 203n30
Salisbury Plain 114
Sallust 126, 131, 169, 215n28–29
Scholes, Robert 50, 200–01n139
Scotland 5, 8–9, 21, 29, 54, 67, 69, 80, 83–84, 103, 179, 194n18–19, 195n24, 206n106, 211n70
Scott, Sir Walter 12, 15, 26, 29, 32, 56–57, 82, 123, 195n30, 198n33–34, 198n42, 221n31
sentimentalism 90–91, 129, 166, 222n58
Shaftesbury, Anthony, Third Earl of 98, 129, 215n37
Shakespeare, William 15, 22–23, 34–38, 43–44, 46, 48, 56, 65, 72, 197n21, 199n70, 199n72, 200n95, 211n73
Shelley, Mary Wollstonecraft 158, 219n20
Shelley, Percy Bysshe 15, 17, 64, 104, 159, 183, 220n20, 220n26, 220n28, 221n53, 224n2
Sheridan, Richard B. 137–38, 143, 217n74–75, 218n79
Simpson, David 59, 61, 203n38–39, 209n9, 212n88
Simpson, Erik 1, 30, 198n50, 202n12
Simpson, Michael 218n89
Siskin, Clifford H. 196n41, 208n9, 209n11
slavery 133, 141–42, 172–74, 218n92
Smith, Adam 21, 179
Smith, Anthony D. 7, 10, 24, 82, 193n11, 197n25, 207n146
Smith, Olivia 59, 203n41
social caricature 67, 70, 205n83
South Sea Bubble 128, 130
Southey, Robert 12, 15, 33, 39, 56, 116, 133, 203n13, 203n23, 207n128, 213n13
Spain 128, 194n19
Spenser, Edmund 33, 48
Stafford, Fiona 5, 82, 207n142
sublime 43, 105, 117–19, 158–59, 162–65,

175, 178, 195n28, 202n11, 211n72, 220n21
Suleri, Sarah 158, 220n21
Sulla 126–27
superstition 39, 54, 73, 78–79, 89, 190
Sweet, Nanora 221n38
Syria 159

Tawney, R.H. 124, 214n17, 214n19
Thelwall, John 117, 120, 132, 147, 210n40, 217n57, 218n80
Thompson, Edward P. 93–94, 120, 209n26, 210n40, 210n50, 213n5, 217n57
Thomson, James 120, 125, 143, 155, 159, 174, 213n1, 214n22, 222n89
translatio imperii 179–80
Trumpener, Katie 1, 5–6, 20, 54, 193n6, 195n30, 203n15

University of Edinburgh 14, 22

Vardy, Alan 122, 213n10
Viswanathan, Gauri 12, 169, 197n17, 222n70
Volney, C.F. 159–60, 163–64, 167, 171, 178, 216n45, 220n25, 221n41, 221n47, 223n119

Wales 3, 5, 8, 9, 30, 51, 54, 57, 114, 194n18–19, 195n24, 203n13
Walpole, Horace 26, 173, 205n96, 222n84
Ward, Stuart 194n18, 222n60
Warrington Academy 172
Warton, Thomas 32
Watkins, Daniel 174, 223n97
Weber, Max 124, 214n17–18
Webster, Noah 35, 199n67
West, Thomas 70, 205n87
Westminster 48, 99
Westmoreland 33, 75, 206n103
Whittaker, Jason 185, 224n8
Wiley, Michael 201n11
Williams, Raymond 13, 64, 89, 91–92, 98, 112, 196n38, 205n71, 208n5, 209n18, 209n21, 210n51
Wilson, Kathleen 195n24
Wilson, William A. 65, 205n73–75, 205n78–79
Winfield-Stratford, Esmé 184, 224n5
Wolfson, Susan J. 156, 161, 219n1, 219n17, 221n32–33, 221n36, 221n38, 221n52, 222n61–62
Wollstonecraft, Mary 14, 154, 158, 173, 219n8, 219–20n20
Woodring, Carl 202n12, 210n50, 218n83
Wordsworth, Dorothy 80, 94, 96, 117, 119, 207n132, 208n154, 211n70, 218n92
Wordsworth, William 1, 4, 6, 11–17, 24, 26, 30, 32–36, 38–43, 49–51, 52–87, 88–119, 132, 148–49, 166, 173, 182, 193n4, 196n37, 196n41, 198n35, 200n109, 201–213, 218n84, 222n72; *Convention of Cintra* 71, 96–97, 205n92, 210n45; *Ecclesiastical Sonnets* 53, 202n11, 203n13; "Essay Supplementary to the Preface" 27, 53, 56, 60–61, 201n8, 203n27, 203n43; "An Evening Walk" 95–96, 210n34; *Guide to the Lakes* 64, 71, 83–84, 202n11, 203n17, 205n68, 205n91, 206n106, 208n151; *A Letter to the Bishop of Llandaff* 89, 95, 208n4; *Lyrical Ballads* 4, 11, 16, 26, 39–40, 52–63, 72–87, 89–90, 93, 95–98, 103–119, 201n1, 202n11–12, 203n13–14, 203n23–25, 204n60, 206n106, 210n50; *Poems, in Two Volumes* 40, 211n70; "Preface" 4, 16, 52–63, 72, 82, 98, 104, 113, 193n4, 196n37, 201n1; *The Prelude* 4, 43, 70–72, 75, 85, 94–96, 101–03, 196n41, 200n109, 201n1, 208n155, 210n35; "Salisbury Plain" 89, 93, 95, 97, 99, 104, 114, 203n13; "The Solitary Reaper" 103–04, 211n70; "Westminster Bridge" 99
Wright, Julia M. 1, 5, 20, 36, 185, 224n8
Wu, Duncan 94, 207n136, 210n31

www.ingramcontent.com/pod-product-compliance
Lightning Source LLC
Chambersburg PA
CBHW051217300426
44116CB00006B/608